The First Two
Quartos of *Hamlet*

The First Two Quartos of *Hamlet*

A New View of the Origins and Relationship of the Texts

MARGRETHE JOLLY

McFarland & Company, Inc., Publishers
Jefferson, North Carolina

LIBRARY OF CONGRESS CATALOGUING-IN-PUBLICATION DATA

Jolly, Margrethe.
 The first two quartos of Hamlet : a new view of the origins and relationship of the texts / Margrethe Jolly.
   p.   cm.
 Includes bibliographical references and index.

 ISBN 978-0-7864-7887-3 (softcover : acid free paper) ∞
 ISBN 978-1-4766-1556-1 (ebook)

 1. Shakespeare, William, 1564–1616. Hamlet—Criticism, Textual. 2. Shakespeare, William, 1564–1616—Bibliography—Quartos. 3. Hamlet (Legendary character) I. Title.
PR2807.J62 2014
822.3'3—dc23   2014014808

BRITISH LIBRARY CATALOGUING DATA ARE AVAILABLE

© 2014 Margrethe Jolly. All rights reserved

No part of this book may be reproduced or transmitted in any form or by any means, electronic or mechanical, including photocopying or recording, or by any information storage and retrieval system, without permission in writing from the publisher.

On the cover: *inset* image on the title page of the First Quarto (1603) and the Second Quarto (1605) of William Shakespeare's *Hamlet*; Scene from Shakespeare's *Hamlet* © Photos.com/Thinkstock

Printed in the United States of America

McFarland & Company, Inc., Publishers
 Box 611, Jefferson, North Carolina 28640
  www.mcfarlandpub.com

In memoriam
Karen Margrethe Elmose Hazell
(1929–1996)

Acknowledgments

The list of people to whom I am indebted must be headed by Dr. William Leahy of Brunel University, whose support and gentle guidance during my doctoral research were liberating and invaluable. Other Brunel staff who have contributed counterarguments and provocative comments include particularly Dr. Sean Gaston, as well as Professors James Knowles and Philip Tew. Professors Willy Maley of Glasgow University and John McGavin of Southampton University have also been encouraging. Associate Professor Anne M. Scott, Dr. Lesley O'Brien and two anonymous Readers are warmly thanked for their editing and critiquing of "*Hamlet* and the French Connection," published in *Paregon* in June 2012.

Many colleagues and friends have tolerated endless discussions about the *Hamlet*s, and to them also I owe much gratitude. First among these is Kevin Gilvary, a fellow Ph.D. student who has generously offered books, and ideas, and above all his time. Among the many others are Lesley Tudor Pole, Marion Peel, David Lewis, Elizabeth Imlay, Richard Malim, Christopher Dams, Dorna Bewley, Penny Edwards, Freya Marsh, Robert Detobel, Alison Williamson, Dr. John Rollett, and Philip Johnson and Dr. Noemi Magri, the last two sadly now deceased. Some outside the field of English have also offered useful advice and comments about methodology. These include Drs. Colin Jolly, Karen Stephens, Andreas Bubel and Helen Jolly, as well as Judge Patrick O'Brien and Chris Rooke.

None of the research would have been possible without the help of library and computing staff. Southampton University library, Brunel University library and Lymington local library have all acquired obscure books and papers for me, from the British Library and the London Library in particular. Dominic Benson at Brunel has patiently facilitated my access to e-journals. Karen Kristensen has also helped with occasional questions about Danish and Denmark.

To all of these, and to all earlier scholars whose ideas sparked this research, thank you. To anyone whom I have omitted, my apologies. And to my patient husband, expert in IT and logical thinking, my heartfelt thanks.

Contents

Acknowledgments	vi
List of Tables	ix
Preface	1
Key Abbreviations, Nomenclature and Conventions Used in the Text	5
Introduction: Nineteen Going on Thirty	7

Part One: Which Came First, Q1 or Q2 *Hamlet*?

1. Dating and Measuring: Initial Evidence	15
2. *Les Histoires Tragiques* and the Quartos	32
3. *Les Histoires Tragiques*, the Quartos and Evolving Ideas	44
4. Hamlet's Return, Nashe and Some Binge Drinking	53
5. Just Like Ben Jonson	62

Part Two: How Certain Is Memorial Reconstruction?

6. Printing, and Contemporary Complaints about Piracy	77
7. Memorial Reconstruction in England	89
8. *The Spanish Tragedy*, and Duthrie's "Objectionable Pronouns"	102
9. Corpses, Stage Directions and Other Anomalies	114
10. Memorial Reconstruction—or Abridgement?	129

Part Three: Was There an *Ur-Hamlet*?

11. "Hamlets" and the Elizabethan Æsop	143
12. Meres and a Contradiction of Scholars	160

Conclusion: Closing with the Consequences	177
Appendix A: Colloquialisms—Q1 and Q2	195

Appendix B: Table of Comparisons from Les Histoires Tragiques,
   Q1 *and* Q2   199
Appendix C: A Summative, Four Way Comparison Between
   Les Histoires Tragiques, *Q1, Q2 and F* Hamlet   211
Chapter Notes   219
Bibliography   231
Index   237

List of Tables

1. Third Person Singular Verb Suffixes — 27
2. Informal or Colloquial Features in Scene 16 of Q1 and Act 5 Scene 1 of Q2 — 29
3. Phrases/Lines Concerning Drunkenness in *Les Histoires Tragiques*, *Pierce Penniless*, Q1 and Q2 — 56–57
4. Details of the Stationers' Register Entries and Printing of the Early Quartos of *Hamlet* — 80
5. *The School for Scandal*: The Characters and Their Lines — 91
6. *The School for Scandal*: The Presence of Any of the Eight Known Characters in Each Scene — 92
7. Q1 *Hamlet*: The Lines of the Suggested Actor/Reporter(s) — 95
8. Q2 *Hamlet*: The Lines of the Suggested Actor/Reporter(s) — 96
9. Q1 *Hamlet*: The Presence of Any of the Three (*Seven*) Actor/Reporters in Each Scene — 97
10. Q2 *Hamlet*: The Presence of Any of the Three (*Seven*) Actor/Reporters in Each Scene — 98
11. Summary of Maguire's Investigations of "Suspect Texts" — 100
12. Animals Mentioned in Nashe's *Epistle* — 150
13. Receipts from Performances 14–16 May, 3–13 June and 15–18 June 1594, in Henslowe's *Diary* — 162
14. A Selection of English Authors Cited by Meres, with Titles of Works — 168
15. Linking the *Hamlet*s — 172

Preface

Seven years ago, a scruffy, patched up copy of George Ian Duthie's book, *The "Bad" Quarto of Hamlet* (1941), slipped through my letter box. It was no longer wanted by the University of Iowa Libraries, but its arrival here was keenly awaited and it now marks the beginning of the research underpinning this volume. *The "Bad" Quarto of Hamlet* focuses upon the relationship of the first two quartos of *Hamlet*, and Duthie writes with a knowledge and passion that makes it easy to see how and why his book has been so persuasive. He brings together in its most complete form the arguments that early references to a *Hamlet* are not to Shakespeare's play, that Shakespeare's first *Hamlet* was the second quarto, and that the first printed quarto was a memorially reconstructed version deriving ultimately from the second quarto of *Hamlet*.

A close reading of the book and the texts it references does, however, reveal a number of peculiarities. For example, the writer of the Foreword, Walter W. Greg, is unsure that Duthie's "monograph will be accepted as offering a final solution of the problem" of the first quarto of *Hamlet*. To a linguist Duthie's missing but implicit modal verbs are rather interesting. Then one of Duthie's quotations from Thomas Kyd's *Spanish Tragedy* is incomplete, suspiciously so. Further on, Duthie admits he is unable to explain to his own satisfaction why Hamlet's age in the first quarto matches the age of the Prince in the source, but is different from Hamlet's age in the second quarto. An obvious question is whether these and other peculiarities matter. The research behind the present work suggests they do.

The First Two Quartos of Hamlet therefore returns to the relationship of the quartos, and re-examines Duthie's hypotheses. Of course, that relationship is commented upon elsewhere. Kathleen O. Irace in *Reforming the "Bad" Quartos: Performance and Provenance of Six Shakespearean First Editions* (1994), Eric Sams in *The Real Shakespeare: Retrieving the Early Years, 1564–1594* (1995), Laurie Maguire as part of her methodical study of forty-one alleged memorial reconstructions from the period in *Shakespeare's Suspect Texts: The*

1

"Bad" Quartos and Their Contexts (1996), and James Shapiro in *1599* (2005) all include discussion of the two quartos as part of their books, and are among relatively recent publications. Two particular books in addition to Duthie's focus upon the *Hamlet* quartos: Thomas Clayton's edition presents a selection of essays all upon *The Hamlet First Published (Q1, 1603): Origins, Form, Intertextualities* (1986), and Paul Menzer offers a study of the cues in *The Hamlets: Cues, Qs and Remembered Texts* (2008). An alternative line of approach is found in books discussing early modern drama on a wider front, such as *A New History of Early English Drama* (1997) edited by John D. Cox and David Scott Kastan, and in several books by Andrew Gurr. Editors of *Hamlet* also usually offer an introduction which mentions the two quartos: Harold Jenkins (1982), Philip Edwards (1985), G. R. Hibbard (1987), and Stanley Wells and Gary Taylor (1988) are obvious examples. Twenty-first century editors include Ann Thompson and Neil Taylor (Q2 in 2006, Q1 in 2007), and Jonathan Bate and Eric Rasmussen (2008). All these scholars refer to the relationship of the quartos. Here that relationship is the sole focus.

Can there be anything left to say? Scholars from Edmond Malone onwards have investigated contemporary allusions to *Hamlet* and the texts of the quartos themselves, but their conclusions are not unanimous, and are often phrased cautiously. The discipline of English literature has developed steadily since Malone and indeed since Duthie. Our knowledge about how drama texts work, about linguistics and about critical methods has undoubtedly advanced. Just occasionally too there is a hint in the literature that our respect for earlier scholars is inhibiting us from questioning, or even disagreeing with, some of their conclusions.

As a result *The First Two Quartos of* Hamlet investigates and reassesses the dominant paradigm describing the relationship of the quartos. It returns to the original texts upon which the "usual" narrative about the *Hamlet*s is based. The book eschews beliefs, it seeks to distinguish between what is evidence and what is speculation, it is almost Gradgrindish in its search for facts, and it defines clearly the methodology underlying different aspects of the analysis. Those original texts include Thomas Nashe's *Epistle to the Gentlemen Students of Both Universities*, Francis Meres' chapter on English poets in his *Palladis Tamia*, and Sir Israel Gollancz's edition of the relevant chapters of the underlying French source, in *Les Histoires Tragiques*, by François de Belleforest. The book includes new examinations of these texts and also a quantitative analysis of the analogy of the memorial reconstruction of Sheridan's *School for Scandal*, a possible reason for why the scenes announcing Hamlet's return to Denmark are so different in the quartos, and an exploration of how some of the characters develop in a clear progression from *Les Histoires Tragiques*, through the first quarto to the second.

The critical aspects addressed are therefore the evidence for the priority of the quartos, for the first quarto as a memorial reconstruction, and for the putative *Ur-Hamlet*. These are all essential to understanding how the quartos are linked. They are also critical to our understanding of how Shakespeare worked as a playwright, and when he was writing.

Not every *Hamlet* is included. While the folio edition of *Hamlet* does receive some attention, it has not been proposed as the anterior version of *Hamlet* and so it remains in the background. And while there is also the question of the origins of *Der Bestrafte Brudermord*, the German version of *Hamlet*—if that is not being too flattering to *Brudermord*—the extant German text dates from 1710, much later than the quartos. *Brudermord* is therefore not part of this study. However, our understanding of that play is likely to be improved if we can first resolve the question of the quartos' relationship.

Ultimately the research reported here demonstrates that there is reproducible evidence which leads to an alternative way of thinking about the quartos, a way rooted in those original texts and contrasting with the most widespread account of the quartos' relationship. For that reason alone this book may not please all. Indeed, pleasing every reader of books upon Shakespeare is probably impossible. Over a century ago one English scholar dismissed another's reasoned doubts on Nashe's *Epistle* with a claim that it was "the unanimous opinion of Shakspearean [sic] critics" that Thomas Kyd was the author of the early *Hamlet*. That sweeping riposte seems to have closed down discussion about Nashe's allusion to "Hamlets," a great pity. This book is no riposte; it does not agree with all of its predecessors, but it could not have been written without their voices proposing, theorizing, suggesting and pushing their ideas to the limits. It is dependent upon those previous studies both acknowledged and consulted for its development of a different approach to analyzing the *Hamlets* and to understanding them. It builds upon its findings to outline a scenario for the quartos' origins, a scenario that, like Duthie's book, will doubtless lead to further debate. But perhaps it will also lead to a fresh examination of the quartos and fresh thinking about Shakespeare, still clearly a genius but perhaps also a grafter.

Key Abbreviations, Nomenclature and Conventions Used in the Text

Abbreviations

Q1	the first quarto of *Hamlet*, printed in 1603
Q2	the second quarto of *Hamlet*, printed in 1604–5
F1	the first folio edition of *Hamlet*, printed in 1623
Les Histoires Tragiques	the title of François de Belleforest's series of volumes of "tragic stories," but herein used to designate the third tale in volume V.

Nomenclature

Refers to characters in, respectively, *Les Histoires Tragiques*, Q1, and Q2.

	Les Histoires Tragiques	**Q1 Hamlet**	**Q2 Hamlet**
1	Horvvendille	Old Hamlet	Old Hamlet
2	ombres, ombre	Ghost	Ghost
3	Le Roy de Norvege, Collere	Fortenbrasse of Norway	Fortinbras of Norway
4	Fengon	The King	Claudius
5	Geruthe	Gertred	Gertrard
6	Amleth	Hamlet	Hamlet
7	quelque belle femme	Ofelia	Ophelia
8	un Gentil-Homme	Horatio	Horatio
9	un ami de Fengon, le conseil	Corambis	Polonius
10	deux des fideles ministres	Rossencraft and	Rosencrans and
11	de Fengon	Gilderstone	Guyldensterne
12	le Roy des Anglois	The King of England	The King of England
13		a centinel	Francisco
14		Montano	Reynaldo
15		Leartes	Laertes
16		Voltemar	Voltemand

Q1 line references are to Irace's edition (Kathleen O. Irace, editor. *The First Quarto of Hamlet* [Cambridge: Cambridge University Press, 1998]), and Q2's to Thompson and Taylor's *Hamlet* (Q2) (Ann Thompson and Neil Taylor, editors. *Hamlet.* (Q2) The Arden Shakespeare [London: Thomson Learning, 2006]), unless otherwise stated.

Quotations from facsimiles of Q1 are taken from *Hamlet: First Quarto, 1603*, with an introductory note by W. W. Greg (London: the Shakespeare Association & Sidgwick and Jackson, Limited, 1951), and William Griggs' *Shakspere's Hamlet: The Second Quarto, 1604* (London: W. Griggs, n.d.).

Conventions

The convention of < > is used to denote inflections, for example <eth>, while / /, for example /k/, indicates symbols from the International Phonetic Alphabet, selectively used to indicate British English pronunciation. The symbols used are:

Vowels	*Consonants*
/ə/ (schwa), for bett<u>er</u> or <u>a</u>bout	/k/ for <u>c</u>at
/æ/ for h<u>a</u>t	/s/ for <u>s</u>ilver
/ɪ/ for <u>i</u>nn	/ð/ for <u>th</u>in
	/z/ for <u>z</u>inc
	/h/ for <u>h</u>at

Introduction: Nineteen Going on Thirty

> *The **Danes**... are an arrogant ass-headed people, that naturally hate learning and all them that love it ... for fashion sake some will put their children to **school**, but they set them not to it till they are fourteen year old, so that you shall see a great boy with a beard learn his ABC, and sit weeping under the rod when he is **thirty** years old.*[1]

The author of this hyperbolic rant in 1592 was Cambridge graduate and wit Thomas Nashe, pamphleteer and writer of erotica. Nashe's figure of a thirty year old Danish student may surprise us, because Hamlet too is thirty years old and he is also Horatio's fellow student at "school in Wittenberg" (I.ii.113[2]). We can be confident about Hamlet's age, for the Gravedigger tells us unambiguously that he has been "sexton here, man and boy, thirty years," from the day that Hamlet was born (V.i.152).

Shakespeare confirms Hamlet's age in the same scene. When the Gravedigger picks up Yorick's skull he points out that it has lain in the earth for "three and twenty years" (V.i.163-4). If Hamlet is recalling memories from when he was about seven years old of riding upon Yorick's back, then Shakespeare is effectively telling us Hamlet is indeed about thirty years old.

At least, this is what we read in the second printed version of *Hamlet*, the 1604-5 second quarto of *Hamlet*, or Q2 for short. It is what we read in subsequent quartos, and also in the third version of *Hamlet* which is found in the 1623 first folio, or F1. Being at school at thirty is a little odd, because in Elizabethan times at Oxford and Cambridge universities the students were generally in their teens. For example, Thomas Nashe attended from 1581 until he gained his bachelor's degree at nineteen in 1586, and Christopher Marlowe, just two months older than Shakespeare, gained his bachelor's degree aged twenty in 1584.

It is more puzzling when we look at the first printed version of *Hamlet*, the 1603 first quarto (Q1). Here the First Clown (Q1's name for the Gravedigger) doesn't tell us Hamlet's age directly, though he does say Yorick's skull "hath been here this dozen year" (16.66³). Hamlet picks up Yorick's skull, and says "I knew him, Horatio... He hath carried me twenty times upon his back" (16.85–6). If we make the assumption that Hamlet is recalling memories from when he was about seven years old, as we do in Q2, then he is around nineteen in the first quarto of *Hamlet* and a much more likely age for being a student, at least in England.

The difference in Hamlet's age is only one of the peculiarities in Q1, which is itself one of the great mysteries associated with Shakespeare. This particular mystery began in 1823 when a certain Sir Henry Bunbury was rummaging in the back of his closet and came across a collection of twelve of Shakespeare's plays. There among plays like *Romeo and Juliet* and the second part of *Henry the Fourth* was a copy of *Hamlet*, the version we now call Q1.[4] It was not a *Hamlet* scholars were familiar with. Two years later in 1825 it was republished. For thirty years it was the only version of the first quarto, but then in 1856 a penniless Irish student walked into a bookseller's called *The Sign of Shakspere's Head*, in Dublin. The student had a copy of Q1 *Hamlet*, and he sold it to the bookseller for one shilling, a mere five pence today in English money.[5] Sir Henry's and the student's first quartos are the only Q1s known to survive. One has the final page missing and the other the title page, but between them they provide us with a whole first quarto. Sir Henry Bunbury's find made *Hamlet* rather special, for it is the only Shakespearean play to survive in three distinct versions.

The "new" quarto must have astonished its early readers, accustomed to Q2 and F1 *Hamlet*s. The first quarto is short, only 2221 lines, next to Q2's 4056 and F1's 3907.[6] Although Q1 is definitely a *Hamlet* play, for the characters and action are more or less the same, there are significant differences in some of the names, in many of the lines, in the order of part of the plot and in one of the events. At the same time, over 450 lines scattered through Q1 are identical to lines in Q2. The title pages for both quartos and the folio *Hamlet* attribute the play to William Shakespeare.

From 1825 onwards the challenge has been how to explain the relationship of the two quarto plays which are both so similar and so different. If we dig a little underneath the mainstream writings about *Hamlet* we find a complex series of speculations and reasoning by nearly two centuries' worth of scholarly detection, but the articles and accounts do not yet reach a consensus. *Hamlet* is like a "cold case"; there are stacks of evidence, hypotheses and contradictions, yet not enough to produce a solid solution.

The early explanation of how the first quarto of 1603 and the second quarto of 1604–5 are related was quite simple. In 1832 Thomas Caldecott saw the first quarto as "the first conception and comparatively feeble expression of a great mind," which was "afterwards wrought into a splendid drama" (Q2).[7] His view was shared by several scholars in the 1830s; they were broadly in agreement that Q1 was the equivalent of a first draft or sketch, and that Q2 represented Shakespeare's revised *Hamlet* or second thoughts. The value of Q1 was therefore in the opportunity to study the poet's growth, in language, intellect and philosophy. However, in 1842 John Payne Collier began to express some doubts about whether Shakespeare was really the author of the first quarto. (Collier was a prolific writer in the arts, but he was occasionally prone to invention and forgery. To this day it is not definite exactly how far his more creative efforts went, or even whether he was the deceiver or the deceived. Nevertheless, his comments planted a seed of suspicion about Q1 *Hamlet*.)

Instead Collier suggested that Shakespeare's Q2 had been performed, that someone in the theatre had taken shorthand notes of the performance, supplemented this from memory or used another inferior writer, and that he or they then scrambled together a somewhat abbreviated *Hamlet*. This, Collier suggested, was what gave us Q1, a *Hamlet* he saw as less than perfect.[8] We might wonder how anyone with paper, quill and ink would have managed to take down any sort of version of a play in the Elizabethan theatre, and especially how it might have been done secretly. It would be a much easier task with today's electronic equipment. In any case, Collier's suggestion was not widely accepted. Much later, in 1949, George Ian Duthie surveyed the methods of shorthand available to the late Elizabethans and early Jacobeans.[9] Duthie gave it as his firm opinion that the kinds of shorthand then in existence were not sophisticated enough to produce anything like a Q1, and produced evidence to support it. Shorthand, or stenography as Collier called it, is therefore not seriously considered as explaining the origins and condition of Q1.

Collier marks the point at which some readers start to feel critical of Q1 *Hamlet*. Instead of it being the first breath of Shakespeare's creation, it begins to be scorned by some scholars as a poor thing, "marred and mangled,"[10] "a maimed and distorted version,"[11] an "imperfect, garbled ... mutilation,"[12] and a "botched text of the play."[13] More recent scholars have added to the list of disparaging terms. For example, in 1992 Q1 is described as "full of passages of bad versification, distorted expressions, [and] misplaced lines that cannot reasonably be thought to derive from any genuine Shakespeare manuscript."[14] Since today we do not have a "genuine Shakespeare manuscript" of any of his plays we cannot be certain what one would look like. Nevertheless many—but not all—scholars today do not believe that Q1 is wholly Shakespeare's.

But if Q1 isn't Shakespeare's, whose is it? The theory which prevails now has its roots in an idea initiated by a German, Tycho Mommsen, in 1857. He proposed that an actor put together the framework of the play and someone else, perhaps a "bookseller's hack," made up the rest of the play from the actor's notes. They cobbled together a *Hamlet*, the one we now call Q1. Mommsen offered several reasons for thinking this. For example, he wrote that there are some "omissions" and "transpositions" in the action, events missing or moved around between the quartos, which might be a result of the actor's incomplete memory of the play. Mommsen also felt it unlikely that a young writer would have written dramas in a shorter form. (He thought the contrary more probable, using the analogy of Schiller's *Don Carlos* and Goethe's *Goetz von Berlichingen*.) He noted that the earlier part of the play was closer in Q1 and Q2 than the later part, and suggested that the actor's patience was greater at the beginning. Mommsen also wrote that "blunders" with regard to meter and scansion were found in the early version.[15]

Twenty years later a scholar called William Henry Widgery won the Harness Essay prize. His essay was on *Hamlet*, and in passing he noted that the lines of ambassador Voltemand in Q2 were almost identical to the lines of ambassador Voltemar in Q1. Widgery pounced on the closeness of the lines, saying: "The speech of Voltemar in act II sc ii is suspiciously correct: he may also have taken the part of the player king, and in him I believe we have the thief who made a copy by stealth."[16]

Then in 1915 another scholar, Henry D. Gray, pointed out that Marcellus' lines in Q2 were similar to his lines in Q1. Gray suggested that instead it was perhaps the actor playing this character who had reconstructed *Hamlet* from memory; it was "Marcellus" who had produced a memorial reconstruction of Shakespeare's *Hamlet* and given us Q1.[17] Duthie took the suggestions much further in a lively, detailed and highly influential book, *The "Bad" Quarto of Hamlet*, in 1941, offering many additional points.[18] The result is that memorial reconstruction (MR) has received extensive support, and it is now the basis of the most widespread narrative explaining the relationship of the first two quartos. However, it is not a universally agreed solution, and there are some matters the theory doesn't explain. It seems odd, for instance, that ambassador Voltemand of Q2 can remember most of his lines remarkably accurately but can't remember his name properly in Q1, where it is Voltemar. There also appears to be very little investigation into whether there might be any other reason for Marcellus and Voltemar/Voltemand having very similar lines in each quarto. Indeed, doubters have described MR as a "house of cards," "an out-moded myth," and even as a "tissue of fabrications, not a material hypothesis."[19] One writer even goes so far as to say that "[i]t is hard to believe that such a theory—one that sounds preposterous on the surface of things—could ever have held sway in modern Shakespearean studies."[20] Yet there are also some who equally forcefully reject the idea that Shakespeare revised. One editor writes: "It is as well therefore to state that all those theories which view

Shakespeare's *Hamlet* as progressing to its final shape via one or more rewritings ... are quite without evidence or plausibility."[21]

Today the theory of MR (also sometimes referred to as MRA, memorial reconstruction by actors) dominates accounts of the relationship of the first two quartos. MR seems the best explanation to many writers on *Hamlet*. Here is a recent summary, carefully and clearly phrased:

> In 1603 appeared an inferior text apparently assembled from actors' memories.... It is our belief that Shakespeare wrote *Hamlet* about 1600, and revised it later; that the 1604 edition was printed from his original papers; that the Folio represents the revised version; and that the 1603 edition represents a very imperfect report of an abridged version of the revision.[22]

Just how cautious this summary is becomes obvious when we realize that "our belief" precedes five separate statements, that is, five separate beliefs. Some readers will not notice the caution, but for those engaged in trying to understand the first two quartos it is valuable to see a clear expression of what authoritative scholars offer at present.

One matter the summary doesn't mention is that those five beliefs depend on another belief, or hypothesis, that allusions to a *Hamlet* play in Elizabethan documents in 1589, 1594, and 1596 are to someone else's drama on the same subject. This early *Hamlet* is sometimes called the *"Ur-Hamlet,"* a label used in this book, without connoting any confirmation of its existence. The *Ur-Hamlet* is distinctly problematic. No one knows what might have been in this putative, unknown text, but there are several proposals about what some of the principal components of this drama might be. For example, Charles Herford thinks that its writer "added the ghost."[23] E. K. Chambers speculates that "[p]robably [Shakespeare] kept the framework of the plot, including the ghost, the play within a play, and the somewhat bloodthirsty final scene."[24] Later scholars think that the Ghost urged "Hamlet to take revenge,"[25] that the ghost, the dumb show and the fencing match,[26] and the "accidental poisoning,"[27] were all added by the author of the early *Hamlet*. Since the hypothetical *Ur-Hamlet* is not known to be extant, scholars can only speculate on its existence and its contents, but if it had existed and had those components already it would have made Shakespeare's task somewhat easier in 1600, if that was when he sat down to write his *Hamlet*. F. J. Furnival, for example, was one who thought this, commenting on "the overwhelming debt that Shakspere would owe to Mr Unknown, if the original of Q1, after Act II, were his, or mainly his, and not, in design and thought, almost wholly Shakspere's own."[28]

There is a third suggestion to explain Q1 and Q2's relationship, one which also depends upon believing that there was an *Ur-Hamlet*. In 1962 Albert Weiner edited Q1; he looked at the reasons put forward for MR, rejected them, and suggested instead that Q1 represented an abridged version of Shakespeare's *Hamlet*. Probably, Weiner thought, there was an acting version of the play which came first, and Q1 was then abridged from that.[29] Certainly Q2 is long; it is closer to a four hour performance than "the two hours' traffic of our stage" that Shakespeare writes about in *Romeo and Juliet*, if that is an accurate time span for performances. There are manuscript plays which survive from the period and they do show that cuts were made on written texts. Abridgement seems a very reasonable possibility.

Although Weiner has received a little support, today MR remains the dominant theory. It means that many scholars believe the order of composition of the two quartos is not the order of publication. If MR is right, or indeed if Weiner's abridgement theory is right, Q1 (published 1603) would have been composed after Q2 (published 1604–5). In contrast, if Q1 is a first sketch and Q2 a revised *Hamlet*, then the order of composition and publication is the same. Nevertheless, scholars do agree about one matter: either Q1 or Q2 represents Shakespeare's first *Hamlet*.

The first major mystery about *Hamlet* is therefore which quarto has priority. There is a second key mystery, closely related to the first: when did Shakespeare write his *Hamlet*? It sounds a simple question. However, the proposed dates for Shakespeare's first composition of the play have varied from 1585, when he was twenty-one, to after the English translation of the play's principal source (which is dated 1608), when Shakespeare was forty-four.[30] It is perhaps mischievous to mention the range, since today there are really only two arguments and two dates, but when scholars read the same contemporary documents and come to strongly contrasting conclusions there is a very significant problem in the literature about *Hamlet*. It is undoubtedly a difficult matter to discuss, with one scholar even saying that anyone attending certain seminars on textual studies "can report tales of psychologically gory frays, furies and frustrations."[31] Yet these same scholars are genuinely striving to discover a solution which has certainty and convinces everyone.

The different beliefs about early references to a *Hamlet* and the origins of the quartos mean we end up with three principal theories explaining the mysteries of the date of *Hamlet* and the relationship of the quartos. These can be summarized in very simplified terms:

1. A very few scholars believe that there was an earlier, pre–Shakespearean *Hamlet*; Shakespeare wrote his Q2 *Hamlet* about 1600; an acting version was prepared; this was then abridged, resulting in Q1. This Q1 was published in 1603, and Q2 in 1604–5.
2. Many believe that there was an earlier, pre–Shakespearean *Hamlet*; Shakespeare wrote his Q2 *Hamlet* about 1600; perhaps he revised it soon afterwards, producing F1; probably an acting version was prepared;

actors performed in this; the actor or actors who played Marcellus and perhaps Voltemand and Lucianus reconstructed the text from memory, resulting in Q1. This Q1 was published in 1603, and Q2 in 1604–5.

3. A small number believe that Shakespeare wrote his first *Hamlet* (Q1) by 1589; it was performed in the late 1580s and in the 1590s; it was published in 1603. At some point after 1598 Shakespeare revised *Hamlet*, resulting in the Q2 published in 1604–5.

These theories are mutually exclusive, and they cannot all be right. It would avoid gory affrays and dissension if only all the matters which scholars have raised could be reconciled, but this appears impossible at present. One reason for the lack of unanimity among scholars is that, of the three principal theories, memorial reconstruction is really the only one to have been explored extensively. Yet *Hamlet* is generally regarded as one of Shakespeare's finest plays, if not the finest, and it would be very satisfying to get a little closer to solving the problems associated with it. The work of past scholars shows how extensive their investigations have been but their disagreements show in their interpretations of documents and texts. Those disagreements are like fracture lines, and to understand them a return to original documents is important, as Alan Nelson recommends.[32] Those same disagreements occasionally also hint at small areas where more research might be useful. The question of Hamlet's age is one of them. It resurfaces in Part One of this book, which focuses on the two quartos, looking for methods to measure unambiguously which came first. In this section a topic which has been surprisingly neglected is explored, namely the quartos' individual debts to the underlying source. Part Two examines and analyses the arguments for MR; in particular it examines the method used for a known MR which took place in 1779, John Bernard's MR of *The School for Scandal*. Part Three returns to the contemporary documents mentioning *Hamlet*, primary evidence which has been interpreted in contradictory ways but which it is well worth revisiting. The new investigation resists theories and aims to identify facts, building on the timeline below. This return to a "cold case" does not intend to ruffle feathers or draw blood; it does not resolve every question, and it cannot agree with every scholar's points, but it does identify weaknesses in the current situation and identifies reproducible evidence which points quite consistently towards one solution.

Significant Records Relating to a Hamlet

1589—Cambridge graduate Thomas Nashe alludes to "whole Hamlets, I should say handfuls of Tragicall speeches."

1594—Theatre manager Philip Henslowe lists a "hamlet" performance at Newington Butts, south of the Thames.

1596—Oxford graduate Thomas Lodge refers to a ghost at the theatre crying "Hamlet, revenge."

1598—Oxford graduate and Rector Francis Meres writes a book which lists the titles of twelve plays by Shakespeare. One play is not known today; *Hamlet* is not mentioned.

1598 or later—Cambridge lecturer Gabriel Harvey annotates his copy of Speght's Chaucer with "his tragedie of Hamlet, Prince of Denmarke, [has] in [it] to please the wiser sort." Harvey attributes it to Shakespeare. He also annotates his copy of Guicciardini's *Detti, et Fatti* with "the Tragedie of Hamlet." Date of annotation unknown; marginalia were added in 1580, 1590 and later.

1600 or later—Theatre-goer Edward Pudsey writes a series of not particularly accurate quotations from *Hamlet* in his commonplace notebook.

1601—Publication of Thomas Dekker's play *Satiromastix*, in which the character Tucca says, "My name's Hamlet reuenge; thou hast been at Parris Garden, hast not?"

1602—*Hamlet* is entered upon the Stationers' Register.

1603—Q1 *Hamlet* is published, attributed to Shakespeare.

1604—Anthony Scoloker, poet, publishes *Diaphantus, or the Passions of Love*, in which he writes a book should "please all, like Prince *Hamlet*."

1604–5—Q2 *Hamlet* is published, attributed to Shakespeare.

(Further quartos largely based on Q2 follow.)

1623—The first folio including *Hamlet* is published, attributed to Shakespeare.

Part One: Which Came First, Q1 or Q2 Hamlet?

1. Dating and Measuring: Initial Evidence

The question of whether Q1 or Q2 is the first Shakespearean *Hamlet* is much disputed, yet the answer is critical. It should, at the very least, inform our understanding of Shakespeare's creative processes and his authorial intentions. Part One therefore offers an open-minded approach to the question of which quarto came first, and shows that even four centuries after the *Hamlet*s were written there is fresh, measurable evidence to be found. (The focus here is almost entirely upon the first two *Hamlet*s, Q1 and Q2, because no one has proposed that F1 is Shakespeare's first *Hamlet*. As a result F1 lies on the margins of this discussion.)

There are good reasons for trying to take a new approach, reasons beyond the scholarly debate and dissension outlined briefly in the Introduction. During the twentieth century scholarship has advanced, and with it has come a change in attitude to the 1608 first quarto of *King Lear* and the 1623 folio *King Lear*. Duthie, the most influential writer promoting the hypothesis of memorial reconstruction for *Hamlet*, jointly edited *Lear* in 1960. A decade earlier, in 1949, he had "imagined" the situation in which *Lear* might have been memorially reconstructed: "I thought of the company as being in the provinces, temporarily deprived of its prompt-book, and desirous of producing a new one; and I imagined its personnel gathered round a scribe, each actor dictating his own speeches in a kind of performance without action." But in 1960 he agreed that Q1 *Lear* "does not look like an actors' reconstruction, and my 1949 theory had better be abandoned."[1] Later exploration of the two *Lear* texts has led to the conclusion that significant, consistent revision had taken place. Contributors to this view have included for instance Steven Urkowitz, in *Shakespeare's Revision of "King Lear,"*[2] and the essayists in *The Division of the Kingdoms*.[3] The two *Lear* texts are now seen as discrete entities, and that change in status is reflected in Wells' and Taylor's *Collected Works*,[4] where both *Lear* texts are printed in full.

If Q1 *Lear* is, effectively, a "first draft," and F1 *Lear* represents Shakespeare's revision of his own play, what about the three extant texts of *Hamlet*? Alfred Hart, after quoting Ben Jonson in *Discoveries*, on Shakespeare's "facility" in writing, declares it is impossible to reconcile that ease in writing with "the patient endurance of the tiresome drudgery required for rewriting the bad quartos, six literary chares more intolerable than the tasks imposed on a teacher of Latin in correcting the exercises of his dullest pupils."[5] Harold Jenkins also rejects the idea of a revising author: "[t]here has been too much irresponsible conjecture about Shakespeare's supposed revisions of supposed early attempts." Jenkins then proceeds to write about his "conception of Shakespeare." Jenkins sees Shakespeare as a "supremely inventive poet," and follows this with his own "conjecture," that Shakespeare "had no call to rework his previous plays when he could always move on to a new one." Jenkins is insistent about that lack of evidence for revision: "the conception of Shakespeare as an artist much given to the revision of his own past work is quite without evidence or plausibility."[6] There is now agreement that Shakespeare revised at least *Lear*. And even if Hart and Jenkins are right about it being a chore to rewrite and about Shakespeare being a "supremely inventive poet," their views about chores and revision are, basically, opinions.

Part One consequently treats Q1 and Q2 *Hamlet* as separate, individual texts, and seeks to find evidence for the priority of either quarto. The chapters avoid evaluative descriptors such as "good" to describe Q2 or "bad" to describe Q1, and also avoid the frequently made assumption that Q1 is an MR. Instead we begin with the recognition that we do not know the time span between the composition of the two texts. If, as many believe, Shakespeare did write Q2 *c*. 1600, and if Q1 is a MR, it has to be written within three years of Shakespeare's original composition, in order to be printed in 1603. If, on the other hand, Q1 is what survives of Shakespeare's first version,[7] as Sams suggests,[8] it could have been in existence by 1589, and it could have been the *Hamlet* referred to by Thomas Nashe in that year. If Q2 is then a revised version, it has to be written by 1604 at the latest, in time for its printing in 1604–5. The range of suggestions for the relationship of the quartos gives us two different time lines and two different time spans between the composition of each quarto. For the MR explanation, or for abridgement, or some combination of the two, there is a possible maximum of three years, but for first draft and revision perhaps as many as twelve to fifteen years. The question then becomes whether with those different time spans it is possible to establish which of the quartos comes first.

There are four principal approaches which scholars use to try to establish when Shakespeare wrote *Hamlet*, and whether he authored Q1. One approach is to examine the allusions to a *Hamlet* play in contemporary Elizabethan literature; they are what we might call the external evidence. Although these allusions have been discussed for over two hundred years, there is no consensus on their interpretation. They are reviewed in Part Three.

Part One, however, concentrates on the three approaches which constitute what might be called the internal evidence, what the quartos themselves tell us. The first of these is the examination of the quartos for historical and literary allusions, in case *Hamlet* is indeed "the abstract and brief chronicles of the times" (II.ii.462–3), as Hamlet says. However, while references and allusions are apparent, their interpretation is also not always agreed, as the sample range discussed below illustrates. The second approach is to compare near parallel lines in the quartos themselves, to see if it is possible to distinguish "better" or definitively "Shakespearean" lines. Once again scholars are not unanimous, as examples will show, though comparisons are a rewarding method of understanding the texts. Lastly, it is possible to take external reference points, both linguistic and literary, and compare the contents of the two quartos against these. This is perhaps the approach taken most recently, and it is the primary focus of most of chapters one to five.

Historical and Literary Allusions

We begin by briefly reviewing a sample of the words, phrases and concepts that some have seen as demonstrating topicality in the quartos, and therefore as indicative of their dates.

There are a number of possible historical allusions which predate any mention of a *Hamlet*. For example, a Katherine Hamlett died by drowning in the Avon on 17th December 1579. It is Chambers' "fancy" that this death by drowning is perhaps recalled in Ofelia/Ophelia's death,[9] though John Dover Wilson thinks the time of year "makes it impossible for the 'setting' to have been drawn upon."[10] When Chambers uses "fancy" we should be aware that his interpretation might not be factual, but more relevantly still, Katherine Hamlett's drowning occurred before any hint of the existence of a *Hamlet* play, so it does not help with dating either quarto. Another example is the unusual description of the Ghost wearing armor, which has led Geoffrey Bullough to suggest that it might derive in part from an engraving of Francesco Maria della Rovere, Duke of Urbino. Titian painted the Duke in 1538.[11] Bullough illustrates this with a picture (an engraving) from Paulus Iovii's *Elogia Virorum Bellica Virtute Illustrium* (1565).[12] Bullough's suggestion has one very distinctive merit, for the story of the play within *Hamlet* is "taken from the murder of the Duke of Urbano [*sic*] by Luigi Gonzago in 1538, who was poisoned by means of a lotion poured into his ears."[13] Bullough may well be right, but both his proposed source and the event precede any date for any *Hamlet*. So does another possible allusion he proposes. Bullough writes that the story of a son revenging his father's murder would have had "considerable topicality between 1587 and 1589," not least because at the time of Mary Queen of Scots' execution in 1587 there were calls by many Scottish nobles for James "to avenge his mother's murder by Queen Elizabeth."[14] This possible topicality is rarely discussed today, but is again early enough to come before any mention of a *Hamlet* play.

Another potential historical reference comes in the mention of "Julius Caesar" in the quartos. Initially it looks as though this might show that the quartos must both be 1599 or later, 1599 being the date by which Shakespeare is supposed to have written *Julius Caesar*. It is in scene 9 of Q1 that Hamlet turns his attention to Corambis, and enquires what he enacted "in the university." Corambis declares, "I did act Julius Caesar. I was killed in the Capitol. Brutus killed me." Hamlet punningly replies, "It was a brute part of him to kill so capital a calf" (9.58–60). Q2 is almost identical: "I did enact Julius Caesar. I was killed i'th' Capitol. Brutus killed me" (III.ii.99–102). It is this mention of Julius Caesar which leads some scholars to place Shakespeare's composition of *Hamlet* as shortly after his *Julius Caesar*. *Julius Caesar*, in turn, is seen as the play that the Swiss tourist, Thomas Platter, "must have seen" at the Globe "in all probability"[15] on 21st September 1599. (Platter doesn't tell us enough for us to be sure that the play was Shakespeare's, which is why there is the hint of uncertainty and authorial persuasion in "must have seen," and "in all probability.") That Shakespeare had written his *Julius Caesar* before 1600 is persuasively demonstrated in John Weever's *Mirror of Martyrs* (1601):

> The Many-headed multitude were drawne
> By *Brutus* speach, that Caesar was ambitious,
> When eloquent *Mark Antonie* had showne
> His vertues, who but Brutus then was vicious?[16]

This includes what seems a very likely reference to when Antony addresses his "Friends, Romans and countrymen," and plays upon "ambitious" and "ambition" (III.ii.73–107[17]). Consequently it is thought that Shakespeare had most likely written *Julius Caesar* by 1600, although how much before is in doubt.

However, the puns in *Hamlet* work regardless of whether *Julius Caesar* was written, or when it was written; they need not even refer to a play about Caesar. They simply work as a pair of puns upon "Capitol"/"capital"[18] and "Brutus"/"brute." Julius Caesar was a popular subject for plays. Chambers mentions *Caesar Interfectus*, probably performed at Christ Church, Oxford in the 1581–2 season, and probably written by Richard Edes.[19] Another play, *The Tragedy of Caesar and Pompey, or Caesar's Revenge*, was "probably" performed during the 1590s at Trinity College, Oxford.[20] But the allusion to Brutus and the Capitol do not need to refer to a play, Shakespeare's or otherwise. As Ann Thompson and Neil Taylor put it: "it is not absolutely necessary to assume that references in one play are 'echoes' of the other ... [or] that a reference to a play about the death of Julius Caesar has to be read as a joke about a play by Shakespeare."[21] The puns in the quartos are rather slight to support the claim that Shakespeare must have written his *Julius Caesar* before writing *Hamlet*; after all, no one suggests Shakespeare had written *Julius Caesar* before mentioning him in *1 Henry VI* (I.i.55[22]).

Of more potential significance for dating are the suggestions of historical allusions where the quartos differ. One of these gains general agreement; it concerns the name "Polonius" in Q2. This is seen as deriving from a book, *De Optimo Senatore*, written by the Polish courtier Wawrzyniec Grzymala Goslicki, and translated into English as *The Counsellor*, in 1598. (Poland was sometimes referred to as "Polonia" at the time, for example in John Gerard's *Great Herball, or Generall Historie of Plantes*, 1597.[23]) If that is so, Q2 (and subsequent quartos, and F1) would seem to date from 1598 or later. It would be useful to argue that the absence of the name Polonius in Q1 means it was written earlier, but the absence of that name tells us nothing.

Other allusions are more tricky, and do not have the unanimous support of critics. One of these is in part of one of Hamlet's speeches, a part exclusive to Q1, which includes these lines:

> Ham.   And do you hear? Let not your clown speake ...
>   ... and my coate wants a cullison:
>   And, your beere is sowre ... [Sig. F2r.26, F2v.3–4].

In 1918 John Dover Wilson notes that two of these are "jests" found in *Tarleton's Jests*, published in 1611. Wilson writes: "But Tarleton died in September 1588, after which a sneer at him would be, to say the least of it, old-fashioned. We are forced to conclude, therefore, that this part of the Q1 text goes back to some period before that date."[24] He repeats this in his *Hamlet* edition in 1934: "two of the 'cinquepace of jests' occur in *Tarleton's Jests* (pub.c.1600)." But now he presents it differently, for he describes the Q1 passage as "an addition" (presumably to the MR of Q2, or a stage adaptation of Q2), and as an "attack upon a particular clown who is accused of using very stale material."[25] By his 1936 edition of *Hamlet* Wilson has changed his note again, and makes a comment instead upon a line in Jonson's *Every Man Out of His Humour*, "Ile giue coats, that's my humour: but I lack a cullisen" (I.ii.145), which may be a "glance at Kempe," the actor.[26] Today it is not suggested that the Q1 passage refers to Tarleton, despite the quotations from his jests, or that it dates from c. 1588, perhaps because Q1 is by most scholars dated after 1600. But since Q1 is for many scholars an MR postdating Q2, and the passage does not occur in Q2, an explanation for the lines would be useful. So the passage is seen as an interpolation, an addition. It may be so, of course, but it is an example of how one hypothesis (MR) needs to be supplemented by another hypothesis (interpolation) to explain what is found in Q1. Wilson has studied and written extensively upon *Hamlet*, so his shifts in position are interesting. It is only fair to add that in 1963 Wilson also effectively writes a "retraction," when he hopes that his essays on Q1 are "out of reach of all but discreet readers."[27]

However, *Tarleton's Jests*—or at least jests which were attributed to Tarleton—were clearly current after his death in September 1588, so perhaps the verbal echoes of two of the "cinquepace of jests" are to his jokes and do not signify the man. Curiously, Wilson offers another possible identification of a contemporary allusion. Q2 has a scene of some sixty-five lines, IV.iv, which is only half a dozen lines in Q1. In Q2 only Hamlet encounters a Captain, who explains he is going to "gain a little patch of land" (IV.iv.17). Wilson picks up the phrase "a little patch of land" and writes:

> From July 2, 1601 till the spring of 1602 the sand-dunes of Ostend were valiantly defended against the Spaniards in many battles and with great loss of life by an English force under Sir Francis Vere, which returned home on March 18. The siege actually continued until Sept. 1604, but the London public would only be interested in the earlier stages [because of the initial involvement of English troops]. There can be little doubt that Sh. is here alluding to these events, which points to the late summer or autumn of 1601 as the date for *Hamlet*, as we have it in Q2.[28]

In his 1936 *Hamlet* Wilson expands upon the note. George Rylands quotes it in his 1969 *Hamlet*.[29] But in 1982 Jenkins rejects it, "even if dates permitted," which, it is assumed here, refers obliquely to his and other scholars' beliefs in a Q2 from *c*. 1600, in other words before the siege of Ostend.[30] In 2007 Thompson and Taylor do not appear to discuss it.

Both of Wilson's suggestions of contemporary allusions would cause problems for the dominant narrative dating Q1 (his suggestion of an early date pre–September 1588) and Q2 (his suggestion of after spring 1601). Both have been dropped. Oddly, while Jenkins rejects "a little patch of land" as referring to the siege of Ostend *c*. 1601–2 because of its date, he mentions the "much disputed" "late innovation" (II.ii.196), which he suggests may allude to the Essex rebellion in February 1601. If that is a correct reading, then Q2 is later than February 1601. Meanwhile James Shapiro suggests that lines further down in the same Q2 scene—about "The imminent death of twenty thousand men" (IV.iv.59)[31]—invite comparison to the loss of life in Ireland during Essex's campaign. This might be so. We should note that Shapiro's suggestion shifts attention away from "a little patch of land" which would hardly describe Ireland. The Essex campaign in Ireland is a little earlier and better for arguing for a *c.* 1600 date for Q2, as Shapiro does.³² As Wilson ruefully writes: "[w]hile it seems to be agreed upon all hands that *Hamlet* is the most topical play in the whole corpus, unhappily when it comes to interpreting the supposed allusion, agreement almost entirely vanishes."³³

These examples do not exhaust the alleged historical allusions, and they are deliberately selected to show the problems of interpretation, and the lack of a consensus. Unfortunately, dating Q1 or Q2 from literary allusions instead is no more helpful. Most of the debts which both Q1 and Q2 may owe to minor Elizabethan literary texts are small. From dumb shows³⁴ to the flowery, euphuistic style of an Osric,³⁵ to the Senecan use of a "ghost" to call for revenge and thus initiate the action of a play,³⁶ to the "sprezzatura" evident in Hamlet himself and in Ofelia/Ophelia's description of him as "courtier, scholar, soldier" (7.185), or the "courtier's, soldier's, scholar's eye, tongue, sword" (III.i.150)³⁷—all can be found before 1589, and are available for either quarto. Michel Eyquem de Montaigne's philosophical *Essais* (published in French in 1580),³⁸ Timothy Bright's *Treatise of Melancholie* (1586), which may have influenced the creation of a melancholic Hamlet, the possible allusion to Robert Norman's book on magnetism ("[H]ere's metal more attractive" [9.63, III.ii.106]),³⁹ and echoes of Philip Sidney's *Defense of Poetrie* (begun in 1579, published in 1595) in Corambis/Polonius' reference to the Players in the compound adjectives in "best for ... pastoral-historical, historical-comical, comical-historical-pastoral" (7.267–8; in Q2, "...pastoral-historical, historical-comical..."⁴⁰ [II.ii.334])—these too are pre–1589, and therefore before the earliest date for either quarto.

There is one phrase in Q1 and in Q2 which has the potential to be useful: "the croaking raven doth bellow for revenge" (9.138–9, III.ii.248). The line appears to blend two lines from the anonymous *True Tragedy of Richard III*,⁴¹ a play that has been dated from 1585 to near 1590. Regrettably, the direction of borrowing cannot be ascertained since those two dates span 1589, the earliest date for a possible *Hamlet*. *The True Tragedy of Richard III* was entered on the Stationers' Register on 19th June 1594.

It is not possible to refer to literary sources without mentioning *Pierce Penniless*, *The Spanish Tragedy*, and the relevant part of volume V of *Les Histoires Tragiques* with its story about Prince Amleth. *Pierce Penniless*, already quoted at the beginning of the Introduction, is discussed in chapter four. *The Spanish Tragedy* is discussed in chapters three and eight, but we can note here that there is no certainty or agreement about its date of composition. J. R. Mulryne, editing the play, suggests it was probably written after 1582, when Thomas Watson's *Hekatompathia* was published, from which *The Spanish Tragedy* adapts material, and obviously before its recorded performance on 23rd February 1592.⁴² Nor is there certainty or agreement about the direction of borrowing. Duthie, for example, believes that the actor/reporter(s) memorially reconstructing (Q1) *Hamlet* drew from *The Spanish Tragedy*, and that therefore *The Spanish Tragedy* came first. *The Spanish Tragedy*, however, has "no major narrative source,"[43] unlike *Hamlet*. *The Spanish Tragedy* does have a plot which mirrors closely some of the plot elements of *Hamlet*'s story, except that it is the son who is killed in *The Spanish Tragedy* and the father who exacts revenge. Its plot and language in some aspects mirror, or reverse, elements of *Hamlet*. Perhaps Kyd noted the plot of *Hamlet* and created his play, for, as Philip Edwards puts it, "If one play copies another, and one is based on a known source and the other isn't, there is a strong argument that the play with the source is the earlier."[44] Until we know more about the dates of either the quartos or *The Spanish Tragedy* we cannot be confident about the direction of borrowing. The evidence, such as it is, is inconclusive.

Fortunately, scholars do agree that *Les Histoires Tragiques* is the underlying source of the *Hamlet*s. It is the subject of chapters two to five.

Lines in the Quartos

Since "source-hunting," with scholars "picking over not only the world's literature, but also any non-literary documentation of actual people and events from history,"[45] does not help us determine either the chronology of the composition of the quartos or their dates, it is not surprising that scholars also scrutinize the two quartos themselves. Wilson gives us a careful comparison of spellings and phrasing variants in *The Manuscript of Shakespeare's Hamlet and the Problems of its Transmission* (1934), and footnotes in any *Hamlet* edition also inform us about differences. However, differences alone do not tell us anything about the date of either quarto. But sometimes there are direct comparisons of specific lines, and sometimes there are contentious assertions. One critic sees these lines in Q1 as "an especially egregious example of memorial muddling":

> *King.* How now son Hamlet, how fare you, shall we have a play?
> *Ham.* Yfaith the Camelions dish, not Capon cramm'd, feede a the ayre [Sig. F2.35–F3v.1].

The critic much prefers Q2:

> *King.* How fares our cosin Hamlet?
> *Ham.* Excellent yfaith.
> Of the Camelions dish, I eate the ayre,
> Promiscram'd, you cannot feede Capons so [Sig. H1r.2–5].

Q1 has "incoherence" against Q2's "rightness."[46] The problem for the critic may start with the way that the King in Q1 asks two questions in succession. Conventionally, in actual speech, when a speaker asks two questions (which happens quite frequently) the listener will reply to just one. In this example, the first question is a "how do you do" polite inquiry, which doesn't often evoke a significant response when another question follows. It does with Hamlet. Hamlet—Shakespeare—appears to choose to subvert the King's expectation of a response to the second question, "shall we have a play?" Hamlet's reply tells us rapidly that he is deliberately not cooperating in an exchange of social niceties with the King; it reminds us of the antagonism between them. The Q1 extract is not fully quoted above; it continues thus:

> *Ham.* I father: My lord, you playd in the Vniversitie [Sig. F2v.35–F3r.2].

As Urkowitz shows,[47] Hamlet's reply here, "I father," does answer the King's second question, "shall we have a play?"

Since the alleged "incoherence" is found in natural speech today when two questions are asked, we could conclude that the composer of these lines has a sharp ear for "real" language. We can also see that Q1's Hamlet is being mockingly dutiful in addressing the King as "father." And then after his two word, cursory reply, Hamlet promptly turns his attention away from the King towards the counselor, Corambis, with "My lord, you playd in the Vniversitie." For the audience or reader who is on Hamlet's side and opposed to the King Hamlet is being deliciously rude. That the intention is rudeness Q2 effectively confirms, for there the King replies dismissively:

> *King.* I haue nothing with this aunswer Hamlet,
> These words are not mine [Sig. H1r.6–7].

Q1 seems not so much muddled as intelligently phrased to "show" rather than "tell" the actor and the audience or reader about the less than amicable relationship between King and Prince. The exchange is more discourteous in Q1— is this something the abridger achieves, or the actor/reporter who is thought to have created a MR? Or could it be something that indicates a sound knowledge of natural speech and stagecraft, executed by Shakespeare slightly differently on the two occasions? Q2 underlines Hamlet's antipathy to the King in a different way when Hamlet describes himself as "Promiscram'd," that is, stuffed with promises that he will be heir to the throne. In both quartos Hamlet sees himself as worse off than a "capon" (which would be fed to be fattened, killed and eaten)—he is merely crammed with promises that are but air. Q1 is effective, and so is Q2 here.

Alternatively, the exchange in Q1 may simply be an occasion when an explicit stage direction like "(*Aside*)" would remove the alleged "memorial muddling":

> *King.* How now son Hamlet, how fare you, shall we have a play?
> *Ham.* (*Aside*) Yfaith the Camelions dish, not Capon cramm'd, feede a the ayre.
> I father: My lord, you playd in the Vniversitie.

It is not the only occasion when an aside is not marked, as chapter eight also shows. Could it be that we are simply not reading Q1 carefully enough here?

There are other examples of differences in phrasing which also convey emotions effectively but subtly differently. In the final scene of Q1 Hamlet confides in Horatio:

> *Ham.* Beleeue me Horatio, my hart is on the sodaine
> Very sore all here about [Sig. I2v.32-3].

"Here" is a proximal adverb; it refers to a place close to, and in this context, as Urkowitz comments,[48] it requires a gesture from the actor towards his heart. The grammar is straightforward: "my hart" is the subject and comes first, "is" is the verb, and the adjectival complement "Very sore" follows. Q2 is fractionally different:

> *Ham.* ... thou wouldst not thinke how ill all's here about my hart, but it is no matter [Sig. N3v.8-9].

The grammar is now a little more complex, or at least less common. The feeling Hamlet has—"ill," the adjectival complement—is brought forward to the front of the clause (before mention of his heart), and therefore receives a little more emphasis.[49] The actor's hand gesture is still expected, because of "here," but having let Hamlet draw attention to his apprehension Shakespeare/Hamlet then plays it down with "but it is no matter." When we compare these versions we see that Q1's version again has merit, but that Q2 is a little more subtle. Urkowitz notes that F1 is different again:

> *Hamlet.* ... I shall winne at the oddes: but thou wouldst not thinke how all here aboue my heart: but it is no matter [F1. V.ii.160-2].

While the proximal adverb "here" again invites that hand gesture, this time there is no "sore" or "ill" to describe the feeling; the adjectival complement has been left unsaid. Hamlet's expression of his feeling appears incomplete, though really it is conveyed in a different manner. After the confident "I shall winne at the oddes" comes a pause. Winning ought to satisfy the Prince, and for a moment Hamlet seems upbeat. Yet he continues with "but," a pivot word which we commonly use to signal a contrast is coming. The expectation of winning is not enough, and Hamlet is still feeling something untoward in his heart. And this time there is a fractionally longer pause, a colon, not a comma, before "but it is no matter," long enough for the gesture and for the audience to understand what is implied. Disconcertingly, this looks like a logical order of development (Q1, then Q2, then F1). It would be an actor/reporter with a relatively fine understanding who recalls Hamlet's momentary hint of pain and apprehension, especially when "Marcellus," "Lucianus" and "Voltemand" are not even on stage in this scene. This matters.

A different set of lines might suggest a possibly different order of composition. Hamlet listens to the troupe of actors, and notes the passion in the voice of the actor merely playing a tragic part. It leads Hamlet to berate himself for being no more than an "ass" and a "John of Dreams," and to ask why if an actor can show that much passion he, Hamlet, cannot do more. The critical lines in each version share a very similar meaning. All ask a question, but they change in their expression:

Q1
   Ham. For Hecuba, why what is Hecuba to him, or he to Hecuba? [Sig. F1r.1].

Q2
   Ham. For *Hecuba*?
          What's *Hecuba* to him, or he to her,
          That he should weepe for her? [Sig. F4v.20–2].

F1
   Ham. For *Hecuba*?
          What's *Hecuba* to him, or he to *Hecuba*,
          That he should weepe for her? [F1. II.ii.591–3].

Q1's line is an unusually long eighteen syllables in a speech otherwise presented as blank verse. It might be seen as a "blunder" (Mommsen's word) made by the alleged actor/reporter, though the whole line presents one thought. Both Q2 and F1 separate the phrase "For *Hecuba*" from the question that follows; both attach "For *Hecuba*" to the words which precede the question. Q2 then presents the question "What's *Hecuba* to him, or he to her" in a regular ten syllable line, by using elision in "What's" and having a string of pronouns: the masculine "him, he" and the feminine pronoun "her." It is not the clearest of the three versions, though it is grammatically standard today. Could it be the first version, from which Q1 ultimately derives? If we look at F1 we find it has Q2's elision, but uses the same mirroring of names and pronouns as Q1: "*Hecuba*" occurs first and last, and just the masculine pronouns "him" and "he" are left. F1 has a twelve syllable line, but its mirrored patterning—chiasmus—and musicality will probably be preferred by most readers and listeners. The meaning is similar in each, and it seems that Q1 and F1 are closer to being parallel. The sequence of composition is hard to determine. If Q1 came first, Q2 might begin the regularization, but F1 show the best of both quarto versions, despite being a twelve syllable line. If Q2 came first, F1 might be the revised version, and Q1's alleged actor/reporter might possibly recall F1's "*Hecuba* to him, or he to *Hecuba*."

Examples such as these suggest that the composer of Q1 was a little more sensitive and able than we might expect an actor/reporter in a minor role or two to have been, as he tried to assemble enough of *Hamlet* to make a MR to be performed, or to be printed as Q1. The first example above has two distinguished scholars locked in disagreement over the value of the two quartos, perhaps because so many (automatically?) reject Q1, seeing it as an MR. But the quotations show differences, not "garbled" incompetence in Q1. Exploring variants is useful, but it too is not conclusive.

Measured Evidence

For over a century scholars have also "measured" the evidence found in the plays themselves, often to try to ascertain the order in which Shakespeare wrote them. Stylistic features have also been examined to distinguish parts of a play that might not be Shakespeare's but perhaps by a collaborator. The information offered by stylometrics is helpful rather than definitive, since we cannot be sure that any play in the form it has descended to us was written at one particular time and not changed subsequently by its principal author or by another. It does not appear that different versions of the same play are consistently examined for specific language and poetic features. Stanley Wells and Gary Taylor's *William Shakespeare. A Textual Companion* includes comparative lists of features for all the plays, but they include them for only one *King Lear*—"Q," the 1608 quarto—and for one *Hamlet*, presumably for Q2 or F1 *Hamlet*. Ants Oras in *Pause Patterns in Elizabethan and Jacobean Drama: An Experiment in Prosody* measures *Lear* and *Hamlet*, but also doesn't specify which version. But because there may be a slight or a significant time span between the two *Hamlet* quartos it may be useful to "measure" these separately.

Early modern English saw a leveling or reduction of verb inflections such as <eth>, found on the third person singular present tense verb, for example "droppeth," which is now "drops." Shakespeare uses a mixture. A quick glance at Portia's famous speech illustrates this (author's emboldening):

> *Portia.* The quality of mercy is not strain'd,
> It dropp**eth** as a gentle rain from heaven
> Upon the place beneath: it is twice bless'd:
> It bless**eth** him that give**s** and him that take**s** ... [IV.i.179–182].[50]

Here the survival of the old third person singular present tense inflection, <eth>, and the presence of incoming modern <(e)s> are both demonstrated.

It may have been convenient for Shakespeare that both existed, for in the second line the two syllables of "droppeth" scan regularly, while the monosyllabic "drops" would have marred the underlying iambic pentameter. The older form was gradually being displaced by the newer ending, as a later writer confirms, in 1643. Richard Hodges noted that although men might write "lead*eth* it, mak*eth* it, not*eth* it, rak*eth* it, per-*fumeth* it & c" yet "in our ordinary speech ... we say lead*s* it, make*s* it, note*s* it, rake*s* it, per-*fumes* it."[51] It is clear that during Shakespeare's lifetime the change from the <eth> ending to the <(e)s> ending was taking place.

If there were only a three year gap between the compositions of the two quartos we might not expect to find much difference in the presence of <eth> in the two texts. If there were perhaps a fifteen year gap, we might see a discernible difference. Sir Brian Vickers, in *Shakespeare, Co-Author*, mentions this linguistic change. He reports on MacDonald P. Jackson's findings of twenty plays up to *As You Like It*, and fourteen from *Twelfth Night*. The first group had 239 old <eth> inflections to sixty-eight modern <(e)s>, but the second group had twenty-nine <eth> uses to 185<(e)s>.[52] This area of linguistic development leads to an obvious question; could these verb endings help to indicate the priority of either quarto?

The results, covering the whole of each quarto, are interesting. Q1 shows no use of the "new" "has," and thirty-seven uses of the "old" "hath." Q2 shows two "has" usages, and fifty-seven of "hath." Allegedly Q2 *Hamlet* "is the first play in which Shakespeare relaxed his preference for 'hath.'"[53] The two occasions of "has" in Q2 are matched by "hath" in Q1, so both "has" must either be forgotten by the alleged memorial reconstructor, or changed to the older inflection by an alleged abridger, if we are to argue for Q2's priority. Modern "does" is used on five occasions in Q1; its usage is up to nineteen in Q2. <[E]th> on other verbs is found ten times in Q1, and four times in Q2. The modern <(e)s> suffix is found widely in Q1 (168) and in Q2 (308). Table 1 summarizes these findings.

Table 1. Third Person Singular Verb Suffixes (All of Q1 and Q2)[54]

Feature	Q1	Q2
has	–	2
hath	37	57
does	5	19
doth	16	17
<*eth*> (excluding *hath, doth*)	10	4
<(*e*)*s*> (excluding *has, does*)	168	308
Total no. of lines (Irace's count)	2221	4056

This indicates that proportionally Q1 demonstrates a higher number of the older forms, and lacks evidence of the more modern "has." Q1, at 55 percent the length of Q2, uses the <eth> inflection more than *twice* as much as Q2. Alternatively, it is accurate to say that there are more uses of the modern "has" and "does" forms in Q2, and fewer of the older <eth> suffixes. The older form of "hath" is still entrenched.

The inflections hint at Q1 being the earlier text. That hint is strengthened by two nearly parallel passages. In Q1 counselor Corambis repeats:

>   *Cor.* ... he closeth with you in the consequence,
>   As you may bridle it not disparage him a iote.
>   What was I a bout to say,
>   *Mon.* He closeth with him in the consequence.
>   *Cor.* I, you say right, he closeth with him thus ... [Sig. D2r.32–36].

The repeated line is a tongue twister, involving the older <eth> inflection and some awkwardly combined consonants, /k, z, ð/ and /s/. In Q2 counselor Polonius repeats:

>   *Pol.* He closes with you in this consequence ...
>   By the matter, I was about to say something.
>   Where did I leave?
>   *Rey.* At closes in the consequence.
>   *Pol.* At closes in the consequence, I marry ... [Sig. E1v.18, 24–7].

This is more modern and less of a tongue twister, with only the awkward /k, z/ and /s/ consonants. Is the older form the preference of the memorial reconstructor (or an abridger)—or did Shakespeare, revising, decide that not only was the "closes" form more modern but that it was also less of a tongue twister?

Examining the <eth> inflection is a useful method to contribute to distinguishing which text might have come first because morphology provides an objective, external reference point and is not an opinion or postulate. A second set of measured data compares the use of colloquialisms across just one scene, the "Gravedigger's" scene, Q1's scene 16 and Q2's act V scene i. The scene is chosen because it contains both prose and blank verse, and while it begins in a relatively informal register, it concludes more formally. Moreover, there is a general agreement that the two quartos diverge more as the play progresses, so to select a scene from towards the end of the play might mean a greater difference. The sampling follows observations by F. O. Waller.[55] This time the external reference point is a perceived trend in Shakespeare's style, that it becomes more colloquial with time, though the usefulness of the reference point is dependent upon scholars' chronology of the plays being fairly accurate. (Tables for selected colloquialisms are given by Wells and Taylor.[56]) Can colloquialisms show any difference between the two *Hamlet* quartos? As with <eth> inflections we might not expect any real difference in colloquial forms if there is only a three year gap between the plays, with Q1 following Q2. A gap of up to fifteen years, with Q2 noticeably later than Q1, might demonstrate a difference.

In the two scenes we can find eleven distinctive colloquialisms. Four are distributed equally. There are nineteen pronoun and verb elisions or contractions (for example "she's"), one noun and verb elision ("funerall's"), one preposition and possessive determiner contraction ("with's" for "with his"), and one contracted interjection (for example "ifaith"). There are also less equal distributions, with Q2 having a greater number of colloquialisms, partly no doubt because of the scene's greater length. Q2 has five verb and pronoun elisions (for example "doo't"), where Q1 has just one, and eight preposition and pronoun elisions (for example "too't") to Q1's two. There are further differences which show that Q2 has a greater range of colloquialisms. While Q1 uses "he" twenty times, Q2 uses "a" for "he" eight times, the spelling reflecting the frequently unstressed status of the pronoun, or a relaxed pronunciation. Additional colloquialisms found only in Q2 include one blend of the infinitive marker "to" and the main verb, "excell," giving "t'excell." The unstressed nature of "the" and its potential for running it into the preceding or following word is also evident. In Q2 there are one proclitic use ("th'inheritor") and five enclitic uses (for example "i'th"). In other words in this scene Q2 shows a higher number of colloquial terms and a wider range than Q1. Table 2 summarizes this.

Table 2. Informal or Colloquial Features in Scene 16 of Q1 and Act V Scene i of Q2

Feature	Q1	Q2
Pronoun and verb elisions, e.g., *she's*	19	19
Noun and verb elision, e.g., *funerall's*	1	1
Preposition and possessive determiner, e.g., *with's*	1	1
Contracted interjection, e.g., *ifaith*	1	1
Verb and pronoun elisions, e.g., *doo't*	1	5
Preposition and pronoun, e.g., *too't*	2	8
he	20	14
a for *he*	–	8
Elision of infinitive, e.g., *t'expell*	–	1
Proclitic "the," e.g., *th'inheritor*	–	1
Enclitic "the," e.g., *i'th*	–	5

While it is important to understand the many differences between the quartos, to establish the priority of one or the other some form of external comparison is necessary. Both <eth> inflections and the colloquialisms are objective evidence that can be found through examining the quartos individually. Both sets of evidence would suggest Q1 is the prior text.

Some may object to this approach. If they support the MR hypothesis, they might say that the compositor(s) setting the text into print preferred particular forms, and that his/their preference explains these differences. This compositorial preference would be another supplementary hypothesis, to add to MR. Or the changes might be attributed to the putative memorial reconstructor(s). We then again need an additional hypothesis to maintain the MR hypothesis, that the actor/reporter(s) remembering the *Hamlet* he'd played in either selectively or accidentally changed some quite specific colloquial forms. (And we meet another problem if we claim that the changes are compositorial preferences, because that would then undermine the use of such measurements in other plays.)

Objectors may also, justifiably, require more extensive linguistic comparisons, not least because Q1's scene 16 is shorter than Q2's V.i. In fact there are still differences when a fuller survey of colloquial features is done. Q1 has a slightly narrower range of types of colloquial features, and Q2 a slightly wider range. Q2 has more examples of verb plus pronoun elisions, like "swear't" (swear it), "see't," "gau't," "pardon't" and "think't." Q2 uses more contractions of the infinitive marker "to" before a verb, giving "t'illume," for example. Q2 also has noticeably more contractions following a preposition, like "neer's" for "near us," and also after conjunctions, for example "ift," for "if it." The enclitic and proclitic use of "the," shown by "it'h" and "th'extravagant" for example, is widespread, with over sixty uses in Q2 against two in Q1. And there is a shift in how "a" is employed when it is not an indefinite article. Q1 sometimes uses "a" to replace "have" and "of," but Q2 generally avoids that and sometimes replaces "he" with "a" instead. The fuller survey—summarized in appendix A—shows the breadth and variety of colloquial terms in Q2. The data show that Q2 has a slightly wider range of colloquial features. If we look at the number of colloquial features, Q1 has slightly fewer, at 10.3 per hundred lines, against Q2's slightly greater number of 10.8 per hundred lines. If there really is a trend in the plays towards a more colloquial style, Q2 is the later text.

We have seen that historical and literary allusions give inconclusive evidence about the priority of the quartos, though it is agreed that Polish courtier Goslicki's book, *The Counsellor*, is the source of the name Polonius, found not in Q1 but in Q2 and F1. There are disagreements about how well written specific, almost parallel lines are in the quartos, with the examples of Q1's lines sometimes different but still effective. When we look at what two different, external reference points tell us, Q1 shows measureable evidence of more, older <eth> inflections, and Q2 shows measureable evidence of a slightly wider and slightly greater range of colloquialisms. These are indications that Q1 may be earlier than Q2. Since stylometrics is still a developing field, since we do not know whether a text was completed in one spell of writing, and since these comparisons are between the quartos rather than across the canon, the findings can hardly be considered incontrovertible proof of which quarto came first. Nevertheless these three approaches—allusions, comparison of lines, measuring stylistic features—show why it is useful, if not essential, to keep an open mind about the priority of the quartos.

There is one particular, further investigation which seems to hold both potential and a challenge. It has its origins in a problem which Duthie notes in his *"Bad" Quarto of Hamlet*. He has difficulty in finding a satisfactory reason for the difference in Hamlet's age in the two quartos.[57] Prince Hamlet is younger in Q1, and about the same age as Prince Amleth in volume V, chapter 3 of *Les Histoires Tragiques*. That French source is also an external reference point, and really we should know what a three way comparison between *Les Histoires Tragiques*, Q1 and Q2 shows. It is a rewarding study, and reported in the following chapters.

2. *Les Histoires Tragiques* and the Quartos

The ultimate source of the *Hamlet* story in Shakespeare was first written down by a Dane, Saxo Grammaticus, who completed his account of Amlethus in his *Historiae Danicae* in the late twelfth century. Saxo's Latin manuscript was first printed in 1514, and later translated into his native language in 1575.

It was François de Belleforest, principally a translator,[1] who produced a French translation of the Latin version, somewhat embellished, with the protagonist now named Amleth, in a collection of several volumes of translations under the title *Les Histoires Tragiques*. The Amleth story appears in volume V. It was popular, being published for example in Lyons in 1576, Paris in 1582, Lyons in 1583 and in 1601, and Rouen in 1604.[2] There is scholarly agreement that Saxo Grammaticus' *Historiae Danicae* was the original source of Belleforest's *Histoires Tragiques*; there is a scholarly consensus that the third story in *Les Histoires Tragiques*[3] volume V is the source underlying Shakespeare's *Hamlet*.

However, exactly how Belleforest's tale is transformed into Q2 *Hamlet* is not agreed. If the MR or abridgement hypothesis is correct, Belleforest translates the story into French, in *Les Histoires Tragiques*, then an English drama (the putative *Ur-Hamlet*) is composed, then comes Shakespeare's Q2, and later—perhaps after F1, perhaps after abridgement, or after a stage adaptation, or some combination of these—comes Q1. It is assumed in this chronology that the memorial reconstructor(s) or abridger(s) of Q1 drew principally upon (acting in) (an adapted) Q2. However, in this scenario it is possible to add further speculations, that memories of the putative *Ur-Hamlet* and/or knowledge of *Les Histoires Tragiques* may have aided the memorial reconstructor(s) or abridger(s). If, on the other hand, the first sketch and revision hypothesis is correct, *Les Histoires Tragiques* remains the first text, then comes Q1, with a later revised version in Q2 (and later still, F1). While these scenarios may well simplify what happened, in the first one Q1 would be more distant than Q2 from the French source, with perhaps F1 and/or abridgement and/or a stage adaptation intervening before Q1 is composed. In the second scenario Q2 would be more distant than Q1 from the French source.

An obvious method of seeking evidence about the priority of the quartos is therefore to examine the parallels between the three texts: the French source, Q1 and Q2. There are investigations into Saxo's Latin tale, and into which edition of *Les Histoires Tragiques* underlies the *Hamlet*s (Bullough quotes for example A.P. Stabler's Ph.D. dissertation[4]), but there seems to be no comprehensive overview of the matching elements in the French source and the quartos as discrete texts. This may be because many scholars assume that there was an *Ur-Hamlet*. This assumption is present in, for example, Jenkins' introduction to his Arden *Hamlet*:

> A question that arises but is hardly possible to answer is whether all that Shakespeare inherited from Belleforest came to him through the *Ur-Hamlet*.... The second alternative presents us with the possibility that some things common to Belleforest and Shakespeare were not in the *Ur-Hamlet*.... Yet it is as inconceivable that the *Ur-Hamlet* did not use Belleforest as it is that Shakespeare did not use the *Ur-Hamlet*....[5]

The *Ur-Hamlet* is hypothetical; *Les Histoires Tragiques* and the quartos exist. If the *Ur-Hamlet* did exist, if Q2 was Shakespeare's first *Hamlet*, if Q1 is a "garbled" MR composed later still, we would logically expect Q1 to reflect *Les Histoires Tragiques* less closely than Q2. Since Q1 is only 55 percent of the length of Q2, we could hardly expect it to retain all the echoes of *Les Histoires Tragiques* that Q2 has (and that the putative *Ur-Hamlet* might have had). And if Q1 has just been remembered and reconstructed, or has been abridged, we might also expect it to have fewer parallels with the source because some would have been forgotten by the actor/reporter(s) or cut by the abridger.

This chapter therefore begins a three way comparison between the French source and the quartos. It starts in the obvious place with the details shared between them, and continues with ideas which have been adapted, discussion of the Ghost, and examples of "transpositions." It concludes with a look at parallels exclusive to one quarto or the other. All French quotations come from Sir Israel Gollancz's edition, *The Sources of Hamlet*. It was printed in 1915, more than half a century after criticisms of Q1 began, and when Voltemand, Marcellus and Lucianus had been suggested as the roles played by the hypothetical memorial reconstructor(s). The presentation of quotations is in the order of publication (*Les Histoires Tragiques*, Q1, Q2), and is not intended to connote or signify the order of composition.

Shared Details in Les Histoires Tragiques, Q1 and Q2

The initial findings are all straightforward. They show the details shared by all three texts, the details which appear to originate in *Les Histoires Tragiques*, and are found adapted, or transposed, or both, in the quartos, and the differences in borrowings. Appendix B gives a comprehensive overview of all the parallels.

We start with the shared verbal matches, plot elements and characters, in all three texts, for these establish the extent to which the source is reflected in the quartos. The verbal matches and shared plot elements begin in the early part of Belleforest's account, which explains how the King of Norway had "deffié au combat" ("challenged to a fight"[6]) Amleth's father Horvvendille, just as in both quartos the King of Norway "Dared to the combat" Hamlet's father (178, 1.73, and I.i.83[7]). The parallels are unmistakable despite the language difference. All three texts describe Amleth or Hamlet's father as "vaillante," or "valiant" (182, 1.73, and I.i.83). When Amleth's father (Horvvendille) or Hamlet's father is murdered by his brother, that same brother marries the widowed Queen, and each text describes this marriage as incestuous. The speed of the marriage is alluded to, and the same image of the beast with such appetites is found in all three texts; "les apetits des bestes" in Belleforest and their obvious English equivalents (210, 2.65–8, and I.ii.144–50) demonstrate how closely the English quartos echo the French source. It may even be that the request of Amleth that his mother should celebrate his funeral ("celebrast ses obseques et funerailles" [230–232]) and the phrase "banquet funebre" ("funeral banquet," [252]) give rise to "the funeral baked meats" (2.94, I.ii.179). Prince Amleth's and Prince Hamlet's distress is evident to the King (a "vilain" or "villain" [210, 5.79, and I.v.106–8]), and the young man's "melancholie" or "melancholy" is noted in each text (236, 7.383, and II.ii.536). Amleth adopts an appearance of insanity; Belleforest tells us this is deliberate. In the quartos Hamlet says he may adopt an "antic disposition" (5.147, I.v.170). The consequence of the conduct of Amleth and Hamlet is the same, for the King and his courtiers question the sanity of the Prince.

Two specific "tests" are borrowed from the source. In the first, a counselor suggests that a young woman is used to test Amleth and discover his true state of mind. In all three texts Amleth/Hamlet loves the young woman. Belleforest writes: "[Amleth] esmeu de la beauté de la fille" ([he was] "stirred by the young woman's beauty" [200–2]), though this is not necessarily evident at this point in the plays. In Q1 and Q2 Hamlet's affection for Ofelia/Ophelia is manifest in the earlier letter Corambis/Polonius reads out; in the actual scene in Q2 Hamlet states, "I did love you once" (III.i.114), and in the graveyard scene he again declares he had loved Ofelia/Ophelia. Perhaps more touching, and another example of a concept in Belleforest influencing the dramas, is that the "belle femme" "l'aymoit des son enfance" ("had loved [the Prince] since her childhood" [202]). (Jenkins sees this as the first hint of that "selfless devotion which is at the heart of Ophelia's tragedy."[8]) The "madness" of Amleth and Hamlet convinces the young woman that he is unbalanced (202, 1.185–6, and III.i.149).

In the second "test" we find more shared details. The same counselor suggests the Queen should speak to her son in her "chambre" or closet, or bedchamber. Each Queen's affection for her son is commented on: Amleth, the Queen's "doux amy" ("sweet friend" [220]) is the son "qu'elle aymoit" ("whom she loves" [230]). The King realizes the same "sweet Hamlet" in Q1 is "the joy and half-heart of your mother," and Claudius notes of Q2's "sweet Hamlet" that "The Queen his mother/ Lives almost by his looks" (2.30, IV.vii.12–13). Each counselor is killed, with a sword, when eavesdropping on mother and son.

Later close borrowings include the plot to remove Amleth and Hamlet. In all three versions the Prince is accompanied by two escorts to England, who carry instructions to the King of England to kill Amleth or Hamlet. The Prince in all the texts intercepts the instructions, and alters them so that the bearers will be killed instead.

At least eleven characters, and possibly twelve, are shared with the source (see "Key Abbreviations, Nomenclature, and Conventions used in the text" preceding the Introduction), and certain themes and motifs surface in each. Revenge is of course the central theme, and recurs on several occasions in each text. There are also allusions to religion, though there is some variation, excessive drinking is mentioned in all three, and the sword is an essential weapon contributing to the action. An image which appears in Belleforest is that of the "filet," a trap or snare, which is probably echoed in the "springes" Corambis and Polonius refer to (204, 3.61, and I.iii.114 and V.ii.291). Accumulatively, the eleven or twelve characters and approximately twenty-five features reported in these four paragraphs begin to establish how securely both the quartos are rooted in the French text.

Ideas and Adaptations

A further set of ideas originates in *Les Histoires Tragiques,* is adapted slightly, and is then found in both quartos. For example, in Belleforest, before they fight, the King of Norway and Horvvendille come to an agreement about the forfeit to be paid by the defeated combatant. In the French source, the agreement is that "celuy qui seroit vaincu perdroit toutes les richesses qui seroit en leurs vaisseaux" ("the one who is vanquished would lose all the riches in his ships/vessels"). In the quartos the fight is between Fortinbras(se) of Norway and Hamlet's father, and the forfeit is instead "all those lands/ Which he stood seized of by the conqueror" (182, 1.7–8, and I.i.87–8). The subsequent murder of Horvvendille and Hamlet's father is "la trahison de frere conte [sic] frere" ("the treason/treachery of one brother against the other"), that is "by a brother's hand" (170, 5.58, and I.v.74). The "Gentil-homme" ("man of gentle birth" [234]) who was brought up with Amleth is similar to Hamlet's confidant and fellow student, Horatio. It is his "compaignons" ("companions" [236]), with whom Amleth discusses "les Philosophes," but Horatio to whom Hamlet says:

> *Hamlet.* There are more things in heaven and earth, Horatio,
>   Than are dreamt of in your philosophy [5.142–3, I.v.165–6].

The suggestion of the counselor that "quelque belle femme" ("some beautiful woman" [198]) tests the Prince's madness is, in the source, presented as a seduction. There the courtiers argue that like all young men the Prince would be so carried away with the pleasures of the flesh that he would be unable to hide his real state of mind ("[un] jeune homme ... est si transporté aux plaisirs de la chair ... qu'il est presque impossible de couvrir telle affection..." [198]). This suggestion is quite a contrast with the quartos, where the counselor has become the father of the young woman. When Q2's Polonius proposes to "loose" Ophelia to Hamlet, sex is presumably not what the father and counselor intends, in either quarto, though we may find the verb disconcerting when the French source is known.

Another adapted borrowing comes with Queen Geruthe. In the "chambre" scene she sees "la vive image" ("the living image") of her former husband's virtue and wisdom when she gazes upon her son, Amleth. In both quartos Hamlet asks that his mother looks upon a physical "picture" of his father (218, 11.23, and III.iv.51). Jenkins notes that Amleth in that scene has decided to speak "rigoureusement" to his mother, while Hamlet vows he "will speak daggers" to her.[9] It is a tiny detail, but the texts are as much linked by the minutiae as by the bigger ideas. Later, Amleth takes the usurping King's sword, and goes to his chamber. King Fengon sees "le glaive nud," the bare sword, in Amleth's hand. Fengon tries desperately to seize Amleth's sword, but that has been nailed into its scabbard. In the quartos Hamlet by chance swaps swords with Leartes or Laertes (256, 17.78, and V.ii.285). This means that in all three texts there is some trickery before the sword swap; in the source King Fengon's courtiers have nailed Amleth's sword in its sheath and thus disabled it, while Leartes/Laertes uses an "[u]nbated and envenomed" sword (V.ii.302).

L'Ombre and the Ghost

While many of these details from the three texts are necessarily reportage, they do establish the breadth and precision of borrowings and echoes, breadth and precision which are in *both* quartos. And a close reading of *Les Histoires Tragiques* does provide us with some surprises. One relates to what Belleforest calls the "ombre," in this context a classical "shade," or the spirit of a dead person. Some scholars, as we have seen, suggest that the author of the putative *Ur-Hamlet* added the Ghost. For example, G. Blakemore Evans claimed that the playwright of the *Ur-Hamlet* added the ghost, the dumb show and the fencing match.[10] The suggestion for this rests on an assumption, that the 1589 reference to "Hamlets" in Thomas Nashe's preface to Robert Greene's *Menaphon*, the 1594 Henslowe entry of a play called "hamlet," and the 1596 mention by Thomas Lodge, all refer to the hypothetical, pre–Shakespearean *Ur-Hamlet*. Lodge's reference comes in his *Wits Miserie*, when "the vizard of the Ghost cried so miserably at the Theator, like an oister wife, Hamlet, revenge," thus establishing the existence of the Ghost in the *Hamlet* known in 1596. (The validity of these texts "proving" the existence of an alleged *Ur-Hamlet* is discussed in Part Three.)

But we don't need an intervening *Ur-Hamlet* dramatist to invent a Ghost. Belleforest himself twice offers a suggestion for a Ghost, enough for a plundering, close-reading dramatist like Shakespeare to notice. Firstly, Amleth sees his mother failing to show respect to the "ombres" (212), the ghost or shades of his father, when she embraces her new husband. This comment occurs in the Queen's "chambre" (the "bedchamber" scene) where in both quartos the Ghost appears, apparently to remind Hamlet of his obligations. The second mention in the source occurs later, when Amleth kills his uncle-father (the equivalent of the last scene in each quarto). Amleth kills the King and demands that he reports the successful act of vengeance to his brother's "ombre":

> Amleth luy donna un grand coup sur le ch[a]i[g]non du col,[11] de sorte qu'il luy feit voler la teste par terre, disant: ... ne faux de compter à ton frere ... que c'est son fils qui te faict faire ce message, à fin que soulagé par ceste memoire, son ombre s'appaise parmy les esprits bien-heureux....
>
> ("Amleth gave [the King] a great blow on the back of the neck, of the type that made his head drop swiftly to the ground, saying ... do not fail to tell your brother ... that it is his son who caused[12] you to bear this message, with the aim that through this memory [of the old King's murder being avenged] his shade/spirit may lie appeased among the blessed/blissful spirits" [256]).

This message has echoes of the classical underworld, found in for example Virgil and Seneca, which Kenneth Muir for one sees Shakespeare as likely to have been familiar with.[13] We might, for instance, remember how book VI of

The Aeneid describes Aeneas' visit to the underworld: "umbrarum hic locus est" ("this place belongs to the shades").[14] Amleth's desire to comfort or appease ("s'appaise" [256]) his father's spirit lets us infer that the spirit was disturbed, or even "perturbed." There is no doubt the dramatist read about the first "ombres," because that reference appears in the scene he used most (the "chambre" scene), nor that he read about the second "ombre," because its mention occurs in the very same sentence as the sword swap and the decapitation of Amleth's uncle-father.

Perhaps the dramatist's concept of a Ghost returning to tell of his own murder is also prompted—at a conscious or subconscious level—by another point in the French narrative. For we are told that Amleth, during the lifetime of his father, had been indoctrinated ("endoctriné") or taught the particular science by which an evil spirit takes advantage of or abuses men and *could advise the Prince about past events* ("Amleth, vivant son pere, avoit esté endoctriné en celle science, avec laquelle le malin esprit abuse ces hommes et *advertoissoit ce Prince (comme il peut) des choses [dé]ja passes*" [236]). (Author's italics.) It is reasonably certain that the dramatist creating a *Hamlet* read this passage with attention, because there are echoes of vocabulary which resurface in both quartos, as Jenkins points out.[15] Q1's Hamlet wonders if the "spirit" he has seen may be "the devil" (7.382), but Q2's Hamlet expands on this:

> Hamlet. The spirit I have seen
> May be a de'il, and the de'il hath power
> T'assume a pleasing shape. Yea, and perhaps
> Out of my weakness and my melancholy,
> As he is very potent with such spirits,
> Abuses me to damn me [II.ii.533–538].

Thus Belleforest's Prince mentions the "ombres" of his father in the "chambre" ("bedchamber") scene and later, at the point when he takes revenge, requests that his dead father's "ombre" or "shade" hears about the successful act of revenge. The dramatist—whether pre–Shakespearean or Shakespeare—appears to have transposed Belleforest's second mention of the "ombre" of the murdered king, who is to learn that revenge has taken place. Instead, in *Hamlet*, the murdered king visits earlier in the story to tell of past events ("des choses [dé]ja passes"), of how he was murdered, and to request revenge. The mention or appearance of the "ombre" or Ghost in the "chambre" or "bedchamber" scene changes from being the first mention of the "ombres" in *Les Histoires Tragiques* to become the last visitation of the Ghost in *Hamlet*. It is consequently unnecessary to propose that the Ghost was invented as an addition to what has been borrowed from *Les Histoires Tragiques*. Arthur Stabler and Jenkins independently also draw attention to the word "ombre" in each context and consider this a possible borrowing.[16]

It seems reasonable to equate the "ombre" with the Ghost. This brings the number of borrowed characters to twelve. And the "ombre" also shows us something else, namely a feature of the original story which has been moved, or transposed, to a different location in the English dramas. "Transpositions" are a feature thought to indicate memorial reconstruction.[17] However, in view of Shakespeare's transformation of aspects of his sources elsewhere the relocation of an idea from one place in the source to a different place in the chronology of a *Hamlet* script would surely have been within his powers. It is illogical to believe that an actor/reporter (of an allegedly "corrupt" text) could manage a transposition, but Shakespeare could not.

Transpositions

Other elements in the source may also be transpositions. Hamlet is not the cunning, bloodthirsty avenger that his French counterpart is. We can see several instances of how the Prince is rendered less vengeful in the quartos. For example, in *Les Histoires Tragiques*, shortly after incapacitating the Danish court with alcohol, Amleth slices off his uncle-father's head. That act of decapitation is "transposed" in both quartos to the King of Denmark's request of the King of England, for beheading is supposed to seal Hamlet's fate. Another transposition might be seen with the references to drink. Excessive drinking is first mentioned in the opening scene of the quartos, but the only mention in *Les Histoires Tragiques* occurs at the funeral banquet coinciding with Amleth's return from England. Here the Prince helps serve the wine (he takes the "office d'eschanson," the role of cupbearer, at the banquet [252]) until many of the King's retainers are "vomissans le trop de vin" ("vomiting from an excess of wine" [254]). There is another transposition, for while in the source the Prince bewails his lack of "advancement" (190) early on, this is a matter Hamlet delays mentioning until scene 7 in Q1 and act III scene ii in Q2. Furthermore, Hamlet's admission of grief occurs near the beginning, in the second scene, with "the tears that still stand in my eyes" (2.34) in Q1, and "the fruitful river in the eye" (I.ii.80) in Q2. Amleth, however, does not mention his grief until he is addressing the Danish people, after he has killed King Fengon. It is in his address that Amleth mentions his distress at the death of his father, and how he has been "tout confit en larmes" ("completely steeped in/overwhelmed by tears" [274]). "Tears" might be an obvious manifestation of grief, and not necessarily a borrowing, but the image in each text shows intensification— "confit" ("steeped/overwhelmed"), "still stand," and "river," which supports borrowing.

There is even a possible transposed borrowing from *Les Histoires Tragiques* which comes from a part of Belleforest's narrative whose events Shakespeare does not draw upon (after Amleth has become king, returned to England, and committed bigamy). Belleforest casually comments on how easily women give promises—"la femme est facile à promettre"—which might be behind the much quoted line, "Frailty, thy name is woman" (306, 2.66, and I.ii.146).

The number of echoes of the French text is now around fifty. The dozen or so examples of a concept originating in *Les Histoires Tragiques*, being changed from the French but then staying constant in the quartos, help to emphasize how closely the quartos are related; they are more closely related to each other than to the French source. But are there differences in the borrowings? Two logical implications of the theory of MR (and of abridgement/adaptation) are firstly that since Q2 has for many scholars the putative status of the anterior quarto, and is in any case the longer quarto, it would have some exclusive borrowings (direct, adapted or transposed), and secondly that it would have *more* borrowings than Q1. Alternatively, we could say that if Q1 is the later of the two quartos and only 55 percent of the length, it is further from the source and shorter and is therefore likely to have fewer borrowings.

Exclusive Borrowings

One small detail which is exclusive to Q2 occurs early on. Belleforest writes that Fengon (Amleth's uncle-father) "avoit incestuesement souillé la couche fraternelle" ("has soiled his brother's bed with incest"), and that his marriage to Geruthe was "d'adultere incestueux" (both "adulterous and incestuous" [186, 188]). Both these passages are reflected remarkably closely in Q2. The Ghost begs Hamlet:

> *Ghost.* Let not the royal bed of Denmark be
> A couch for luxury and damned incest [I.v.82–3].

Q2 uses not just the colloquial "bed" but an additional verbal echo in "couch." The same precision is found in the Ghost's description of his brother as "that incestuous, that adulterate beast," juxtaposing the same two words as the French source (188, I.v.42). Q1 is slightly less damning; the King is "an incestuous wretch" (5.37), though in both quartos the new couple do lie in "incestuous sheets" (5.37 and 2.70, I.ii.157). Other echoes appear; Amleth is waiting for the time, means and opportunity, or "occasion" for taking revenge— "[t]outs fois faut il attendre le temps, et les moyens et occasions"—while only Q2's Hamlet opens one speech with "How all occasions..." (216, IV.iv.31).

Another example can be found in Belleforest's presentation of Amleth's two choices. He could take "les armes au poing" ("his sword/weapons in his hands") or suffer the shame which tortures "nostre conscience," and the cowardice which withholds the heart from "des gaillards enterprises" ("gallant/brave enterprises/schemes"). Jenkins too notes that this is closely echoed in Hamlet's "To be or not to be" speech, in "conscience does make cowards ... and enterprises of great pitch...." Q1 has simply "this conscience makes cowards of us all" (226, 7.135, III.i.55–87). Jenkins also comments that just as Amleth is "le ministre et executeur" of revenge, so Hamlet, in only Q2, is the "scourge and minister" who brings it about.[18]

There is also one change which might hint at a possible actor/reporter recalling the sense of what he was trying to remember, but not the exact word; Amleth complains that he wants "advancement." This is also what Hamlet in Q2 mentions, twice, in act III scene ii: "For what advancement..." and "I lack advancement...." In Q1 a synonym is used, "preferment" (194, 7.231, III.ii.52, 331). Finally, one small plot element is shared between *Les Histoires Tragiques* and Q2. Amleth hears or understands that he will be sent to England ("entandant qu'on l'envoioit en la Grande Bretagne" [230]), while Q2's Hamlet knows "There's letters sealed" (III.iv.200).

These details which are exclusive to Q2 suggest MR is a possibility at this point. It is of course necessary to pose the question the other way, and ask if there are any differences in borrowings which suggest Q1 is closer to the source.

One such difference brings us back to the starting point of this book, to Hamlet's age. Belleforest tells us that Amleth's decision to simulate madness to protect himself is because he has not yet come "à perfection d'aage" (to adulthood, or the age of majority). His youth is clearly mentioned on several occasions: "un jeune Prince," "le jeune seigneur," "[l]'Adolescent," and "du jeune Prince." It is confirmed when he speaks to his mother, and asks why she has not thought "de sauver vostre enfant" ("of saving your child"), "cest enfant" ("this child"). Later the Queen embraces Amleth "avec la mesme amitié qu'une mere vertuese peut baiser, et caresser sa portee," in other words with the same love as a virtuous mother kissing and caressing the one she carries in her arms. The distribution of the page references for these in Gollancz's edition—192, 194, 202, 254, 282, 214, 218 and 220—illustrates unambiguously that Belleforest's characterization of Amleth as youthful is pervasive. It is also consistent.

And it is exactly what we find in the characterization of Hamlet in Q1. Horatio refers to "young Hamlet," Ofelia to "young Prince Hamlet," Corambis to "the young Prince Hamlet" and "young Hamlet." The First Clown declares that Yorick's skull has rotted for "this dozen year" (16.66), and refers to "young Hamlet's father." Hamlet's recollections of riding piggy back on Yorick are from perhaps the age of seven, making Q1's Hamlet about nineteen years old.

(Perhaps eighteen, Thompson and Taylor write.[19]) Again the references (scenes 1, 6, 7, 11 and 16 in Q1) are pervasive, and consistent. It is true that Q2 has three references to a "young" Hamlet. The first is from Horatio in I.i. Horatio's age is indeterminate, for he seems to be a fellow student but also old enough to know what Hamlet's father looked like in battle. (This may be dramatic license, since Horatio needs to confirm that the Ghost resembles Hamlet's father; it could also be argued as a sign of a part of the play which was not fully revised by Shakespeare.) But the other two references are by men noticeably older than Hamlet. One is by Polonius and the other by the Gravedigger who began his trade thirty years earlier, on the day Hamlet was born. The Gravedigger is therefore clearly older than Hamlet, whom he, like Polonius, might consequently see as "young." The Gravedigger also makes Q2's Hamlet thirty years old. Moreover, Yorick's skull has lain in the earth "three and twenty years" (V.i.163–4), also confirming Q2's Hamlet as significantly older.

Is thirty years just a "humorous and palpable exaggeration on the Clown's part?" Duthie is swayed by this suggestion by V. Østerberg, and adds "after all, had Shakespeare intended to force Hamlet's age upon our attention, he would surely have done so more effectively."[20] Yet the dramatist is perfectly effective in drawing the audience's attention to Hamlet's age in Q1, just as Belleforest gave us a clearly youthful Amleth. The Princes in *Les Histoires Tragiques* and Q1 are both portrayed as young. The age issue is problematic. If MR is the explanation for Q1, the memorial reconstructor must have systematically added references altering Hamlet's age from older in Q2 to younger in the Q1 text he is preparing. It would presumably also be sheer coincidence that the change such a composer might make would bring the new text closer to the original source than the one he was attempting to recall. The change in age does not sensibly support MR.

Nashe's picture of Danes still learning their ABC at the age of thirty and quoted at the opening of the book is so hyperbolic it is hard to think Shakespeare read *Pierce Penniless* and actually believed a Danish student at university in Wittenberg would be that age. But if Q2 were a revision it would be possible to speculate that Q2's older Hamlet in 1604–5 was to permit an older Richard Burbage, aged about thirty-six at this time, to (continue to) play Hamlet convincingly. It might also explain why it is in Q2 that the Queen says of Hamlet "He's fat" (V.ii.269), an adjective that critics "do not want [it] to mean 'overweight,'"[21] while Q1 lacks such an epithet.

There are other small examples of where Q1 is nearer to Belleforest than Q2 is. When the counselor proposes "quelque belle femme" ("some pretty woman") is used to test whether Amleth's madness is real, the verb Belleforest employs is "atraper" ("to entrap"). In Q1, counselor Corambis claims Hamlet wants "to entrap the heart" of Ofelia, in order to take advantage of her (198,

3.68). The verb is not, it is true, used in precisely the same context in each text; it appears transposed. It is not used at all in Q2, but all three texts do have several entrapments. Another, minor example, mentioned earlier, occurs when Amleth speaks of how he was "tout confit de larmes" ("completely steeped in/overwhelmed by tears") at his father's death, which Q1 picks up straightforwardly as "tears." In Q2 Hamlet speaks in metaphor, of "the fruitful river in the eye" (274, 2.34, 1.ii.80). It has been suggested that a memorial reconstructor or abridger is likely to simplify, and might therefore have removed the image. Perhaps that is the case, but the accumulation of details where Q1 is closer to the source than Q2 does need an explanation if MR is correct.

It is rather disconcerting to read the French source and recognize how often *Hamlet* echoes it. Together the shared borrowings show how extensively each quarto draws upon *Les Histoires Tragiques*. A small number of details are exclusive to Q2, and a different group of minor details is exclusive to Q1, though one of those details—Hamlet's age—is significant. But there is not yet enough evidence to support any of the hypotheses—MR, abridgement, first draft and revision—wholly convincingly. It becomes quite a different matter when we ask whether there is any sign of development across the three texts, of the evolution of ideas which originate, as they must, with *Les Histoires Tragiques*.

3. *Les Histoires Tragiques*, the Quartos, and Evolving Ideas

While we have already established that there are over fifty parallels between the French source and the quartos, this does not exhaust what the source shows us about the quartos. In a small number of instances an event in the three texts is clearly linked, but it is slightly different in each. If we can isolate these instances, we might be able to see if they are simply variations, or whether there is evidence of an idea evolving across the texts. Since we know that *Les Histoires Tragiques* came first, the question is whether the idea evolves from *Les Histoires Tragiques* through Q2 to Q1, or whether it evolves from *Les Histoires Tragiques* through Q1 to Q2.

The "Nunnery" Scene

The first of these events concerns what is often referred to as the "nunnery" scene in *Hamlet*. It is where Ofelia or Ophelia is talking to Hamlet, with her father and the King eavesdropping. The idea originates in *Les Histoire Tragiques*, which is necessarily the first text against which to compare the two quartos. Here King Fengon is concerned about the apparent madness of the Prince, and his courtiers advise him to discover the truth behind Amleth's "tromperie" ("deception/fraud" [198]). They suggest Amleth should be entrapped by a "belle femme" ("beautiful woman") in a secret place; they elaborate on the pleasures of physical intimacy and how when thus engaged the Prince will not be able to dissemble ("dissimuler" [198]) his true feelings, and then they initiate the entrapment. All this occurs in less than a page, without any diversions.

Q1 appears to follow this idea fairly closely. It is true that counselor Corambis is now the father of the woman, Ofelia, and it is true that he does not suggest she seduce the Prince. However, the sequence is still similar to the source, in the making of the proposal and its immediate implementation. So in Q1, in scene 7, Corambis proposes the King and he should "stand close in the study"; five lines later Hamlet enters, briefly soliloquizes, and then talks to Ofelia within the hearing of the eavesdroppers.

In Q2, act II scene ii, Polonius makes a similar proposal, but before it is put into practice a series of conversations intervene. Firstly, Polonius has a conversation with Hamlet; then Hamlet speaks to Rosencrans and Guyldensterne; next Polonius and the Players enter; then, in III.i, the eavesdroppers hide, Hamlet soliloquizes at greater length, and finally—*nearly 600 lines later*—he speaks to Ophelia and the trap is sprung.

Q1's approach is straightforward. Q2 keeps the audience in suspense about when the entrapment will occur and what will be revealed. Q1 follows the French source closely. It might be a dramatist's first version of the play, as he uses his source and before he has interleaved some of the themes and parts of scenes that are present in Q2. Q1's "nunnery" scene is located in the same place as the source. The way the position of the "nunnery" scene in Q1 is in an identical place to where it is found in the source is not explained by MR or abridgement. It is hardly satisfactory to say that Q2's location of the scene is "transposed" by an actor/reporter(s), or an abridger, coincidentally back to where it was in the source. To claim that as a "transposition" and as evidence of MR is surely unconvincing.

Interestingly, the MR hypothesis with Q2 preceding Q1 is so well disseminated that one modern writer does describe the different position of Q2's "nunnery" scene like this: "This particular episode is ... transposed from its position in Act 3 of Q2/F1 to the early position of Q1...."[1] The writer *assumes* the hypothesis of MR is correct, but we must pause when Q1 is closer to the source than Q2 is. If we just look at the three texts it would be simplest to see Q1 borrowing directly from the source, and Q2 deliberately building up suspense, making the audience wait to see what will happen. And we would of course note that, like Q2, F1 is also more distant from the source than Q1.

The "Bedchamber" Scene

The second entrapment also shows a development of ideas. It occurs in the Queen's "chambre," where Amleth is asked to attend upon his mother. Now at the first entrapment Amleth received two explicit warnings that he was entering a trap, one from a childhood friend and one from the "belle femme" herself (200, 202). So it is not surprising that Amleth enters his mother's "chambre" full of suspicion and with the expectation that here is another trap. Belleforest as a novelist underlines this by placing Amleth in the chamber, and in the very next clause indicating Amleth's suspicions: "[il] se douta de quelque trahison..." ("[he] suspected some treachery"). Then, before he even speaks to his mother, Amleth feigns his "folles et niaises" ("mad and naïve/simple") mannerisms as usual, and like a cock bird beats all about with his wings (206). This action means he discovers the counselor hiding behind the quilt, and upon this discovery the Prince immediately thrusts his sword through the quilt and the man. Only after the counselor is dead and disposed of does Amleth return to his mother and start to address her.

In Q1, in the fourth line after his entrance, Hamlet declares "but first we'll make all safe" (11.6). It is a half line that has no stage business to support it, but it makes complete sense if we come to it from the French source. That odd half line appears to reflect the suspicions of the Prince in *Les Histoires Tragiques*. In Q2, Hamlet lacks that half line and its implicit suspicions. Yet in other respects the quartos are closer to each other here than to the source, because after that the sequence of events is the same in the quartos. In both quartos, within a few lines of entering, Hamlet begins to address his mother (Amleth poked around with his sword and killed the counselor before speaking to his mother), in both quartos Hamlet is interrupted by firstly the Queen's and secondly the counselor's call for help, in both Hamlet kills him, and then continues to speak to the Queen.

The presence of Q1's half line, "but first we'll make all safe," suggests the playwright was in places reading and/or remembering Belleforest quite closely. A simple explanation might be that a drafting playwright followed the source for Q1, but in revising noted that Q1's half line had no stage business to support it. He decided he wanted his Hamlet free of such suspicions and excised the half line in writing Q2. Q1 hints at being an intermediate stage; it shares one aspect with Belleforest, and one different aspect with Q2. It is difficult to explain logically why an abridger or memorial reconstructor of Q2 might make Q1's Hamlet suspicious, especially as the abridger/reconstructor does not provide a context or a hint for such suspicions.

The second example in the "chambre" scene blends a transposition with an apparent evolution of ideas. The borrowing occurs from a scene in the French source which is not used by Shakespeare for the plot, but which seems to have some verbal echoes in the quartos. Amleth kills his uncle-king, and survives. He then addresses the Danish people to explain why the King is dead and to persuade them that he, Amleth, should become their King. The Prince declares that one of the reasons that he had killed the King was to wash away the spots which had blackened the reputation of the Queen ("j'ay lavé les tasches, qui denigroient la reputation de la Royne" [280]). In both quartos the concept is echoed in the "bedchamber" scene; the verbal echo is transposed. In Q1 these are still the Prince's words; he "tells" not a general populace but the Queen his mother:

> *Hamlet.* I'll make your eyes look down into your heart
> And see how horrid there and black it shows [11.20–1].

But in Q2 it is not Hamlet who is "telling" the Queen and the audience. Instead Shakespeare presents Q2's Queen as so distressed by the picture Hamlet paints of the contrast between "Hyperion" (old King Hamlet) and the "moor" (Claudius) that it is now she who expresses the thought; she "shows" the effect Hamlet's words have had upon her. She says:

> *Queen.* Thou turn'st my very eyes into my soul
> And there I see such black and grieved spots ... [III.iv.87–8].

The characterization of the two Princes has changed. Q1's Hamlet is more obviously determined to make his mother recognize what she has done. Q2's Hamlet is more anguished, uncomprehending, revolted, and sets out to "wring" her heart, but he is less accusatory. The Queen's response in Q2 also contributes to Shakespeare's presentation of her, for her suffering means that she gains a little sympathy as a tragic figure. Her response "shows" how deeply she is affected. A progression again seems apparent: Belleforest's Prince, addressing a crowd, claims to have removed the black spots from his mother's reputation; Q1's Prince, still the speaker, now addresses the Queen and says her eyes will see how black her heart is. In Q2 it is now the Queen who speaks, and admits to Hamlet that her eyes see the black spots in her soul. The changes in speaker and audience suggest both an evolution across the texts (from *Les Histoires Tragiques*, to Q1 to Q2) and the close relationship of all three.

A fourth example also shows an evolution from *Les Histoires Tragiques* to Q1 to Q2. It concerns the three Queens' different promises to the Princes. Two issues lead to the French and Q1 Queens making these promises, namely revenge, and the motives for revenge. Those motives are closer in Belleforest and in Q1, for the same word is used in both French and English. In *Les Histoires Tragiques*, Amleth explains that one reason for taking revenge is to wipe out the "infamie" associated with his mother's renowned family name (216). In Q1 Hamlet's motive is also to erase his mother's "infamy" (11.94) with its connotations of earthly shame and reputation. Q2's Hamlet, on the other hand, refers to his mother's "trespass"; he asks his mother to "confess" and "repent" her "trespass," which has connotations of offending divine law (III.iv.144–48). We need to ask how or why an actor/reporter or abridger, recreating Q1, would happen to use such a distinctive word, found also in the source. (Some might say the actor/reporter is recalling something in the hypothetical *Ur-Hamlet*, though we need to be wary of making an assumption that the *Ur-Hamlet* hypothesis is right as well as the MR hypothesis.) If MR explains all, then a sequence of Belleforest and "infamie,"

Q2 and "trespass," changing to Q1 and "infamy" must, somehow, be seen as credible.

A second reason for revenge is put bluntly in Belleforest and Q1. Fengon is "le meurtrier de mon pere" ("my father's murderer" [210]), and Q1's King is "[he]/ That slew my father" (11.39–40). Q2 is more oblique or circumlocutory, for after he kills Polonius, Hamlet agrees it was:

> *Hamlet.* A bloody deed—almost as bad, good mother,
> As kill a king and marry with his brother [III.iv.26–7].

The obvious question is whether the proximity of *Les Histoires Tragiques* and Q1 is due to chance improvisation and the simplification of the memorial reconstructor/abridger, or reference to the putative *Ur-Hamlet*, or consultation of *Les Histoires Tragiques*, or whether Shakespeare has revised Q1 and created a more subtle text.

There is another difference. Belleforest presents Amleth from the beginning as thinking about how to avenge his father's death, "s'en venger" (194). In the "chambre" scene Amleth declares his intention to take revenge, in a long and passionate speech to the Queen ("j'espere d'en faire une telle, et si haute vengeance, qu'il sera jamais parlé en ces terres"—"I hope to take such great vengeance that it will be spoken about forever in these lands" [216]). In Q1 the Ghost appears, Hamlet recalls his task of revenge, and asks for his mother's assistance ("assist me in revenge" [11.93]). In other words, in the source and in Q1 the intention to gain revenge is explicit.

Once again Q2 appears to be drawing away from both the source and Q1, for we see that Q2's Hamlet is not as direct. There Hamlet refers to "Th'important acting of your dread command" (III.iv.105) when he addresses the Ghost. This line only *alludes* to "revenge," because it requires the audience/reader to recall the Ghost's request some scenes earlier to "Revenge his foul and most unnatural murder" (I.v.25). Once again several reasons might be proposed for this difference in Q2: perhaps the Q1 script has been revised, and is made into a more demanding Q2, perhaps because the latter is intended to be a literary text, as Lukas Erne argues.[2] Or is it that the alleged abridger or actor/reporter of Q2, in creating Q1, simplifies the role of the Prince and spells out his desire for revenge, by chance as in the source?

Immediately after his declaration to take revenge Amleth asks the Queen to say nothing about the matter: "rien informé de cecy," where "cecy" ("this") deictically refers to his intention to take revenge. The Queen promises to keep Amleth's intended revenge secret. She will feign a lack of knowledge about the matter, and she promises that she will keep secret both his wisdom and his brave enterprise ("duquel je feindray ne sçavoir rien je tiendray secrette, et ta sagesse, et ta gaillarde enterprinse" [222]). Her words have prominence because

3. Les Histoires Tragiques, *the Quartos, and Evolving Ideas*   49

of the sibilance (author's emboldening) and the Latinate grammatical structure "et ... et," "both ... and." It is a dramatic moment. In Q1 it is rendered slightly differently. Here Q1's Queen volunteers a promise to keep his plan concealed in a very similar way to Queen Geruthe:

> Queen. I will conceal, consent, and do my best,
>   What stratagem soe'er thou shalt devise [11.97–8].

Her lines also gain prominence, through alliteration on the plosive /k/ (author's emboldening), and through the rhetorical triplet.

But in Q1, oddly, Hamlet does *not* solicit this concealment. (He has asked her to "Forbear the adulterous bed," and said that if she assists him in revenge, her "infamy shall die" [11.90, 94]). Q1's Queen's promise, however, seems to answer the request of the French Prince Amleth. Her promise "I will conceal..." opens a series of four consecutive clauses which do not altogether cohere with the preceding dialogue, just as the half line "but first we'll make all safe" at the beginning of the "bedchamber" scene lacks cohesion with its context. Thus both "I will conceal..." and "but first we'll make all safe" seem to echo Belleforest's version, but lack an immediate context in the Q1 text. Neither are abridged versions of anything in Q2. It is as if the dramatist has included the Queen's promise because there was a (request and) promise in the source he was working from.

Again Q2's Queen is different. Hamlet does not declare to her that he will exact revenge. He does, however, make an explicit but *different* request, for secrecy; his mother must not let Claudius know her son is only "mad in craft." The Queen's promise is remote stylistically and semantically from the French and from Q1, for in Q2 the Queen utters:

> Queen. Be thou assured, if words be made of breath
>   And breath of life, I have not life to breathe
>   What thou hast said to me [III.iv.195–7].

Her answer does, however, cohere linguistically with its context; it does promise the secrecy Hamlet has asked for. And again the answer achieves prominence, through its literariness; it is largely monosyllabic, with native vocabulary, and its resulting simplicity gives it a poignancy which moves us to sympathy for the Queen. The two lines are lyrical and rhythmic, not least because of the use of chiasmus. It is perhaps surprising that their patterning is not remotely recalled by a potential actor/reporter or reproduced by the abridger. In their promises, Q1's Queen is closer to the source, and Q2's is again drawing away from the source and from Q1.

Alternative Explanations

The proximity of the Queen's promise in Q1 to the French source is explained differently elsewhere. Duthie's explanation for the Queen's promise in Q1 is a confident one. He asserts that *The Spanish Tragedy* is the source of Gertred's promise.[3] Duthie quotes rather selectively; the critical lines are given in full below:

<u>Les Histoires Tragiques</u>
   Geruthe: je tiendray secrette, et ta sagesse, et ta gaillarde enterprinse.
                 ("I will keep secret both your wisdom and your brave enterprise" [222].)

<u>Q1 Hamlet</u>
   Queen: I will conceal, consent, and do my best,
                 What stratagem soe'er thou shalt devise [11.97–8].

<u>The Spanish Tragedy</u>
   Hieronimo: And here I vow, so you but give consent, } (*omitted by Duthie*)
                 And will conceal my resolution ... }
   Bellimperia: Hieronimo, I will consent, conceal;
                 And aught that may effect for thine avail
                 Join with thee to revenge Horatio's death.
   Hieronimo: On then, whatsoever I devise
                 I will ere long [IV.i.42–4, 46–49].

It is reasonable to suggest that *Les Histoires Tragiques* offers enough to inspire the Queen's lines in Q1, in phonological and syntactic patterning, and in meaning. While there are interesting parallels in Kyd's play, there is no certainty regarding the direction of borrowing. We have already noted that it is not known when *The Spanish Tragedy* was written. It was probably after 1582, when Thomas Watson's *Hekatompathia* was published, from which *The Spanish Tragedy* adapts material, and obviously before its performance on 23 February 1592.[4] This places it securely before the publication of Q1 in 1603, but in an ambiguous position in relation to the *Hamlet* which is mentioned by Nashe and whose authorship is uncertain. So the date of Kyd's play does not help. Of course, some have suggested that the possible *Ur-Hamlet* was written by Kyd, in which case they may believe that Q1's Queen's lines do echo Kyd's *Spanish Tragedy*. But it is peculiar that *The Spanish Tragedy* repeats "conceal" and "consent," presumably to draw attention to them. Duthie omits this repetition, curiously. Deliberate repetition is sometimes done very knowingly to ensure the reader/audience "gets" the allusion. Since we are uncertain about the dates of the plays' composition, we need to remember it might be Kyd who is borrowing, which would mean *The Spanish Tragedy* might not be the source of Q1's two lines.

3. Les Histoires Tragiques, *the Quartos, and Evolving Ideas* 51

Other scholars propose an alternative explanation for the apparent link between Q1 Queen's promise and Belleforest's Queen's promise:

> [T]he part of Gertrude in performances of the lost play [i.e., the putative *Ur-Hamlet*] would have been taken by a boy actor; a boy actor of the late 1580s or early 1590s could well be a hired man in 1600–3, playing parts like Marcellus and Voltemand ... a simple mechanism for contamination exists....[5]

It is of course possible, though it means we must construct a sequence of composition resembling this: *Les Histoires Tragiques* (a known text) is followed by an *Ur-Hamlet* (a hypothetical text); Shakespeare writes Q2, which may be abridged or adapted, before a hypothetical MR is made by an actor who is assumed to have played Gertred (*c.* 1589) in the *Ur-Hamlet* (a hypothetical text), who is now playing "Marcellus" and/or "Voltemand" (*c.* 1600?), thus being able to contribute to the production of Q1. While the narrative explaining the origins of the quartos is no doubt complex, this sequence seems exceptionally complicated and depends on several speculations. (And it is presumably disappointing for the actor concerned, who could play a Queen in the 1580s—before his voice breaks?—but play only a sentinel or ambassador in the 1600s.) The same scholars, discussing *Hamlet* in some detail but in general terms on the subject of the character of the Queen, also note that "it is intriguing that the part of Gertrude contains ... the only feature in which Q1 agrees with earlier narrative accounts, against Q2 and F1."[6] This chapter, and the preceding one, show that the Queen's part is *not* the only feature of Q1 which is closer to the source than Q2 is. (The French and Latin sources are the only known "earlier narrative accounts.")

The position of the "nunnery" scene, the half line "but first we'll make all safe," the change in speaker and development of the Queen's character in seeing spots in her soul, the infamy of the Queen, the intention to take revenge, the promise of the Queen—all these features in Q1 are significantly closer to the source than Q2's equivalents are. Moreover, the source details listed in chapters two and three show that Q1 echoes the source as much as Q2 does. This means that Q1's density of borrowings is almost double that of Q2.

How might the findings best be explained? It is possible that if we were certain that an *Ur-Hamlet* had existed then we could argue that the *Ur-Hamlet* itself was even closer to the French source than Q1 or Q2, and that the putative memorial reconstructor(s) recalled the *Ur-Hamlet* in his/their reconstruction. That requires four different assumptions or hypotheses to be right. Firstly, the *Ur-Hamlet* must have existed, secondly the *Ur-Hamlet* must have been closer to the French source, thirdly the memorial reconstructor(s) must have been familiar with the *Ur-Hamlet*, and fourthly he/they must have recalled parts of the *Ur-Hamlet*, or even more of the *Ur-Hamlet*, in preference to Shakespeare's *Hamlet*.

If we prefer economy of hypothesis we might consider the first sketch and revision proposal. Perhaps it could be argued that Shakespeare wrote an early *Hamlet*, transferring one or two half thought-through ideas (like the suspicions of a safety conscious Hamlet), and some years later revised the play, having skim-read the French source again and with his own first version of *Hamlet* in front of him. Certainly we should consider carefully whether the evolution of ideas suggested by the juxtaposition of scenes here is from the hand of an actor or abridger.

One matter which emerges from this three way comparison is just how close some of the parallels, or borrowings, are. And since Q1's scene 14 and Q2's act IV scene vi differ substantially, perhaps it is worth examining the French text to see whether it throws any light upon how the writer of each quarto reports upon Hamlet's return to Denmark.

4. Hamlet's Return, Nashe and Some Binge Drinking

By now the French source has shown not just a substantial number of parallels between it and the two quartos, but also that there are a number of borrowings which suggest Q1 is closer to the source than Q2 is. *Les Histoires Tragiques* is still not exhausted, however. Today we are likely to see an edited Q2 or F1 *Hamlet* first, or perhaps a conflation of those texts. It is less likely that we will look at Q1, and it is even rarer that the French source is read. But we can gain a quite different perspective if we try to make the French source more prominent in our minds, and if we try to put ourselves in the position of the dramatist who first came across the Amleth story and thought about making it into an English play. For that French source also offers further hints, about how Hamlet's return is handled, about drinking, and about gaps in the narratives.

Hamlet's Return

One scene in each quarto is surprisingly different. It is the scene where in Q1 Horatio tells the Queen that her son has returned to Denmark and where in Q2 Horatio learns from a letter that Hamlet is back on Danish shores. Discussion about the two scenes is not extensive.

Q1 has just two characters, Horatio and the Queen, in scene 14. Q2 has a minimum of five, indicated by the stage directions including "Horatio and others" and "Saylers," in act IV scene vi. Superficially, to have only two actors in scene 14 does appear to support abridgement, if we think that Q2 preceded Q1. But the scenes work quite differently. In Q1 Horatio is already aware of Hamlet's return, and his role is to inform the Queen (and us) that Hamlet's back. In Q2 Horatio learns of Hamlet's return at the same time as we do. The Queen is not present in Q2, though she is to receive a letter about her son's return. She does not learn of his return in as immediate, direct and confidential a way as in Q1.

Once again the source, which must have come first, is instructive. In *Les Histoires Tragiques* Amleth asks his mother to arrange a funeral banquet for one year from his departure to England (she should "celebrast ses obsequies et funerailles" [230–232]). He tells her she will see him return ("...elle le verroit de retour" [232]). Amleth's mother therefore expects him to come back, so she prepares the banquet (this is the "banquet funebre" [252]), and he does indeed return at the given time.

In Q1 scene 14 Horatio's opening line, addressed to the Queen, is:

> *Hor.* Madame, your sonne is safe arriv'de in *Denmarke* [Sig. H2v.5].

Where does the emphasis lie in this line? For readers coming to the scene and knowing Q2, "your sonne is safe arriv'de in *Denmarke*" is simply an announcement of Hamlet's return. But to come to it from *Les Histoires Tragiques* permits the inference that Q1's Queen was anyway expecting her son and that what Horatio does is specifically to confirm Hamlet's arrival is "safe" (iambic pentameter naturally gives "safe" one of the line's five stresses). The idiom survives today; we may comment on the "safe arrival" of someone, and the important information is not the arrival, which is anticipated, but the "safe" aspect of it. The Q1 scene appears to reflect an aspect of *Les Histoires Tragiques* which is not translated explicitly into the play. This interpretation is supported by the distancing in the relationship between mother and son in Q2, which Chapter 3 mentioned and which Chapter 5 will illustrate further. An alternative way of putting it is that in Q1 this scene shows that "Gertred seems more closely allied to Hamlet against the king than she appears in Q2 and F."[1] However, we might also note that it is a respect in which Q1 is closer to the source. As we have already seen, for example, in Q1 Hamlet does inform the Queen he will avenge his father's death, but in Q2 he does not confide any such intention to the Queen. It is one of the little details with which Shakespeare isolates Hamlet more in Q2, with the result that he is more of a lonely and tragic figure. A Q2 scene which does not ensure the Queen is among the first to know of his return contributes to that isolation.

That Q1's scene is closer to the French source may be reinforced by another feature which *Les Histoires Tragiques* and Q1 share. The French Queen, in her concern for her son, asks him "conduire sagement tes affaires, n'estre haste, ny trop boüillant en tes entreprinses" ("to conduct the matter [the act of revenge] wisely, being neither too hasty nor too impetuous in your enterprise/action" [222]). In Q1 the Queen, also concerned for her son, asks Horatio to "Bid him [Hamlet] a while be wary of his [the King's] presence" (14.19). That expression of concern is not present in Q2.

While the Queen is more prominent in Q1's scene 14, Hamlet is more prominent in Q2's IV.vi. It is part of a trend between the two plays. Hamlet is closer to the Queen and more explicit in what he says in Q1 (as indeed in the source). Hamlet is more isolated and less confiding in Q2. In scenes such as the "closet" one Hamlet has a greater proportion of the lines in comparison with the Queen than he does in the matching scene in Q1. The change in the two scenes contributes to that, and once more to the priority of Q1.

Binge Drinking

The importance of sources in helping us to understand how *Hamlet* evolved is evident again in another close analysis of an extract from *Les Histoires Tragiques*. It "is apparent" that another literary influence is Shakespeare's debt to Nashe's *Pierce Penniless*, writes one critic.[2] *Pierce Penniless* was published in 1592, three years after Nashe's *Epistle* with its first reference to a *Hamlet*. In *Pierce Penniless* Nashe exclaims over the "bursten-bellied sots," as he calls the Danes, and writes at length about them, and about drink. Superficially this looks as though the dramatist might indeed have drawn upon *Pierce Penniless* for some details in *Hamlet*. However, the French source which underlies the quartos includes a major scene of excessive drinking, when Amleth returns to Denmark. There the Danish court drink until they are utterly incapacitated. Amleth actively encourages this and manipulates it to his own advantage, but he does not participate in the drinking. (Amleth, like Hamlet, stands outside the world of drunkenness.) The scene is the "banquet funebre" ("funeral banquet"), that distinctive juxtaposition which might even have suggested to Shakespeare the "funeral baked meats" of both quartos.

It is suggested that Nashe's reference to the Danes as "bursten-bellied sots ... [the Italians] mortally detest this surley swinish generation"[3] gives rise to Q2's:

> Hamlet. This heavy-headed revel east and west
> Makes us traduced and taxed of other nations:
> They clepe us drunkards [I.iv.17–9].

But a closer parallel than Nashe's—much closer—is found in the French source. Drunkenness, Belleforest writes, is a "vice assez familier, et à L'Alemant, et à toutes les nations et peuples Septentrionaux" ("a vice known well enough both to the Germans and all the northern nations and people" [254]). And Nashe's use of "this surley swinish generation" is supposed to suggest to Shakespeare "with swinish phrase" (I.iv.19). But the image of a pig and overindulgence in alcohol is also present in the French source. There the courtiers are "gisans par terre comme porceaux" ("lying (= helpless) on the ground like swine/pigs"

[252]). There are some further words which are also allegedly drawn from *Pierce Penniless*: "carouse," "manners," "vice." But these are not unsurprising lexis in the discussion of drunkenness, and Shakespeare does use all of them elsewhere, as Crystal's *Shakespeare's Words. A Glossary & Language Companion* shows. Consequently, while Shakespeare is very likely to have read Nashe, *Pierce Penniless* is *not* critical for the observations on drink. The French source is more closely echoed.

Table 3 summarizes the key parallels concerning drink. The order reflects publication dates, and is not intended to connote the sequence of borrowing. The lines from the four texts are presented to show parallels, and follow the order of the phrases in *Les Histoires Tragiques*.

Table 3. Phrases/Lines Concerning Drunkenness in *Les Histoires Tragiques*, *Pierce Penniless*, Q1 and Q2

Les Histoires Tragiques (1582) (Translation)	*Pierce Penniless* (1592)	Q1 (1603)	Q2 (1604)
"banquet funebre" (252) (the funeral banquet)		"the **funeral baked meats**.../ Did coldly furnish forth the marriage tables" (2.94, 95)	"the **funeral baked meats**/ Did coldly furnish forth the marriage tables" (I.ii.179–80)
	"this unnecessary vice" (105) "mens **manners**" (105)		"some vicious mole" (I.ii.24) "plausive **manners**" (I.iv.30)
	"one beastly imperfection" (105) "like lees and dregs" (105)		"From that particular fault: the dram of eale" (I.iv.36)
	"his **carousing** cups" (105)	"taking his **carouse**,/ Drinking drunk" (10.23–4)	"When he is drunk" (III.iii.89)
"vice assez familier, et à L'Alemant, et à toutes les nations et peuples Septentrionaux" (a vice known well enough	"Danes are burstenbellied sots ... [the Italians] mortally detest this surley swinish generation" (77)		"This heavyheaded revel east and west/ Makes us traduced and taxed of other

Les Histoires Tragiques (1582) (Translation)	Pierce Penniless (1592)	Q1 (1603)	Q2 (1604)
both to the Germans, and all the northern nations and people)			nations:/ They clepe us drunkards" (I.iv.17–9)
"gisans par terre comme **porceaux**" (lying (=helpless) on the ground, like **swine**/pigs) "**yvrongne**" (308) (drunkard)	"foul drunken **swine**" (104) "this surly **swinish** generation" (77)	"**drunk**" (6.23)	"with **swinish** phrase" (I.iv.19) "drinking" (II.i.25) "o'ertook in's rouse" (II.i.56)

However, it is of course *Pierce Penniless* which is quoted at the beginning of the Introduction. That particular passage pertaining to the mature age of the still-at-school Dane does not seem to be discussed by commentators, even though it is in the same pamphlet as the comments upon drinking. The passage about Danes and schooling occurs in a subsection of *Pierce Penniless,* one entitled *The Pride of the Danes*. It is there that Nashe claims "they [the Danes] are an arrogant, ass-headed people, that naturally hate learning...." It is followed by *The Danes Enemies to all Learning: No rewards among them for Desert*. This ends a page later, with the section quoted earlier: "...they set them [children] not to it [school] till they are fourteen year old; so that you shall see a great boy with a beard learn his ABC & sit weeping under the rod when he is thirty years old." Hamlet, as we have already noted, is thirty years old in Q2, and wishes to return to Wittenberg. It is difficult to conceive that there is a link between that part of Nashe's essay and Q2's Hamlet, aged thirty, but *if* Hamlet's age in Q2 is explained by this, it would confirm Q2's date as later than 1592.

"Disparity Gaps"

Studying *Les Histoires Tragiques* is instructive for so much, including now both Hamlet's return and the drunkenness of the Danes. An awareness of the French source also helps with other tiny peculiarities in the quartos, which, since they share similarities and need a label, we shall call "disparity gaps." The label is intended to refer to those moments when a feature of the original story casts its shadow over the *Hamlet*s, for there are occasions when the plot in the French source is clearer than in the quartos, or when reference to the French source clarifies vagueness in a *Hamlet*. A major example occurs in the "nunnery" scene of both quartos. At some point during this scene Hamlet has to realize that there are eavesdroppers, though there is nothing in the plays which tells either the actors or the readers that this is the case.[4] The moment of realization can of course be provided by the actors—for example a nervous glance in the direction of the eavesdroppers by Ofelia/Ophelia—but it is not explicit in the text. It *is* explicit in *Les Histoires Tragiques*; we have already noted that Amleth is warned both by his friend and by the young woman herself that this is a trap. The writer(s) of Q1 and Q2 seems to know it was a trap and writes the scene as a trap, but does not leave a trace of how the Prince recognizes the trap in either quarto.

The second example follows straight on, and was noted earlier. When Q1's Hamlet enters his mother's bedchamber, he retains just a hint of the suspicions of Amleth entering his mother's "*chambre.*" Amleth "se douta de quelque trahison" ([he] "suspected treachery") and checks the room out. Q1 Hamlet says "but first we'll make all safe." But Q2's Hamlet is more distant— we might almost say more trusting—and does not contain that half line and the small "disparity gap."

The third example is in the slippage between the Prince's request and the Queen's response. It is perfectly straightforward in the French source. There Amleth says that the King must not learn about Amleth's plans for revenge ("le Roy ny autre ne soit en rien informé de cecy" [218]). The Queen responds relevantly, saying that she will feign ignorance, and keep secret both the plan and her son's gallant or brave intentions ("duquel je feindray ne sçavoir rien ... je tiendray secrette, et ta sagesse, et ta gaillarde enterprinse" [222]). But in Q1 Hamlet asks the Queen to "Forbear the adulterous bed tonight" and "assist me in revenge" (11.90, 93), and her response is noticeably less relevant. From a linguistic perspective her response lacks cohesion with his lines. She says "I will conceal" (she has not been asked to conceal anything), "consent and do my best,/ What stratagem soe'er thou shalt devise" (11.97-8). Q1's Queen's response actually answers the request of the source's Prince better than the request of Q1's Prince Hamlet. Q2's Hamlet has a noticeably different request. He asks that the Queen should not

> *Hamlet.* Let the bloat King tempt you again to bed ...
> Or ...
> Make you to unravel all this matter out
> That I essentially am not in madness
> But mad in craft [III.iv.180–1, 184–186].

Q2's Queen again answers relevantly:

> *Queen.* Be thou assured, if words be made of breath
> And breath of life, I have no life to breathe
> What thou hast said to me [III.iv.195–7].

4. Hamlet's Return, Nashe and Some Binge Drinking 59

It seems that Q1's exchange incompletely echoes the French source. If the playwright is following that text as he writes Q1, this could explain the lack of cohesion in Q1. But Q2's exchange has moved right away, to a different request and response. A Q1 > Q2 sequence of revision removes the need for the putative actor/reporter(s) to depend upon knowing or playing in *The Spanish Tragedy* (the reasoning of, for example, Duthie).

A last hint of a "disparity gap" is the opening line to the scene unique to Q1, scene 14, examined above: "Madame, your sonne is safe arriv'de in *Denmarke*." The line appears to let us infer the Queen is expecting Hamlet's return, which is exactly the case in the source. Together these four examples show how *Les Histoires Tragiques* casts a shadow over the quartos, or suggest that the author of Q1 was very familiar with *Les Histoires Tragiques*. But while each "shadow" affects Q1, only the first (Hamlet's awareness of eavesdroppers in the "nunnery" scene) still affects Q2. The apparent resolution by Q2 of three of the four "disparity gaps" is another reason for deducing that Q1 is the earlier text, and that Q2 represents a revised version.

The evidence of those "disparity gaps" does not support MR or abridgement in any logical way. To include that textual evidence in the MR or abridgement hypotheses we must propose another hypothesis, that the reconstructor(s)/abridgers supplemented their recollections or cuttings with reference to and a preference for the French source. Or we must argue that the hypothetical *Ur-Hamlet* happened to be closer to the French source in those respects and that the reconstructor(s)/abridger(s) supplemented their recollections or cuttings with reference to and a preference for the hypothetical *Ur-Hamlet* for those details.

A last piece of evidence to be emphasized here concerns the density of parallels between the source and each of the quartos. Q1 has slightly more parallels, but it is only 55 percent of the length of Q2. That means Q1 has almost double the density of borrowings. This would not be expected if the abridger was cutting Q2's length, nor if the reconstructor was struggling to remember what was in Q2, even if we should be talking about not Q2 but a stage adaptation of Q2.

Chapters one to four have taken a systematic approach to comparing Q1 and Q2 as individual texts, and attempt to establish the priority of one or the other. The three principal techniques are found elsewhere in Shakespearean studies, even if they have not been applied to these two quartos before. The use of an external reference to linguistic change has been used by Jackson, and the identification of a trend towards a more colloquial written style over a playwriting career was identified by Waller. The use of the underlying source and how it may reflect upon the two versions of *The Taming of the Shrew* is mentioned in Brian Morris' edition.[5] It is not so much that *Les Histoires*

Tragiques has been neglected, for Stabler's and Jenkins' examinations are very enlightening. It just happens their investigations do not focus on the individual debts the quartos may owe to the French source.

The chapters contribute several pieces of significant, reproducible evidence to add to the dates at the end of the Introduction. However the relationship of the quartos is described, the description needs to accommodate both the dates and this objective evidence.

The evidence lies in the higher number of dated <eth> inflections in Q1 (or the higher number of more modern verb endings in Q2), and in the wider range of colloquialisms, and slightly higher proportion, in Q2 (working on the assumption that Shakespeare's trend towards a more colloquial style is correctly identified). Further evidence lies in Q1's greater proximity to the source. This is shown in how Amleth's and Q1 Hamlet's ages match, in the position of the "nunnery" scene, in small echoes of the source like "but first we'll make all safe" and "Madame, your sonne is safe arriv'de in *Denmarke*," in the Princes' explicit intention of taking revenge, in the Queen's expression of concern for her son, and in similarity of the Queens' promises. More evidence is seen in Q1's higher number of borrowings from the source, and in the fact that Q1's density of borrowings or parallels is almost double that of Q2.

This does not overlook the few verbal echoes like "couch," and the proximity of "adulterate" and "incestuous" which make Q2 closer to the French source. Only these points support MR or abridgement, even with an intervening stage adaptation. But supplementary hypotheses are needed to account for all the points in the preceding paragraph. A first draft and revision approach accommodates all the findings; we simply have to see Shakespeare skim-reading *Les Histoires Tragiques* again as he revises, if indeed he does not recall these minor verbal echoes. This is an uncomplicated explanation, with only one speculation or supplementary hypothesis needed, that Shakespeare glanced again at *Les Histoires Tragiques*.

It does lead to a matter that is impossible to evidence. It is very difficult to estimate the point at which Shakespeare started writing, because of the lack of knowledge of his education and his whereabouts during the "lost" years. The only contemporary records relating to the Free School in Stratford in the 1570s give the names of the masters (Simon Hunt, Thomas Jenkins, and John Cotton).[6] There is no list of pupils, and no account of its curriculum. Shakespeare is assumed to have attended; the curriculum is assumed to be similar to, for instance, what is known of Leicester's Free Grammar School, and aspects of what he learnt is inferred from the plays and the then current educational books.[7] Nothing is known of his facility in learning, whether he was exceptional as an eidetic or echoic pupil, or how he became a polyglot, though the plays prove familiarity with at least Latin, French, and Italian, according to

Muir in *The Sources of Shakespeare's Plays*.[8] Katherine Duncan-Jones, for whom Shakespeare was an "early starter," points out that Richard Field, also from Stratford, went to London, was apprenticed (aged eighteen) to the Huguenot printer Vautrollier, and was involved in publishing books in, for example, French, Italian, Spanish and Welsh, the implication being that Field must have acquired a facility in some modern languages.[9] While it is known that Shakespeare was lodging with a French Huguenot family in 1604,[10] that is too late for him to learn French for the source of *Hamlet*, or indeed for the French conversation in act III scene iv in *Henry V*, published in 1600.

We can reasonably assume that Shakespeare was familiar with French because of one of the historical allusions present in both quartos. It is to a legal case which was reported in French, and it pre-dates the earliest mention of *Hamlet*, in 1589. This is the Hales v. Pettit case. Sir James Hales committed suicide by drowning in 1554; the lawsuit followed in 1560 and the reports were published in Law French in 1571–8. They were not translated into English until the eighteenth century.[11] Shakespeare alludes to this case in the "gravedigger's" scene. The triumph of Shakespeare's argument is that "it puts what is a crucial issue in Ophelia's death in a way that precisely mimics the typical legal argument," writes Jenkins.[12] This means that either Shakespeare was familiar with French or the allusions, which run over several speeches in the penultimate scene, are not Shakespeare's. Logically, if Shakespeare knew the French for alluding to that case, and for the scene in *Henry V*, it is perfectly possible that he read *Les Histoires Tragiques*. If there were only one occasion when it appeared that Shakespeare knew French, it might be possible to assume that he had help or heard an English version. But since there are several occasions, it seems reasonable to deduce that he was a fluent reader of French.

Chapters two, three and four have shown parallels with the French source,[13] how ideas rooted in that text have evolved in the quartos, and some of the ways in which Q2 draws away from *Les Histoires Tragiques*. Chapter 5 now looks briefly at what we know about revision of plays in Elizabethan and Jacobean times, and whether there is further evidence for revision in the *Hamlet* quartos.

5. Just Like Ben Jonson

Q1 *Hamlet* is often referred to as the "Bad" quarto, a label which is uncomplimentary and biased. The descriptors quoted in the Introduction— "maimed," "mangled," "imperfect," "distorted" and so forth—also show their users' disapproving responses to Q1. Yet there are others who have praised the play, particularly as a performance text. Its first recorded performance in 1881, put on by William Poel, received the comment: "the First Quarto is an excellent acting play."[1] Peter Guinness, in the 1985 performance of the so-called "Bad Quarto" at the Orange Tree Theatre, Richmond describes it as:

> an express train that roars out of the station at the beginning of the play, and heads for the next two hours at accelerating speed towards a dead-end at the far end of the track. The audience knows that disaster is coming, and the excitement builds simply because of the speed at which the play moves.[2]

A reviewer of Guinness in Hamlet's role in Q1 wrote: "I shall never think of it as the Bad Quarto again."[3]

Graham Holderness and Bryan Loughrey front their Introduction to their 1992 Q1 *Hamlet* with a selection of "phrases of positive celebration," responses to the 1985 performance: "Enormous dramatic economy and force...," "a brisk, exciting play...," and "vitality." It is true that those accolades do not have the mentions of "subtlety," "poetry" and "great lines," all associated with Q2.[4] There is a critical distinction necessary here, between a good theatrical text, and a great, poetic, theatrical text. If Q2 is the latter, it does not exclude Q1 from being the former.

So the question of whether Q2 shows signs of being a revised version of Q1 is important. In his F1 paean to Shakespeare Ben Jonson appears to suggest the playwright did revise. The metaphor Jonson uses to describe Shakespeare's approach, to "strike the second heat/ Vpon the *Muses* anuile,"[5] is interpreted by Schoenbaum as Jonson understanding that "part of [Shakespeare's] greatness was bound up in his gift for second thoughts."[6] It may even be that the length of Q2 exemplifies another of Jonson's comments on Shakespeare, that "he flowed with that facility that sometimes it was necessary he should be stopped: *Sufflimandus erat*, as Augustus said of Haterius."[7] And Shapiro, who suggests Shakespeare was revising Q2 shortly after its completion, writes that Shakespeare "tinkered obsessively."[8] It means that we can feel reasonably confident that Shakespeare did revise, though we may not be certain what he revised or how much.

In *Revising Shakespeare* Grace Ioppolo assembles examples of emendations, or revisions, to contemporary plays. Some of these emendations are identified from handwriting upon manuscripts and books, while others may be deduced from the differences between printed versions. The first group cannot be proved with regard to Q1 and Q2, because no such manuscripts or corrected books are known. (It is, however, interesting to read Brian Vickers' comments on Shakespeare's possible hand in *Sir Thomas More*. Vickers writes: "[o]ne peculiarity of the handwriting on these pages is the amount of space Shakespeare allowed himself." It is "as if he were allowing himself ample space for interlinear additions and corrections."[9] Such comments invite further speculation upon whether Shakespeare was a reviser, and even whether he expected to revise.) The examples of emendations in the first group of manuscripts and books include: marginal additions (some written at ninety degrees to the main text), interlineations, inserted slips, and insertions of major speeches on separate leaves and in the margins. The second group include: alterations to spelling and punctuation, correction of errors or rewriting of some unclear words, addition of stage directions, added topical allusions, substitutions of one word with a whole speech, additional characters, development of another character, a whole scene omission, single word or line substitutions, transpositions, deletions, and additions.

It is easy to find examples of the latter group in Q2. The "rewriting of an unclear word" might come at the beginning of act V scene i, when Hamlet is speaking to Horatio about the bones the Clown is finding. In Q1 Hamlet comments that a nearby box:

> *Ham.*   ... will scarce
>   Hold the conveyance of his [a lawyer's] land and must
>   The honor lie there? [Sig. H4v.7–9]

It is thought that "honor" was a misreading of "owner." In Q2, the word is not "owner" but a more formal, less easily mistaken, near synonym, "inheritor" (sig. M2v.35).

The opening scenes of the quartos offer a range of single word "substitutions," another revision feature. For example, the phrase "yonder star" (Q1, sig. B1v.12) may be substituted by "yond same starre" (Q2, sig. B1v.22), and "But loe, behold" (Q1, sig. B2v.7), with "But soft, behold" (Q2, sig. B3r.1).

"Substitutions" is an awkward word in this context, for it is also used in discussing MR. When "substitutions" is used about vocabulary in Q1, it invites the reader to accept that the different vocabulary in Q1 has come second, replacing a word in Q2. The technique is not objective; it works from an assumption, that Q1 is a later text than Q2. For example, Q1 mentions "upon your watch" (sig. B1r.3), in comparison with "vpon your houre" in Q2 (sig. B1r.6). If we see Q1's "watch" as a "substitution," we are assuming Q2 came first.

If instead we say Q2's word is the "substitution," we are connoting that Q1 came first (and then the "substitution" would be a revision). So although we can find examples in Q2 of words which might be "substitutions" and revisions, this too may be seen as biased. Only if we know which word really came first can we call the other a "substitution," and with these it is not easy to declare one vocabulary choice is noticeably better than another. There are advantages to using "variants," a neutral word, like "differences."

Further examples of typical, potential revisions can be found. For instance, a "single line substitution" or difference in phrasing begins the play: Q1's "Stand: who is that?" (sig. B1r.1) can be paired with Q2's "Whose there?" (sig. B1r.1). Minor changes in punctuation are also evident. Horatio speaks in Q1 of how Fortinbrasse:

> *Hor.* ... did forfeit with his life all those
> His lands which he stoode seazed of by the conqueror [Sig. B2r.30–1],

while Q2 breaks up the rather complex sentence, placing the adverbial "(with his life)" in parenthesis, and pausing with a useful comma between the verb ("seaz'd of") and the indirect object ("to the conquerour"):

> *Hora.* Did forfait (with his life) all these his lands
> Which he stood seaz'd of, to the conquerour [Sig. B2v.1–2].

"Transpositions" of words are noticeable, too. When in Q1 Horatio speaks of the cock crowing at dawn and awakening the god of day, one line of his speech runs thus: "Whether in earth or ayre, in sea or fire" (sig. B2v.32). In Q2 the same line is "Whether in sea or fire, in earth or ayre" (sig. B3r.29). In terms of the sense, the alternative ordering of the two sets of elements is not significant. All are monosyllables, and the slight phonological patterning between the second of each pair in each quarto hints at a weak internal rhyme ("fire"/"ayre") in a manner no other combination of the four words would. This is retained in each quarto. The same is true of another alternative ordering. Q1's Marcellus speaks of the time when our savior's birth is celebrated as "So gratious, and so hallowed" (sig. B3r.5), while Q2 has an alternative order, "So hallowed, and so gratious" (sig. B3v.1).[10]

"Deletions" and "additions" are further revision techniques, like the above-mentioned "transposition," though again all these terms are usually associated with MR when discussing the *Hamlet* quartos. These terms too need to be approached with caution, since each implies the direction of change and could consequently influence a reader regarding the chronology of the quartos. For example, only Q2 has a soliloquy beginning "How all occasions" (act IV scene iv). To comment that the same soliloquy is an "addition" to the script of Q2 when it was revised implies Q1 existed first. The soliloquy would then be an example of revision. If we say that Hamlet's "How all occasions" soliloquy is "deleted" or "omitted" in Q1 we are implying that Q2 existed beforehand and that the compiler of Q1 had some degree of choice about whether to include the soliloquy in Q1.

If we *assume* Q1 preceded Q2 and *assume* that first draft and revision is correct, more examples of the revision features which Ioppolo identifies are easy to find. Shakespeare "deletes" his first method for returning Hamlet to Denmark ("Being crossed by the contention of the winds" ([14.5]), and "adds" the story of the "pirate of warlike appointment" (IV.vi.15–16). Shakespeare "transposes" the "nunnery" scene from its position just after Corambis' suggestion of using Ofelia to discover if Hamlet is mad with love, to nearly 600 lines later in Q2, leaving the audience/reader waiting in suspense. These two examples are logical enough if the case for revision is to be argued, but in reality the quartos are merely being measured against each other. Much more significant are the examples of revision that can be argued by bringing in a third text with a known position in the chronology. This is why, for instance, the earlier positioning of the "nunnery" scene in Q1 is so valuable, because it is similar to that of the earlier Belleforest; that example is superior to either of the examples beginning this paragraph.

Ioppolo also sees the development of character as a sign of possible revision. The King of Q1, for instance, is a more manipulative, smooth-speaking character in Q2, as both his opening speeches and his "prayer" scene speeches show. This is a "development of character" if we accept Q2 as the posterior script. But those advocating abridgement or memorial reconstruction would see the more streamlined characters of Q1—such as the King—as evidence of the possible simplification that occurred with abridgement, or the lack of detail in the recall of the actor/reporter(s). Hart, who sees a "bad" quarto as most probably "a corrupt, garbled, ungrammatical and probably mutilated version" of an original manuscript,[11] suggests that "literary" revision began with Jonson,[12] though it was not a concern of all dramatists.[13] (We should at the very least challenge Hart's label of "ungrammatical." This is an unsupported statement; "ungrammatical" would make the meaning of the text difficult to understand because of non–Standard English, or it would be characterized by a strong dialect that is not Standard English, and neither is true.) But the way that Hart is happy to acknowledge Ben Jonson as a reviser is interesting; Hart doesn't seem to think that rewriting is too great a "chare" for Jonson.

Ben Jonson

Jonson is a useful analogy with regard to revision. His revision of *Every Man in His Humour* was carried out between its first publication in 1598—when it included a list of actors headed by William Shakespeare—and 1616, when it was republished in Jonson's collected works. Jonson's revisions included:

- an added prologue
- varied lengths of acts
- the number of scenes, increased from twenty to thirty-three
- the location of the action, changed from Italy to England
- the renaming of most of the characters
- hundreds of verbal and phrasal changes
- additions of less than two or three lines, on the whole
- the excision of many lines and some short passages, and
- an addition of thirty lines to one speech, and the removal of another of thirty-one lines.

How does Q2 *Hamlet* rate against that list, in comparison with Q1, if Q1 > Q2 is momentarily assumed? Q2 includes:

- an added soliloquy,
- varied lengths of acts
- the number of scenes is increased from seventeen to twenty
- a minor change in the location of the place in which Hamlet is separated from his two escorts, from "set ashore" after a storm to a pirate ship,
- some characters gain names and two are renamed
- many verbal and phrasal changes
- varied numbers of lines added
- the excision of some lines and the removal of part of Q1's speech beginning "Let not your clown speak more…" (9.17–28), and
- an addition of twenty-nine lines to Claudius' opening speech and the removal of scene 14.

In general the types and extent of changes between Q1 and Q2 are very similar to those listed for Jonson. Since the types of alterations and revisions are found across a range of authors' scripts, and differences between Q1 and Q2 bear resemblances to Jonson's style of revision, we cannot simply dismiss the first sketch and revision hypothesis for Q1 *Hamlet*.

This analogy with Jonson's revisions, or rewriting, provides one way of looking at Q2. Hart comments: "The excessive difference between Jonson's two plays, *The Case Is Altered* (2525 lines) and *Every Man Out of His Humour* (4452 lines) is partly explained by his habit of rewriting and expanding the original manuscript of the acted play prior to publication."[14] Shakespeare might have revised for the same reason, perhaps for a reading public, as Erne considers.[15] If so, it offers one possible explanation for why Shakespeare, an experienced playwright by 1600, would write a play so much longer than the "two hours traffic" of the stage, if that really was the approximate limit to a play's duration. For a *reading* public the dramatist is free to choose the length at which he wishes to write. Shakespeare might even have been one of those playwrights who "vsed a double sale of their labours, first to the Stage, and after to the presse," as Heywood complained in 1608.[16]

Ioppolo herself recognizes that the concept of "extensive authorial revisions in *Hamlet* has been critically acceptable only since the 1980s." However, her discussion begins with her acceptance that "Duthie established in 1941 that Quarto 1 was a reported text of the acting version."[17] Her view combines a belief in the memorial reconstruction of Q1 with a Q2 that is revised into F1. But it cannot reasonably be assumed that Shakespeare was beyond using any of the types of emendation or revision techniques that Ioppolo has found or which Jonson used. The pertinent question is whether it was just Q2 which was revised to give us F1, or whether Q1 was also revised, to give us Q2. Revision is, after all, commonplace in literature. Few professional writers do not revise, though the rejected version may not survive to prove the process has occurred. That literary writers do change texts substantially is shown by, for instance, the two versions of *Tender Is the Night* by F. Scott Fitzgerald. The novel consists of three "books," which in the first version were presented in the order of 2, 1, 3, in terms of the chronology of the story. But after the relative lack of success of his novel in that shape, Fitzgerald "transposed" the first "books," which were then published in chronological sequence, 1, 2, 3. The former is the usual version found today (the rearrangement didn't improve the book's popularity). Thomas Hardy's *Return of the Native* and John Fowles' *French Lieutenant's Woman* offer different endings, Hardy at the request of his publishers, and Fowles as a creative and experimental author. William Wordsworth produced two versions of *The Prelude*, in 1805 and 1850. The former is usually preferred, despite the fact that the latter offers his considered revisions. There are many such examples.

Chapters one to four provide evidence indicating a trajectory from *Les Histoires Tragiques* through Q1 to Q2. There is a further reason for proposing that revision is the best explanation. This concerns the differences in some of the characters between the quartos, differences which are more than the extra lines in a single scene, as for Claudius in I.ii, and which span several scenes. While "differences" is appropriately neutral terminology, the following discussion illustrates a development of some characters and their relationship from (Belleforest to) Q1 to Q2. The argument stems, once again, from familiarity with *Les Histoires Tragiques*. It is that text (in the absence of any putative *Ur-Hamlet*) which is therefore used as the starting point. Three sets of characters in particular demonstrate these differences: the relationship of the Prince and the Queen, the portrayal of the King (and his relationship with Leartes/Laertes, who is *not* part of *Les Histoires Tragiques*), and "deux des fideles ministres de Fengon" ("two of Fengon's faithful servants" [232]), that is, Rossencraft and Gilderstone, and Rosencrans and Guyldensterne.

The Queen and the Prince

We start with the relationship between the Queen and the Prince, and again with the French source. There can be no doubt that the French Queen loves her son. She calls him "mon filz, et doux amy" ("my son, and sweet friend" [220]), and King Fengon comments upon "[Amleth] qu'elle [Geruthe] aymoit" ("[Amleth] whom she [Geruthe] loves" [230]). Amleth in turn is appalled by her betrayal of his father in marrying Fengon (her "infamie," infamy). Nevertheless, it is she in whom he confides his intention to take revenge, it is she who promises to keep silent about his intentions, and it is she whom he asks for help. She asks him not to be too hasty and impetuous in taking revenge. Her role is to prepare the "banquet funebre," the funeral banquet, for a year hence when he will return. She looks for his return, and prepares the banquet he has asked for. He is able to slip in, ensure all those celebrating are completely drunk, reach the King's room, and kill him.

There is also no doubt in Q1 that Gertred loves Hamlet. He too is "Sweet Hamlet" (11.45), and the King says directly to Hamlet that he is "the joy and half heart of your mother" (2.30). In the "bedchamber" scene Hamlet is also appalled by her remarriage (her "infamy"), and tells her that he will exact revenge. She too promises to "conceal" his intentions, and "do my best" (11.97) to help him. Scene 14 then begins with "Madame, your son is safe arrived in Denmark" (14.1), which may permit us to infer that she is expecting his return.

It may be Horatio who first hears of Hamlet's return, but the playwright presents it so the Queen (and the audience) hears about it from Hamlet's confidant, Horatio. And in her concern for her son Gertred asks Horatio to tell Hamlet to be careful: "Bid him [Hamlet] a while be wary of his [the King's] presence" (14.19).

But in Q2 there is just a little more distance between Gertrard and Hamlet. He is still "sweet Hamlet" (III.iv.94), and she refers to him as "O gentle son" (I.iv.118). Claudius still notes that "The Queen his mother / Lives almost by his looks" (IV.vii.12–3), though this comment comes later (as indeed in *Les Histoires Tragiques*). In the "bedchamber" or "closet" scene however, Hamlet does not confide in his mother in quite the same way. He is appalled by her remarriage ("trespass," now), and describes his killing of Polonius as "almost as bad.../ As kill a king and marry with his brother" (III.iv.26–7). This is almost an aside on Polonius; it is not the separate and explicit statement in each of the other two versions which declares that Fengon/the King is a murderer. Moreover, Hamlet does recall the Ghost's "dread command" (III.iv.105), which the audience knows from act I is that Hamlet should exact vengeance. But Hamlet does not explicitly tell his mother that he will take revenge. The Queen does not know what Hamlet means when he addresses the Ghost, which is why the Ghost comments that "amazement on thy mother sits!" (III.iv.108). It is only the audience who are in the know. And when Hamlet does return to Denmark, his confidant Horatio hears it at the same time as the audience. The Queen is not even present in this scene. There is nothing to suggest she expects his return. The Queen is relegated to hearing about his return in a letter, this arriving a scene later when it is only the King and Laertes present. Interestingly, in the two quarto "bedchamber" scenes the Queen's contributions change from about 28 percent in Q1 to 22 percent in Q2, another way of showing her role is less in Q2 here. Her role is fractionally diminished, quite consistently, in Q2.

These are all small points, but cumulatively it results in the Queen's role being slightly less prominent in Q2 than in Q1 or the French source. Her relationship with the Prince is also less close than in Q1; Q1 is a little nearer to *Les Histoires Tragiques* in this respect too. The alternative way of expressing this is that the Queen's role is a little bigger in Q1 and that she is a little closer to her son in Q1 than in Q2. If we are to accept MR or abridgement, we need to explain why the abridger or actor/reporter(s) might *expand* the Queen's role in Q1, in a shorter text. And we must explain how and why the abridger or actor/reporter draws closer to the source. Must we speculate again upon the actor/reporter'(s) familiarity with the putative *Ur-Hamlet* (which cannot be proved, of course), or the actual French source?

The King

Something different occurs with the character of the King. Belleforest's treatment of Fengon's murder of Horvvendille is confused. On the same page Belleforest describes the murder in two ways. In one it is public—"en un banquet" ("at a banquet")—and in the other it is a totally different, private one, where he had killed his brother whom he had found at the point of killing the Queen ("s'estant trouve sur le poinct qu'il taschoit de la massacrer" [186]). This enables Fengon (the new King) to claim he was protecting the Queen. Shakespeare uses neither murder method. But on the preceding page Belleforest has, prior to the murder, explained why there is no suspicion of Fengon. For there existed "un tel nœud d'alliance et de consanguinité," such a close knot of alliance (kinship) and blood relationship (between Horvvendille, his wife Geruthe, and his brother Fengon), that no one would have expected one brother to murder the other. Rather they would have expected that the only outcomes of that family relationship would be virtuous and courteous or chivalric ("les effetz pleins de vertu et courtoisie" [184]). In other words, the first of Belleforest's three approaches to the murder tells the reader that Fengon is completely free of any potential suspicion in the death of his brother. This is similar to Q1's first presentation of the King in scene 2. Here the King's opening speech is ten lines; it informs the lords that he has written to Fortinbrasse, and he is now dispatching Cornelia and Voltemar to Old Norway. The King shows no need or desire to explain to the court or the audience why he is King. There appears no suspicion in the court, and the playwright shows no need or desire to explain.

In the theatre this is unproblematic, since audiences accept being placed *in medias res*, and the pace of the play is such that there is little chance to wonder about the King. Moreover, the back story is revealed in other ways, through Hamlet and the Ghost, for example. However, in Q2 King Claudius has thirty-nine lines, nearly four times as many as in Q1, in his first speech. He starts by offering an exposition, telling us about the death of his brother and his own marriage to the widow. He moves then to express respectful grief for that brother; then he acknowledges—flatters—the wisdom of the lords, offers more exposition regarding Fortinbras, and, finally, dispatches Voltemand and Cornelius to Old Norway. Claudius' style here is authoritative and statesmanlike, sufficient to gain for example L. C. Knight's admiration and praise of him as a pragmatic and promising King: Knight calls him an "excellent diplomatist and King."[18]

Thus in Q2 any questions that the more leisurely reader may have (or that the revising playwright may anticipate?) about the circumstances underlying the situation—the prequel, effectively—are forestalled by Claudius' longer opening speech. Claudius is immediately a much more substantial and kingly figure and consequently more menacing. So is Claudius "cut," or is he half forgotten, to become the King of Q1 in scene 2? Or has Shakespeare, if revising Q1 and creating Q2, decided there is a need, or opportunity, to provide his version of why no suspicion falls upon the new King? Does Shakespeare have *Les Histoires Tragiques* to hand, note (again?) on a second reading[19] why Fengon is above suspicion, re-read Belleforest's two, alternative murder descriptions which the playwright had rejected the first time, and then see how Fengon is also described as "vn fin et rusé Conseiller" (184), a shrewd/astute and crafty counselor? Might it be that Belleforest's epithet is the origin of Q2's Claudius at the beginning of act I scene ii? Few would disagree that Claudius is shrewd or astute or crafty or all three in his opening speech.

However, it is not in just one scene that the King and King Claudius differ. The dramatist authoring Q1's scene 14 uses Horatio to announce to the Queen that her son is "safe arriv'de in *Denmarke,*" news he reports from a letter. The scene backgrounds Hamlet's return, but shows the Queen as affectionately maternal, alert to the treachery and potential displeasure of the King, and it explains that Gilderstone and Rossencraft have met their doom. The short scene—thirty-five lines—is effectively and dramatically framed by the King's last words in scene 13, that Leartes "shall heare that you do not dreame vpon" (i.e., Leartes will shortly hear that Hamlet is already dead [sig. H2v.4]), and by the King's first, incredulous words in scene 15: "Hamlet from England! is it possible?" (sig. H3r.7). Dramatically this is effective; dramatically, the end of scene 13, the whole of scene 14 and the beginning of scene 15 cohere well. Either the original dramatist, or an abridger, or an actor/reporter has structured this very carefully. "Garbled" it is not.

Then Q1's scene 15 races ahead, with the King swiftly laying out the "plot" he has devised, of a "keene sword," "deadly poyson" and a "potion," three chances to kill Hamlet. In both scenes 13 and 15 the King remains evil, treacherous and powerful. Meanwhile, Hamlet's vulnerability continues; the command of his father to seek revenge awaits execution. For the audience the suspense is acute.

Q2's dramatist shows Horatio learning of, rather than announcing, Hamlet's return, via a letter brought by a sailor. The introduction of pirates offers a credible and topical reason for Hamlet's rapid return. In the later part of Elizabeth I's reign pirates were a problem in the Great Sound/Belt between Elsinore on Zealand and the south of Sweden and the English court were complaining about them.[20]

The device of reading aloud a letter purporting to come from Hamlet places him at the centre of the scene. It also marks the beginning of those final stages of the play where Horatio is allied to Hamlet and Hamlet is otherwise isolated. It also means that Horatio must bear a letter to Claudius, which delays the King's discovery of Hamlet's return in the next scene. Instead in the first thirty-five lines of IV.vii the King claims the absent Prince has "Pursued my life," and explains the problem of punishing a man for whom his mother and the general public have a "great loue" (IV.vii.5, 19). It is now that the King alludes to the news he assumes he will shortly receive. The audience (in the know) savors the dramatic irony of it, and then a messenger enters with letters from Hamlet. The news briefly halts Claudius, but soon the "fin et rusé conseiller" of act I scene ii's opening lines reappears in all his craftiness. Claudius manipulates the vengeful, mourning Laertes through flattery—"such a masterly report"—and a hint of doubt—"are you like the painting of a sorrowe?"—and a challenge—"what would you vndertake..." (IV.vii.94, 106, 122). Claudius is more deceitful than in Q1; he is a more dangerous and subtle adversary. He leads Laertes to accept cheating—"a little shuffling," and a "sword unbated"—and Laertes himself, in his eagerness for revenge, adds the third method of cheating, the use of "an unction of a mountebank" (IV.vii.135, 136, 139).

While there are still three methods to ensure Hamlet's death, now only two are proposed by Claudius. This contributes to the sense in this scene of a manipulative Claudius thinking on his feet, as "Let's further think of this" and "soft let me see" (IV.vii.146, 152) suggest. The scene has more "showing" than Q1's King, who "tells," saying "mark the plot I have laid" (15.9). And Q2's scene underlines Claudius' malevolence and self-interest when his only comment after the news of Ophelia's death is:

> *King.* How much I had to do to calm his rage,
> Now fear I this will give it start again [IV.vii.190–1].

The subtle changes in the characterization of the King occur across more than one scene and suggest a creator with a clear aim, adjusting his characters and their lines. This surely permits another of Hart's comments to be dismissed. Hart thinks that "[if] Shakespeare rewrote the bad quartos, some of his additions suggest he was rather capricious in his choice of the characters whose parts he increased."[21] "Capricious?" Or selective and purposeful? We would have to ask whether an actor/reporter or an abridger would be seeking to make character changes or indeed any changes across a *series* of scenes. If we accept the actor/reporter(s) or abridger as the agent of these changes, we need to ask why he/they might do it.

If an actor/reporter has a faulty memory he might "forget" the pirates. He might "forget" that Q2 announces Rosencrans and Guyldensterne's deaths in the final scene, not in scene 14 as in Q1. But it is difficult to explain why he introduces the Queen into Q1's scene 14. It cannot be to economize on actors, since while Q2's version requires five actors, several roles are already ended and actors therefore available (Voltemand, Marcellus, Barnardo, Francisco and the Ghost are a few examples). An abridger has no need to cut or change actors either, nor does he have to change the location of events. But if Q1 were the first sketch of a young (upstart) dramatist laying down the skeleton of the play, it would be possible to see the revised Q2's act IV scene vi as embedding topicality, intensifying suspense, heightening the vulnerability of Hamlet, and transposing the announcement of the two courtiers' deaths to the final scene to add to the dénouement.

It would be reasonable to suggest that an abridger cut the opening thirty-five lines of I.ii in Q2. It has been suggested that "Marcellus" as actor/reporter was offstage, and therefore didn't hear them. But it may be instead that a reviser inserted them, as a prelude to changing the character of the King. Claudius is presented consistently in act IV scenes v and vii, and that portrayal matches his manipulative political persona in I.ii. The change in the King is credibly explained by a great playwright, Shakespeare, revising; it requires an abridger to be outstandingly skilful in paring down the King's role in both Q1's scenes 2 and 15. Yet those Q1 scenes contain the seeds of Q2's I.ii and IV.vii. We must consider whether it is a plausible scenario that a playwright first created *Hamlet* from the French narrative, interweaving the subplot and Players, transforming a vengeful and violent Amleth to a deeply hurt and philosophically inclined Hamlet, and shaped a workable plot for the whole play (Q1). Then, later, might he return to revise, to elaborate, to round out his characters and refine them, to "show" more and "tell" less, and to sharpen the play's dramatic import? It would not be an unrealistic composition and revision approach.

We have by now noted that there are three separate occasions where the drama and suspense are heightened in Q2 in comparison to Q1. The first is the "nunnery" scene; the use of Ofelia to "test" Hamlet is almost immediately after Corambis' suggestion, with only the "To be" soliloquy intervening. In Q2 there is a delay of nearly 600 lines as well as the soliloquy; the audience must wait. Secondly, in Q1 the King learns immediately after scene 14 (when we hear of Hamlet's return) that Hamlet is back. In Q2 we begin IV.vii knowing that Hamlet is back, and we wait for the King to hear of Hamlet's return, to discover what Claudius' next move will be. In the first thirty-five lines the King explains to Laertes that Hamlet has not been punished because of the love of the Queen and the people. But of course, says the King:

> *King.* ... you must not think
> That we are made of stuff so flat and dull
> That we can let our beard be shook with danger
> And think it pastime [IV.vii.31–4].

Then just as we wonder what the King will admit to (or even brag about), "*Enter a* Messenger *with letters*," and the King learns Hamlet is back. The third example is the announcement of the two escorts' deaths. In Q1 we hear about this in scene 14, but in Q2 it is delayed until the last scene. These three examples which heighten the drama would be quite understandable changes by a revising dramatist. It is harder to see why an actor/reporter would place these events earlier. It is even harder to see why an abridger might change these, since presumably he would have a script in front of him to remind him where events occur.

The Escorts

A last example of some change in characterization between the quartos is again related to the underlying source. In *Les Histoires Tragiques* there are "deux des fideles ministres de Fengon" ("two of King Fengon's faithful/loyal servants/ministers" [232]), who translate in Q1 to Rossencraft and Gilderstone, and in Q2 to Rosencrans and Guyldensterne. These are the men whom the King calls upon to escort the Prince and a letter to the King of England, in all three texts. Later in the French source the same two "ministers" are called "les deux serviteurs du Roy Fengon" ("two of King Fengon's servants" [248]). There can be no doubt that in the source Amleth's escorts to England hold their allegiance first and foremost to King Fengon; there is no suggestion otherwise.

In Q1 Rossencraft and Gilderstone appear first in scene 7, where the King greets them as "Right noble friends" (7.1). Rossencraft describes the pair of them as the King's "liegemen" (7.11), and Hamlet is "the prince your son" (7.14). All of these phrases distance the pair from Hamlet. This language may be predictable in the context of the two men addressing the King, but it also aligns them with him. Hamlet greets them later in the same scene as "kind schoolfellows," but in his very next speech questions the purpose of their visit. He seems very suspicious; as Gilderstone says, Hamlet "puts us off" (8.7). That level of suspicion is sustained in scene 9, where he accuses them of being a "sponge that soaks up the king's countenance" (9.182). Hamlet obviously perceives them as the King's men. Later he makes it clear he does not wish to tell them where Corambis is. Their "doom" at the hands of the King of England is merely alluded to (15.27)—Hamlet expresses no concern for them.

Once again, Q2 is a little different. The King does address the two men as "dear" (II.ii.1), and later as "friends" (IV.i.33), but their closeness to the King is played down a little. It remains clear that he uses them as tools, to try to find out the reason for Hamlet's "transformation," to send Hamlet to the Queen's bedchamber, to extract from Hamlet where the body of Polonius is, and to bear letters to the King of England. For Hamlet they have been "friends"

(II.ii.219, 239), and their banter on their first meeting in the play seems to confirm this, but Hamlet still wants to hear *why* they are in Elsinore. However, twice Rosencrans and Guyldensterne reveal that they are no more than the King's pawns. When they speak to Hamlet in act III scene ii Guyldensterne offers a brief courteous request—"Good my lord, vouchsafe me a word with you"—before he goes straight to their task, with "The King, sir..." (III.ii.291). This reveals instantly who has directed them, and makes it obvious that it is because of the King's request that they are speaking to Hamlet. In act IV scene ii Rosencrans and Guyldensterne are even more forthright. They reveal both their knowledge of the death of Polonius and that Hamlet will know where the corpse is with their question: "What have you done, my lord, with the dead body?" (IV.ii.3–4). There is no preamble, no courtesy. In Q2 it is for Hamlet and the audience to deduce from what they are shown rather than told, namely that Rosencrans and Guyldensterne work for the King. Much later, when Hamlet updates Horatio about events in England, Hamlet confirms what he and we have inferred, Rosencrans and Guyldensterne's "insinuation" into the King's service. Hence "[t]hey are not near my conscience" (V.ii.58–9).

By now Part One is showing a range of different reasons, all evidence based, which indicate that Q1 was written before Q2. It is not just the larger number of older verb forms in Q1, nor the wider range of colloquialisms in Q2, nor the higher density of parallels with the underlying source in Q1, though these do all suggest Q1's priority. There are specific points at which Q1 is clearly closer to the source. The source may also explain the differences in the accounts of Hamlet's return, as well as the "disparity gaps." This chapter adds to the measureable evidence, illustrating how Q2 has revision features typical of contemporary plays. It also shows how there are signs of character developments in Q2 which run across scenes quite consistently. It is not unreasonable to speculate that these changes are from Q1 to Q2, for they fit a first sketch and revision scenario. If we return to the possible time spans for the composition of the quartos we might speculate that the difference in the poetic quality of the quartos suggests Q1 was an early version with (major) revision taking place some years later to create Q2. The examples may not be exhaustive, but they are very suggestive.

However, as the Introduction showed, many scholars believe that Q1 is a MR and the later quarto. It is unlikely that evidence for Q1's priority alone will change many minds. Part Two therefore turns to examine the principal reasons for scholars' belief in MR, and to evaluate exactly how secure the hypothesis of MR is.

Part Two: How Certain Is Memorial Reconstruction?

6. Printing, and Contemporary Complaints About Piracy

The hypothesis that Q1 *Hamlet* was memorially reconstructed has not been proposed as a result of a comparison of the morphology or colloquialisms of the two quartos. Nor was a comprehensive three way comparison between the French source and the two quartos carried out before or as the hypothesis was developed. As we have noted, when stylistic comparisons of particular features in the canon are made, for example for colloquialisms in verse or pause patterns,[1] those for *Hamlet* are usually given once, as if there were one *Hamlet*, not three. There isn't always any indication of which *Hamlet* is being measured, though we may guess at Q2 or F1 or a conflation. Indeed, the two quartos are not often examined in equal or similar detail, which may reflect how many scholars accept MR as the explanation for Q1.

Although this may seem a rather negative manner in which to begin examining the concept of MR, we do need to understand the context in which it emerged and developed. Scholars in the eighteenth century recognized both the genius of Shakespeare and also how little we knew about him and his works. The rediscovery in the nineteenth century of a Q1 *Hamlet* without some of *Hamlet*'s most well-known lines and speeches must have astounded many. It is like going into a beautiful garden at its midsummer best one day, and visiting another time to find little trace of the best blooms, even though the paths and hedges are still in place. The image may begin to suggest how those familiar with Q2 *Hamlet* might have felt when they later met Q1, for it is unlikely that many people today have read or seen Q1 first. While some moving from Q2 to Q1 have seen Q1 as the "first conception" of a "great mind,"[2] others have presumably felt the whole effect of Q1 lacked so much of the quality of Q2 they have felt it necessary to explain Q1's existence as something other than Shakespeare's first conception.

It is now more than a century since Mommsen and his successors first began to suggest that certain characteristics of Q1 point towards a MR or

MRA (or abridgement). They take several distinctive approaches to arguing for MR. Some scholars, reading Q1, have simply described the text with derogatory terms like "maimed," or "marred," or "garbled," as the Introduction mentioned. This is a rather vague and general attack upon Q1. Occasionally these descriptors are applied to a specific part of Q1, such as "a farrago of nonsense" to the Q1 "To be or not to be, ay there's the point" soliloquy.[3] One example—Hamlet's reply to the King—is discussed in Chapter 1.

The second approach begins with Mommsen, in 1857. He began listing features of Q1 *Hamlet* which he did not attribute to a Shakespearean *Hamlet* (though his attention was principally on Q1 *Romeo and Juliet*). These features include "very striking inconsistencies of the action, owing not only to omissions or transpositions, but also to certain alterations of the text." Mommsen also writes about the "blunders of the mutilated *Hamlet*" and "discern[s] two hands employed ... the one being probably an actor ... the other that of a bad poet, most probably a 'bookseller's hack.'" Indeed, Mommsen states that "the most curious misunderstandings of every kind are found on almost every page."[4] While this is only a small collection of the points Mommsen makes, it is unfortunate that he does not give examples of the features he finds. (It is tempting to suggest it is a little like a detective at a crime scene giving his summary of the crime without giving reasons.) And there are several ideas Mommsen puts forward which do not find support elsewhere, such as: "the new names, which we find in the *Hamlet* of 1603—Corambis for Polonius and Montano for Reynaldo—might be traced to the same source, if we think them pieced out from *Cor.* and *Mon.*, which might mean *Courtier* and *Man of Polonius.*"[5] If some of Mommsen's ideas are not accepted, perhaps more should be checked. Part One has already shown that one of his key ideas, a "transposition," can actually be an example of where in reality Q1 follows the underlying source (the position of the "nunnery" scene). However, that misunderstanding does not invalidate all Mommsen's suggestions. Later scholars have added to the list of features seen to be characteristics of MR, particularly Duthie. For instance, he presents what he considers to be the actor/reporter'(s) recollections of words and phrases from other Shakespearean plays and from *The Spanish Tragedy*, as well as singling out "objectionable" pronouns attributed to an inferior hand in Q1. Duthie gives examples of all of these (they are examined in Chapter 8). Laurie Maguire goes further; she methodically identifies, brings together and examines a host of details which are supposed to be typical of MRs, in thirty-eight plays and three parts of plays which have been suspected of being MRs, including Q1 *Hamlet*. The texts include not just some Shakespearean titles but also perhaps less well-known titles, such as the anonymous *Arden of Faversham*, Chapman's *Blind Beggar of Alexandria*, and Marlowe's *Doctor Faustus*.

A third approach relates to the mechanics of how MR is supposed to have occurred. A number of scholars have proposed who might be the agents of the putative MR. Widgery suggested Voltemand was the "thief who made a copy by stealth,"[6] Gray proposed "the player who acted the part of Marcellus,"[7] and Lucianus. Irace, in *Reforming the "Bad" Quartos* (1994), added the actor of the Prologue.[8] In her Q1 *Hamlet* in 1998, however, she no longer includes the "Prologue." J. D. Wilson did add a "Player," the "Second Gravedigger," the "'churlish' Priest" and the "English Ambassador" in *The Copy for Hamlet, 1603, and the Hamlet Transcript, 1593*, in 1918; the same actor might also be present sometimes as a super or extra.[9] However, these are presumably the text and the ideas which he retracts later. It is not what we find in his later *Manuscript of Shakespeare's Hamlet*. This paragraph includes all the roles suggested whose actors might have contributed to a MR.

A fourth approach is the scholars' search for indications in the literature of the time that MR did actually take place, whether in the printing of the quartos or in writing about other plays. This we may call external evidence. Part One has already touched upon the derogatory descriptors, so Part Two investigates the features which are used to support the hypothesis of MR and/or abridgement, the proposed mechanics of MR, and what contemporary documents tell us. All the main reasons given to suggest how the alleged MR of Q1 took place are reviewed. The final chapter in the section addresses the question of abridgement, which a small minority argues is the explanation for Q1's state.

Contemporary Documents: The Stationers' Register and the Printing of Hamlet

We start with the obvious question of whether the printing of Q1 demonstrates any irregularity that would signal the script was in any way "pirated," as Pollard might have called it. E. K. Chambers gives an invaluable summary of the plays' entries in the Stationers' Register, the dates, printers and publishers, and of the title pages in *William Shakespeare. A Study of Facts and Problems*, volume I.

From this we can deduce that a "normal" registering and printing process begins with a date, title and entry to a given person on the Stationers' Register, followed by a play printed by a different person for the named individual on the Stationers' Register. For example *Troilus and Cressida* is entered to Richard Bonian and Henry Walleys on 28th January 1609, and duly imprinted for them by G. Eld in 1609.[10] This "norm" is found for editions of *2 Henry VI*, *Richard III*, *The Taming of the Shrew*, *Richard II*, *The Merchant of Venice*, *1*

Henry IV, 2 Henry IV, Much Ado and *Henry V*. A considerable number of variations also occur, from registration without printing (*As you like y^t* was "staid" in the Stationers' Register, probably on 4th August 1600, but not printed until 1623),[11] printing without an entry (Q1 *Love's Labours Lost*, 1598),[12] to the entry on the Stationers' Register also being the printer's name (*Titus Andronicus*, 1594).[13]

The names of those involved in the registering and printing of Q1 and Q2 *Hamlet* overlap in ways which suggest continuity rather than piracy. Thus the entry on the Stationers' Register on 26th July 1602 is made for James Robertes, who is also the printer for Q2 ("I[ames] R[oberts]"). Q1 is printed for N[icholas] L[ing] and Iohn Trundell; Q2 is printed for N[icholas] L[ing], who in turn transfers *Hamlet* to John Smythick in the Stationers' Register entry in 1607, preceding Q3's printing for Iohn Smethwick (i.e., Smythick) in 1611. Moreover, the first three quartos of *Hamlet* all bear Shakespeare's name upon the title page. We can see these details and their links most easily in table 4.

Table 4. Details of the Stationers' Register Entries and Printing of the Early Quartos of *Hamlet*[14]

S.R.	Q1	Q2	Q3
Play	Hamlet	Hamlet	Hamlet
S. R. date	26.7.1602	–	19.11.1607
Entered for	James Robertes	–	John Smythick
Transferred from	–	–	N Linge
Players	Lord Chamberleyne his servantes	–	–

Printing	Q1	Q2	Q3
Play	Hamlet	Hamlet	Hamlet
Date	1603	1604–5	1611
Players	His Highness' Servants	–	–
Printed by	(Valentine Simmes)	I(ames) R(oberts)	–
Printed for	N(icholas) L(ing), Iohn Trundell	N(icholas) L(ing)	Iohn Smethwick
Author	William Shake-speare	William Shakespeare	William Shakespeare

Chambers' summary of the plays' printings shows that four out of the five men named here are also involved in the publishing of other Shakespearean plays. The Stationers' Register has, for example, an entry for James Roberts for *The Merchant of Venice* on 22nd July 1598, and he is printer for a Q1 *Merchant* in 1600.[15] Valentine Simmes or Sims is the printer of, for example, *Richard II* and *III* in 1597,[16] and *I Henry IV* in 1604.[17] The Stationers' Register records an entry to John Smethwick "from Nicholas Ling" for *Loves Labours*

Lost in 1607 as well as for Q3 *Hamlet*.[18] Only John Trundell seems to appear just once.

It is true that Q1 does not quite follow the "normal" registration and printing, for Q1 is printed for Nicholas Ling and John Trundell rather than the James Roberts named on the Stationers' Register entry. But we can see that Q2, the supposedly genuine Shakespearean text, follows the "norm" even less closely, because there is no Stationers' Register entry. It is difficult to argue for any irregularity in Q1 here. The variations found in other Shakespeare play printings would indicate that the registration and printing of the first three *Hamlet* quartos in 1603, 1604 and 1611 are not significantly atypical, even if they are not the "norm." (Walter Greg found that about a third of the books published in the late Elizabethan period were not entered.[19]) Robert Burkhart also reasonably questions why printers of "bad" quartos would have received permission to publish legitimate plays.[20] It is odd that James Roberts and Nicholas Ling were still able to publish Q2 if their involvement with Q1 *Hamlet*'s publication was not legitimate.

Q2's title page is also debated. Does its claim to be "Newly corrected ... according to the true and perfect Coppie" permit readers to infer that Q1 was not "true?" It is an inference that those supporting MR would find useful. We can see that "newly corrected..." is formulaic and perhaps like a sales patter. Q3 *Richard III*, for example, claims to be "Newly Augmented," though Chambers comments that "There are no augmentations."[21] A similar "sales patter" is found fronting the French source of *Hamlet*, *Les Histoires Tragiques*, which claims to be "reveu, corrigé & augmenté" (revised, corrected and augmented/supplemented) in the Paris 1582 edition.[22] A reasonable explanation for the descriptor might be that Q2 *Hamlet* was sufficiently different for the printer to wish to reassure potential purchasers that it was a valid edition. Or perhaps the publisher wanted to ensure readers would buy a second copy of a book which had been on sale only the previous year.

Hints of "Piracy"?

Nevertheless there are contemporary hints of "piracy," of what might loosely be called (intellectual) copyright, in Elizabethan and Jacobean times. In 1565 William Griffith printed *The Tragedie of Gorbodvc*, played in front of the Queen in 1561. This was a pirated copy, printed when the two authors were away from London. In 1570 John Day printed it under the title *The Tragedie of Ferrex and Porrex*, making it very clear that the first publication had been pirated. Day's version has "Seen and allowed" placed prominently in the centre of the title page, with about six lines of white space above and below, to emphasize that this is an authorized publication. Day's *Preface to the*

Reader criticizes the previous, unauthorized edition of 1565: "one W.T. getting a copie therof at some yongmans hand that lacked a little money and much discretion ... put it forth excedingly corupted."[23] We might note that there is no such complaint from Shakespeare or from any of those associated with the printing of any *Hamlet*.

A piracy is not the same as a MR. However, neither *Hamlet* quarto bears "seen," or "allowed," or "cum privilegio" on the title page, though this was not unusual. Nor does the second quarto have any such useful preface or prolegomena lamenting the corruption of a play which has not been intended for publication. We might also reasonably infer from Q1's title page that the play has been allowed, since Q1 *Hamlet* has, according to its title page, been "diuerse times acted by his Highnesse seruants in the Cittie of London: as also in the two Vniversities of Cambridge and Oxford, and else-where." Since Q1 comes out in 1603, and Elizabeth only dies on 24th March 1603 there's not a lot of time for "diuerse" performances by "*his* Highnesse seruants" (author's italics), though we might speculate that in deference to the new King James no reference is made to his predecessor.

Much closer to the date of the printing of the *Hamlet* quartos, playwright Thomas Heywood addresses the reader at the front of his *Rape of Lucrece* (1608) complaining that plays had been "corrupt and mangled, (coppied onely by the eare)."[24] The adverbial "by the eare" indicates that the written text he complains about had been performed, and it was a version of that spoken performance which he claims had been returned to the written medium before publication. Heywood's address does appear to hint at the existence of memorial reconstructions. Much later, in 1637, he returns to the issue, blaming the indifferent quality of the first edition (1605) of *If You Know Not Me* upon a stenographic copy: "some by Stenography, drew/ The plot: put it in print: (scarce one word trew)."[25] However, in *Elizabethan Shorthand*,[26] Duthie concludes decisively and convincingly that the shorthand methods available at the time were not suitable for reproducing a *Lear*. By extension those early styles of shorthand were unlikely to be appropriate for transcribing a stenographic copy of Heywood's play in 1605. The idea of a reconstruction of any Elizabethan or early Jacobean play by the stenographic methods then available has not been pursued since Duthie's book. Discussion about Heywood's claim hasn't resolved what he meant. G. N. Giordano-Orsini's view is that Heywood is mistaken, or that if shorthand were used, it was supplemented. William Bracy comments that the "plot" could mean a sketch or paraphrase or outline of a literary work.[27] Maguire considers that the belatedness of Heywood's second complaint—it is thirty-two years later—renders it less reliable, and that if Giordano-Orsini's view is correct, Heywood actually "had no idea how his text had been reconstructed."[28]

It is therefore uncertain exactly what and how much might have been reconstructed by memory, though there is no doubt that versions of "memorial reconstruction," or written reports of the spoken word, existed and exist. In Tudor times, some of Queen Elizabeth's speeches were committed to writing after she had delivered them. For example Camden reported her 1559 speech, made after the Commons' petition that she marry.[29] The theatre-goer Edward Pudsey, who wrote down extracts from *Hamlet* and other Shakespearean plays in his commonplace book, (mis)quoted from *Hamlet* with, for example, "To perseuer in obstinate sorrow ys impious stubbornnes, vnmanly greef, y^t shows a will most incorrect to heauen."[30]

Playwrights also referred variously in the plays to writing down others' words. Hamlet himself refers to his "tables" (5.81, I.v.98 and 107), which appears to draw from a contemporary custom of noting striking turns of phrase or ideas in a commonplace book. Maguire mentions Marston's *Scourge of Villainy* (1598): "when of playes or Plaiers he did treat/ H'ath made a commonplace booke out of playes" (which coincidentally partly describes Pudsey's practice).[31] Maguire notes Marston's *Malcontent* (1604), where Sly has seen the play often enough to be able to "give them [the players] intelligence for their action: I have most of the ieasts here in my table-booke."[32] This sounds similar to a collection such as *Tarlton's Jests*, published in 1611. The possibility of the plot being sufficiently well remembered for the outline to be expanded by another writer is suggested by two further plays Maguire cites. The first is Robert Taylor's *The Hog Hath Lost His Pearl* (*c.* 1613), in which the character Haddit fears a player has:

> *Haddit*: ... learned [the text of a written entertainment] by heart, if you haue powdred vp my plot in your sconce, you may home sir and instruct your Poet ouer a pot of ale, the whole method on't.

In the second example, the dedicatory sonnet to Chapman's 1605 edition of *All Fools*, Chapman decides to publish "least by others stealth it be imprest,/ without my passport, patcht with others wit."[33]

These wide-ranging examples demonstrate that the variety of what might have been reconstructed by memory is considerable, though the frequency of references over the Elizabethan and early Jacobean period to such practices is low. Even today the level of accuracy of some reporting may not be high. Wells and Taylor cite a modern misquotation from Senator Sam Ervin, where the videotape preserves his accuracy in speech, but the official stenographic report has errors.[34] Other evidence of memorial reconstruction is also offered by Taylor. This includes the pirated text of Macklin's *Love à-la-Mode* (1759), of the first English adaptation of *Le Mariage de Figaro* (first written by Beaumarchais in 1788), and of a 1601 pamphlet containing "A Declaration of the Practices & Treasons attempted and committed by *Robert* late Earle of Essex," including "the Speeches of Sir *Chr. Blunt* ... as neere as they would be remembered."[35] It is perhaps unsurprising that the Oxford English Dictionary records that the first use of the noun "plagiarism" was in 1621.

    The evidence of Heminge and Condell in their address "To the Great Variety of Readers" is that Shakespeare's "writings" in the first folio are "as he conceiued them," and no longer the "diuerse stolne, and surrepticious copies, maimed, and deformed by the frauds and stealthes of iniurious imposters."[36] This does not indicate which plays were thus described, nor the method by which "stolne" or "surreptitious copies" of Shakespeare's plays might have been obtained—from a (complete or incomplete) collection of actors' parts, or from a playhouse prompt-book, or from Shakespeare's manuscript or foul papers, with or without the kinds of revisions noted by Ioppolo on other contemporary plays. All of these would be "copies" of the written word. Whether "copies" could be used to signify a MR of performances by actor/reporters, which would be returning the spoken medium of performance to a written medium, is unclear. Modern usage employs "copy" for a physical tape or disc or dvd of the spoken word in the spoken mode, but that usage and definition would be anachronistic here. The quotation does share the concept of "stealth" with Chapman's complaint. It is unfortunate that Heminge and Condell are not more specific. It is assumed here that Heminge and Condell's line is not merely promotional in intent, to persuade readers that the folio offered better versions of plays, though that possibility does exist. The folio contains different versions of around half the plays, so the statement by Heminge and Condell may function to forestall any contemporary complaint about the folio plays being different from earlier editions, and to ensure that potential readers believe the purchase of every one of the plays in such a collection was worthwhile.

    Later still, Humphrey Moseley, in his address to the reader before the 1647 folio of Beaumont and Fletcher's plays, assured those readers that they would read "All that was Acted, and all that was not; even the perfect full Originalls without the least mutilation." Moseley explained that some actors had supplied plays to their friends, transcribing what they acted (presumably their "part"). This would suggest that some copying went on. Paul Werstine wonders whether multiple texts through such copyings were not unusual.[37]

    Thus to "write downe," or learn "by heart," copy "onely by the eare" or "by stenography" a play, and the copying or transcribing of the actor's part, are all methods suspected or known by some Elizabethan and Jacobean playwrights and printers over a period of more than half a century. The concept of "stolne" copy appears to exist, but seems to apply to a written copy of a part or script. This seems generally suggestive that piracy might have occurred on occasion and that copying from scripts did take place. However, there is nothing conclusive about whether MR in the way that it is supposed to have happened for Q1 *Hamlet* did exist.

A Spanish Analogy?

A kind of piracy has been found in the Golden Age of Spanish literature, a piracy that some see as analogous to the possible MR of *Hamlet*.[38] Fred M. Clark, in *Objective Methods for Testing Authenticity and the Study of Ten Doubtful Comedias Attributed to Lope de Vega*,[39] sees the authorship of Spanish plays of doubtful authenticity resulting from three factors: the lack of copyright protection, a publisher's attribution of the name of a famous playwright to a play of a lesser writer in order to promote sales, and to the collaborative efforts of two or three authors. He notes that a playwright then could even take a play of a known author, rewrite it in part, and consequently take the credit for its composition and profit. Clark comments that the manuscripts of *comedias* might be used and altered so much they could no longer be attributed to the original author; the censor might intervene, or the theatre manager might modify a script to become an acting copy, or it might be passed from hand to hand, and someone would copy off the parts, for example.[40] This, however, would not be memorial reconstruction, because the changes are occurring to a *written* script. This is different from Greg's definition of a "process of transmission which involves the memory," the definition which underlies reporting and memorial reconstruction.[41]

Much of what Clark outlines is confirmed by the playwright Lope Felix de Vega Carpio himself (1562–1635). He produced his first play in about 1593, and ten years later is complaining about the pirating of his plays, and their inaccuracy in the written version. Hugo Albert Rennert in his *Life of Lope de Vega*[42] reports on volumes of de Vega's plays published in 1620 and 1621. These feature a prologue entitled *El Teatro à los Lectores*, including the comment: "The author of these comedias is fulfilling the promise he made by publishing those which come into his hands, or to his feet, begging for correction."[43] In his Prologue to *Decimaseptime Parte de las Comedias de Lope de Vega Carpio* ... Lope de Vega explains that the theatre is "weary of the complaints of managers of companies who say that *their comedias are printed to the injury of their property.*" Legal proceedings were twice taken up against booksellers, because writers were offended "to see so many strange *coplas* and so many absurdities concerning the ill understood plots and histories."[44] This demonstrates the poor state of some publications in Spain, and that some texts were recognized as corrupt. As a result Spanish writers were allowed to make corrections, and new imprints were more accurate. The different practices which could lead to these "injured" plays include theatrical managers stealing a play from one another, and "a play running the gauntlet of villages, servants, and men who live by stealing them and adding to them," with the result that the play is "so disfigured as to be scarcely recognisable."[45] It appears too that an actor owning a play which the public had received well would not wish to part with the original, but for a financial consideration would allow another play to be written up with the same plot and situations.[46] Lope de Vega, dedicating *Los Muertos Vivos* to the successful poet Salucio del Poyo, gives further information about Spanish practices when he explains that because Poyo has a good reputation:

> theatrical managers, when they have any comedias whatever, with the author of which they are not satisfied, adorn their placards with your name, and since most of these comedias, being written by some ignorant fellow, are so detestable, you would lose reputation among those who know, if the injury to you did not reach those that esteem you at the same time as its discovery.[47]

However, these practices are not principally memorial reconstructions.

It is in another Prologue, to *Trezena Parte de las Comedias de Lope de Vega Carpio* ... in 1620 that de Vega refers to the *memoriones*, whom Wells and Taylor and Maguire also describe. Lope de Vega comments on "the stealing of comedias by those whom the vulgar call—the one *Memorilla*, and the other *Gran Memoria*, who with the few verses which they learn, mingle an infinity of their own barbarous lines...."[48] If we disregard the hyperbole here, the description would appear to resemble what is understood by memorial reconstruction of some English Renaissance plays. Rennert also quotes Cristobal Suarez de Figueroa describing a young man who could apparently recite entire *comedias* after hearing them three times.[49] Learning by heart still occurs today (for example in societies where knowing the Koran well is expected), though if the young man could achieve such a recitation after three performances it is impressive. *El major alcalde, el roy* (*The King, the Greatest Alcalde*), by Lope de Vega, is approximately 2410 lines; remembering the whole accurately would seem demanding.

Yet if this young man and other *memoriones* could reproduce *comedias* so accurately, then their versions would not need the correcting de Vega refers to. In fact, de Vega himself doubts the existence of such a skill. His Prologue to *Trezena Parte de las Comedias de Lope de Vega Carpio* ... continues by offering the reader the corrected version of his plays with this additional comment[50]: "...you may not believe that there is anyone in the world who can take down a comedia from memory, on seeing it represented; and if there were such a person I should praise him and see him as standing alone with this power."⁵¹ Figueroa's account and de Vega's don't quite tally. However, it does seem that some Spanish plays which were plagiarized comprised an element of learning by heart and substantial invention by the plagiarizer. These created new texts of the type de Vega complained about and, very loosely, resemble a MR. That there was a degree of corruption in such stolen texts is proved by José Ruano de la Haza, who compared a manuscript of de Vega's with a printed version. The changes include for example a less inspiring text, one that is shorter, which omits the breadth of imagery, and simplifies characters and plot.⁵² The records of such a practice in Spain therefore appear to bear a resemblance to the *proposed* practices in English theatres, perhaps by actors or publishers. Two kinds of plagiarism existed there: firstly a text might be partly rewritten and claimed as the rewriter's, or adapted and interpolated so often it was very different from the original, and, secondly, due to the *memoriones*, a play might be heard, partly or substantially written down from performance(s) and patched up.

Lope de Vega is explicit, vocal and critical of such practices affecting his work in at least four prologues. But in England there are no accounts of *memoriones*, which significantly weakens the use of the Spanish situation as an analogy. Q1 *Hamlet* did appear with Shakespeare's name on the title page. Q2 *Hamlet*'s title page does offer a reason for differing from Q1, stating it is "Newly imprinted and enlarged to almost as much againe as it was, according to the true and perfect Coppie." Some may infer this means Q1 was not the "true ... Coppie," but the difference between the two could be abridgement, adaptation, or revision, the latter explaining the description "enlarged" on the title page in Q2. Or it could simply be to "sell" Q2. The formulaic nature of the phrasing does not indicate anything out of the ordinary regarding Q1; at best, it does not exclude Q1 as a memorial reconstruction. Heminge and Condell's comment in the first folio about "stolne" copies is made on behalf of Shakespeare, not by Shakespeare, a contrast with de Vega, and Heywood. If Heywood could complain, why not Shakespeare, especially if, as is alleged, several of his plays were "pirated?" However, an absence of a complaint from Shakespeare does not remove the possibility of "stolne" copies or MRs.

Although MR seems to bear a resemblance to some Spanish practices, it remains a hypothesis as an explanation for some of the different versions of plays in England on the evidence so far. The examination of the entry in the Stationers' Register and the information about the printer shows no signs of Q1 having been a pirated text. Q1 does bear Shakespeare's name, and Q2 is published by some of the men associated with the printing of Q1, which together might suggest Q1 was a legitimate edition. The description on the front of it being "Newly imprinted and enlarged to almost as much againe as it was" is accurate for a Q1 > Q2 sequence and relationship. Shakespeare himself is not known to have complained about any piracy or copying by the ear or stenographic plagiarism.

Yet hints of some sorts of plagiarism or pirating—*Gorboduc*, Heywood, "stolne" copies—linger. It is more than a century and a half before MR is indisputably known in England, and a good account survives for the mechanics of how that occurred. The question is whether that account helps us understand how an MR of *Hamlet* might have come about.

7. Memorial Reconstruction in England

We do know that memorial reconstruction occurred in the eighteenth century in England. Wells and Taylor mention the pirated texts of Macklin's *Love à-la-Mode* (1759) and of the first English adaptation of *Le Mariage de Figaro* (first written by Beaumarchais in 1788).[1] Duthie offers two accounts of reconstructions of English plays. The two men responsible for these, Tate Wilkinson and John Bernard, employed methods Duthie considers "similar to those we can assume in memorial reconstructions of the Elizabethan period."[2] Wilkinson's and Bernard's methods are therefore critical to an understanding of how and why Duthie and others consider memorial reconstruction might have happened.

Memorial Reconstruction of The Duenna

The first memorially recreated play Duthie mentions is *The Duenna*, originally by Richard Brinsley Sheridan (1751–1816). Wilkinson constructed a version of his own, which was first performed on Easter Monday, 1776. His account of its reconstruction states that he "saw it several times," locked himself up in a room, and set down first the jokes he remembered. Then he "laid a book of the songs" before him, and "with magazines kept the regulation of the scenes," and "by the help of a numerous collection of obsolete Spanish plays," produced "an excellent opera."[3] *The Duenna* is a three act comic opera, with a combination of successful songs from other composers, some traditional ballads, and new compositions by Thomas Linley the elder and his son, Thomas Linley the younger. The existence of a book of the songs and other relevant material must have been of considerable assistance. Certainly they would provide a substantial amount of written text, so that Wilkinson did not have to depend only upon his memory. His reconstruction therefore:

- was intended and planned for performance;
- was reconstructed only by him;
- was based in part upon written materials he had access to, and
- followed several documented viewings of *The Duenna*.[4]

Memorial Reconstruction of The School for Scandal

The second account is fuller, and is actor John Bernard's description of his "compilation" of Sheridan's *School for Scandal*. His reason for compiling it was that the play had already been successful in Bath, and there was an opportunity to put it on in Exeter. However, the play was not published and the copies which did exist had been obtained on the condition that they were not permitted "to become the parents of others," in other words they were not to be copied. Like Wilkinson's, Bernard's motive was performance. He offered to recreate the play specifically for performances in Exeter, and to ensure his compilation was destroyed after the run. Bernard was in a fortunate position for the reconstruction; he had played three different roles in the play, those of Sir Benjamin, Charles Surface and Sir Peter Teazle. Two fellow actors provided him with their parts by post, which means that Bernard was also given some written materials. These were the roles of Joseph Surface and Sir Oliver. Bernard's wife had also played two parts, Lady Teazle and Mrs Candour. "Old Rowley was in the company" (Bernard's words) presumably means that Rowley's part was also accessible. Each of these eight roles is a major one. Additionally, Bernard comments on his "general knowledge of the play collected in rehearsing and performing it above forty times." (Linguistically this is ambiguous; it could mean rehearsing an unspecified number of times, and, separately, performing it above forty times, or a total of above forty rehearsals and performances altogether.) Consequently he was able to reconstruct the five act comedy in about a week. Although Bernard was provided with two written parts and presumably some context for them, the majority of his reconstruction is from memory.

The number of roles he had access to is important. The eight roles from which he could draw are eight out of the ten largest parts, on a simple line count; six of the eight roles are the biggest in the play. In total, Bernard had played or had access to 78.09 percent of the lines in the play, or nearly four fifths of the text, not counting their cues. This begins to sound like a reasonably plausible "memorial reconstruction." Table 5 shows the number of lines belonging to each actor, and the percentage of the play for each role. Ordinary print is used to indicate the roles known to Bernard through his own acting or through his wife and friends; italics are used to name the other characters.[5]

Table 5. *The School for Scandal*:
The Characters and Their Lines

Character	Number of lines/ 3128	Number of lines as a %
Sir Peter Teazle	530	16.94
Joseph Surface	399	12.76
Charles Surface	376	12.02
Sir Oliver Surface	362	11.57
Lady Teazle	300	9.59
Rowley	189	6.04
Lady Sneerwell	*181*	*5.79*
Mrs Candour	164	5.24
Crabtree	*135*	*4.32*
Sir Benjamin	123	3.93
Moses	*71*	*2.27*
Maria	*70*	*2.24*
Snake	*69*	*2.21*
Careless	*63*	*2.01*
Trip	*34*	*1.09*
Sir Harry	*32*	*1.02*
Servant	*15*	*0.48*
Gentleman 1	*6*	*0.19*
Gentleman 2	*4*	*0.13*
Maid	*4*	*0.13*
All	*1*	*0.03*
Bernard + fellow reconstructors		**Total:** 78.09 percent

A relevant issue to understanding the mechanics of this reconstruction must be how many of the scenes of the play any of the characters appeared in. Logically, recreating a scene during which an actor is resting backstage and has not had to learn his own lines nor the cues from other actors is more difficult than reconstructing one in which an actor *has* had to learn his lines and his cues. Bernard was fortunate in his reconstruction, for every scene of the play is covered by at least one actor. Act III scene ii has only one of those contributing actors present, but every other scene has at least two of the characters, and for more than half of the scenes three or more actors. Table 6 lists all the scenes of the play, and which of the eight critical characters are present.

John Bernard's account is detailed enough for the mechanics of his reconstruction to be understood, for the memorial element to be credible, and for the reconstruction to be convincing, because

Table 6. *The School for Scandal*: The Presence of
Any of the Eight Known Characters in Each Scene
(NB: all scenes are included)

Act	Character(s) present
I i	Joseph Surface, Mrs Candour, Sir Benjamin
I ii	Sir Peter, Rowley
II i	Sir Peter, Lady Teazle
II ii	Mrs Candour, Joseph Surface, Sir Benjamin, Sir Peter Teazle, Lady Teazle
II iii	Sir Oliver Surface, Rowley, Sir Peter Teazle, Sir Oliver Surface
III i	Sir Peter Teazle, Sir Oliver Surface, Rowley, Lady Teazle
III ii	Sir Oliver
III iii	Charles Surface, Sir Oliver Surface
IV i	Charles Surface, Sir Oliver Surface, Rowley
IV ii	Sir Oliver Surface, Rowley
IV iii	Joseph Surface, Lady Teazle, Sir Peter Teazle, Charles Surface
V i	Joseph Surface, Sir Oliver Surface, Rowley
V ii	Mrs Candour, Sir Benjamin, Sir Oliver Surface, Sir Peter Teazle, Rowley
V iii	Joseph Surface, Sir Oliver Surface, Charles Surface, Sir Peter Teazle, Lady Teazle, Rowley

- he offers a motive for that reconstruction;
- he had access to 78.09 percent of the lines through fellow actors, through eight roles, including some written materials;
- at least one of those fellow actors was present in every scene, and
- rehearsals and performances were over forty, which gave plenty of time to learn roles thoroughly.

Bracy, while not offering any analysis or percentages as above, gives it as his opinion that a "reasonably good text" might be achieved through repeated participation or attendance at regular performances.[6]

The Hypothetical Memorial Reconstruction of Hamlet

Our question must be how close Wilkinson's and Bernard's MRs are to what is suggested for *Hamlet*.

The motive or reason for recreating *Hamlet* is uncertain. Pollard at one point suggests "arranged piracy at the instigation of a London Stationer," though he later changes his mind.[7] R. Crompton Rhodes theorizes that "certain players turned strollers, profiting by the accidental retention of their parts, and reconstructing the rest from memory, made prompt-books for the companies they joined."[8] Duthie comments that a surreptitious copy of a prompt-book might occur, but that the time needed for copying would render discovery certain. Besides, such copying should present a sound copy, which is not an apt description of Q1's relationship with Q2 or a likely abridgement of it.[9] Wells and Taylor consider actors with the greatest motive for preparing such a text would be those "with no economic or personal loyalty to the company." These might be major actors who have moved to another company, or "hired men," freelancers,[10] a point also made by Hibbard: "A hired player who was eventually discharged after serving the purpose for which he had been engaged, would be exactly the sort of man to join another company, and to concoct a version of *Hamlet* for that company to put on."[11]

Hibbard, summarizing, considers that Duthie "showed beyond all reasonable doubt" that Q1 is reported and put together "for, in all probability, a band of actors playing outside London."[12] We should note that "probability" here denotes an educated guess, however, not certainty. The comment also ignores Q1's title page and the statement that "it hath beene diuerse times acted by his Highnesse seruants in the Cittie of London." Maguire sees the "raison d'être of reconstruction" as "performance, with publication very much an afterthought."[13] This is also effectively Jenkins' position,[14] though Chapman and Heywood seem to assume publication.

On the whole, scholars think that the motive for creating a memorial reconstruction of *Hamlet* might have been to provide a version for touring in the provinces, or perhaps to make a profit from the printing of the play. This contrasts with the apparently legitimate printing of the text. A profit for the players is perhaps unlikely; Peter Blaney notes that "printed plays never accounted for a very significant fraction of the trade in English books."[15] There has been some discussion about whether the short texts were adapted for the needs of touring companies and provincial audiences. The former might be correct, though some of those audiences in the "provinces" were, after all, accustomed to the long cycles of the Mystery plays and did not necessarily require a simpler, shorter version (and one would hesitate to identify "the two Vniuersities of Cambridge and Oxford" as the "provinces" in need of a shorter version). Of course, the act of "pirating" a play to a printer might not render the pirate(s) popular with the theatre manager, playwright or fellow actors. Gerald Johnson, exploring the concept of a smaller troupe of players for *Merry Wives*, concluded that it is "unlikely that the quarto text was deliberately adapted for a reduced company."[16] When Scott McMillin examined Q1 *Hamlet* he suggested ten men and three boys were required, one player more than for Q2, simply because the longer version with more dialogue provides more time for actors to change clothes and role.[17]

All these possible reasons for a MR of *Hamlet* remain speculative in comparison with Bernard's reasons for recreating *The School for Scandal*. If *Hamlet* was memorially reconstructed, we don't know whether it was for performance, whether in the provinces or in London, or for publication, and whether it was done by actors who were freelancers, or discharged, or disaffected, or even financially embarrassed.

Which actors might have been responsible for the reconstruction? Widgery suggested "Voltemar" was the actor involved in the reconstruction. Widgery appears to contradict himself in his Harness Essay. He states: "The speech of Voltemar in Act II sc ii is suspiciously correct: he may also have taken the part of the player king."[18] Widgery believes that Nicholas Ling "got the player who took the part of Voltemar to get a hurried transcript of Shakespeare's older play: that he sent pirates into the theatre to take shorthand notes of the first two acts in order to give this stolen transcript a more colourable likeness...."[19] Yet thirty pages later[20] Widgery writes of reading Q1 and later Q2: "that we are viewing a continuous growth and evolution will be borne in upon us ... the first quarto [is] the spiritual father of the second." It would seem Widgery blends literary theft, copying and revision in his essay, but because he identifies the similarity in Voltemar and Voltemand's speeches, he seems to be the one who suggested the actor for that role participating in the reconstruction.

Other suggestions follow. Gray proposes "Marcellus" and perhaps "Lucianus"[21]; John Dover Wilson briefly puts forward both those roles, plus a "Player," the "Second Gravedigger," the "'churlish' Priest," the "English ambassador," and thinks the same actor (Wilson calls him the "traitor-actor"[22]) might also be present sometimes as a super or extra.[23] Irace has also for a short time seen the actor of the Prologue as a possibility.[24] (The Prologue has all of three lines.) Strikingly, none of these eight are major roles. They are, however, carefully chosen by a range of scholars as the roles where the match between the lines in Q1 and Q2 is closest, or where there is least "fluctuating correlation," as Irace might put it. Hibbard writes that "the basis for this theory is the demonstrable fact that these two parts [of Marcellus and Lucianus] are rendered with considerable fidelity to the authentic [Q2] text—Lucianus being almost word perfect...."[25] (Hibbard does not draw attention to the fact that Lucianus has a mere six lines, nor discuss just how useful or otherwise "Lucianus" might be in remembering a whole play of 4000 lines or so, nor whether the "demonstrable fact" has other explanations.) However, even though some of the proposed memorial reconstructors have relatively few lines, it is they and their lines which must be examined.

Consequently the next two tables show the same analysis as for *The School for Scandal*, and indicate the percentages of the lines in the play that these minor characters learnt.[26] The first table, table 7, gives the percentages of those characters' roles as a proportion of Q1 and shows that the "largest" of the parts suggested is that of Marcellus, who has 2.79 percent of Q1's lines. If only the three actors for Marcellus, Voltemand and Lucianus reconstructed a *Hamlet* from a *Hamlet* of Q1's length, they would have begun with knowing 4.05 percent of Q1's lines, not counting their cues (i.e., the same calculations as for *The School for Scandal* above). If the actors for *all* the suggested parts worked together they would originally have learnt 6.03 percent of Q1's lines. (NB It has not been proposed, and is not proposed here, that all those actors jointly compiled a version of *Hamlet*. The prospect and the percentage are offered solely to demonstrate the most favorable terms for the argument concerning the hypothetical memorial reconstruction of *Hamlet*.)

Wells and Taylor do comment that the different quality of texts like Q1 and Q2 *Hamlet* may be due to the number engaged in the reconstruction and their parts.[27] If it is thought that there were more actor/reporter(s) involved, some discussion of whom and how might suggest how a higher percentage of lines might be known by the actors.

Table 7. Q1 *Hamlet*: The Lines of the Suggested Actor/Reporter(s)

Characters	*Number of lines/ 2,221 (Q1)*	*Number of lines as % of total*
Marcellus	43 + 3 + 12 + (4) = 62	2.79
(Gent +) Voltemar	1 + 21 = 22	0.99
(Murd.[erer]) Lucianus	6	0.27
Player	17 + (6) = 23	1.04
Prologue	*3*	*0.14*
Second Clown (gravedigger)	9	0.41
Priest	6	0.27
First (English) Ambassador	3	0.14
	Total 90 or *134*	Total 4.05% or *6.03%*

( ) denotes lines are shared with another character.
Italics denote actor-reporters briefly considered to have contributed to memorial reconstruction by J. D. Wilson (and Irace, "Prologue" only), and totals including them.
W. W. Greg's facsimile of Q1 has been used for the line counts of the characters, and Irace's figure of 2221 lines is for Q1 as a whole.

Table 7 is a generous way of calculating what those actors might have brought to the reconstruction of the play; it is the "best case" scenario. Since Q1 is supposedly a memorial reconstruction of Q2, the numbers of lines might be more accurately assessed as percentages of Q2's 4056 lines. If just "Marcellus," "Voltemand" and "Lucianus" were involved in reconstructing Q2 from memory, they would have learnt 2.22 percent of the lines (4.28 percent if all the proposed actors were counted).This is the "worst case" scenario, though since Q2 might have been adapted for the stage, or abridged, or both, the total percentage of lines known to the proposed actors would be a little higher. In the absence of the existence of any abridgement or adaptation no parallel calculations can be made, but the percentages are unlikely to change significantly.

Table 8 therefore shows the same players' parts but now as a proportion of Q2. One obvious objection to this method of calculation is again that each actor would be familiar with the line or half line which cues his speech turn. This is especially significant for Marcellus, who has nearly thirty single lines or half lines to utter (and therefore as many cues). Shakespeare uses stichomythia for part of the scenes where Marcellus is speaking, and indeed also for the Second Clown/Man. Even if we generously double the percentages to include every cue each actor needed to learn, the total number of lines the putative reporters would have learnt is still about one in twenty or 5 percent.[28] A comparison with the figures and method for *The School for Scandal* illustrates rapidly the difficulty of memorial reconstruction for the proposed actor/reporter(s) of *Hamlet*.

Table 8. Q2 *Hamlet*: The Lines of the Suggested Actor/Reporter(s)

Characters	Number of lines/ 4,056 (Q2)	Number of lines as a % of total
Marcellus	43 + 2 + (5) +12 = 62	1.53
Voltemand	(1) + 21 = 22	0.54
Lucianus	6	0.15
Player	*48*	*1.18*
Prologue	*3*	*0.07*
Other (gravedigger)	14	0.34
Doct.	*13*	*0.32*
Embassador	*6*	*0.15*
Actor-reporters	Total 90 (*or 180*)	Total: 2.22% (*or 4.28%*)

( ) denotes lines are shared with another character.

Italics denote actor-reporters briefly considered to have contributed to memorial reconstruction by J. D. Wilson only, and totals including them.

W. Griggs' facsimile of Q2 has been used for the line counts of the characters, and Irace's figure of 4056 is for Q2 as a whole.

How many of the scenes do those characters appear in? Bernard had all *School for Scandal* scenes covered by his group of contributing actors. The "best case" scenario gives us eight *Hamlet* roles, and the actors present for some or all of the time, mainly singly, in eight out of seventeen scenes or 47 percent (in Irace's Q1 scene division), and in eight out of twenty scenes or 40 percent in Q2. In other words, the proposed memorial reconstructors are on stage for less than half the scenes of either quarto. If only the three actors—"Marcellus," "Voltemand" and "Lucianus"—are counted, they are present in only six out of seventeen scenes (35 percent) in Q1, or six out of twenty scenes (30 percent) in Q2. Again, supporting tables are found below, table 9 for Q1 and table 10 for Q2. The second table, table 10, demonstrates for example that none of the nominated reporting actors was on stage at all in act IV. The number of scenes when none of the three (or eight) characters is present is high, and presumably it must be assumed that the potential actor/reporter(s) is/are carefully listening from the side of the stage or just off stage, or, as Wilson suggested, is/are supers.

The absence of actor/reporters from whole scenes is not prominent in discussion. Duthie alludes to it when he comments that "actors would be more efficient with their own lines than with other characters, and more efficient as a whole with scenes in which they appear than with others."[29] "[O]thers" is a masterly euphemism for the scenes with a total absence of any of the proposed memorial reconstructors. Irace too expresses a logical expectation that an actor/reporter is likely to remember his own lines best because he is "required to memorise" them, and certainly "more accurately than the lines spoken by others on stage with him."[30] The absence of any actor/reporter on stage for other scenes merits discussion at the very least, and more than a suggestion that, for example, supers or extras supplied whole scenes.

Table 9. Q1 *Hamlet*: The Presence of Any of the Three (*Seven*) Actor/Reporters in Each Scene (NB: All scenes are listed)

Scene	Characters present	Scene	Characters present
1	Marcellus	10	–
2	Gent. (Voltemar), Marcellus	11	–
3	–	12	–
4	Marcellus	13	–
5	Marcellus	14	–
6	–	15	–
7	Voltemar, *Player*	16	Second Clown, Priest
8	–	17	First Ambassador
9	Player, Prologue, (Murd.[erer]) Lucianus		

These tables (9 and 10) demonstrate at a glance that the situation for the actor/reporters recreating *Hamlet* Q1 was much less favorable than for John Bernard recreating *The School for Scandal*. Wilson was perhaps recognizing some of the difficulty with the general theory and its application to Q1 *Hamlet* when he proposed that supers were also further actor/reporters; otherwise, it

Table 10. Q2 *Hamlet*: The Presence of Any of the Three (*Seven*) Actor/Reporters in Each Scene (NB: All scenes are listed)

Act/scene	Characters present	Act/scene	Characters present
1.1	Marcellus	3.4	–
1.2	Voltemand, Marcellus	4.1	–
1.3	–	4.2	–
1.4	Marcellus	4.3	–
1.5	Marcellus	4.4	–
2.1	–	4.5	–
2.2	Voltemand, *Player*	4.6	–
3.1	–	4.7	–
3.2	*Player, Prologue*, Lucianus	5.1	*Other Man, Doct.*
3.3	–	5.2	*Embassador*

must be assumed parts of the reconstructed Q1 *Hamlet* were "remembered" by actors who were off stage. Duthie, who towards the beginning of his book saw Bernard's account as "similar" to what must have happened for *Hamlet*, enlarges upon that by the end, thinking Q1 was:

> a memorial reconstruction ... by an actor who had taken the part of Marcellus and perhaps another part or parts in the full play [the full Q2?] and who was able, when his memory failed, to write blank verse of his own ... he had access ... [to] the manuscript part of Voltemar, or a copy of that.³¹

This is moving away from the "similar" scenario of what happened in *The School for Scandal* MR. Nevertheless, Marcellus, a vague other actor who had perhaps taken "another part or parts in the full play" and Voltemar's "part" do not constitute the eight out of ten major parts that Bernard's team of co-reconstructors did. The case for Q1 *Hamlet* as a memorial reconstruction would be considerably strengthened if the issue of the composition of scenes where none of the proposed actor/reporters are present is addressed and resolved. Perhaps more potential actor/reporters from other scenes could be identified, or the method of reconstruction could be brought closer to that of *The School for Scandal*, the very play which Duthie saw as a "similar" case, to explain how memorial reconstruction might come about. Duthie did of course retract his thoughts of memorial reconstruction for Q1 *King Lear* (1960), where he wrote that his "1949 theory [of a memorial reconstruction of *Lear* made by the whole company] had better be abandoned."³²

The last point of comparison concerns the frequency of performance. (There is no contemporary evidence for rehearsals, and speculation regarding this, and how many plays were being performed when, is not attempted here.) The lists of performances in Henslowe's *Diary* illustrate variety of performance first and foremost. A random selection of plays from five pages—202 performances over two to three years—shows *Titus Andronicus* performed just three times in seventeen months, *Harey the vj* performed three times in seven months, *Tamberlaine* seven in twenty-nine months, with *The Jew of Malta* or *The Jew* performed seventeen times in twenty-five months. If seventeen performances occurred closely enough together and used the same actors one aspect of *The School for Scandal*'s recreation is nearly achieved. It is true that Middleton's *Game of Chess* was performed from 6th to 16th August in 1624 (and then banned), which shows that some runs did take place. However, it is noticeable that Henslowe's *Diary* does not include runs of a play, which is where the greatest familiarity with the script is likely to occur. It would be interesting to know if there is any correlation between large numbers of known performances of a play and suspected memorial reconstructions. Logically, frequent performance would indicate popularity as well as potential opportunity for memorial reconstruction. A *Hamlet* is mentioned just once in Henslowe's *Diary*, though Q1's title page of course boasts performances in Oxford, Cambridge, London and elsewhere.

The analogy of Bernard's recreation of *The School for Scandal* does not help the hypothesis of memorial reconstruction for Q1 *Hamlet*, certainly not with the selection of actors who have been proposed. Indeed, this examination of Bernard's method and its application to a Q1 *Hamlet* might well be seen as ruling out memorial reconstruction. The counterarguments are fourfold:

- Bernard clearly stated a credible motive. Motives for an MR of *Hamlet* are proposed, but are speculative: for performance on tour, perhaps in the provinces, perhaps for printing.
- Bernard's group of actors knew eight major roles and between them 78.09 percent of the lines. The actors proposed as possibly responsible for the *Hamlet* MR had minor roles and would have together learnt less than 6 percent of the total number of lines.
- Bernard's group of actors appears in all the scenes, often several together. For Q1 *Hamlet*, the number of scenes those three (to eight) actors appear in are less than half of the total in the most favorable scenario.
- Bernard had performed at least forty times in the play. We do not know about the frequency of performances of *Hamlet*. However, Q1 claims it has been performed "diuerse times," and a *Hamlet* must have been reasonably well known for Nashe to allude to it in 1589, for Lodge to allude to it in 1596, and for it to be mentioned in *Satiromastix* (1601). We may infer that a *Hamlet*—"*Ur-*," Q1?—was performed sufficiently frequently over a twelve year period to at least be well known. More than that can only be speculation.

Maguire has systematically surveyed the evidence for memorial reconstruction in forty-one Elizabethan and Jacobean plays or part plays. Her findings are that none of the plays she considers is "unquestionably memorial reconstruction." Table 11 summarizes her findings.

Table 11. Summary of Maguire's Investigations of "Suspect Texts"[33]

Status	Number of plays/38
Unquestionably Memorial Reconstruction	0
A Strong Case can be made for Memorial Reconstruction	4
A Case can be made for Memorial Reconstruction	3, includes *Hamlet*
Probably not Memorial Reconstruction	2
Not Memorial Reconstruction	29, and 3/3 part plays

She finishes by writing that "[a] strong case can be made for memorial reconstruction" in *Merry Wives*, and *The Taming of a Shrew*, and "[a] case can be made for memorial reconstruction" for *Pericles* and *Hamlet*. She identifies as "[p]robably not memorial reconstruction" *Contention, Henry V, Romeo and Juliet*, and *The True Tragedy of Richard Duke of York*. The general accuracy of Q1 *Hamlet* when compared to Q2—which is the approach those favoring memorial reconstruction take—does show quite a low level of identical lines, around 19.8 percent. On the whole the scenes in which the proposed actor/reporters were performing are those which most closely resemble Q2, but even this is not totally accurate. For example Q1's scene 7 has Voltemar present and 20 percent of its lines match with Q2's equivalent. Q1's scene 13 has 24 percent of its lines match with Q2's equivalent—and no Marcellus, Voltemar or Lucianus in sight. This does not appear to be discussed, but it needs to be explained. (Probably it is because the scene includes Ofelia/Ophelia's songs, which may have been widely known as folk songs.) The question remains; is the match in lines between certain characters due to memorial reconstruction, or to revision, or to adaptation, or perhaps to Weiner's theory of abridgement?

In his essay *Texts with Two Faces: Noticing Theatrical Revisions in Henry VI, Parts 2 and 3* Urkowitz writes of the "dominant paradigm 'memorial reconstruction'...."[34] So far, Part Two indicates that the general theory of that "dominant paradigm" for *Hamlet* is surprisingly weak. There are enough suggestions to show how the hypothesis of memorial reconstruction arose. There is clear evidence that there is noticeable correlation between the lines of the putative reporters in Q1 and Q2. Indeed, Irace concludes her chapter on memorial reconstruction with a confident certainty about the origins of four quartos—*Hamlet, Merry Wives, Henry V* and *Richard Duke of York*. Irace writes: the "pattern of fluctuating variation" "demonstrates that these four short quartos were reconstructed from the reporters' memories of the familiar longer versions."[35] However, what she actually demonstrates is a strong match between the selected reporters' roles in Q1 and Q2, not the *reason* for that strong match. The practices described in Spain, whereby *memoriones* learnt a proportion of a play by heart after watching performances, and wrote that up with linking text, may seem to resemble the postulated reconstruction underlying Q1 *Hamlet* in general outline, but *memoriones* are not recorded as part of the English scene.

The reconstructed Sheridan plays, which Duthie sees as similar to what would have happened with "bad" quartos, offer detail, and suggest the efforts involved. Wilkinson's account showed that he depended substantially on written materials. Bernard's account is more relevant to memorial transmission. We need not assume that Bernard's account of his compilation is the only kind of account that could be convincing. We can show that Bernard had motive and opportunity which are not paralleled in the speculation about Q1 *Hamlet*'s theoretical reconstruction. The comparison between Bernard's reconstruction of *The School for Scandal* and the suggestions for Q1 *Hamlet*'s reconstruction demonstrate three substantial challenges to the would-be Q1 "pirates," namely the minor roles—with few lines—played by the so-called actor/reporters, the few scenes they appear in, and a shortage of evidence for long runs or frequent performances for gaining familiarity with the scripts. These differences are not addressed in the scholars' texts examined and cited, but must be significant issues in the memorial reconstruction theory. It is difficult not to conclude that alternative explanations need to be sought and evaluated for the similarities found in certain actors' roles in the two—or three—versions of *Hamlet*. There are genuine grounds for doubt, as well as doubters, for example Sams: "[T]he entire theory should now at last be officially and formally abandoned,"[36] and Holderness and Loughrey: "[E]ven if the theory of memorial reconstruction is correct...,"[37] and Urkowitz, *inter alia*.

Superficially, the existence of a definite example of MR and a clear account of how it worked seem a solid plank in the argument for Q1's MR. However, when we look carefully at the analogy of *The School for Scandal*'s recreation, it simply serves to show the frailty of the link between the matching lines of minor characters in the *Hamlet*s and MR. The circumstances and opportunities for a MR of *Hamlet* are very different from those for *The School for Scandal*, so different that the analogy undermines rather than supports a MR of *Hamlet*.

The analogy of the memorial reconstruction of *The School for Scandal* is only one aspect of Duthie's wide-ranging collection of points arguing for MR, and others too need reviewing.

8. *The Spanish Tragedy*, and Duthie's "Objectionable" Pronouns

The arguments for memorial reconstruction do not rest solely upon the existence of accounts like Wilkinson's and Bernard's. There are many features in Q1 itself which are used to argue for MR, particularly by Duthie. His book shows such passion and such a breadth of knowledge about Elizabethan plays that it seems discourteous to ask whether his enthusiasm might on occasion be misplaced. He has created a very detailed picture of how his actor-cum-reporters might have assembled a *Hamlet*, a picture which we might in our eagerness to understand Q1's origins be tempted to accept as it stands, with all its multi-faceted splendor. He gives examples for all his ideas and methodically explores how MR might have come about.

Three of the threads in his argument are the focus of this chapter. Duthie proposes that some words and phrases in Q1 are recalled by the "reporter" because he recalls them from other Shakespeare plays. Other words and phrases, Duthie argues, are remembered from the reporter's performance in another major revenge tragedy of the time, *The Spanish Tragedy*. And to demonstrate the weakness of the technical skills of the reporter, Duthie draws our attention to what he sees as "objectionable" pronouns in the scene unique to Q1, scene 14, where Hamlet's return is announced.

Before reviewing these aspects we might recall that it is the character of Q1 itself which has led to a search for an explanation other than Shakespeare's authorship of the play. Approximately 19.8 percent of the lines in Q1 do match lines found in Q2, and on the whole these lines occur most frequently in the scenes where the alleged memorial reconstructor(s) performed. (For example, Q1's scene 3 has 26 percent of its lines matching Q2's I.iii, though scene 13 has 24 percent of its lines matching lines in Q2's IV.v.) However, we meet another divergence of opinions here, for scholars have not agreed about how extensively Shakespeare's hand is seen in the play. When Boas comments on Q1 he writes that "the bulk of the blank verse in the three later acts is, in my opinion, unmistakably pre–Shakespearean."[1] Wilson comments in 1918 that the non–Shakespearean fragments of Q1 are from the *Ur-Hamlet* over which Shakespeare had not yet worked, though this is not a view he maintains.[2] Edward Dowden writes that "Shakespeare's hand can be discerned throughout the whole of the truncated and travestied play of 1603," and nothing "looks pre–Shakespearean."[3] Meanwhile Duthie finds it "absurd that anyone could attribute it [Q1] to Shakespeare."[4] Duthie even questions whether a memorial reconstructor is "intellectually capable of reproducing" parts of Q2 and F1, and refers to "defective memory."[5] It is obviously problematic that there is no consensus on the extent of Q1's Shakespearean qualities, not least because it is difficult to define Shakespeare's style satisfactorily if the lines which are his cannot be incontrovertibly identified. The inclusion of Q1 and any other "bad" quarto will alter his style from the style considered Shakespearean if Q1 and other "bad" quartos are excluded.

So Duthie, having questioned whether Q1 could possibly be attributed to Shakespeare, offers a series of points to show how a memorial reconstructor, or a "hack-poet," or reporter (possibly with "defective memory") "used his own powers of ingenuity and inventiveness in fitting the fragments [from Shakespearean and occasionally other plays] together and in connecting them with short pieces of original matter."[6]

"Fragments" from Shakespeare

The "fragments" from Shakespeare are indeed small fragments. Duthie takes as his starting point what he calls "the 'good' texts" and the "authentic texts,"[7] partial language clearly connoting his views, and compares what is in them with Q1. He notes that "the 'good' texts" include the word "Possess" in Hamlet's first soliloquy: "…things rank and gross in nature/ Possess it merely" (I.ii.137). The "reporter" in Q1's scene 11 wrote "It is not madness that possesseth Hamlet" (11.87). Duthie suggests that the "reporter" may "[j]ust possibly … have vaguely remembered a passage in another play: consider for example, *Titus Andronicus*, IV.i.15–17":

> Boy.   My Lord, I know not, nor can I guess,
>   Unless some fit or *frenzy* do *possess* her.

Or, Duthie writes, the "reporter" may even have borrowed from *King John*, V.iii.17:

> King John.   "*Weakness possesseth* me, and I am faint."[8]

We need to think carefully about this. It may be easy to assume that the occurrence of a particular word in one context has only one explanation for its presence in another, but it is rather like saying that the only reason a car won't go is because its battery is flat. A surer way is to consider whether there are other reasons which might also be valid for the occurrence of the word (or which might also explain the car engine's silence). Duthie is right to say that the same verb is found in Q1, Q2, *Titus Andronicus*, and *King John*. It is possible that the italicized nouns ("frenzy," and "weakness") may have seemed to Duthie to be in the same lexical field as "madness," though he does not write that. Would it, however, be that surprising if Shakespeare who used the same relatively common verb in three plays, in the same metaphorical way, also used it in Q1, even if it were not in the same scene? Or is it more likely that a "reporter" who perhaps played a Boy in *Titus Andronicus* or the King in *King John* recalls one word from a different play, and to be honest from a different context, in his alleged reconstruction of the "bedchamber" scene? Alternative reasons for these features need to be considered for a balanced evaluation of their possible origins.

Another single word trigger for the "reporter," Duthie suggests, is "unpardonable." He writes: "One line in the Q1 soliloquy seems to be an appropriation from another play."[9] Q1 reads: "O these are sins that are unpardonable" (10.7). Immediately Duthie presents us with "a very close parallel in *3 Henry 6*, I.iv.106: 'O, 'tis a fault too unpardonable.'" This is one of Queen Margaret's lines. Should we believe that the "reporter" also played or knew this role, or might it be that Shakespeare—again?—used a word twice?

In another example Duthie offers more than a single word trigger. Q2 reads:

> *King.* Hamlet, this deed, for this especial safety,
> Which we do tender ... [IV.iii.40–41].

Q1 reads:

> *King.* Well sonne Hamlet, we in care of you: but specially
> in tender preservation of your health ... [11.155–6].

Duthie proposes that the verb "tender" (Q2) "has formed in the reporter's mind an association-link with *Henry V* II.ii.56–8:

> *King.* ... We'll yet enlarge that man,
> Though Cambridge, Scroop and Gray, in their dear care
> And tender preservation of our person....

The "alteration entails a borrowing (with modifications)," Duthie explains.[10]

The vocabulary here overlaps: "(e)special(ly)," "tender," "care" and "preservation." Each is of course an extract from a speech designed for the role of a King, which might lead a playwright to produce some stylistic similarities, and the concept of apparently expressing a concern for someone's wellbeing is commonplace. And chapters two to five earlier explored verbal parallels between the French source and the quartos, and some of those parallels are fragmentary. However, *Les Histoires Tragiques* is known to predate the *Hamlet*s (we cannot be certain that *Titus Andronicus, King John, 3 Henry VI* and *Henry V* all predate the text of Q1, since the date of Q1 remains hypothetical). Additionally, *Les Histoires Tragiques* is also known to be the (direct or) underlying source of the *Hamlet*s, and individual words or "fragments" like "infamie"/ "infamy" occur in the same context in the source and Q1. Duthie's examples of how the alleged reporter "may have vaguely remembered," "quoted inaccurately," made an "association-link," had a "vague recollection," or made a "borrowing (with modifications)" provide ingenious cross-references to other plays. Some readers may be convinced. The question, however, must always be whether other explanations are possible, such as whether Shakespeare used the same vocabulary on a number of occasions, and whether those explanations are more credible. We must also note that for Duthie to be right the hypothesis of MR needs another supplementary hypothesis, that the actor/reporter had performed in a number of other Shakespearean plays and that he remembered odd words from them.

"Fragments" from The Spanish Tragedy

Another of Duthie's key arguments is that the putative reporter also drew upon *The Spanish Tragedy*. From Malone onwards its author, Thomas Kyd, has been linked to the phrases "*Hamlets*," the "Kid in Æsop" and the list of criticisms in Nashe's preface (discussed in Chapter 11), for it was Malone who first suggested that Kyd was "perhaps" the author of the "early" *Hamlet*. Duthie lists ten alleged borrowings from *The Spanish Tragedy*. These borrowings, Duthie claims, show parallels between lines in Kyd's play and Q1 in lines not present in Q2 or F1. Duthie argues that the memorial reconstructor had previously performed in *The Spanish Tragedy* and recalled these lines, because of similarities in the plots, and incorporated these into his memorially reconstructed *Hamlet*. Duthie's argument includes the assumption that *The Spanish Tragedy* must have preceded a Q1 *Hamlet*, and in the following discussion that assumption is respected. We have already noted that the date of *The Spanish Tragedy* is problematic; it is probably after 1582, and definitely before its performance on 23rd February 1592.[11] The date range places it securely before the publication of Q1 in 1603, but in an ambiguous position in relation to the *Hamlet* mentioned by Nashe. There is no agreement, or unambiguous evidence, upon which came first. Bullough records E. E. Stoll's belief that *The Spanish Tragedy* was written first.[12] Jenkins suggests the reverse (alluding to the so-called *Ur-Hamlet*).[13]

The "reporter," who recalls about 10 percent of Q2 or reconstructs a Q1 with not quite 20 percent of its lines matching Q2's, is, in Duthie's opinion, able to bring to mind ten partial quotations from *The Spanish Tragedy*, and embed them in his MR of Q1. The quotations are not from a single role which the "reporter" might have taken. Instead they come from six different roles: Hieronimo (four times), Bellimperia (thrice), Lorenzo (twice), and Isabella, Balthasar and Castile (once). Duthie doesn't mention that the quotations are from different roles, nor comment on whether he thought the "reporter" played one or more of the roles, merely that the "reporter" "borrowed" from them, or "confused similar situations."[14] Duthie's suggestion for the source of these Q1 lines is supported by Frederick Boas and John M. Robertson.[15] It is reasonable to consider whether the putative actor/reporter would find it easier to recall and borrow from a role he had played, or whether he would just have a general memory for the whole performance.

The alleged borrowings or recollections are worth examining. Two are a single word: "friends," and "prevailed." Two are two words: "drown" and "tears," and "noble mate" and "nobler mate." Three borrowings are three words: "woe," "grief," "relief," and "like not [the]/[this] Tragedy," and "to try [your]/[my] cunning." Once it is four words: "And how for [this]/[that]?," and "Excellent," the latter occurring at a space of several lines.[16] Duthie does not quote all of these in their context. So the last example, for instance, is presented as follows:

Q1
   Leartes.   And how for this?
   King.   Mary Leartes thus ...
   Leartes.   T'is excellent ... [XV.14–15, 37].
Cf. *Spanish Tragedy*:
   Lorenzo.   And how for that?
   Hieronimo.   Marry, my good Lord, thus ...
   Lorenzo.   O excellent! [IV.i.74, 126].[17]

The line references here, which Duthie himself gives, should be noted. They show how far apart the apparent parallels are in their own texts, fifty-one lines apart in the last example. It is perhaps hard to see that any of these words and phrases is sufficiently striking to be immediately recalled and be at the tip of the actor/reporter's quill for his reconstruction, but that is a subjective opinion.

There is also a whole clause, which seems more promising: "I never gave you cause." However, this could easily be an echo of the French source—"Ce n'est sans cause" (214)—it seems to be an idiom in both languages at that time. And like every one of the above examples, it too is used by Shakespeare elsewhere. We find the complete clause in *Othello*, when Cassio exclaims to Othello, "Dear General, I never gave you cause" (V.ii.302[18]).

Laurie Maguire in her study of supposed memorial reconstructions comments on only two of Duthie's ten. She then simply rejects those two alleged parallels with *The Spanish Tragedy* as "innocuous recollection," a considerable contrast with Duthie's identification of them as explaining how the memorial reconstructor recreated a *Hamlet* in Q1. Maguire requires "1) a run of lines, containing 2) distinctive vocabulary" for a borrowing to be proved.[19] The vocabulary in the alleged recollections above is not unreasonably described as undistinguished.

This can be confirmed by a brief glance at some of Duthie's alleged "borrowings." "[F]riends," with various meanings from "lover" to "relative" to "well-wisher," can be found in *Love's Labours Lost*, *All's Well* and *Merry Wives* respectively, for example. "[P]revailed," denoting "win" and "succeed in seduction," is used by Shakespeare in, for instance, *Coriolanus* and *1Henry VI*. "[D]rowned" is also found in *Twelfth Night*, and "cunning" and "cause" with several different meanings are each present in over a dozen of Shakespeare's plays. "Tragedy" is a recurring word in several play titles. It is true that Duthie's suggestions do not appear in Crystal and Crystal's list of one hundred "Frequently Encountered Words" at the front of their *Glossary*, but despite this we can hardly see any of Duthie's examples as "distinctive."

The last, most promising and most interesting of Duthie's parallels is also the most problematic. It does hold some "distinctive vocabulary," though not "a run of lines." It is the promise of the Queen in Q1, which Duthie sees as deriving from *The Spanish Tragedy*, but which chapter three shows could derive quite straightforwardly from *Les Histoires Tragiques*. In the quotations below the lines with a grey background (from *Les Histoires Tragiques* and four lines from *The Spanish Tragedy*), and are *not* given by Duthie, and they do *not* play any part in his discussion. It may be that in his enthusiasm to link Q1 and *The Spanish Tragedy* Duthie overlooked the "grey" text; it is ungenerous to suggest that he was deliberately selective in his quotations. Chapters two to five have shown that the source is echoed frequently in the *Hamlet*s, and indeed that the Queens' promises are worth studying in parallel.

Les Histoires Tragiques
Geruthe: je tiendray secrette, et ta sagesse, et ta gaillarde enterprinse (222). ("I will hold/ keep secret both your wisdom/wise plan and your gallant/ brave enterprise.")

Q1 *Hamlet*
Queen: I will conceal, consent, and do my best,
What stratagem soe'er thou shalt devise ... [11.97–8].

The Spanish Tragedy
Hieronimo. And here I vow, so but you give consent,
And will conceal my resolution,
I will ere long determine of their deaths
That causeless thus have murdered my son.
Bellimperia. Hieronimo, I will consent, conceal,
And aught that may effect for thine avail,
Join with thee to revenge Horatio's death.
Hieronimo. On then; and whatsoever I devise,
Let me entreat you, grace my practices [IV.i.42–50].

Duthie asserts that Q1 here is "substantially an importation," from *The Spanish Tragedy*.[20] Oddly, despite quoting selectively twenty or so lines of Belleforest,[21] Duthie does *not* quote Geruthe's promise. Instead Duthie insists: "As has already been noted, the last two lines [Q1, 11.97–8] contain not the words of Gertrude in any authentic version of *Hamlet*, but of Bellimperia in *The Spanish Tragedy*."[22] It would be discourteous to suggest Duthie is deflecting readers from *Les Histoires Tragiques*, though that might be an inadvertent result of his statement. It is worth stressing that the "bedchamber" scene—"la chambre de la Royne" in the source—is where Amleth's mother makes her promise, and it is the scene offering the largest proportion of parallels to any scene in *Hamlet*. Several ideas from the French source are closely mirrored in Q1: the hiding of the counselor (206, 11.2), the making safe of the chamber (206, 11.6), the Prince's determination to speak (210, 11.10), and the charge of murder directed at the new King (210, 11.40). Amleth refers to the ghost or "ombres" of his father, while Q1's Ghost appears (212, 11.56); the Prince draws attention to the contrast between the two kings, and admits to seeming possessed by madness (214, 11.88); he comments on the "infamie"/"infamy" of his mother (216, 11.47 and 11.94), and on his intention to take revenge (216, 11.93). Amleth asks his mother not to tell the King of his intentions, which she promises she will hold secret ("je tiendray secrette..." [218]); Hamlet asks for assistance, and his mother, unprompted, volunteers to "conceal and consent..." (11.93, 11.97).

The accumulation of echoes of the source and the closeness of the source show that there is enough to launch Q1's version of the scene and to explain Gertred's promise. But the precise lexis "conceal," "consent," in conjunction with "revenge" and "devise" in Q1 and *The Spanish Tragedy* is disconcerting, the more so because in the latter Kyd appears to be deliberately and emphatically repeating "conceal" and "consent." Hieronimo requests that Bellimperia will "give consent,/ And will conceal my resolution..." which two lines later

Bellimperia echoes (and Duthie starts to quote): "I will consent, conceal ... revenge," with Hieronimo also using "devise." It is peculiar that Duthie gives an edited version of this from *The Spanish Tragedy*—did he wittingly suppress the repeated "conceal" and "consent?" The deliberate repetition of words is not uncommon in Kyd, but the vocabulary is still noticeably close to Q1.

Several explanations may be mooted, depending on the reader's beliefs. Some will accept Duthie's argument because they believe that Kyd wrote the putative *Ur-Hamlet*, which cannot be (dis)proved. Or they may believe that the putative "reporter" played in a putative *Ur-Hamlet*, which too cannot be (dis)proved. The possibility that Kyd's repetition is witty, even parodic, and intended to invite readers/audiences to recall a *Hamlet* should be included among the possibilities, though this also cannot be proved. However, the early *Hamlet* in 1589 is alluded to in ways which suggest it is well-known (see Chapter 11), and a playwright might like to ride on the coat tails of another successful play by echoing it deliberately.

The inconvenience to Duthie's argument of the more prominent borrowings from Belleforest is underlined by his reluctance to endorse the conclusion of another scholar, Giovanni Ramello, that the compiler(s) of Q1 consulted Belleforest.[23] Instead, in Duthie's own words: "the reporter ... remembered material from the Closet-scene in the old *Hamlet* [the putative *Ur-Hamlet*] ... he then immediately proceeded, intentionally or involuntarily (by memorial confusion), to borrow a passage from *The Spanish Tragedy*."[24] Reference to what is still a putative source, the *Ur-Hamlet*, doesn't prove Duthie's claim, despite its ingenuity. And we are again left with the need for a supplementary hypothesis to prop up the MR hypothesis. This time it is that the actor/reporter(s) had also performed in or was familiar with up to six roles in *The Spanish Tragedy*.

"Objectionable" Pronouns

A third aspect of Duthie's proposal does, however, support his statement that we can see "throughout Q1 ... the handiwork of someone connected with the theatre."[25] This concerns what he calls the "misuse of personal pronouns," of the "faulty" or "objectionable" use of pronouns. This proposed misuse occurs in Q1's scene 14, when Horatio tells the Queen that Hamlet is back in Denmark.[26] The "rule" in modern Standard English is that a pronoun should refer in case, number and gender to its antecedent, that is, to the preceding noun which matches it. This would be applicable today in writing, and it is helpful in speech too. However, it does not mean that we should assume the modern "rule" also applied in Shakespeare's time.

Duthie's first example is the Queen's reply to Horatio. In these lines Horatio and the Queen are discussing Hamlet and the King, both third person singular masculine nouns. The subject pronoun "he," the object pronoun "him," and the possessive determiner "his" can therefore be used of either Hamlet or the King. Here the composer has consistently used "<u>he</u>" to denote Hamlet, and "**his/him**" to denote the King of Denmark (author's underlining and emboldening added for clarity). The sense is easily understood in the context, but does not follow the modern "rule."

> Hor. Madame, your sonne is safe arriv'de in *Denmarke* ...
> ... <u>He</u> will relate the circumstance at full.
>
> Queene. Then I perceiue there's treason in **his** lookes
> That seem'd to sugar o're **his** villainie:
> But I will soothe and please **him** for a time,
> For murderous mindes are always jealous,
> But know ye not *Horatio* where <u>he</u> is? [Sig. H2v.5, 13–18].

Horatio uses the pronoun "<u>He</u>" to refer to the subject of his opening line here, the Queen's son, in other words to Hamlet. The Queen's first four lines in her speech are then effectively an aside to herself and the audience about her husband the King of Denmark. The aside alerts the audience to her watchfulness and her intention to be vigilant regarding the King; it shows us that she is on Hamlet's side, and sees the King as capable of treason, villainy and murder. She does not name **him**; in natural speech she need not, in "thinking aloud" we might not, and besides by now—it is scene 14—the audience is aware of the King's "murderous mind" and his targeting of Hamlet. That her first four lines are an aside is confirmed by her use of Horatio's name (the vocative "*Horatio*") in the last line, when she turns her attention back to Horatio and answers him. In her question she now returns to her son, Hamlet, "<u>he</u>," whom Horatio has just mentioned. Gertred uses the same pronoun as Horatio, "<u>he</u>." On stage her aside can be conveyed by her turning away from Horatio for those four lines, probably facing the audience, and appropriately *not* confiding her suspicions of her husband and his King to Horatio. As such, this is well-written, speech-like, completely comprehensible, and theatrically effective. The pronoun usage in the Queen's first four lines is hardly "objectionable"; it demonstrates an implicit knowledge of how stage conventions work. If the composer of the lines had written: "*Gertred.* (Aside) Then I perceive..." we would probably not give the grammar of these lines a second thought.

But it is those lines that Duthie then wishes to use as an analogy for his second example of "faulty" pronoun usage, shortly afterwards in the same scene. Again, "<u>he</u>" denotes Hamlet, "**his**" the King. (The composer of the scene is impressively consistent.)

8. *The Spanish Tragedy, and Duthie's "Objectionable" Pronouns* 111

> *Queene* ... lest that <u>he</u>
> Faile in that <u>he</u> goes about.
> *Hor.* Madam, neuer make doubt of that:
> I thinke by this the news be come to court:
> <u>He</u> is arriv'de, obserue the king, and you shall
> Quickely finde, *Hamlet* being here,
> Things fell not to **his** minde.
> *Queene* But what became of *Gilderstone* and *Rossencraft*?
> *Hor.* <u>He</u> being set ashore, they went for *England* ... [Sig. H2v.24–32].

The pronoun "<u>he</u>" of the Queen's first line refers back to the subject of her "mother's care," in other words her son. Horatio's first pronoun usage is identical: "<u>He</u>" means Hamlet. When Horatio mentions the King—"obserue the king"—the text now holds a second masculine singular noun, which in English can be problematic. The playwright resolves this by creating another aside, "*Hamlet* being here," which is grammatically a non-finite subordinate clause; we could say it is in parenthesis to the main content of the speech. As such it need not have the emphasis or volume or pitch of the preceding and following words about the King. Strictly speaking, the use of "**his**" is not modern, formal, written Standard English, but it is entirely understandable in its context. It is far less clumsy than repeating the noun "king" as follows:

> *Horatio.* Observe the king, and you shall quickly find,
> Hamlet being here, things fell not to the king's mind."

Duthie argues a third instance of these "objectionable" pronouns, following the Queen's question:

> *Queene.* But what became of *Gilderstone* and *Rossencraft*?
> *Horatio.* <u>He</u> being set ashore ...

"<u>He</u> being set ashore" now refers deictically (and semantically) to the man who accompanied Gilderstone and Rossencraft, not, as it would grammatically, to the King. The characters and the audience know that Hamlet has been sent off with Gilderstone and Rossencraft, so with "<u>He</u>" (again) the audience is likely to think it means Hamlet. Hamlet has been abroad, so "set ashore" will be associated with Hamlet, and thus any possible momentary confusion is rapidly resolved.

The expectations of "correct" pronoun usage that Duthie holds here are both a more modern standard than Shakespeare's, but are also those expected in written English. However, the playwright is attempting, and achieving, the naturalness of speech, where grammar is a little different, and where deixis is more common. Moreover, non-verbal clues are expected on the stage. Duthie uses the apparent non-standard usage to argue that "obserue the king" is an interpolation (and also an exhortation to the audience), and argues that this is attributable to the "reporter." But if Duthie had not made his objection, we might note instead that the playwright has mirrored the relative inexplicitness of speech in a context where the known concerns of the two speakers, and the nouns—"sonne," "king," and "*Gilderstone* and *Rossencraft*"—clarify any ambiguity in pronouns that Duthie may notice. Even with Duthie's query the use of pronouns in all the examples is hardly problematic, and it is consistent. Usage is certainly not "objectionable" or "faulty" to anyone who is following the plot.

Additionally, the playwright makes this demand upon his audience not at the beginning of the play where it might have been confusing but at a point where the audience's understanding can be assumed, and the speakers' concerns cannot be mistaken. Rather, these examples seem a sophisticated handling of several threads: what has happened to Hamlet, how the King is conducting himself, the Queen's suspicions of the King and her concerns for her son, and the hint that Gilderstone and Rossencraft are dead.

One possible issue here (regarding "things fell not to his mind...") is that Q1 appears to bury a rhyming couplet, "...finde ... minde":

> *Hor.* ... obserue the king, and you shall
> Quickely finde, *Hamlet* being here,
> Things fell not to **his** minde.

Indeed, Irace re-aligns this part of the text in her Q1 edition (1998) to disinter that rhyming couplet:

> *Horatio.* Observe the king and you shall quickly find,
> Hamlet being here, things fell not to his mind [14.23–4].

It might have been a chance rhyme; it might have been a form of delayed internal rhyme (Shakespeare plays with these from time to time, for example in Sonnet 135), or it might have originated as a rhyming couplet, though that would have been more likely at the end of the scene. Because there are other quite reasonable explanations, neither rhyme or pronoun usage here proves memorial reconstruction in this scene.

Many scholars have been swayed by Duthie's carefully constructed description of the methods employed by the "reporter" who is supposed to have recalled a Shakespearean *Hamlet*, and cobbled together Q1. Greg writes that it is "the fullest and most detailed exposition ... of the theory that the 1603 *Hamlet* is nothing but a memorial reconstruction of the complete version, upon which it is almost entirely dependent."[27] Hibbard comments on "the most careful and thorough-going examination Q1 has ever been subjected to."[28] Certainly Duthie is very observant and does pay close attention to Q1,

8. The Spanish Tragedy, and Duthie's "Objectionable" Pronouns 113

and he does produce a very full description of how he thinks MR occurred. Thomas describes it as "Duthie's convincing analysis."[29] These are just a few of the tributes that have been paid to *The "Bad" Quarto of Hamlet*, a genuinely exciting read, and a genuine and necessary attempt to push to the limit the hypothesis of MR to explain Q1.

The three aspects considered in this chapter all demonstrate how well Duthie knew both Q1 and other Elizabethan plays. But the re-examination of these aspects does raise troubling questions. Since Shakespeare could use identical vocabulary elsewhere, it need not be a "reporter" who is remembering; it could be Shakespeare using some relatively common words more than once. Since the *Hamlet*s are derived ultimately from *Les Histoires Tragiques*, we ought to consider whether that text is the potential source for Gertred's promise. Since we can only guess at whether *The Spanish Tragedy* came before or after the first *Hamlet*, we can wonder whether Kyd alluded to that *Hamlet*, rather than whether a "reporter" hypothetically drew upon a few lines of Kyd's play. And since modern rules of grammar for written texts are not known to have governed Shakespeare's scripts for the stage, we could see those "faulty" pronouns instead as intelligent stagecraft.

Duthie's choices of vocabulary tend to suggest a less than competent "reporter." Yet the "reporter" supposedly uses his "ingenuity" and "inventiveness," "vaguely remembers" and makes "association links," and seems to be acquainted with quite a wide range of roles in several other plays. He even recalls words Shakespeare knows and uses elsewhere. The "reporter" doesn't look at the source, Duthie seems to think, but we can see that the "reporter" does have considerable knowledge about the theatre and how to embed stage directions in scripts.

The foci of this chapter are three significant parts of Duthie's argument. Each can be explained without a "reporter," despite Duthie's enthusiasm and personal conviction. It means that this chapter, like chapters six and seven, must also challenge the MR hypothesis. Chapter nine considers other arguments which have been proposed to support MR.

9. Corpses, Stage Directions and Other Anomalies

Sometimes scholars express their views with vehemence:

> Objectors to "memorial reconstruction" as the explanation for the bad quartos have sometimes complained that there is no contemporary "testimony" to such a practice; but if you come upon a mutilated corpse you don't deny a murder because nobody has reported one.[1]

We are encouraged by this to share the writer's assumption that an absence of evidence about MR is not critical, and his opinion that Q1 is like "a mutilated corpse." Yet we know that some directors and actors have found Q1 to have pace and energy. Q1 may be a "skeletal version," but at the same time it's "the ... absolute dynamo behind the play," says Peter Guinness.[2] The contrast between "corpse" and "dynamo" is almost as marked as between seeing Q1 as MR and as Shakespeare's first draft. These contrasts in opinion reinforce the need for a re-evaluation of those first two quartos, the status of Q1 in particular, and MR as the explanation for Q1.

So far Part Two's reassessment of the arguments for MR has found that several characteristics of Q1 which have been thought to indicate MR have straightforward, alternative explanations. While chapters six to eight have examined the major lines of reasoning indicating MR, this chapter draws together a host of disparate points made by a number of scholars who see Q1 as MR or who have investigated it.

Stage Directions

The first concerns descriptive stage directions, which have been seen as the "hallmark of the reported text." Descriptive stage directions might result from the reporter trying to recall something he didn't know accurately in the first place, according to Harry Hoppe.[3]

In Q1 scene 13 this seems at a first glance to be fulfilled by one stage direction. Ofelia enters "playing on a lute, and her hair down, singing" (scene 13, between lines 14 and 15). It is a more visual and detailed description than Q2's, where Ophelia merely "Sings." Yet the most complicated set of stage directions in the quartos, for the dumb show, is clearly more complex in Q2. Q1 offers simply:

> Enter in a dumb show, the KING and QUEEN. He sits down in an arbour. She leaves him. Then enters LUCIANUS with poison in a vial and pours it in his ears and goes away. Then the Queen cometh and finds him dead and goes away with the other [9.67 onwards].

while Q2 offers:

> Enter a king and a queen, the queen embracing him and he her. He takes her up and declines his head upon her neck. He lies him down upon a bank of flowers. She seeing him asleep leaves him. Anon comes in another man, takes off his crown, kisses it, pours poison in the sleeper's ears and leaves him. The queen returns, finds the king dead, makes passionate action. The poisoner with some three or four come in again, seem to condole with her. The dead body is carried away. The poisoner woos the queen with gifts. She seems harsh awhile but in the end accepts love [III.ii.128 onwards].

The contrast is considerable, with Q2 giving a much fuller description of the action, and Q1—where the actor/reporter may be recalling the visual side of the performance—a briefer account. The evidence from the two sets of stage directions is contradictory in *Hamlet*, or rather the difference in detail does not support the idea that a remembered text has more detailed stage directions.

An associated puzzle comes with Lucianus, fingered as a potential memorial reconstructor. He has a double role in Q1, where he is named as the poisoner in the dumb show and speaks six lines when he apparently reappears later in the scene as the Murderer. In Q2 he may be "another man" in the dumb show—he is not named—but he still has six lines, now under his own name. If, as actor/reporter, Lucianus played "another man," it is rather odd that he recalls such a meager account of the dumb show, where he has his major scene. This isn't what might be expected of a remembered text.

In her study of a breadth of features across forty-one plays, Maguire notes a range of more or less descriptive stage directions across several different texts, both suspect and not, and she concludes that descriptive stage directions are not consistently indicative of memorial reconstruction.[4] The samples of stage directions in *Hamlet* quoted above support her conclusion.

"Extra-metrical Connectives"

A second point concerns "extra-metrical connectives." Hart considered that "the initial 'O' is the sign-manual of the pirate."[5] It is true that in the equivalent of act 1 of Q1 there are twenty-one uses of "O," while in Q2 there are twenty. What is more difficult to discern is whether this is significant. Twelve of the uses are the same. For example, each Ghost says "O horrible" (5.62, I.v.80), and after the Ghost's exit each Hamlet begins with "O all you host of heaven! O earth..." (5.72, I.v.92). But it isn't as simple as finding that Q1 uses the same as Q2 and then adds one more, for the distribution is a little different. In Q2, Hamlet's speech beginning "O all you host of heaven! O earth..." goes on to have more uses of "O," in "O most pernicious woman," and "O villain..." (I.v.105, 106). It is difficult to see logically how an overall higher number of "O's" in this part of Q1 shows the actor/reporter(s) at work, while parts of the same act in Q2 which have a higher proportion of "O" cannot signify the actor/reporter'(s) memorial efforts (and aren't discussed). It is less difficult to believe that the shared examples of "O" are kept by a reviser, who reduces the use slightly overall, but *increases* their use where Hamlet is particularly despairing.

In another example of repetition, Hamlet laments to his two "kind schoolfellows" that man does not delight him, "no, nor woman too," while in Q2 the negative particle, "no," is absent. But it *is* present in F1:

Q1
Hamlet. This great world you see contents me not; no, nor the spangled heavens, nor earth, nor sea; no, nor man, that is so glorious a creature, contents not me; no, nor woman too, though you laugh [7.233–5].

Q2
Hamlet. Man delights not me—nor women neither, though by your smiling you seem to say so [II.ii.274–6].

F1
Hamlet. Man delights not me—no, nor women neither, though by your smiling you seem to say so [II.ii.344–6].

This variability points to the close relationship of the three texts, but not to such "insertions" as proof of the memorial reconstruction of Q1.

Maguire describes F1's "no" as an example of extra-metrical pleonasm—"Man delights not me; [no,] nor Woman neither"—and comments that "extra-metrical pleonasm is almost as plentiful in non-suspect texts as it is in suspect texts."[6] Extra-metrical features might be attributed to an unpolished text or to the putative actor/reporter(s), but that requires the assumption that the playwright's aim was metrical regularity (perhaps like Alexander Pope in his poetry). Ironically, probably the most famous line in Shakespeare lacks that metrical regularity in Q2 and in F1—"To be, or not to be—that is the question"—but achieves it in Q1—"To be, or not to be; ay, there's the point." It is not easy to distinguish between repetition which might be emphatic or unnecessary. If we return to Hamlet and his reaction to the Ghost's revelations we find that in Q2's "O all you host of heaven..." speech Shakespeare/Hamlet has more repetition; for instance "smile"/"smiling" occurs three times as in Q1 while "villain" is found four times, once more than in Q1, but this does not seem to cause concern. And Q1's Ghost has just "O horrible, most horrible!" (sig. E4v.17), all of eight syllables, while Q2 has "O horrible, ô horrible, most horrible" (sig. D3r.38), all of twelve syllables. Extra-metrical, yes; repetition for emphatic and emotional effect, or pleonastic? Searching for examples of these features which are proposed as indicative of MR is frustrating, because the findings are not consistent.

"Aural Error" and "Honor"

Thus "insertions" are unreliable indicators. The same can be said of "aural error," a third point. The ear can be an uncertain instrument; it would not be surprising that if there were a "reporter" attempting to write down all he had heard that he makes an error. In the "gravedigger's scene" Q1 reads "and must the honor lie there" (16.40), while Q2 reads "and must the inheritor lie there" (V.i.105). Those who favor memorial reconstruction suggest that the "reporter" misheard "owner," and took it as "honor." However, Maguire identifies the same error—"homonymic"—in Massinger's *Duke of Milan* (1623), not a suspected memorial reconstruction.[7] The two words "honor" and "owner" are not homophones in modern British Received Pronunciation ("honor" begins with a short monophthong, "owner" with a diphthong). The misremembering of the compositor as he slots individual letters backwards into the letter stick is a possible reason, because the compositor probably looked at each word only once or twice, while the actor/reporter had presumably heard the play much more frequently, and, theoretically, might be more familiar with the meaning of the text.

We might look carefully at "honor" and its context. This is Hamlet's speech in Q1:

> *Ham.* Looke you, there's another *Horatio.*
> Why mai't not be the scull of some Lawyer?
> Me thinks he should indite that fellow
> Of an action of Batterie, for knocking
> Him about the pate with's shouel: now where is your
> Quirkes and quillets now your vouchers and
> Double vouchers, your leases and free-holde,
> And tenements? why that same boxe there will scarce
> Holde the conueiance of his land, and must
> The honor lie there? O pittiful transformance!

> I prethee tell me *Horatio*,
> Is parchment made of sheep-skinnes? [Sig. H4r.34–H4v.1–11].

The speech contains what Duthie might have cited as more "objectionable" pronouns ("he" and "him" refer to the skull/lawyer, with the contracted "his" in "with's" referring to "that fellow" digging the grave), but again they are perfectly understandable in the context. It is humorous, of course, with Hamlet's suggestion that if it were a lawyer's skull it should indict the Clowne for battery with a shovel. Shakespeare/Hamlet also shows off some legal knowledge, with the list of lawyer's jargon. Hamlet then gestures to a "boxe," "that" and "there" indicating the presence of the box at a slight distance from him. It is a box (perhaps the skull itself, which would then be called "skull," "pate" and "box" here[8]) that will scarcely hold another legal term, the "conueiance of his land." Hamlet rounds off his wry comments with "and must/ The honor lie there?" Is this what a powerful legal person comes to, a skull that is knocked about by a gravedigger? It looks as if "honor" could be the intended word in Q1, ironic in tone, particularly when Hamlet concludes (mockingly?) "O pittiful transformance!," underlining the transformation from legal power to a disrespected skull.

It is true that Q2 uses "inheritor," but it is also true that the speech is not identical. It is perfectly possible to read "inheritor" as correct in Q2: "The very conveyance of his lands will scarcely lie in this box, and must th'inheritor himself have no more, ha?" (V.i.103–5). If we did not know that "inheritor" was in Q2, would we challenge "honor" in Q1? It is very difficult to come to Q1 impartially, to read what is there rather than what isn't Q2. It is also enlightening to find someone who is not very familiar with the play and ask them how they would read Q1's speech as a whole, and "honor" as part of it.

"To Be or Not to Be"

It is impossible to discuss the differences between the quartos without referring to that most famous soliloquy, which in Q2 begins "To be or not to be; that is the question." One scholar comments on how that opening line is so well known that Q1's opening line, "To be or not to be, ay there's the point" immediately unsettles an audience: "Hamlet's first wrong turn of language meets with polite titters, but as the mistakes multiply, the titters quickly expand into guffaws."[9] It is understandable but nonetheless unfortunate that disparaging and partial terms like "wrong" and "mistakes" are used here. The point the scholar makes and inadvertently reinforces is that, in effect, it is almost impossible to give a fair hearing to Q1's speech, because virtually everyone will have met Q2's version first. On the other hand, Peter Guinness says that in performance the opening line can also produce "a smile of delight, because somehow it's a much more muscular line to deliver."[10]

Certainly the Q1 speech has been forcefully and vigorously criticized:

> One who can believe, for example, that the Q1 text of Hamlet's "To be or not to be" soliloquy is the work of Shakespeare, can believe anything.
>
> No one can seriously contend that Shakespeare wrote this farrago of nonsense at any stage of his career, let alone in his creative prime.
>
> [H]ow else explain the complete collapse of sense and syntax in this major speech than as the desperate improvisations of a reporter jumbling together the bits and pieces supplied by his fallacious memory?[11]

Hyperbole is an art form which can give much pleasure. It is part of rhetoric's palette, and requires a little care. One of the possibilities this book is trying to keep open is that Q1 is not necessarily the jumble of "bits and pieces" the "reporter" fallaciously reassembles, but that Q1 might be the early *Hamlet*; it might be the first draft of our Q2 *Hamlet*. It might date back as far as 1589, when Shakespeare was twenty-five, and when he may not have reached his "creative prime." After all, no one seems to have suggested that Shakespeare wrote the Q1 "To be or not to be" soliloquy in his "creative prime." The only suggestion has been that if Shakespeare authored it, he wrote it early on in his playwriting career. (Only Andrew Cairncross seems to have thought Q2 might have been written by 1589.[12])

The same vigorous critic speaks of "the complete collapse of sense and syntax in this major speech." An analogy might be appropriate here. A little while ago there were (November 2010) headlines about Jane Austen's "poor grammar," and a sample of *Pride and Prejudice* in her own handwriting. The quotations in the newspapers actually show writing which is grammatically standard, but demonstrates a (now) non-standard punctuation and the use of underlining for emphasis. The style and tone of the quotations are undoubtedly Austen's, who did revise.

Another analogy might also be revealing. In act 1 scene ii of *The Winter's Tale*, Leontes soliloquizes, with some words and phrases addressed to his son Mamillius, while on another part of the stage Hermione and Polixenes talk and gesture. Leontes is descending into jealous insanity, in which he interprets his pregnant wife's friendliness in her role of hostess as indicating instead that she has been unfaithful. Leontes even begins to doubt that Mamillius is his. The language is convoluted, not a modern written standard, and it is dense with wordplay. It is perhaps "the obscurest passage in Shakespeare" according to van Doren.[13] Some of the features are easily illustrated with a brief extract:

> *Leontes* ... yet were it true
> To say this boy were like me. Come, sir page,
> Look on me with your welkin eye: sweet villain!

> Most dear'st, my collop! Can thy dam?—may't be?–
> Affection! thy intention stabs the centre;
> Thou dost make possible things not so held ... [I.ii.134–139].

The sense and syntax are initially challenging here. The first line of the quotation uses inversion of subject "it" and the verb "were," "yet were it true," which may be subjunctive in force (line 134). Leontes' reference to his son, "this boy," uses a proximal demonstrative adjective, "this," which tells the actors as well as the audience how physically close Mamillius is to his father, perhaps that Leontes is gesturing to the nearby Mamillius. However, it is a third person reference (line 135). After the caesura, Shakespeare changes to an imperative, "Come," and a vocative, "sir page." This vocative doesn't include Mamillius' name, but we know that Leontes has now switched to addressing his son directly, for it is confirmed by the second person possessive determiner "your" in line 136. "[W]elkin eye" acts as a compressed simile, meaning something like "your eyes which are as blue as the sky." The explanatory version immediately shows how concentrated Shakespeare's writing is here. The interjection "sweet villain" is oxymoronic, requiring the audience to think quickly why both labels might be appropriate in Leontes' eyes. The phrase following, "Most dear'st," appears to miss out the head word, presumably "son." The next phrase, "my collop," denotes a small piece of meat and conveys "flesh of my flesh" and keeps the question of Leontes' suspicions of Hermione's fidelity firmly in mind (line 137).

By now the lines have moved from declarative mood ("To say this boy were like me...") to imperative ("Come," "Look"), to exclamatory ("sweet villain!"), and now an incomplete interrogative begins: "Can thy dam?" The main verb is not included; the audience must supply their own version of it ("have betrayed me sexually?"), and quickly too, for Shakespeare/Leontes is already alluding to the same suspicion in another inexplicit question, "may't be?" (line 137) before his thoughts change direction and he shifts to an apostrophe, "Affection!" Which meaning does he intend? Lust? Passion? A feeling of great intensity is certain, and the personification of "affection" is evident in "thy." Leontes' own pain is revealed in "stabs," and the audience may barely grasp this before the inexplicitness of "Thou dost make possible things not so held"—a strength of feeling makes possible things which were not believed to be possible, or believable. More could be said, but this brief passage from *The Winter's Tale* surely shows demanding and occasionally non-standard syntax, and a sense or meaning which lies somewhere between what Leontes says and what we can infer.

The Winter's Tale is generally taken to be a later play, a mature comedy (perhaps even written in Shakespeare's "creative prime"), and passages like this demonstrate a writer who can manipulate language for its meaning and its

9. Corpses, Stage Directions and Other Anomalies   121

effect. It is not necessary to understand exactly what Leontes means on stage (though in the study it is desirable), because the characterization shows so well a man tortured by his own suspicions. At some point Shakespeare—this writer assumes—experimented with language; at some point he was not as skilful. Q1 might possibly be an example of this. So does Q1's "To be" speech really demonstrate a "complete collapse of sense and syntax?"

This is the speech in its entirety. (Matches with Q2 are *italicized*.)

> *To be, or not to be*, I there's the point,
> *To Die, to sleepe*, is that all? I, all:
> No, *to sleepe, to dreame*, I mary there it goes,
> For in that dreame of deathe, when wee awake,
> And borne before an euerlasting Iudge,
> From whence no passenger euer *retur'n*d,
> *The vndiscouered country*, at whose sight
> The happy smile, and the accursed damn'd.
> But for this, the ioyfull hope of this,
> *Whol'd beare the* scornes and flattery of the world,
> *Scorn*ed by the right rich, the rich curssed of the poore?
> The widow being oppressed, the orphan wrong'd,
> The taste of hunger, or a tirants raigne,
> And thousand more *calamitie*s besides,
> *To grunt and sweate vnder* this *weary life*,
> When that he may his full *Quietus make*,
> *With a bare bodkin*, who would this indure,
> But for a hope of something after death?
> Which *pusles* the braine, and doth confound the sence,
> Which *makes vs rather beare those* euilles we *haue*,
> *Than flie to others that we know not of.*
> I that, O this *conscience* makes *cowards* of vs all,
> Lady *in thy orizons, be all my sinnes remembred* [Sig. D4r.27–E1v.12].

The question is whether the soliloquy is partly "mutilated" by a reporter, or whether it is a first draft; it is whether Q2 represents the original soliloquy, or a redrafting. Since Q1 is measurably closer to the source of the play, which means its priority must be a possibility, could we defend this speech? This is not to suggest that the speech matches the quality of its equivalent in Q2, but just to query whether it is entirely devoid of merit. Some of its characteristics, allegedly due to a memorial reconstructor, have a possible, reasonable explanation.

We might wonder, for instance, whether the strongly phrased criticisms of the speech occur partly or principally because of the existence of Q2. Such criticism might begin with the use of "I," "aye," as a filler three times in the opening three lines. This may be seen as diluting the impact, manifestly contrasting with the concentration of Leontes' speech. (It probably doesn't help that today we don't spell "aye" as "I," so some readers may be momentarily distracted by the semantics here.) Leontes' speech, however, is intended to convey a racing, tortured mind, overwhelmed by suspicions; Hamlet's speech is supposed to convey the musings of a tortured young man (he is about nineteen in Q1) over whether to live or not. If he is handling a "bare bodkin," and touching one end—"I, there's the point"—the first "I" might be judged acceptable, for the speaker is implying that he is contemplating killing himself. The second line's usage might be justified as a dramatic pause, maintaining the audience's apprehension about the Prince's intentions. The deliberate repetition of "all" suggests the disillusionment and disappointment weighing down the Prince. In the third line, "I mary there it goes" is weak. On the other hand it separates the two sequences of "to sleepe, to dreame" and "that dreame of death," rather than letting them follow each other on the same line (and in the same ten syllables) without a break. That phrase, "I mary there it goes," permits the writer to create a pattern of two pairs of interlinked infinitives, each pair on a separate line, followed by a noun phrase—"that dreame of death"—which makes more concrete the Prince's thoughts, and keeps the focus on "sleep," "die," "dream." We might even wonder whether the speech starts slowly and then gains momentum to reflect how the Prince is aware of thinking the unthinkable, of the act of suicide.

A second criticism might be "that dream of death" is ambiguous in meaning, if that ambiguity is perceived as problematic. Does it mean the dream *about* death, or the dream *belonging to, following*, death? "Of" does not indicate which. "When we awake" suggests the latter might be what is intended; it is the concept of falling asleep, dying, and waking up again (which for example John Donne plays with in his sonnet, "Death be not proud"). Of course, the ambiguity may be deliberate.

There is undoubtedly non-standard grammar in "when we awake/ And borne...," for "awake" is an active verb, and "borne" is a passive—we are borne— but lacks its auxiliary verb, "are." In terms of the grammar "when we awake,/ We're borne..." would be much better. It would give that part of the sentence (from "No, to sleepe" to "the accursed damn'd") a subject, which is in the line above at present. "We're" would also provide in "'re" the missing auxiliary verb. The non-standard grammar may require us to look twice to recover the sense, but it is exaggerating to call it the "complete collapse of ... syntax."

We might be critical of "this," in "But for this, the ioyfull hope of this." It is a rather vague demonstrative pronoun which bundles together death being a sleep, a dream, followed by an awakening, where the "happy smile." Here singular "this" means plural "these." The same occurs with "who would this indure." Now "this" refers to the "calamities" which have just been listed, and

9. Corpses, Stage Directions and Other Anomalies   123

which are wide-ranging as we would expect. Idiomatically it would be unusual to find "these," although "these things" would have been acceptable.

Another point would relate to the line beginning "From whence no passenger euer retur'nd," a subordinate clause which *follows* "the vndiscouered country" in Q2. But does the clause refer back to "death," or that "dreame of death?" "Death" is a little distant—one and a half lines previously—yet this speech represents a young man thinking through one of the most profound questions we can pose. His ideas may well ebb and flow, and Shakespeare may present him returning to a half thought through line. Grammatically too there is another issue; in Q1, if the subordinate clause had followed "the vndiscouered country" (as in Q2), then the next phrase, "at whose sight," is separated from the noun it refers to, and "sight" would now refer to "the passenger" ("The vndiscouered country from whence/ No passenger euer retur'nd, at whose sight..."). In other words, Q1's line/word order is logical, not garbled or incoherent here, even though the line or clause order is different in Q2.

The agentive phrase "by the right rich," immediately followed by "the rich curssed" may appear clumsy. The line may have eleven syllables, and perhaps a surplus "right." It might be an idiom familiar to the audience, "curssed" could, of course, be accented to provide that extra syllable, "cursèd," and it might be that in speech "of the" would be elided ("o'th"). The line is irregular. On the other hand it has three stressed syllables in each patterned half line, which gives a distinctive rhythm. Elsewhere such a change in rhythm might gain praise, for a long soliloquy benefits from variation:

— ᴜ ᴜ — — ᴜ — — ᴜ ᴜ —
Scorned by the **right rich**, the **rich curssed** of the **poore**.

The remainder of the speech offers a coherent argument, though some would argue for an indefinite article before "thousand." The relative pronoun "which," beginning "Which pusles the braine" is perhaps better today with a different pronoun "That pusles the braine" ("that" would also avoid the repetition of "which"), but it is comprehensible.

The vigorous critic despairs over this speech. It does lack the power of the emotional impact, some of the most memorable imagery (where are those "slings and arrows of outrageous fortune?"), the more controlled pace and the wiser thought of Q2. It still conveys the sense of a melancholic debating with himself whether to live or die, considering the ills of the world, the temptation of "his full *Quietus,*" but rejecting that. And "Quietus" is correctly spelled in Q1. Those claiming memorial reconstruction can point out the speech's shreds and patches, but it has also the skeleton of Q2's speech, and rhythms that surprise and delight. It has two missing auxiliary verbs ("And [are] borne," and "Who'd beare.../ [be] Scorned..."), and a missing subject, but that is about as far as its collapsed syntax goes. We might ask whether a Shakespeare in his early twenties could have written that, and revised it and produced Q2's "To be" speech in his mid– to late thirties, some fifteen years later. We might ask when Shakespeare's "creative prime" actually was. (We might even ask what state a script would be in after several years with a theatre company, if Q1 was printed from a script from *c.* 1589.) The possibility that the speech is not completely remembered cannot be eliminated, but likewise the possibility that it is the skeleton of Q2's soliloquy cannot be eliminated either.

"A Moral Agenda"

Maguire's methodical study of the characteristics of alleged memorial reconstructions permits her to comment on some additional features that might be typical of a "reporter." One suggestion she makes is that there is apparently a "moral agenda" in Q1, the implication being that this is unusual in Shakespeare.[14] An example of a line she identifies as indicating a "moral agenda" is the second of the two below:

> *King*: My wordes fly vp, my sinnes remaine below.
> No king on earth is safe, if Gods his foe [Sig. G1v.39–40].

Is this second line particularly "moral," or unusually moral, for Shakespeare? It slips neatly into the position of the second line of a rhyming couplet that rounds off the King's insincere "prayer." It contains a two part contrast just as the first line does, so a degree of linguistic patterning is sustained across the couplet. It explains why the King prayed (effectively, as an insurance precaution), and it foreshadows the death the audience is expecting and willing to fall upon him. It may even glance sideways at the divine right of kings. It is about as "moral" as "Uneasy lies the head that wears the crown" (*2 Henry IV*, III.i.31)—not outstandingly or didactically so. Or as sonnet 94, which begins "They that have power to hurt and will do none," and concludes "Lilies that fester smell far worse than weeds." Or even as Q2's "Words without thoughts never to heaven go" (III.iii.97–8). If Q1's line conveys a "moral agenda" it is not really different from other occasional overtly "moral" lines in Shakespeare.

"Fluctuating Correlation"

A sixth and final aspect for consideration in this chapter relates to a recent study on the so-called "bad" quartos (*Hamlet, Henry V, Romeo and Juliet, Merry Wives, Contention*, and *Richard Duke of York*). The analysis is both recent (1994) and thorough. It gives the number of lines which, bar spelling, correspond between the Q1 and Q2/F1 *Hamlet*s, and the number of lines where more than half the words correspond. These are then separated into lines spoken by a character, and overheard by a character (on the logical assumption that an actor will know his own role best, but will also be familiar with the roles of characters on stage with him). This confirms firstly that the four characters whose lines match most closely are Marcellus, Voltemar/Voltemand, Lucianus and the Prologue,[15] and secondly that when these characters are on stage the number of Q1 and Q2/F1 lines which match is higher than when the four characters are off stage. These contrasting levels of correspondence the writer calls a "fluctuating correlation." Tables are presented demonstrating this for *Hamlet*, and for different roles in the five other "bad" quartos.[16] The argument is twofold: that there is an "unmistakable pattern of fluctuating correlation," and that the fluctuating correlation is the "strongest" of clues pointing to memorial reconstruction.[17]

The most striking correspondence is found in Voltemar and Voltemand's speech in scene 7 and act II scene ii, when he reports to the King on the outcome of his ambassadorial visit to the King of Norway. Their speeches of twenty-one lines are almost identical; it is unquestionably the part of the play where the two quartos are closest for longest. Spelling, punctuation, italicization and morphology, not fully standardized at the time, account for all bar two differences, the figure—"three thousand" (Q1), or "threescore thousand" (Q2)—and a modal verb—"would" (Q1) or "might" (Q2). The correspondence of those twenty-one lines *en bloc* is exceptional in the two quartos, which makes it all the more odd that Q2's Voltemand apparently doesn't remember his name correctly.

Several questions can and should be posed. Q1 has a closer correspondence with Q2 in some lines and scenes than in others, but does that correspondence prove the *cause* is memorial reconstruction? Are there other possible explanations? For example, if Q1 is a first draft it could be that Shakespeare was satisfied with those characters and parts of the play and simply made minimal revisions to the characters and their lines in comparison with the changes he made elsewhere.

Secondly, the theory of memorial reconstruction depends on an actor/reporter(s) who is only present in 30 percent of Q2's scenes. As we have noted, there isn't much discussion about how the rest of the play, with its lower number of corresponding lines, is reconstructed. (Supers or extras and listening backstage are too vague to prove or disprove, unless one really believes that "a little listening at the stage-door after his exit would explain everything."[18]) This problem is linked to another, why in a couple of other scenes—that is, ones in which the alleged memorial reconstructors did *not* appear—a reasonable number of lines still match.

One response to the awkwardness of the differing levels of correspondence has been that perhaps some form of abridgement has taken place, or was also carried out in the reconstruction.[19] This is a reasonable speculation, bearing in mind the substantial differences between Q1 and Q2, the length of Q2, and the perhaps "two hours traffic" length of play upon the Elizabethan stage. The sequence of texts would then be Q2 > *abridgement/adaptation* > Q1 (with F1 possibly intervening too). Since the intermediate, italicized text is not extant, the degree of change it includes is unknown, but that change might—or might not—have been so drastic that the extant Q1 actually reflects the hypothetical abridgement more closely than Q2. This possibility cannot be ignored. However, the absence of any such text renders this speculation impossible to prove or disprove. In the analytical study under discussion, abridgement before the creation of Q1 is seen as unlikely, with there also being an expectation that "the roles of the reporters [would] reflect the same cuts as are evident in the rest of the play," with these reporters' lines being "disproportionately preserved."[20] We must however, be wary of "cuts," since the word implies a reduction from Q2; it is another biased word, connoting an assumed Q2 > Q1 sequence, while the sequence itself is still a hypothesis.

"Abridgement" is problematic for another reason. It denotes a reduction in length, implicitly without sacrificing meaning or significance.[21] Marcellus has one function in being part of the exposition, another in contributing to the atmosphere, another as being a witness to the Ghost, and at least one more as a foil to Horatio in scene 1. Arguably all these functions are important, and are achieved economically and effectively in Q1 and in Q2. A judicious abridger—or reviser—will be evaluating not so much a proportional excision as an appropriate one, one which does not significantly mar the whole. For example, an abridgement was made in the 2009 *Hamlet* with Jude Law as Hamlet, where the *whole* of the dumb show was omitted, not a proportion of it. This abridgement did not mar the meaning for the audience. (Possibly few of the audience would know of the scholarly discussion about whether the King sees this re-enactment of his alleged murder of his brother.) A reduction of 45 percent—the reduction of Q2 to Q1's length—is very unlikely to have been achieved through "proportionality."[22]

The correspondence of certain lines exists. But the correspondence itself is not proof that Q1 *Hamlet* must be memorially reconstructed. In mathematics "correlation" is normally used to indicate the dependence of one item upon another or the relationship of one item to another. In the context of Q1 "correlation" appears to be used to support the proposed causal relationship, the proposed dependence of Q1 on Q2. But "correlation" in the context of the *Hamlet* quartos really means "correspondence." The fact that some lines do match does not show the *cause* of that matching. The higher level of correspondence in lines when Marcellus, Voltemar and Lucianus are present may simply signify a coincidence, or instead a pattern in Shakespeare's revision. "Fluctuating correlation" and memorial reconstruction offer a limited and questionable explanation for a text which averages just over 50 percent accuracy when the hypothetical reconstructor(s) is on stage, which is for less than 25 percent of the whole text.

Chapters six to nine have reviewed the major arguments for memorial reconstruction, remembering to consider whether the various features discussed might have an alternative explanation. A series of at least ten further, significant facts emerge, to add to those at the end of the Introduction, and those in Part One.

These significant pieces of evidence start with Q1's printing, which shows no signs of having been "pirated" in any way. Then there is no contemporary evidence for memorial reconstruction in England, only occasional suspicions. While this may not disturb every scholar, it must be a concern. The analogy of the memorial reconstruction of *The School for Scandal* nearly 200 years after the alleged memorial reconstruction of *Hamlet* does not support Q1 as a memorial reconstruction. Instead it undermines it. The contrast in motive, potential memorial reconstructors, and the numbers of lines they knew and scenes they performed in bear little resemblance to what is suggested for Q1 *Hamlet*. Next, we can hardly find it surprising that some of Q1's words and phrases also occur in other Shakespearean plays. It is a fact that Shakespeare used quite a few words more than once. Duthie's selective quotations from *The Spanish Tragedy* and his omission of the French source in the only significant parallel between *The Spanish Tragedy* and Q1 *Hamlet* distinctly weaken his argument. Duthie's "objectionable" pronouns in the one scene that is exclusive to Q1 (and hence exclusive to the alleged actor/reporter[s]) simply demonstrate the skills of the playwright.

This chapter shows that the "corpse" of Q1 may have been blasted with rhetoric, but that stage directions, insertions of "O," and aural errors are not limited to alleged memorial reconstructions. It shows that while Q1's "To be" speech is not Q2's, it has two non-standard items of grammar, not a "complete collapse of sense and syntax." The hint of a moral agenda can be matched elsewhere in Shakespeare. The correspondence of lines in the quartos, what has been called their "fluctuating correlation," does not prove that the speakers of those lines were "reporters." "Correlation" is not the same as "cause." The correspondence can also be explained by Shakespeare selectively revising and expanding the play.

Effectively, supporters of memorial reconstruction pose the question: "In which Q1 scenes do the lines spoken and overheard by a particular character most closely match and therefore show memorial reconstruction?" Their answer is scenes 1, 2, 4, 5, and parts of 7 and 9. An alternative question is: "Which scenes does Shakespeare revise least?" The answer is principally scenes 1, 2, 4, 5, and very small parts of 7 and 9. Only one question can be correct.

This chapter has begun to touch upon another explanation for the relationship of the quartos. Abridgement is rarely discussed today, but all the same it should not be dismissed without examination.

10. Memorial Reconstruction— or Abridgement?

It is hardly surprising that abridgement features as a possible explanation for some of the differences between the two quartos when their lengths differ so much. There is also plenty of evidence that contemporary texts were abridged or cut. Those who favor abridgement as the primary reason for the differences in Q1 and Q2 tend first to argue against MR, next to argue for the value of Q1, and then proceed to explain why they think Q1 is mainly the result of abridgement. Unfortunately, exactly where in the processes of composition of Q1 and Q2 (and F1) this proposed abridgement took place is not a matter of agreement. And as we have only the three surviving *Hamlet* texts to examine, and none of the hypothesized theatrical adaptations, it is rather difficult to prove or disprove any of the scholars' proposals.

Evidence of Abridgement

We can, however, start with confidence to consider abridgement, for there are several explicit statements testifying to the practice in Elizabethan and Jacobean times. Abridgement might be the reason for the declaration on the title page of, for example, the 1600 quarto of Ben Jonson's *Every Man Out of His Humour*: "As it was first composed by the Author B.I. Containing more than hath been Publickely Spoken or Acted."[1] This suggests that the increase in contents is explained by the abridgement of the original text rather than by Jonson's revisions before publication. A clearer indication of abridgement comes in the 1623 quarto of John Webster's *Duchess of Malfi*. This proclaims unambiguously on its title page: "As it was Presented privately, at the Black-Friers.... The perfect and exact Coppy, with diuerse *things Printed, that the length of the Play would* not beare in the Presentment."[2] It appears *The Duchess of Malfi* had been cut for performance. Later, in 1647, Beaumont and Fletcher's

F1 begins with a note from "The Stationer [Humphrey Moseley] to the Reader," claiming that:

> here are no omissions ... when these comedies and Tragedies were presented on the stage the Actours omitted some scenes and passages with the author's consent as occasion led them: and when private friends desired a copy they then, and justly too, transcribed what they acted. But now you have both all that was then Acted, and all that was not, even the perfect full originals without the least mutilation.³

This too indicates the existence of abridgement. Nor was the sole purpose of abridgement to shorten the texts, if we can believe Ben Jonson's characters in *Bartholomew Fair* (published 1614). Here Jonson mocks the less intelligent of his potential audience, effectively acknowledging that texts may be simplified. In act V Master Bartholomew Cokes peers into the basket of puppets "Master Lanterne" holds. Cokes asks, "do you play it according to the printed booke?" Lanterne, mouthpiece for each of his puppets, announces that he does it:

> Lanterne. A better way, Sir, that is too learned and poeticall for our audience; what doe they know what *Hellespont* is? Guilty of true loues blood? or what *Abidos* is? Or the other *Sestos* hight?

Consequently Lanterne has taken "a little paines to reduce it to a more familiar strain for our people," and "made it a little easie and *moderne* for the times" (V.iii.109–117).⁴

Even the verb "abridge" occurs in a pertinent context. In Webster's *Induction* to John Marston's *Malcontent* (published 1604). Sly asks, "What are your additions?" and Burbage answers:

> Burbage. Sooth, not greatly needful; only as your sallets to your great feats, to entertain a little more time, and to abridge the not-received custom of music in our theatre.⁵

Shakespeare is one of several writers who hint at the typical performance time of a play. He refers to the "two hours traffic of our stage" (*Romeo and Juliet*: Chorus, line 12), which might suggest an average performance time. Shakespeare of course could hardly have referred to "the two and a half hours and somewhat more traffic of our stage"; the phrasing is wordy, clumsy, and does not scan, and Shakespeare always had regard for the ear. Hence his desire for a poetic line may have resulted in the timing mentioned in *Romeo and Juliet*. Jonson, however, in *Bartholomew Fair*, drew up articles of agreement that theatre personnel and "the said *Spectators* and *Hearers* ... doe severally covenant and agree to remain in the places their money, or friends have put them in, with patience, for the space of two houres and one half, and somewhat more," implying that even two hours and a half might be exceeded.[6] We are unlikely to be surprised by this, since Ben Jonson's longer than usual plays (for instance *Every Man Out of His Humour* was 4452 lines[7]) weren't included in Hart's calculations for Jacobethan plays. But two and a half hours wasn't the limit either. Urkowitz reports that "the front matter of the 1647 Beaumont and Fletcher Folio speaks of 'the three howers spectacle' offered by a play; again, in the play house 'few here repent/ Three hours of pretious time, or money spent.'"[8]

Hamlet itself refers to cutting or abridging a text for performance. In act II scene ii lines 436–7 Polonius declares of one Player's speech, "This is too long." Hamlet responds with "It shall to the barber's with your beard." The two lines are virtually identical in Q1, Q2 and F1. Hamlet's advice to the Players is not to adlib ("let not your Clowne speake/ More than is set downe" [Q1, sig. F2r.26–7]). Yet Hamlet also wishes to "insert" "[s]ome dozen or sixteene lines" (Q1, sig. E4v.26) in a play he requests the Players to perform. These make it certain that Shakespeare at least knew about cuts and additions.

The plausibility of abridgement as the explanation behind Q1 seems to be supported by Hart's studies on play lengths in *Shakespeare and the Homilies*. Here Hart shows that average play lengths in the 1594–1616 period were 2490 lines.[9] This average includes Shakespeare's plays, but excludes Ben Jonson's, which can be exceptionally long. It means that Hart's average isn't an average for all plays. On the other hand, a 2490 lines average does fit in well with the probable start time of two o'clock in the afternoon for performances that would be "don betwene fower and fiue" as a letter by Henry Lord Hunsdon stated in 1594.[10] Q1 at 2221 lines is an appropriate length for an afternoon performance.

However, it seems peculiar that Q1 *Hamlet*, if it is an abridgement of Q2, is reduced to well below that average of 2490 lines. Yet there are some plays shorter than 2490 with passages still marked for excision. *John a Kent and John a Cumber* began with 1672 lines and was reduced to 1638, and *Edmund Ironside* dropped 196 lines to 1865. Other plays which were abridged do not necessarily drop below that 2490 average. So *Charlemagne* loses a mere five of its 2656 lines, and *The Honest Man's Fortune* loses 40 lines from 2742.[11] Hart prints a table of sixteen plays where twelve have abridgements of anything from five to 467 lines. There is no immediate pattern to the extent of the abridgements (it could of course be due to the subjective judgment of the abridger), in that there is no obvious proportionality to cutting, no obvious attempt to reduce plays to a particular length. And not one play in Hart's list is cut to anywhere near the extent that Q1 must have been if it is an abridgement of Q2. A five line cut from 2656 for *Charlemagne* is a 0.18 percent cut and the smallest Hart lists. 467 lines cut from 2689 in *Sir Thomas More*, the largest cut in Hart's list, is a 17 percent cut. But 1835 cut from Q2 *Hamlet*'s 4056 is a 45 percent cut, nearly three times greater. The dramatic difference in percentages for the two quartos does not fit in straightforwardly with Hart's findings. It suggests that more than mere abridgement accounts for Q1's relative brevity, *if* abridgement is the reason. And the shortness of Q1's text in comparison with Q2's really does need explanation.

This brings us to how a range of scholars have proposed abridgement as part of the process of composition between Q2 and Q1. Their proposals contrast. For example, early in the twentieth century Greg considers that Q1 represents an abridgement of an intermediate version which was an adaptation of Q2. Wilson (1918) proposes that there was an early *Hamlet* text (the *Ur-Hamlet*), partly revised by Shakespeare (which would presumably explain the presence of the lines shared by Q1 and Q2); that text was then abridged for the purpose of "provincial use."[12] It contrasts dramatically with, for example, Hart's view: "I cannot reconcile what they [Shakespeare's contemporaries] tell of him with painstaking revision of another man's work."[13] Instead Hart thinks that "bad" quartos were "corrupt abridgements of acting versions,"[14] the *Hamlet* acting version deriving from Q2. In the late twentieth century Irace also sees abridgement as an intermediate stage, when she discusses the apparent evidence of a deliberate theatrical abridgement in the context of her detailed argument for the MR of Q1.[15] Shapiro considers abridgement necessary for performance not just for "provincial use" but for London as well. He writes that when Shakespeare was done with the "new draft" (F1?) he "turned it over to his fellow players; a significant abridgement would still be necessary before it could be performed at the Globe."[16] Shapiro's focus is not upon the relationship of the *Hamlet*s, so it is understandable (but nevertheless disappointing) that he does not expand a little on why he states this.

Arguing for Abridgement and Q1

In between the early twentieth century measurements of Hart and the early twenty-first century ideas of Shapiro come three particular studies which see abridgement as the principal cause for the difference in the lengths of Q1 and Q2. Robert Burkhart looks at the so-called "bad" quartos in *Shakespeare's Bad Quartos: Deliberate Abridgements Designed for Performance by a Reduced Cast*. William Bracy concentrates primarily but not exclusively on *Merry Wives* in *The Merry Wives of Windsor. The History and Transmission of Shakespeare's Text*. Albert B. Weiner is the author of the third of these, and writes at length upon Q1 *Hamlet* in his introduction to his 1962 edition of Q1 *Hamlet*.[17]

Like those who believe in MR, these scholars place Q2 as the anterior text, with Q1 ultimately deriving from it. They also share the belief that a shorter text than Q2 would have been necessary for touring. However, they diverge considerably from those believing in MR when it comes to the value of Q1. The group believing in abridgement sees Q1 as a theatrically effective text while the second group, believing in MR, tends to regard Q1 as "corrupt." The promoters of abridgement have support in their evaluation of Q1 from for instance Madeleine Doran, who finds the variant quartos too good dramatically to have been pirated and to be seen as "garbled."[18] (It is true that the 1881 performance viewed by William Poel gained only faint praise: "The performance was certainly up to the average of amateur performance of a high class," and "on the whole the company may be congratulated on a satisfactory performance of an entirely untried and very difficult play..."[19]). Some in the acting fraternity also view Q1 in a positive light as the beginning of Chapter 9 shows. Hardin Craig too has commented upon Q1 as a sound performance script; he had watched the Ben Greet Company play Q1, based on Frank Hubbard's text, and the performance was "not lacking in dramatic interest."[20] Craig's view is complemented by Peter Guinness' opinions as an actor in Q1 in 1983, about Q1 being a "*working* text," one with "an energy and edge that the Folio in all its refinement, particularly its poetic refinement, doesn't have."[21]

Burkhart, Bracy and Weiner argue against MR partly because as the most widespread account of Q1 *Hamlet* it must be overturned before an alternative view can gain any momentum, and partly because they wish to reclaim some of the aspects given as "evidence" for MR as "evidence" of abridgement instead. Burkhart argues that bit parts, or minor characters, may be cut in variant quartos, major characters may have their roles reduced, and many elaborate and rhetorical speeches are shorter or a paraphrase. There may also be precision in noting properties.[22] All these, he suggests, are deliberate and consistent parts of an abridgement process.[23] Consistency militates against (memorial) reporting, he feels.[24] We might, however, question his assumption of a Q2 > Q1 sequence (including any intermediate acting versions). Once again we need to drag out the antonyms; we need to ask whether bit parts or minor roles have instead been *added* in Q2; if major characters have had their roles *expanded*; whether speeches have become longer with *additional* elaboration and rhetorical flourishes, and whether descriptions of properties have been *changed*. These are all possibilities and could be explained by a first draft and revision scenario.

Bracy also identifies similar characteristics in his proposal that *Merry Wives* Q1 was an abridgement of its F1 version. His examples, in exploring one play, are often detailed, and exemplified. He concludes that "excursions into the arid realms of philosophy, sage reflections on life, conduct and character, over-much moralising, unnecessary displays of learning and classical allusions ... may be cut because they are inessential to the action."[25] This description could loosely be applied to the absence of Hamlet's soliloquy "How all occasions..." (IV.iv), from Q1. Once again, while such "excursions" might be "cut," we should also ask whether a mature Shakespeare might not desire to add such flourishes to his play in the process of revision. We might also remember Erne's suggestion that Q2 is a literary text, intended for the study rather than the stage. A play with elements of "philosophy" and "displays of learning and classical allusions" might be better appreciated in the study rather than upon the stage. After all, many of those who prefer Q2 to Q1 are literary scholars rather than stage practitioners.

It is Weiner who focuses specifically upon the *Hamlet* quartos in his discussion of abridgement. He challenges the terms "anticipations" and "recollections" which proponents of memorial reconstruction use, for both depend on whether one starts from the belief or assumption that a word did occur, or should have occurred, earlier or later.[26] He draws attention to the pointing in Corambis' speech when he advises Leartes, a feature likely to be copied from a written text, for "Surely the reporter never *heard* Corambis' punctuation."[27] Certain changes in the text Weiner sees as thoughtful, such as the cut to the act IV scene iv with Fortinbrasse. On tour with perhaps ten actors, the players might find it hard to create an "army" after a series of scenes where several actors are on stage, and Weiner sees that a cut (this "cut" is a feature of F1 too) eliminates the problem.[28]

Problems with the Abridgement Hypothesis

Weiner's approach has occasional problematic aspects, such as his discussion of the names of Corambis/Polonius and Reynaldo/Montano. "It seems to me," Weiner writes, "that Shakespeare wrote at least two versions of *Hamlet*."[29] Even though that clause is selectively quoted and decontextualised, it is disconcerting. Weiner has introduced the prospect of another *Hamlet*, because it is "debatable whether Q1 is based upon an earlier or later version than Q2."[30] And he undermines his own argument in the act of abridgement being carried out upon Shakespeare's "foul papers"[31] when he notes that Ofelia's songs are not pointed in Q1,[32] even though he has previously drawn attention to how Corambis' speech *is* punctuated as if copied. Weiner's two examples are not consistent.

There are over twenty features which have been interpreted as indicative of abridgement. If there were a certainty that abridgement had occurred, they might not be disputed, despite inconsistencies. But the interpretation of many of those features is problematic, for they may be used to support any of the explanations for the quartos' relationship. There *is* a "streamlining of action," or at least there is "streamlined action," when Ofelia "tests" Hamlet just after Corambis' suggestion, but this is also one respect in which Q1 is closer than Q2 to the French source, and can therefore also indicate a Q1 > Q2 sequence. The same example is also an instance of a "dislocation of scene," or a "shifting of scene," or a "rearrangement of scene." In reality, it is not agreed at present which way the alleged "dislocation" occurred, though the French source is an impartial and logical way of determining this. There are indeed "shorter speeches," such as the King's at the beginning of Q1's second scene, which "hastens the presentation of a dramatic situation" and brings the important character of Hamlet to the fore "more rapidly."[33] It may be, however, that Q2 expands the speech and the role and character of the King, in the process naming him as well. There *is* a smaller cast (Q1 lacks a Norwegian Captain, a Sailor and a Messenger), but it is uncertain whether this is a "reduction" or "elimination" since Shakespeare might instead have expanded the cast slightly in Q2. It could be argued that Marcellus' and Voltemand's speeches are examples of the "careful transference of whole lines from one text [Q2] to another [Q1]," though these might also be lines a revising playwright chose to transfer with little alteration from Q1 to Q2. There are also less careful "transferences," where the playwright might have transferred the gist of the speech but revised its phrasing as he did so. Hamlet's "To be or not to be" speech does have markedly "less imagery" in Q1 than in Q2, though again it may be that Q2 expands upon the character, his philosophy and his poetic voice. It is a speech which is indeed in a "condensed" or at least shorter form in Q1, though whether it was "condensed" from Q2 is a different matter. The vocabulary used in these discussions frequently connotes the writer's view rather than being impartial (like "variant" or "difference"), and examinations of the arguments show that virtually every supposed characteristic of abridgement—or indeed of memorial reconstruction—is capable of more than one interpretation.

Evaluating the proposal that that abridgement is a part or the principal part of the process giving us Q1 is therefore highly problematic. And there are several points which do not indicate that either MR or abridgement are part of that process. The most obvious of these is probably the extent of the cuts. Q1 *Hamlet* is a dramatic 45 percent shorter than Q2. It is not just that percentage, however. Q1 shares 456 lines with Q2; that is, 456 of Q2's lines are present in Q1. This can be expressed as 456 of Q2's 4056 lines; that is, about 11 percent of Q2's lines are present in Q1.

An alternative way of looking at this is that 89 percent of Q2's lines are excised or altered in some way in the proposed abridging of Q2. Even with the possibility of an intermediate adaptation for the stage that is a very substantial level of cuts and changes. Rewriting is a more accurate description.³⁴ It is vastly in excess of the highest number of cut lines Hart reports upon, 17 percent (467 from *Sir Thomas More*'s 2689 lines³⁵). Weiner suggests that the abridgement was carried out on foul papers of *Hamlet*, and was upon a text which was difficult for the compositor to read, but the difference in the texts is still huge. And if some cut texts remained over that average 2490 lines (*The Honest Man's Fortune*, 2702 lines or 1 *Richard II* [sic] at 2830³⁶) it is difficult to understand why Q2 would have been cut to noticeably below that 2490 level. The dramatic level of change would confirm the suggestion of, for example, Hart and Greg that abridgement alone could not account for the difference between Q1 and Q2 (and possibly F1). Wherever the argument places the abridgement process, for example Q2 > abridgement > memorial reconstruction producing Q1, or Q2 > acting version > abridgement producing Q1, even with the inclusion of F1, it would appear that if abridgement is a contributory factor to the form of Q1, it cannot be the sole explanation.

A second significant objection to abridgement occurs when we contrast specific passages in Q1 and Q2. Let us consider, for instance, the opening lines of Q2:

Q2
>   *Barnardo.* Whose there?
>   *Francisco.* Nay answer me. Stand and unfold yourself.
>   *Barnardo.* Long live the King.
>   *Francisco.* Barnardo?
>   *Barnardo.* He.
>   *Francisco.* You come most carefully upon your hour.

Q1 uses three lines to convey similar information:

Q1
>   1.   Stand: who is that?
>   2.   Tis I.
>   1.   O you come most carefully upon your watch.

Q2 is dense with information. The script gives readers/actors the names (why would they be forgotten or cut in Q1?), and the spoken text gives the audience the name of one of them, Barnardo. The brevity of the question, omitting the more predictable "Stand," hints at urgency. This is rapidly confirmed when we realize that the first guard to speak is *not* the one on duty, for it is the second challenger ("*Francisco.* Nay answere me. Stand and vnfolde your selfe.") who is taking the watch, and ready for his shift to end. Both are on edge. We see that in Barnardo's response, which does not give his name but a response which says first and foremost that he is loyal to the King. In other words, it is a cautious reply. It is left to Francisco to identify Barnardo to the audience, perhaps showing that Francisco knows Barnardo's voice well enough, or that Barnardo has advanced sufficiently far forward to be recognized; actors have two options here. The atmosphere in Q2 is darker, more suspicious, less predictable, gives us one name, and tells us that these are the King's guards.

Q1 is noticeably different. Every line is changed, even though "hour" and "watch" are not dissimilar. It gives no names. It does not have the challenge that each sentinel offers, only one of them. It begins what we would now probably see as a clichéd imperative and question, which does not necessarily convey any anxiety upon the part of the speaker, just a routine exchange. The second sentinel does not give us his name, though we do realize that "1" must recognize "2," since the response with "you" is instant, and we then learn that this is the time when the two guards change shift.

The number of changes between the two texts in a mere three to five lines is surprisingly large. Q1 is functional, arguably just as a MR or abridgement or first draft might be. A number of names do change between the quartos, but if Q1 was a MR or abridgement, why are the names forgotten or omitted? And if an abridger wanted to reduce the number of lines to three (as Q1 has) why didn't he just score (~~score~~) through a few lines (as below) and swap a couple of names (as underlined below) around?

~~Barnardo.~~ *Fran.*	Who's there?	
~~Francisco.~~	~~Nay, answer me. Stand and unfold yourself.~~	
~~Barnardo.~~	~~Long live the King.~~	
~~Francisco~~. *Barn.*	Barnardo?~~.~~	
~~Barnardo.~~	~~He.~~	
Francisco.	You come most carefully upon your hour.	

If Q1 was a first draft it is easier to understand why names and atmosphere are *added* to Q2, and why both guards are apprehensive, and what Shakespeare has achieved *if* he revised it. It is less logical to see how and why the changes occur with a Q2 > Q1 sequence.

There are many sets of lines which raise similar questions. Another example might be the opening of scene 14 and act IV scene vi. The Q2 scene could quite easily have been edited to convey the information that Hamlet was back in Denmark without needing to "add" the Queen, which is what we must believe happened if Q2 is the anterior text. Q2 opens with:

Enter Horatio and others.

Horatio.	What are they that would speak with me?
Gentleman.	Sea-faring men, sir. They say they have letters for you.
Horatio.	Let them come in.
	I do not know from what part of the world I should be greeted if not from Lord Hamlet.

Enter Sailors.

Sailor.	God bless you, sir.
Horatio.	Let Him bless thee too.
Sailor.	'A shall, sir, an please Him. There's a letter for you sir—it came from th'ambassador that was bound for England—if your name be Horatio, as I am let to know it is [IV.vi.1–12].

It could have been edited to open as follows (lines "cut" are scored through (~~through~~), and a couple of minor adjustments are added and underlined):

Enter Horatio and another.

Horatio.	What are ~~they~~ you that would speak with me?
Gentleman.	~~Sea-faring men,~~ A sailor, sir. ~~They say they~~ I have letters for you.
Horatio.	~~Let them come in.~~ I do not know from what part of the world I should be greeted if not from Lord Hamlet.

~~Enter Sailors.~~

~~Sailor.~~	~~God bless you, sir.~~
~~Horatio.~~	~~Let Him bless thee too.~~
~~Sailor.~~ Gent.	'~~A shall, sir, an please Him.~~ There's ~~a~~ letter ~~for you~~ sir—it came from th'ambassador that was bound for England—if your name be Horatio, as I am let to know it is [IV.vi.1–12].

If abridgement was the primary aim this would function to reduce the number of speakers from five (Horatio and others/Gentleman, Sailors) to two (Horatio, Gentleman/Sailor), and reduce the number of words in this particular extract to 70 percent of Q2's. The level of effort is minimal, and the scene begins with the essence of what Q2 says. But that isn't anything like what we find in Q1. If the difference is MR then the actor/reporter must have forgotten the scene and had to invent one, but why would an abridger create a quite different scene?

We can look at this differently. Superficially, scene 14 between Horatio and the Queen in Q1 appears to function chiefly to inform the audience of the fact and method of Hamlet's return, and to create anticipation of what this much-wronged Prince might do. In Q1 two characters are required, which is indeed fewer than in Q2, which must require in total at least three speakers plus two non-speaking actors. Q1 is therefore undoubtedly more efficient in terms of cast. Considering the scene from this angle alone renders abridgement quite reasonable. But the method of delivering the information is also different. Q2 lets the audience see how and when Horatio receives the information, and hear Hamlet's own account of his escape from his escorts. In contrast (the proposed abridged) Q1 presents a Horatio who is already acquainted with Hamlet's return and who conveys this to the Queen. However, the involvement of the Queen in Q1 but not in Q2 is consistent with Q1 deriving more immediately from *Les Histoires Tragiques* than Q2 does, as Chapter 5 shows. In the context of abridgement the issue is whether it was impossible to cut Q2's scene without introducing the Queen. It is actually quite easy to assume the role of an abridger and quickly change the opening of the scene to just two characters, as the above "abridgement" shows.

While the suggested abridgement is obviously not perfect, it leads straightforwardly into the rest of the Q2 scene, having reduced the number of actors to two, as in Q1, and having cut three lines. This suggests it was not necessary for an abridger to change the scene so dramatically. If an abridger deliberately changed this it would suggest he rejected, or missed, how Q2's Hamlet is developed, for Q2 presents a Hamlet more isolated than in Q1, and likely to evoke more sympathy than in Q1. Q2 prepares the audience for Hamlet's increasing use of Horatio as a confidant in act V, and for Hamlet's last instruction to Horatio, "To tell my story" (V.ii.333).

Yet, if abridgement or memorial reconstruction is to be believed, the composer of the Q2 > Q1 variant is sufficiently subtle to have begun to change the relationship between Hamlet and the Queen in the "bedchamber" scene, and is now quietly continuing that change in another scene which he is composing from scratch. Such changes indicate a sophisticated abridger or memorial reconstructor. They are the kind of alteration we would expect of an author, not of an "editor" (be he abridger or reconstructor). Moreover, that abridger/memorial reconstructor coincidentally matches how in the source the Queen asks Prince Amleth to be careful, and tucks a few lines into Q1's scene 14 which also have Q1's Queen desiring Prince Hamlet to be wary:

> *Queene.* ... bid him a while
> Be wary of his presence, lest that he
> Faile in that he goes about [Sig. H2v.19–21].

Perhaps scholars would suggest this maternal advice is just a natural touch. But it is present in *Les Histoires Tragiques* and Q1, and it is absent in Q2.

The scene has further differences. The account of Hamlet's escape in Q1 is vague, for he has simply been "set ashore" (sig. H2v.28). In Q2 the escape is more detailed; his ship has been boarded by pirates, who take him alone as prisoner. Why might that version be ditched by the alleged abridger? It would have had a contemporary resonance, since English sailors had been troubled by Danish pirates in the Øresund from 1588 onwards.

Q2 includes another aspect which Q1 lacks. In Q2 Horatio quotes from Hamlet's letter, which means that although Hamlet is offstage (for three scenes) while he is supposedly in England, the audience "hears" his voice; the protagonist is "present." And while Q1 informs the audience of Rossencraft and Gilderstone's fate, Q2 more dramatically withholds that information until the final scene. The audience is again required to wait, in true thriller style, for that detail in the dénouement. If this were an example of abridgement, Q2's manuscript might reasonably have been in front of the abridger. Why would the abridger, without the stimulus of the idea in front of him in IV.vi, relocate the deaths of Rossencraft and Gilderstone (from V.ii) in scene 14? This again merits discussion. It is again the kind of change which might be attributed to a reviser rather than to any kind of abridger/reporter.

It means that the two scenes as a whole have differences which appear to be much more extensive than need occur with abridging. There appear no satisfactory answers offered at present to why these changes occurred in the course of abridgement. To say they were a result of memorial reconstruction is little better, for then the composer would seem to have consulted *Les Histoires Tragiques* (or the putative *Ur-Hamlet*, some might suggest). That would only explain the Queen's expectation of Hamlet's return, and her warning. The more closely these scenes are examined the more difficult it is to suggest that the difference in them is explained by abridgement, or indeed by MR.

A third set of problems with abridgement are identical to those problems with MR, and have been explored in Part One. Neither MR nor abridgement sensibly accounts for why Q1 has more dated inflections and Q2 more modern ones. Nor do MR and abridgement account for the greater number of colloquial, orthographical features found in the sampling and comparisons in Chapter 1. Most significantly, neither MR nor abridgement can accommodate why Q1, half recollected or substantially abridged, has almost double the density of verbal parallels with the French source, or the change in the "nunnery" scene, or the shift from the more intimate confidences between Prince and Queen to more distant in Q2 (and F1). All those distinct parallels to the external reference point, *Les Histoires Tragiques*, are straightforward if Q1 is permitted to be the prior text, the first sketch or first draft, and Q2 a revision. All those distinct parallels need to be credibly explained to sustain the MR or abridgement hypothesis.

And, of course, abridgement complicates the question of Hamlet's age. Why would an abridger make the Prince younger and bring the play back closer to the source, and render Hamlet that vulnerable near adult who has lost his father, who has watched his mother remarry "incestueusement" and who has seen his own "advancement" vanish, just as in the source?

Part One provides reproducible evidence which cumulatively points strongly to Q1 as the anterior text, evidence which is linguistic and source based. Part Two examines the principal arguments of those scholars who have

10. Memorial Reconstruction—or Abridgement?

sought to explain the distinctive differences between the two *Hamlet* quartos as primarily due to MR and/or abridgement. Scholars may like to think that the analogy of *The School for Scandal* MR generally supports the same method of MR for Q1, but the quantitative analysis seriously undermines that. Duthie and others might like to think that ten words and phrases with disputable parallels in *The Spanish Tragedy* suggest MR, but there are other reasons for those apparent parallels. Abridgement may initially seem a sensible explanation, but a 45 percent cut from Q2's length to Q1's accompanied by a drastic 89 percent of Q2's lines being omitted or changed does not suggest abridgement is the primary explanation. Some may not believe that Shakespeare revised, but the subtleties found in the texts suggest otherwise (and that Shakespeare revised Q2 into F1 is not generally disputed). We may choose to disregard Shakespeare's name on Q1's title page and the apparent legitimacy of its printing, but there is no hard evidence to doubt either of these. We can be amused by the descriptions of Q1 as a "mutilated corpse," and of its "To be" speech as a "farrago of nonsense," but perhaps we should be more suspicious of these rhetorical flourishes when practitioners see Q1 as the skeleton of Q2, as dynamic, and as having distinct energy.

Of course, both MR and abridgement hypotheses, in whatever form scholars suggest, depend upon the existence of an *Ur-Hamlet*, a *Hamlet* play preceding any *Hamlet* attributed to Shakespeare. Not all scholars believe such a play existed, and it is not known today, but many have been inclined to credit the speculation that there was a pre–Shakespearean *Hamlet*. And there is no doubt that a *Hamlet* play existed before the date at which Shakespeare is supposed to have written his Q2, *c.* 1600. Part Three therefore turns to the contemporary texts mentioning *Hamlet*, and how they too have been variously interpreted.

Part Three: Was There an Ur-Hamlet?

11. "Hamlets" and the Elizabethan Æsop

It is sometimes difficult to remember that the *Ur-Hamlet* is merely hypothetical. It does not exist in any known form today. It is not a concrete, extant text; it is simply the label given to the *Hamlet* of 1589 and the 1590s by those who believe that the sixteenth century *Hamlet* wasn't Shakespeare's. However, it is an integral part of the most widespread account of the relationship of the quartos, that Q1 is a memorial reconstruction. The hypothesis advocating the existence of an *Ur-Hamlet* begins with Edmond Malone, and is developed in the late nineteenth and early twentieth century. The peak of debate about it seems to occur in 1905 and 1906. The hypothesis persuades enough scholars for some to write about it as a certainty, sometimes even firmly attributing it to Thomas Kyd.

For example, Robert Miola, writing in 2000 about Shakespeare's reading, alludes to the *Ur-Hamlet* as the "lost revenge thriller,"[1] and in the nineteenth century Frederick Gard Fleay refers without qualification or doubt to "Kyd's *Hamlet*, the Corambis *Hamlet*."[2]

Whether there was an *Ur-Hamlet*, and whether it was by Kyd or someone else is critical for our understanding of the *Hamlet*s and to the relationship of the quartos. Consequently Part Three returns to Malone and his reasoning for the existence of a pre–Shakespearean *Hamlet*, and reviews the series of allusions to a *Hamlet* prior to the publication of the quartos. For not only is *Hamlet* unique in existing in three versions, but it is also a play which has a relatively high number of contemporary references to it.

This chapter focuses upon a crucial text, Nashe's prefatory *Epistle* to Robert Greene's *Menaphon* in 1589, its mention of "Hamlets," and how it has been interpreted. Other relevant references are considered in Chapter 12, beginning with Henslowe's entry at Newington Butts, and Malone's curious comments upon it.

Edmond Malone and His "Attempt to Ascertain the Order of Shakespeare's Plays"

It was in 1778 that Malone published his "Attempt to Ascertain the Order of Shakespeare's Plays," the first ever effort to create a chronology for Shakespeare's plays.[3] At this point Malone was only acquainted with Q2 and F1 *Hamlet*, for Q1 would not be rediscovered until eleven years after his death. His date for *Hamlet* in his first "Attempt to Ascertain" is 1596. He reluctantly classes it as a pre–1600 play. The play (Q2 or F1) does not appear to be early to him, and he prefers a date "five or six years later than 1596,"[4] in other words 1601 or 1602. Several factors influence his suggested date. At the time of compiling the first chronology Malone was familiar with Dr. Richard Farmer's "Essay on the learning of Shakespeare" (1767), which refers to Thomas Lodge's pamphlet of 1596, the *Wits miserie and the worlds madnesse*. This pamphlet includes a contemporary allusion (discussed in Chapter 12) to a "ghost who cried so miserably at the Theatre, like an oister-wife, Hamlet, revenge."[5] Malone concedes that Lodge indicates that a *Hamlet* play is known by 1596, but speculates that it was "probably but a rude sketch of that which we now possess."[6] Malone was also aware of Nashe's *Epistle to the Gentlemen Students of Both Universities*, with its mention of "whole *Hamlets* ... handfuls of Tragicall speeches."[7] In 1778, in his first "Attempt to Ascertain," Malone accepts Farmer's conjectural date of 1591 for Nashe's *Epistle*, though in a footnote he acknowledges that Mr Oldys[8] "on I know not what authority" has attributed an even earlier date of 1589 for the *Epistle*, which Malone sees as "still less probable"[9] as a date for a Shakespearean *Hamlet*. Today we know that the *Epistle* was first printed in 1589.

Malone's "Attempt to Ascertain" tackles one of the biggest challenges in studying the plays, namely trying to identify the dates of each and the order in which Shakespeare wrote them. The information Malone had available to him was considerable, but not quite as much as we have today. In 1778 he did not know Q1 *Hamlet*, and he had not yet seen the records Henslowe kept of play performances. These include details of play performances with a small number of Shakespearean titles, including "hamlet" at Newington Butts in 1594. The papers were only made available to Malone in 1790, twelve years after he had published his "Attempt to Ascertain," and therefore did not affect his initial "Order." One of the reasons we must examine Malone's ideas carefully is because we do have more knowledge than he did, and we do have a Q1 to study. It is also tempting to linger momentarily on his speculation that a pre–Q2 or F1 *Hamlet* by Shakespeare was "probably but a rude sketch of that which we now possess," and to wonder whether Malone would have used that description again if he had seen Q1.

Malone read Nashe's *Epistle*, and claimed that there were three principal objections to interpreting the passage as Nashe referring to a Shakespearean *Hamlet*:

1. The whole passage refers to the trade of "Noverint," or law clerk, which Shakespeare is not known to have followed;
2. Shakespeare does not appear to be at all indebted to the translations of Seneca, and
3. Nashe's phrase—"'whole *Hamlets* ... of Tragicall speeches' ... might have only meant a large quantity" and need not entail a reference to the play.[10]

These are points we return to later in the chapter. The final version of Malone's chronology was published posthumously in the 1821 *Third Variorum*, and suggests a date of *c.* 1600 for *Hamlet*.[11]

At some point after his 1778 "Attempt to Ascertain" Malone records that he has revisited a 1589 text of Nashe's *Epistle* to Robert Greene's *Menaphon* (his initial examination of this text appears to have been of an edition later than 1589). Malone now views its interpretation differently:

> Not having seen the first edition of this tract [by Nashe] till a few years ago, I formerly doubted whether the passage referred to the tragedy of *Hamlet*; but the word *Hamlets* being printed in different character from the rest, I no longer have any doubt upon the subject. It is manifest from this passage that some play on the story had been exhibited before the year 1589; but I am inclined to think that it was not Shakespeare's drama, but an elder performance, on which, with the aid of the old prose *Hystorie of Hamblet*, his tragedy was formed.[12]

Malone's idea or inclination about the "elder performance," formed with "the aid of the old prose *Hystorie of Hamblet*," comes partly from reading Dr Richard Farmer (1767). Farmer argues that Shakespeare derives most of his plots from English texts, and that *The Hystorie of Hamblet* is the source for *Hamlet*. Since the only surviving edition of *The Hystorie of Hamblet* is dated 1608, and because it clearly *follows* the English play in at least one place,[13] *The Hystorie* is now understood to postdate the *Hamlet* quartos. This part of Malone's reasoning has therefore been superseded.

Malone is nevertheless the scholar who initiates the idea of a pre–Shakespearean *Hamlet*. And he is the one who first speculates on that play's possible author, when he writes that "Perhaps the original *Hamlet* was written by Thomas Kyd."[14] It is a view which has cast a long shadow. Although all three *Hamlet* texts—Q1, Q2 and F1—bear Shakespeare's name, there is, however, an undoubted unwillingness in Malone and among many scholars to see Shakespeare writing a version of *Hamlet* that early in his career. A similar unwillingness among many scholars to attribute Q1 *Hamlet* to Shakespeare continues to today.

The result is that some scholars accept without question that Nashe's allusion is to a *Hamlet* by Kyd or by someone else, but not by Shakespeare. Fleay and Miola have already been mentioned. Sir Sidney Lee too feels that "Nashe's English Seneca may safely be identified with Thomas Kyd,"[15] and Dowden acknowledges that it is his "opinion" that Kyd was the author of the *Ur-Hamlet*.[16] In 1906 John Cunliffe even goes so far as to declare that Kyd as author of the early *Hamlet* was "the unanimous opinion of Shakspearean [*sic*] critics."[17]

Except that Cunliffe exaggerates. Certainly many scholars are very tempted. Nashe's editor, Boas, reviewing the number of apparent allusions in the extract, concludes that "evidences of Kyd's authorship of it have become practically conclusive."[18] (Chambers, nearly thirty years later, would use the antonym, "inconclusive."[19]) Duthie's examination of the extract and its commentators shows he is particularly persuaded by V. Østerberg's argument from 1920, which comes "very near to proving an allusion to Kyd."[20] Peter B. Murray, writing on Kyd, notes firstly that there is "some reason to believe [Kyd] wrote the original version of *Hamlet,*" and four pages later advances to saying the *Ur-Hamlet* was "probably written by Kyd."[21] The vocabulary here indicates neither proof nor complete belief in Kyd's authorship: "practically conclusive," "very near to proving," "some reason," and "probably."

There is a marked hesitancy on the part of some scholars to join Cunliffe's group of allegedly unanimous critics. J. Schick, who edited *The Spanish Tragedy* earlier, in 1898, is uncertain. His willingness to accept the attribution seems assured when he writes "Surely Nashe points here with his very finger to the person of Kyd," but then Schick acknowledges that "we have no absolute proof." However, he decides, "we may be allowed to interpret it in some such way,"[22] leaving us a distinctly vague and contradictory series of comments. In 1902 Ashley H. Thorndike writes at one point "Thomas Kyd was the author ... and probably, as Dr Sarrazin has shown, of the old *Hamlet,*" though curiously Thorndike has shifted his position forty-three pages later, with "we have not gone to the extent of accepting Sarrazin's conjecture that Kyd was the author."[23] Some just recognize the interpretation of Nashe's *Epistle* as a battleground. Hibbard accepts the putative *Ur-Hamlet* but simply reports the attribution to Kyd as a "long drawn out and inconclusive conflict."[24] The element of conflict is best illustrated by A. E. Jack.[25] In 1905 he questions the reading of the whole Nashe passage. It is Jack's essay which is sweepingly dismissed by Cunliffe with his declaration that Kyd as author of the early *Hamlet* was "the unanimous opinion of Shakspearean [*sic*] critics." Cunliffe doesn't even respond to Jack's points. Again the vocabulary used by these scholars does not indicate certainty or even unanimity: "Surely," "no absolute proof," "probably," "conjecture," and "conflict."

Some scholars remain at a distance from the battleground. Chambers, in 1904, is circumspect, with the adjective "probable" qualifying the "existence of a pre–Shakespearean *Hamlet*." In fact Chambers distances himself from the theory. He uses the impersonal third person ("It"), the passive voice ("has been suggested"), and a qualifying prepositional phrase ("with some plausibility"): "It has been suggested with some plausibility that this early *Hamlet* was written by Thomas Kyd."[26] In his later study of the chronology of the plays Chambers phrases it a little differently, since "the old play" implies his acceptance of a pre–Shakespearean *Hamlet*. Nevertheless Chambers does not believe the *Epistle* necessarily carries the inference that Kyd was the earlier author.[27] Much more recently, in 2007, Thompson and Taylor are noticeably circumlocutory. While referring to the "general agreement" that stylistically, the texts of *Hamlet* printed in 1604–5 and 1623 (Q2 and F1) "cannot belong to the years before 1590," they also comment that "nevertheless it is not logically impossible" that the 1596 reference by Lodge did refer to Shakespeare's *Hamlet*.[28] (The use of the double negative and the absence of reference to Q1 are interesting.) Sams stands out as one who simply accepts Nashe's allusion is to a Shakespeare *Hamlet*: Shakespeare is "the Senecan playwright lampooned by Thomas Nashe, and hence (as common sense confirms) the author of the early *Hamlet*."[29]

In other words, these examples of scholars' views on how to interpret Nashe vary from seeing him as offering proof of a Kyddian *Hamlet*, to proof of a pre–Shakespearean *Hamlet*, to proof of Shakespeare's play existing by 1589, with all the shades of certainty or uncertainty in between. Collectively they do not agree. They cannot all be right. And yet our reading of Nashe's text is fundamental to understanding the quartos. On Nashe's text also depends another critical hypothesis, the hypothesized chronology of the *Hamlet* quartos. That chronology is vital to determine the quartos' relationship and which of the hypotheses of MR, first sketch and revision, or abridgement, or some combination of all of them, is right.

1589: Nashe's Epistle to the Gentlemen Students of Both Universities

Nashe's *Epistle* is therefore vital both to whether Shakespeare was writing in the 1580s, and to whether a Shakespearean *Hamlet* was in existence by August 1589. Since there is no unanimity in the interpretation of Nashe's *Epistle*, it is perhaps superfluous to state that Nashe is not the easiest author to understand today. The challenge of reading his *Epistle* results from a number of different factors, such as his use of irony, exaggeration, metaphor, ambiguity, contemporary reference, his sustained use of alliteration as part of his euphuistic and rhetorical style, dramatic switches in tone, and a desire to display his wit and erudition to his contemporaries. All of these can blur his intended meaning for the modern reader. The passage, however, merits a careful reading.

The critical lines are given in full below, and are about a fifteenth of the whole *Epistle*. Ronald McKerrow's edition has been used; he printed from the 1610 edition.[30]

Extract from Nashe's prefatory *Epistle* to Robert Greene's *Menaphon*:
TO THE GENTLEMEN STVDENTS OF BOTH VNIVERSITIES
But lest I might seeme, with these nightcrowes, *Nimis curiosus in aliena republica*, I will turne backe to my first text of Studies of delight, and talke a little in friendship with a few of our triuiall translators.... It is a common practise now a days amongst a sort of shifting companions, that runne through euery Art and thriue by none, to leaue the trade of *Noverint*, whereto they were borne, and busie themselues with the indeuours of Art, that could scarcely Latinize their neck verse if they should haue neede; yet English *Seneca* read by Candlelight yeelds many good sentences, as *Blood is a begger*, and so forth; and if you intreate him faire in a frostie morning, hee will afford you whole Hamlets, I should say handfuls of Tragicall speeches. But O griefe! *Tempus edax rerum*, whats that will last always? The Sea exhaled by droppes will in continuance bee drie, and *Seneca*, let blood line by line and page by page, at length must needs die to our Stage: which makes his famished followers to imitate the Kid in *Æsop*, who enamoured with the Foxes newfangles, forsooke all hopes of life to leape into a newe occupation; and these men, renouncing all possibilities of credite or estimation, to intermeddle with Italian Translations: wherein how poorely they haue plodded, (as those that are neither prouenzall men, nor are able to distinguish of Articles,) let all indifferent Gentlemen that haue trauelled in that tongue discerne by their two-pennie Pamphlets. And no maruell though their home borne mediocritie bee such in this matter; for what can be hoped of those that force *Elisium* into hell, and haue not learned, so long as they haue liued in the Spheres, the iust measure of the Horizon without an hexameter? Sufficeth them to bodge vp a blanke verse with ifs and ands, and otherwhile for recreation after their Candle-stuffe, hauing starched their beards most curiously, to make a Peripateticall path into the inner parts of the Citie, and spend two or three howers turning ouer French Dowdie, where they can attract more infection in one minute than they can do eloquence all daies of their life, by conuersing with Authors of like argument ... [pages 315–316, lines 21–25].

There are three essential questions to ask about the passage. Does "Hamlets" refer to a *Hamlet* play? Does "the Kid in *Æsop*" refer to Thomas Kyd? And does the whole passage link the group being criticized, "Hamlets" and/or "the Kid in *Æsop*" in such a way that we can conclude that the *Hamlet* mentioned here links to Kyd, or to another playwright, or even to Shakespeare?

The first question stems from Jack's ultimate conclusion that it was not "perfectly clear that Nash knew of a Hamlet drama."[31] McKerrow's footnotes to the relevant passage reveal that in the 1589 edition "Hamlets" was italicized and capitalized. The footnote for the relevant line, line 33, simply reads "*Hamlets* 89."[32] In modern typography the capital letter and the italics would suggest a title, and indeed in the *Epistle* italics are used for titles, for example Greene's "*Arcadian Menaphon*" (312), and Nashe's promotion of his own writing, "*Anatomie of Absurdities*" (324). It is true italics are used for other purposes, such as Latin, fictional Latin names, classical authors' names, fifteenth and sixteenth century names, places, apparent quotations and for "Dowdie." (For example, Latin—"*Tempus edax rerum*" [pages 315–6]; fictional Latin names—"*Boreas*" [311]; classical authors' names—"*Tully*" [312]; fifteenth and sixteenth century names—"*Peter Ramus*" [313]; places—"*Cambridge*" [317]; apparent quotations—"*Blood is a begger*," though this is not known [315], and "*Dowdie*" [316]. "*Dowdie*" appears to anticipate Pepys's use of it as a noun to denote a plain or homely woman, though in Nashe "turning ouer French *Dowdie*" may connote visiting a prostitute.) "Hamlets" occurs in the same sentence as the Roman playwright, Seneca, who is associated with revenge tragedies, and "Tragicall speeches." Typography and context make it a reasonably safe interpretation that "*Hamlets*" refers to a play, one Nashe is probably gently mocking. Today this interpretation does not seem to be questioned.

The second question requires us to address "the Kid in *Æsop*." Cunliffe and others considered "Kid" alluded to Thomas Kyd, as well as denoting a young goat. Like "Hamlets," "Kid" is capitalized. In fact the *Epistle* contains a surprising number of animals, as table 12 below shows, and fifteen out of seventeen, or 88 percent of them, have capitals. It is not surprising to find an inconsistent use of capital letters in English Renaissance writing, because the use of capitals is not standardized in British English until about 1800. However, it is clear that Nashe or his publisher have been fairly consistent in typography, in capitalizing animals. As a result, the presence of an initial capital letter alone does not prove any connection between "Kid" (small goat) and "Kyd"/"Kydd"/"Kidd" (Thomas Kyd).

"Kid" and "Kyd"/"Kydd"/"Kidd" are undoubtedly homophones. Of course, to rest the argument for Kyd as the author of an early *Hamlet* upon a homophone alone would be to make a very precarious case. And McKerrow does draw attention to Nashe's earlier reference to Æsop and his fable of the ape and the glowworm, and how no one sees that as an allusion to a Mr Glowworm.[33] It is only because there *was* a contemporary writer called "Kyd" that the link between a "kid" and "Kyd can be proposed.

Duthie rightly points out that Nashe can and does pun on names. In Nashe's *Anatomie of Absurdities*, parodying Philip Stubbes' *Anatomie of Abuses* (1583), Nashe writes about those who are "pretending to anatomize abuses

Table 12. Animals Mentioned in Nashe's *Epistle*

Animals with capitals	Reference (page/line)	Animals with capitals and associated with Æsop and "Æsop"	Reference (page/line)	Animals without capitals	Reference (page/line)
Bull	311, 24	Glowworme	314, 19–20	nightcrowes	315, 21–2
Mouse	312, 21	Apes	314, 20	swallows	323, 12
Goats	314, 1, 6	Kid	316, 5		
Panther	314, 25	Foxes	316, 5		
Asse	315, 12, 20 321, 25				
Oxe	315, 13				
Crowes	320, 31				
Swallowes	320, 32				

and stubbe vp sin by the rootes."[34] This is an unmistakable parody, for three reasons. Firstly there is the play on Stubbes' surname, secondly the deliberate paralleling in phrasing of *Anatomie of Abuses* and *Anatomie of Absurdities*, and thirdly the recognition of what Stubbes was trying to do, to erase what he perceived as "sin."

But that isn't what is happening with "Kid." The "Kid" is clearly postmodified with "in *Æsop*." In the passage Nashe gives us an anecdote, a little story, about a kid goat that was "enamoured" by something newfangled shown to it by a predatory fox. The kid falls for the object, and consequently "forsook all hopes of life." There is no story in Æsop about a kid goat and a fox, so we rightly wonder what is happening with "the Kid in *Æsop*." However, a page earlier in the *Epistle* (314) Nashe has demonstrated that he *is* familiar with Æsop, the ancient teller of fables. On that page Nashe suggests that "vnexperienced and illiterated Punies' will value the tale of Joan of Brainford's will ("she bequeathed a score of farts amongst her frends"[35]) as much as the best of Tasso's poems. These "Punies," says Nashe, will value dross as much as gold, loss as much as gain, and mistake a glowworm for actual fire, like the foolish ape in Æsop's fable. Æsop, who may have composed, or is at least associated with, as many as six hundred fables, does narrate a fable about an ape and a glowworm, as Nashe clearly knows. Nashe accurately refers to an Æsop story here, and draws a close parallel with the point he is actually making. "[V]nexperienced and illiterated Punies," like the foolish ape in Æsop, will value wills about farts and value dross and loss, just as the ape in Æsop mistakes a glow-worm for fire.

So why "the Kid in *Æsop* ?" It is more than a century since Koeppel noted that the story about the kid and the fox in Nashe's *Epistle* draws upon *The May Eclogue* in Spenser's *Shepherd's Calendar*.[36] Spenser tells the tale of a "Kidd" or "kiddie" who is left at home while its mother "Gate" ([goat]: the spelling is supposed to represent a northerly pronunciation[37]) goes out. The mother goat has warned the kid not to open the door. But along comes a "Foxe," disguised as a sheep and a "pedler," offering wares. The kid is "enamored with newell," the "newell" being a "glasse" or mirror offered by the fox. The kid leans into the basket to pick up another novelty. Immediately the fox closes the lid, and the kid is trapped, paying "to dere a prise"[38] (the price is his life) for succumbing to the temptation of having something new.

Just as Nashe has earlier used an Æsop tale to make an amusing point about those of limited intelligence and their lack of appreciation of Tasso's poems, Nashe now uses Spenser's tale to make a point about "a sort of shifting companions." Nashe's parallel version of Spenser's tale sees those who change their profession also "enamoured" by novelty. Their novelty is a "newe occupation" (just as Spenser's kid leans into the fox's basket to pick up another novelty), like intermeddling with Italian translations. But the followers are so poor at it they effectively "[forsake] all hopes of life" (Spenser's kid is carried off by the fox), for they are "renouncing all possibilities of credite or estimation." Nashe's point is that Spenser's kid and the writers Nashe criticizes are equally foolish in falling for a newfangled trinket or a new occupation. Duthie's argument is—following V. Østerberg—that the parallels present "violent contrasts," and therefore the analogy seems "very imperfect."[39] Nashe's extended metaphor may seem a little extreme in our more literal age, but it was hardly strained at a time when extravagant images were deliberately concocted to entertain, such as the conceits sometimes found in Metaphysical poetry. For example, within a decade of Nashe's *Epistle* John Donne devises a comparison between a pair of compasses and the love he and his mistress shared, in "A Valediction: Forbidding Mourning." This conceit is applauded for its outrageousness rather than being seen as "very imperfect." In fact the parallels between Spenser's "Kid" and the "shifting companions" or the "followers" of Seneca enable Nashe to show off his knowledge of a successful contemporary writer's popular works. And it is clear that Nashe wishes to entertain with his extravagant phrasing, his "swelling bombast of bragging" prose (311), to borrow his own words in the *Epistle*.

Like the analogy between the *Anatomie of Abuses* and *Anatomie of Absurdities* there are clear verbal echoes. Spenser uses "Kidd," "Kiddie," "enamored," "with newell" offered by the "Foxe," and paid "to dere a prise" (his life).

Nashe alludes to the story using "Kid," "enamoured," "with the Foxes newfangles," and "forsooke all hopes of life." In his extended metaphor, Nashe sees "[Seneca's] famished followers imitat[ing] the Kid in *Æsop*," for they "leape into a newe occupation" where they "intermeddle with Italian Translations," thus "renouncing all possibilities of credite or estimation."

This explains the allusion to the story of the "Kid" in Spenser's *May Eclogue*, but not "in *Æsop*." Enlightenment is simple. It comes from the notes which accompanied Spenser's *Shepherd's Calendar* then and which still follow it now. These notes give a fairly lengthy "Glosse," initialed at the end "E. K." "E. K.," the provider of the "Glosse," is considered by scholars to have been Edward Kirke, Spenser's fellow student at Cambridge.[40] E. K.'s "Glosse" to *The May Eclogue* comments quite explicitly that "This tale is much like to that in Æsops [*sic*] fables...."[41] McKerrow also considers the gloss to have given rise to "*Æsop*" here.[42] "*Æsop*" is a quite understandable label because both Æsop and Spenser are moral writers. Indeed, the gloss to *The May Eclogue* also overtly and explicitly comments on the "morall of the whole tale."[43] Another eclogue with a similar moral story, and glossed to emphasize it, is *Februarie* (the story/fable of the Oake and the Bryer). We can have no doubt that to Nashe's contemporaries "the Kid in *Æsop*" meant Spenser, the Elizabethans' "Æsop." Today Spenser is probably better known for *The Faerie Queene* (1590), not so much a fable as an allegory, another moral, literary genre.

In the context of the whole *Epistle* it is obvious that Nashe is trying to ingratiate himself with anyone who might give him a chance to write for them. Robert Greene, for whose *Menaphon* Nashe is writing the *Epistle*, is one he compliments, and another is Edmund Spenser. In the *Epistle* Nashe calls Greene his "sweet friend," unsurprisingly since Nashe's *Epistle* prefacing Greene's novel is the first opportunity Nashe has to get into print.[44] Later in the *Epistle* Nashe calls Spenser "diuine Master *Spencer*, the miracle of wit" (323). This context demonstrates that "the Kid in *Æsop*" does indeed refer to the fable of the kid and the fox in *The May Eclogue*, by the Elizabethan "Æsop," Spenser. Here "Kid" need mean no more than a small goat.

But there are other reasons why Kyd has been connected with this passage. The extract contains Nashe's rant about a "sort of shifting companions," that is, a group of people who shift their occupation or profession. Scholars note that the passage is criticizing these "sort of shifting companions" who "leaue the trade of *Noverint*," and claim that phrase is what identifies Kyd. The two quotations encapsulate the next line of argument to examine, the first concerning the use of plurals—"sort of shifting companions"—and the second the list of criticisms, some of which are seen as alluding to Kyd.

In the passage under discussion Nashe uses twenty-one plurals. Grammatically the objects of his ridicule are plural: noun phrases such as "a sort of shifting companions" and "famished followers" show this, as does the use of plural pronouns ("they," "themselves," "them"), and the plural possessive determiner ("their"). Boas, for example, declares that the use of plurals is a "mere rhetorical device, as so elaborate an indictment could only be aimed at a single personage."[45] Are the plurals simply a rhetorical device "aimed at a single personage," or is Nashe attacking a group? This is a difficult question, because it is easy to find examples of when rhetorical writers use plurals when a singular is intended. A recent, modern example can be found in an article in the magazine, *Compass*, printed for Hampshire, England in 2010. An extract from it reads:

> Disillusionment has set in. It probably started with the MPs' expenses debacle. Labour **MPs** may have been among the worst **culprits** but what sticks in the mind, and the throat, are the expense **claims** made by Conservative **MPs** for cleaning out the moat and the building of duck **houses**. Then there was the gall of one Conservative MP, Antony Steen, who claimed that the public response was "about jealousy; I have a very, very large house"....[46]

Some readers will remember the newspaper revelations about the British Members of Parliament's expenses. The plurals above (author's emboldening added) would suggest that more than one Conservative MP claimed for moat cleaning, and more than one for a duck house. In reality the allusion to moat cleaning refers to only one MP, Douglas Hogg, who wanted to claim for his one moat being cleaned, and the allusion to duck houses to only one MP, Peter Viggars, who wanted to claim for his duck house. It is only when the writer, Truman, quotes a single individual and names him that Truman switches from the rhetorical plural to the accuracy of the singular.

If Nashe had wished the target of his satire to be clearly identified, he could have chosen to use the singular. In the wider context of the whole *Epistle*, Nashe offers, to borrow his own phrase, a "large fielde of inuectiue" (318). (This indicates some honesty on Nashe's part, though it is perhaps still an understatement.) He attacks a considerable number of different categories of unnamed people. The very first target in the whole *Epistle*, who "abhorreth the English he was borne too" appears singular (pronoun "he"), but the noun subject in the preceding line is "euery mechanicall mate" (311). The premodifier, "euery," immediately renders the grammatically singular "mate" the equivalent of a plural. After that, all bar two of Nashe's quite creatively phrased targets are in the plural: "ideot Art-Masters" (311), "Schoolemen or Grammarians" (312), "vnsatiate humorists" (313), "vnexperienced and illiterated Punies," and "quadrant crepundios" (314), all precede a "sort of shifting companions," while "Diuinitie Dunces," "bungling practitioners" (318), and "reformatorie Churchmen" (321) are among his subsequent targets. It is not easy to discover whether any of these are attacks on one individual. If they were, that might add some conviction to the argument that Kyd is Nashe's target where those twenty-one plurals are used.

If Nashe really wishes to sneer at Kyd the playwright, he is *not* specific. The *Epistle* attacks a number of groups which name no one explicitly. But Nashe does not hesitate to name or signal very clearly two individual men he does wish to deride, and the titles of their writings. Firstly, Nashe jeers openly at "Maister [Richard] Stanihurst" (an Oxford scholar), who had translated the first four books of *The Aeneid*. Nashe declares Stanihurst's writing is not much better than the "extremitie of clownerie" (319), and quotes from him. No inference is needed; Nashe is quite unequivocal. The second example we have already considered, Nashe's "*Anatomie of Absurdities*," a tract which he had already written but had not yet had printed. That title is an unmistakable parody of Stubbes' *Anatomie of Abuses*. In other words, Nashe can be explicit if he so chooses, and he does choose twice in the *Epistle* to identify his target clearly. We might also note that Nashe is writing here as a university man (a university "wit") to university students, and Kyd is not a member of that exclusive group. If Kyd is Nashe's target, why is Nashe not as obvious in his attack as in his rant against Stanihurst, who *is* a university man?

So Nashe doesn't choose to name Kyd, which in the context of the whole *Epistle* might suggest Kyd isn't his specific target. There is still the list of criticisms in Nashe's rant against the "sort of shifting companions." These "shifting companions" allegedly:

1. "runne through euery Art"
2. "leaue the trade of *Nouerint*"
3. "busie themselues with the indeuours of Art"
4. do not know enough Latin to save their necks with "neck verse," in other words to be able to recite for example Psalm 51, and get themselves transferred from the stricter secular court to the more lenient ecclesiastical court
5. borrow from Seneca
6. "intermeddle with Italian Translations," "poorely"
7. "force *Elisium* into hell"
8. "bodge vp a blanke verse with ifs and ands"
9. starch their beards
10. spend time with "French *Dowdie*."

One of the reasons allegedly identifying Kyd as a likely object of this diatribe is that his father is recorded to have been a "Nouerint"[47] (point 2 above),

"Noverint," being the beginning of the Latin phrase *Noverint universi per praesentes*, which began many of the legal documents in Elizabethan times. Nashe is criticizing people who "leaue the trade of Nouerint, whereto they were borne," and it is perhaps because Kyd's father was a scrivener that Kyd might be seen as born to the trade. The trade is unlikely to have been uncommon at the time. It could also be that Nashe is suggesting metaphorically that these "shifting companions" aren't capable of much more than copying, and deliberately juxtaposing the concept of merely copying with the (creative) "indeuours of Art." Certainly Kyd was one of many Elizabethans who busied himself with the Arts (3). He drew upon Seneca (5) and he translated from Italian, not particularly successfully (6). (Boas writes that Kyd's "English version of Tasso's *Padre di Famiglia* is crowded with blunders and fully deserves Nashe's sneer,"[48] which appears to justify "poorely."[49]) There were other Italian translations being printed at that time[50] which might possibly also have been Nashe's target. After that, three criticisms may, or may not, refer to Kyd. In his *Spanish Tragedy* Kyd does borrow from Virgil's *Aeneid* book VI, which describes the Elysian fields, to fashion a picture of hell (7), though not "forc[ing]" them. Andrew Gurr, in his *Introduction* to Mulryne's recent edition of *The Spanish Tragedy*, points out that in Marlowe's *Faustus*, scene 3, 57–8, Mephistophilis has two lines which appear pertinent: "This word damnation terrifies not him,/ For he confounds hell in Elysium."[51] *Faustus*'s date is also uncertain, so it cannot be determined who first phrased the sentiment, but Nashe and Marlowe were acquaintances, and collaborated on Marlowe's *Dido, Queen of Carthage*. "[I]fs" and "ands" are spoken by Kyd's character Lorenzo: "What villain, ifs and ands?" (II.i.77).[52] Boas sees this as a fair comment on those lines. But G. Sarrazin prefers to quote two other extracts from *The Spanish Tragedy*:

> *Balthazar.* And with that hand he fiercely waged war,
> And in that war he gave me dangerous wounds,
> And by those wounds he forced me to yield,
> And by yielding I became his slave [II.i.122–125].

and

> *Hieronimo.* If love's effects so strive in lesser things
> If love enforce such moods in meaner wits,
> If love express such power in small estates ... [III.xiii.98–100].[53]

though in none of the examples are the words or lines "bodge[d] vp." If these last two criticisms are directed at Kyd, Nashe is exaggerating, unsurprisingly, since hyperbole is one of his stylistic traits. One criticism is undeserved; Kyd's Latin was sound, good enough for "neck verse" (4). The remaining criticisms, such as the more personal elements of, for example, beard starching, do not appear to be recorded, or discussed, for Kyd.

We can summarize by saying that four of the ten criticisms appear to be applicable to Kyd: his father was a scrivener, Kyd did busy himself "with the indeuours of Art," he did borrow from Seneca, and he was not altogether successful "with Italian Translations" ("poorely"). Three are weak hits if Kyd is the target: Kyd was better than merely competent at Latin; he didn't "bodge vp" "ifs" and "ands," and he didn't "force *Elisium* into hell." Three are unknown. Kyd seems very unlikely as Nashe's sole target, although he may be one of a number of targets. Even Shakespeare—another writer who was not university educated, who would "run" through the arts of acting and writing, busy himself with the "indeuours of Art," and draw upon the revenge theme found for example in Seneca, and began sequences of lines in *Titus Andronicus* with "And,"[54] and had a beard, starched or otherwise—might have been seen as one who should have been no more than a scrivener, by a university wit like Nashe, as Duncan-Jones suggests.[55] Consequently we can safely say that Kyd may, or may not, be included in Nashe's targets here, and that "the Kid in *Æsop*" refers to Spenser's fable, but it is not clear whether "Kyd" and "Kid" are any more than chance homophones.

The third question is whether there is any connection between "*Hamlets*" and Kyd, if, for a moment, we accept that Kyd is one of the "shifting companions" alluded to here. The context of "Hamlets" is distinctive. The word comes in a little linguistic quirk which Nashe employs. The relevant excerpt is: "hee will afford you whole Hamlets, I should say handfuls of Tragicall speeches." Stylistically it is very similar to another, later in the same *Epistle*: "whose heroicall poetry, infired, I should say inspired, with a hexameter furie (319)." Both of these include a deliberate self correction, signaled by "I should say." Both include grammatical and phonological play. In the first the noun phrase "whole Hamlets" is replaced or "corrected" by another noun phrase "handfuls," both noun phrases being post-modified by "of Tragicall speeches." In the second example the verb "infired" is replaced or "corrected" by another verb, "inspired," both verbs being post-modified by "with a hexameter furie." Each time the first word—"Hamlets," and "infired"—is not a standard word in the context. Each time the replacements, or corrections, *are* standard—"handfuls" and "inspired." And the two pairs of words are linked by their sound patterning. "Hamlets and "handfuls" are two syllables, alliterate, have the same consonant and vowel sound (/hæ/) in the first syllable, and the same initial stressed syllable. The second pair is also linked. "[I]nfired" and "inspired" begin with the same vowel and consonant (/ɪn/), and have the same stress on the second syllable. These two quirky excerpts indicate that when Nashe uses "Hamlets" he is concerned with his style, concerned with "Hamlets" providing the right word play, and perhaps concerned with providing a witty cross cultural reference for his audience.

The next question is whether Nashe is also trying to link "Hamlets" with one possible candidate (Kyd) in his rant about "a sort of shifting companions." We now need to examine another characteristic of Nashe, his occasional movement between second and third person pronouns. Elsewhere in the *Epistle* Nashe addresses Greene with a vocative "(sweet friend)" in parenthesis and the second person singular, "thy": "I come (sweet friend) to thy *Arcadian Menaphon*" (312). Nashe also addresses, at least grammatically, "the Gentlemen students of both Universities," beginning the whole *Epistle* with a complimentary vocative, "Cvrteous and wise" ("gentlemen" is understood in this ellipsis [311]). Most of the time in the *Epistle* Nashe refers to people in the third person, as he does in most of the key passage above. But in the middle of the passage, he swaps from talking about a group of people in the third person to using the second person "you" (author's marking up):

> It is a common practise now a days amongst a sort of shifting companions, that runne through euery Art and thriue by none, to leaue the trade of *Noverint*, whereto they were borne, and busie themselues with the indeuours of Art, that could scarcely Latinize their neck verse if they should haue neede; yet English *Seneca* read by Candlelight yeelds many good sentences, as *Blood is a begger*, and so forth; and if you intreate him faire in a frostie morning, hee will afford you whole Hamlets, I should say handfuls of Tragicall speeches. But O griefe! *Tempus edax rerum*, whats that will last always? The Sea exhaled by droppes will in continuance bee drie, and Seneca, let blood line by line and page by page, at length must needs die to our Stage: which makes his famished followers to imitate the Kid in Æsop, who enamoured with the Foxes newfangles, forsooke all hopes of life to leape into a newe occupation; and these men, renouncing...

This switch to the second person is disconcerting. Nashe appears to be offering an aside, a little comment effectively in parenthesis, about how Seneca's plays can give his readers ideas for tragic speeches. Grammatically, the "aside" is disconnected from the main part of the extract because it switches to the second person pronoun. We can remove the "aside" and the sense still flows quite coherently:

> ... yet English *Seneca* read by Candlelight yeelds many good sentences, as *Blood is a begger*, and so forth. But O griefe! *Tempus edax rerum*, whats that will last always? The Sea exhaled by droppes will in continuance bee drie, and Seneca, let blood line by line and page by page....

It means that the part of the passage mentioning "Hamlets" is not a necessary or integral part of the whole. We could also note that "Hamlets" appears two sentences before "the Kid in *Æsop*." The two key words and ideas aren't even in the same sentence. Nashe's anecdote about "the Kid in *Æsop*" starts a whole two sentences after mention of "Hamlets." To make a link between the homophones "Kid" and Kyd, to see Thomas Kyd as perhaps *one* of the "sort of shifting companions" and link him with "Hamlets," and then to credit Kyd with the authorship of a non-extant *Ur-Hamlet* is at best highly speculative.

We are left with several findings. These concern Malone, and the three questions about whether "*Hamlets*" means a *Hamlet* play, whether Kyd is alluded to, and whether Kyd is fingered as the author of a pre–Shakespearean *Hamlet*.

Malone initially thought that "Hamlets" might simply mean a plural quantity in this passage. Since that is what "handfuls" suggests, Malone's comment is reasonable. In the context of Seneca and "Tragicall speeches," to take "Hamlets" as an allusion to a *Hamlet* play as well is also reasonable, and widely accepted. The *Hamlet* plays surviving today do have Senecan undertones—a Ghost, a revenge theme—despite Malone's comment about Shakespeare not being indebted to Seneca.

The "Kid in Æsop" is straightforwardly explained as alluding to the Elizabethan "Æsop," Spenser, and his story of the kid and fox in *The May Eclogue*, glossed as similar to Æsop's fables. Nashe's extended metaphor fits well into his rant about "shifting companions" trying a new occupation, and paying the price of credit and estimation. Østerberg feels that Nashe "awkwardly wrenches the story of the kid"[56] to place it in the *Epistle*, but actually "Kid in Æsop" complements Nashe's obvious intention to praise "divine Master Spenser."

Nashe is criticizing a group in a "sort of shifting companions," just as most of his *Epistle* rants against groups. His list of criticisms here is long and while some may be applicable to Kyd, some are not. Malone notes that Shakespeare is not known to have been a "Noverint" or law clerk, but Nashe's point may be simply that some people are making endeavors in "art" when such upstarts are born to be no more than copyists. Nashe does unambiguously single out two contemporaries for ridicule, Stanihurst and Stubbes. Nashe does not unambiguously single out Kyd. Nashe doesn't indicate that he is making any link between "Hamlets" and Kid/Kyd. We can feel confident that "Hamlets" is used as part of Nashe's word play, because the whole line provides a linguistic quirk paralleled very precisely later in the *Epistle*. "Hamlets" is probably also a witty cross cultural link intended for his readership. (These are "*the Gentlemen Students of Both Universities*," universities actually named on Q1's title page.) Further, the second person clauses including mention of "Hamlets" are grammatically an aside, separate from Nashe's criticisms.

Nashe does not give us enough to make any link between "Hamlets" and Kyd, or to assert that this *Epistle* identifies Kyd as the author of a *Hamlet* existing by 1589, or that the *Epistle* identifies Shakespeare or anyone else as its author. All Nashe does is let us infer that a *Hamlet* play existed by 1589, and that his casual reference to it means he expects it to be known to his readership.

This chapter has examined "Hamlets" and "the Kid in *Æsop*" and their context in detail, because the hypothesis of a pre-Shakespearean *Hamlet* is so important to the current narrative about the *Hamlet*s. What we need is corroboration that Kyd, someone else or Shakespeare was the author. But Nashe is not the only writer who is called as a witness to the *Ur-Hamlet* hypothesis. Chapter 12 examines more, beginning with Henslowe, Lodge and Meres.

12. Meres and a Contradiction of Scholars

In 1594, five years after Nashe's *Epistle* was published, theatre manager Philip Henslowe recorded the names of plays performed at Newington Butts, south of the Thames. One of these was "hamlet." Two years later Thomas Lodge's *Wits Miserie* glanced at "the Visard of ye ghost which cried so miserably at ye Theator, like an oister wife, Hamlet, revenge."[1] In 1598 Francis Meres wrote about Shakespeare's writings in his *Palladis Tamia; Wit's Treasury*, but did not mention *Hamlet*. Many think that these show that while there was a *Hamlet* play in the 1590s, it was not Shakespeare's. After Meres there are a series of allusions to Shakespeare and/or *Hamlet*, by Gabriel Harvey, Thomas Dekker and Anthony Scoloker, and in *The Parnassus Plays*, most of which seem to be taken as referring not to a putative *Ur-Hamlet* but to Shakespeare/*Hamlet*. It is the first group of allusions which are critical, because of their date. Scholars' interpretations of these are varied and not a source of agreement. The allusions are again vital to the question of whether the *Hamlet* of the late 1580s and the 1590s is an *Ur-Hamlet* or Shakespeare's, and consequently they are the focus of this chapter.

1594: Henslowe's Diary

Henslowe's papers were rediscovered in 1790, shortly after Malone had completed his first "Attempt to Ascertain the Order of Shakespeare's Plays." Malone had early access to the manuscripts. He read the entry at "Newington, my Lord Admeralle and my Lorde chamberlen men" about a performance of "hamlet." The entry records the date of the performance, and the sum received ("Rd") in shillings. The entry reads:

    9 of June 1594   Rd at hamlet   viijs[2]

Malone made a note: "I have stated my opinion that there was a play on the subject of *Hamlet* prior to our author's, and here we have a full confirmation of that conjecture."[3] Regrettably, especially as Malone was trained in the law, and called to the bar in 1767, this statement is a *non sequitur*. It is not confirmation of any such "conjecture." All the entry shows us is that a play entitled "hamlet" was performed. The entry mentions no author. If the *Hamlet* Nashe mentions were pre–Shakespearean, Henslowe's might be the same, or it might have been a version by Shakespeare. If the *Hamlet* Nashe mentions were Shakespeare's, this Newington Butts performance might, or even might not, be Shakespeare's.

Malone's respect for Shakespeare's achievement in Q2 and F1 *Hamlet* is implicit in his first reason for this erroneous conclusion: Malone claims we cannot "suppose that our poet's play should have been performed but once in the time of this account." (Henslowe's entries are not continuous, but include some of his theatrical activities from 1592 to 1609.) We should note that Henslowe's *Diary* at no point claims to record all performances of "our poet's play." Henslowe also presumably only recorded the performances he was involved with, not those in every inn yard and theatre in and around the city of London and elsewhere.

The second reason also implies Malone's respect. He is surprised that Henslowe only drew "the sum of eight shillings" for "hamlet."[4] While Malone's view reflects the high value he places upon *Hamlet*, the size of the gate money does not prove, or disprove, the authorship. The absence of further entries for *Hamlet* does not in itself attest the play was unappreciated. However, the entry and its context are worth further examination.

In 1594 the theatres reopened after the closure due to the plague. Henslowe had remodeled his Rose Theatre during the closure, but the Privy Council kept it closed from 16th May to 15th June 1594. As a result Henslowe held performances at Newington Butts from 3rd to 13th June. This was not a particularly popular theatre, since it was a mile south of the Thames, and a tedious trek. The Privy Council understood "the tediousness of the way."[5] Moreover:

> In Shakespeare's day the southern side of the Thames opposite London consisted chiefly of flat, open country, large areas of which were below the river's daily high-water mark. Much of it was swampy ... and after a heavy rain ... would be covered with water that might remain for weeks.[6]

The drainage channels, known as sewers, were supposed to be kept clear by the owners of the adjacent properties. The owners often did not do so, despite orders from the Surrey magistrates, and flooding resulted. We might therefore not be very surprised to see that the receipts from the three performances at the Rose from 14th to 16th May, and afterwards from 15th June are markedly higher than the receipts from the unpopular Newington Butts from 3rd to 13th June, as table 13 below shows.

Table 13. Receipts from Performances 14–16 May, 3–13 June and 15–18 June 1594, in Henslowe's *Diary*[7]

14th–16th May (the Rose Theatre)

Rd at the Jewe of malta 14 of may 1594		xxxxviijs
Rd at the Rangers comodoey the 15 of maye 1594		xxxiijs
Rd at the Cvtlacke the 16 of maye 1594		xxxxijs

3rd–13th June (Newington Butts)

3 of June 1594	Rd at heaster & ashweros	viijs
4 of June 1594	Rd at the Jewe of malta	xs
5 of June 1594	Rd at andronicous	xijs
6 of June 1594	Rd at cvtlacke	xjs
8 of June 1594	Rd at bellendon	xvijs
9 of June 1594	Rd at hamlet	viijs
10 of June 1594	Rd at heaster	vs
12 of June 1594	Rd at the tamynge of A Shrowe	ixs
13 of June 1594	Rd at the Jewe	iiijs

15th–18th June (the Rose Theatre)

15 of June 1594	Rd at bellendon	iij^{li} iiijs
17 of June 1594	Rd at cvtlacke	xxxvs
18 of June 1594	Rd at the Rangers comodoey	xxijs

The average receipts for the three sets of dates, chronologically, are 41 shillings (the Rose), approximately 9 shillings and 4 pence (Newington Butts), and approximately 40 shillings and 4 pence (the Rose). In other words, receipts at Newington Butts are noticeably below those at the Rose.[8] At 8 shillings, the gate money for *Hamlet* was just below the average of about 9 shillings and 4 pence at the unpopular Newington Butts. Two further reasons for the low receipts are possible: perhaps Henslowe had to pay rent for this theatre and subtracted that from the takings, and perhaps the weather was less than inviting. Dr. Simon Forman comments on the wet weather in 1594:

> This moneths of Juen and July were very wet and wonderfull cold like winter, that the 10 dae of Julii many did syt by the fyer, yt was so cold; and soe was yt in Maye and June; and scarce too fair dais together all that tyme, but yt rayened every day more or lesse. Yf yt did not raine, then yt was cold and cloudye.[9]

This weather was hardly likely to add to the delights of attending a theatre in a swampy location.

Malone's third reason is also mistaken. He claims that if one of "our poet's" plays "had been performed, we should certainly have found more." Charles Knight points out that "the very next entry is 'at the tamynge of a shrewe [*sic*]'" (actually one entry later, for "heaster" intervenes. See table 13.), which Malone, in a note, described as "the play which preceded Shakespeare's."[10] Also performed at Newington Butts was "andronicous." Other apparently Shakespearean titles are found in Henslowe's *Diary*: *harey the vj*, and *kinge leare*.[11] No author's name is attached to these either.

Malone identifies "the tamynge of A Shrowe" as a version which preceded Shakespeare's in his first "Attempt to Ascertain." In 1778, Malone places Shakespeare's *Shrew*'s date as 1606, but by the (posthumous) 1821 edition he has revised his ideas and places it at 1596.[12] It is worth recalling that Malone issued his first "Attempt to Ascertain" in 1778, twelve years before he received the Henslowe papers, in 1790. We might wonder whether he would have constructed his chronology differently if he had had access to the papers before that first attempt, for suddenly he would have had documentation showing performances of several Shakespearean titles: *Andronicus, Hamlet, Shrew, Lear, Henry VI*. In Malone's second "Attempt to Ascertain" his chronology actually dates some texts later, including *Hamlet*.

A careful examination shows that Malone is wrong to claim the Newington Butts entry was "confirmation" of his "opinion" or "conjecture" about a pre–Shakespearean *Hamlet*. Malone is understandably biased but still mistaken in suggesting the receipt of only eight shillings indicates that the "hamlet" Henslowe lists was not Shakespeare's play, and Malone (probably) errs in claiming that there are no others by "our poet." Indeed, as we have noted elsewhere, Malone is incorrect in speculating that Shakespeare used "an elder performance" of *Hamlet* and *The Hystorie of Hamblet* to create his own drama, since the date of printing (1608) and one or two details in the content of *The Hystorie* show it postdates both quartos of Shakespeare's *Hamlet*. (In *Les Histoires Tragiques*, in the "chambre" scene, Amleth feels something hidden under the quilt, uses his sword, pulls out the half dead counselor and finishes him off.[13] Then follows the gruesome description of Amleth cutting up the body, boiling it and throwing it to the pigs. There is no mention of a rat. In Q1 Hamlet says, "I a Rat, dead for a Duckat" (sig. G2r.17), and in Q2 "How now, a Rat, dead for a Duckat, dead" (sig. I2r.32). But in *The Hystorie*, mainly a translation of the French source, Hamblet also cries, "A rat, a Rat!" which appears to show knowledge of either Q1 or Q2 *Hamlet*, and which is why *The Hystorie* is seen as postdating *Hamlet*.) We could wonder again whether Malone would have reached different conclusions, had he known Q1 and the date of *The Hystorie*.

Henslowe's *Diary* shows that a play called "hamlet" was performed on 9th June 1594. The entry does not offer information about the author, and the entry neither implies nor excludes Shakespeare's authorship. There is no corroboration that *Hamlet* was Kyd's or another's. We might be surprised at how little discussion of the entry can be found today.

1596: Thomas Lodge's Wits Miserie

Two years later, in his 1596 *Wits Miserie*, Thomas Lodge writes of the ghost who cried "Hamlet, revenge." This reference is also taken by many to be to a pre–Shakespearean *Hamlet*, partly because the precise phrase "Hamlet, revenge" does not occur in Q1, Q2 or F1 *Hamlet*. Yet there is nothing to say that Dr. Lodge knew about or was obeying twentieth and twenty-first century rules for quotations in scholarly essays. The phrase may be a succinct summary, a "soundbite" uniting protagonist and genre. We can find an analogy supporting this idea in 1598, in *Palladis Tamia*, where Meres refers to "chast *Matilda*," for example, as one of the writings of "*Michael Drayton Tragœdigraphus*."[14] The actual title of Drayton's text, published in 1594, was *Matilda the faire and chaste Daughter of Lord Robert Fitzwater*. Meres offers a reference which is not a precise quotation from or of the title, but Drayton's text would have been recognizable to his contemporaries by its soundbite summary, just as Lodge's "Hamlet, revenge" would have been. Meres gives several of Michael Drayton's titles as soundbites, so the actual title of the story of "great *Gaueston*" is *The Legend of Piers Gaveston*, and "the downfal[s] of valiant *Robert of Normandy*" is actually *The Tragicall Legend of Robert, Duke of Normandie*.[15]

Interestingly, in 1778 Malone did accept Lodge's reference as signifying a Shakespearean *Hamlet*. This is rarely discussed today. Nevertheless, Lodge, like Nashe and Henslowe before him, still offers no indication of authorship, Shakespeare's or another's. It means that we now have three references to a *Hamlet*, but none to an author. Equally frustratingly we can gain little from a later entry in Henslowe's *Papers*. A small number of properties inventoried on 10th March 1598 appear potentially relevant to *Hamlet*:

> Item, … ij Danes sewtes, and j payer of Danes hose
> Item, … j gostes sewt, and j gstes bodeyes.[16]

Nothing links these explicitly to *Hamlet* or Shakespeare. They do occur in the same papers as properties which may be linked to other Shakespearean plays, for example:

> Item, Harye the v. velvet gowne
> Item, Harye the v. satten dublet, layd with gowld lace[17]
> A purpell satten welted w^t velvet and silver twist Romeos.[18]

(*Henry V* was "staied" in the S.R. on 4th August 1600, and Q1 *Romeo and Juliet* was published in 1597.) However, as Foakes writes, "perhaps little reliance is to be placed upon the connecting of a property with a specific play."[19]

By now the "ghost" of a *Hamlet* play has haunted Elizabethan literature for ten years.

1598: Francis Meres' Palladis Tamia: Wits Treasury

Later in 1598 another publication emerged, one which places Shakespeare firmly at the forefront of Elizabethan literature, and indeed of English literature. This is Francis Meres' *Palladis Tamia*, entered on the Stationers' Register on 7th September. After a section entitled "Poets" and before that entitled "Painters" comes a chapter entitled "A comparative discourse of our English poets, with the Greeke, Latine and Italian Poets."[20] Paragraph 24 reads:

> As *Plautus* and *Seneca* are accounted the best for Comedy and Tragedy among the Latines: so *Shakespeare* among ye English is the most excellent in both kinds for the stage; for Comedy, witness his *Gentlemen of Verona*, his *Errors*, his *Loue labors lost*, his *Loue labours wonne*, his *Midsummers night dreame*, & his *Merchant of Venice*: for Tragedy his *Richard the 2. Richard the 3. Henry the 4. King Iohn, Titus Andronicus* and his *Romeo and Iuliet*.[21]

Editors frequently use this list to contribute to their propositions for dating Shakespeare's plays, but they do not use it consistently. For example, one editor of *The Taming of the Shrew* comments that "[t]he omission of *The Shrew* from Meres' list is not particularly surprising since he was not aiming for completeness."[22] On the other hand an editor of *As You Like It* concludes that "[t]he date of the play is fixed by the fact that it does not appear in the list Meres gives in the *Palladis Tamia*, in 1598."[23] A different editor, this time of *Much Ado*, is puzzled by that play's omission from Meres: "The play is not named in *Palladis Tamia*.... The omission might be accidental, but it creates a strong supposition that the play was not known when he completed his list, and so suggests the middle or latter part of 1598 as the earliest date of composition."[24] Another editor of *Much Ado* is equally surprised: "That *Much Ado* is not named is in no way conclusive that it was not in existence, but the quality of the play makes it likely that had Meres known it he would have named it."[25] Thus editors interpret Meres in several different ways:

1. Meres was not offering a complete list;
2. If a play is not mentioned by Meres Shakespeare has not yet written it;
3. Meres may have accidentally omitted a play, and
4. A play of quality is likely to have been mentioned by Meres.

These editors cannot all be right; collectively their views are contradictory, and one or more must be wrong.

One editor footnotes his comment on *Hamlet*'s date and Meres: "It [*Hamlet*] cannot have been known to Francis Meres in the autumn of 1598..." with a reference to Chambers' *William Shakespeare*, vol. II, 193–4.[26] Chambers, however, quotes only briefly and selectively from Meres, and gives no context. While it would be fair to say that not everyone will be riveted by Meres' style, a return to the original chapter is valuable for accurately evaluating Meres' evidence regarding the dates of some of Shakespeare's plays.

Don Cameron Allen is probably the scholar who has completed the most detailed study of this chapter of *Palladis Tamia*. His analysis is of Meres' sources for the chapter. Allen tells us that much of the content is drawn from J. Ravisius Textor's *Officina* (1520, with seven reprints before Meres), with material also from, for example, W. Webbe's *A Discourse of English Poetrie* (1586), George Puttenham's *The Arte of English Poetry* (1589), Petrus Crinitus' *De Poetis Latinis* (1518), Erasmus' *Parabolae sive Similia* (1514) or Mirabellius' *Polyanthea* (1503).[27] While Allen's focus is not upon Shakespeare but upon those sources, Allen's conclusion is nevertheless pertinent; he sees Meres' chapter on the literary figures of the past and present as a mixture of "pseudo-erudition and bluff."[28] Allen, in other words, does not see Meres as an expert in the field of literature.

What we are more concerned with is Meres' style. The "comparative" aspect of Meres' title is systematically sustained. The fifty-nine paragraphs, bar five or six, have a virtually identical structure. The paragraphs begin with the same lexeme, "As...," usually followed by a Greek, Latin or Italian writer or number of such writers, plus their claim to fame. This half of the sentence is concluded by a colon to mark where Meres' comparison pivots, and the second half of the sentence is then initiated by the continuer "so," followed by the English writer'(s) name(s), and his/their claim to fame. Most of the time the numbers of classical writers match the number of English authors or the numbers in each national group are the same. The majority of these balanced sentences focus on fame in the literary sense, though not quite all. The exemplar paragraph below, chosen for its brevity and its typical syntactic parallelism, leans more towards infamy in a non-literary sense:

As	Anacreon	died by the pot	:
(*begins comparison*)	(*Greek writer*)	("*fame*")	(*colon/pivot*)
so	George Peele	by the pox.[29]	
(*continuer*)	(*English writer*)	("*fame*")	

Again and again identical numbers of writers are cited. Paragraph 1 offers three Greek (Orpheus, Linus and Musæus), three Latin (L. Andronicus, Ennius and Plautus) and three English poets (Chaucer, Gower and Lydgate). Paragraph 2 offers Homer, Petrarch, and Chaucer as "Princes" and the "God" of Poets. In paragraph 24, the paragraph we are examining, the symmetry is broken: the two Roman playwrights Plautus and Seneca are accounted the best for comedy and tragedy, but just one English playwright, Shakespeare, is mentioned. One inference might be that Meres saw Shakespeare as just a prolific a playwright as Plautus (twenty plays) and Seneca (ten attributed to Seneca in Thomas Newton's 1581 collection) together. Meres offers twelve titles for Shakespeare. Those titles predictably follow the endlessly repetitive pattern Meres has established, so that six comedies (Plautus wrote comedies) are balanced by six "tragedies" (Seneca wrote tragedies). This neat patterning alone should prompt readers to question whether Meres was offering the titles of *all* Shakespeare's plays known by 7th September 1598, or simply another balanced list to continue his by now well-established appositive style. We should also question whether Meres gives all the titles of the works of the other English writers he cites.

In fact we can see that Meres does omit Shakespearean plays known by this date, such as *1 Henry VI*, known from Nashe's pamphlet *Pierce Penniless* in 1592, *2 Henry VI*, known from the Stationers' Register 1594 and Q1 (*Contention*), and *3 Henry VI*, from 1595. Meres therefore does not list all the Shakespearean titles known to have been in existence by this date.

Nor does Meres give complete information about other English writers. He refers to Marlowe six times, but includes no titles of any of Marlowe's plays (though Meres tells us that Marlowe is an "imitator" of Musæus, "who wrote the loue of Hero and Leander"[30]). Meres also names Thomas Kid, Benjamin Johnson [sic], Thomas Watson, Anthony Munday, Porter and Heywood, without including a single example of their works. However, for a small number of contemporary writers Meres does give titles. For Philip Sidney he mentions *The Countess of Pembroke's Arcadia*, and for Spenser *The Faerie Queene* and *The Shepherd's Calendar*. Yet these are not complete backlists for Sidney and Spenser by 1598, for Meres omits for example Sidney's *Astrophel and Stella* and Spenser's *Colin Clout comes home*. Table 14 on page 168 gives examples of several English writers whom Meres mentions, writers whose pre–1598 titles are *not* all given.

Despite omitting some publications by authors he cites, Meres does reference Everard Guilpin's *Skialethia*, entered on the Stationers' Register on 15th September 1598, eight days after his own book was registered. This demonstrates that Meres chose to be up to date with some authors.

What of Meres' ability to discriminate? One editor believes that the quality of *Much Ado* would have merited citation, if it had been written by this date. However, while Meres does mention Shakespeare nine times, Michael

Table 14. A Selection of English Authors Cited by Meres, with Titles of Works

Author	Times cited	Titles cited	Examples of pre-1598 titles *not* cited
Michael Drayton	12	Polyolbion England's Heroical Epistles	Idea, the Shepherd's Garland (1593)
Shakespeare	9	Venus and Adonis Lucrece sonnets, 12 plays	1, 2, 3 Henry VI (1594/95) (Hamlet [1589/94/96]) Taming of the Shrew (1594/96)
Philip Sidney	6	The Countess of Pembroke's Arcadia	Lady of May (1578) Astrophel and Stella (1591) Defence of Poesie (1591)
Edmund Spenser	9	Faerie Queene Shepherd's Calendar	Astrophel (1596) Colin Clout comes home (1595) Amoretti (1596) Epithalamium (1596)
Warner	5	Albion's England	Pan his Syrinx (1595) Translation of Plautus' Menæchmi (1595)
George Buchanan	1	Iephthe	De Jure Regni apud Scotos (1579) Rerum Scoticarum Historia (1582)

Drayton is mentioned more times than any other writer (twelve). Meres praises Drayton's "vertuous disposition" in "these declining and corrupt times, when there is nothing but roguery in villanous man, & when cheating and craftines is counted the cleanest wit, and soundest wisedome."[31] Meres' fondness for Drayton, who is barely read today, suggests perhaps a significant difference in taste, or that Meres lacked discrimination, or that Meres had been persuaded to promote Drayton (and perhaps Guilpin's *Skialethia*).

This brief examination of *Palladis Tamia* establishes that Meres does not offer a complete list of Shakespearean titles in his *Comparative Discourse*, or a complete list for other Elizabethan writers. Meres cannot be used to prove whether or not Shakespeare had written *Hamlet* at this point. The editor who suggested an "accidental" omission implies his expectation that Meres intended to include all, but this is demonstrably not Meres' achievement, nor his implicit intention. Which plays he did not know cannot be proved. Additionally, Meres' taste or discrimination is different from today's. His testimony in *Palladis Tamia* is limited, merely confirming the existence of some titles, and unfortunately it is of no value for dating Shakespeare's *Hamlet*.

Gabriel Harvey

Our next witness to *Hamlet* is Gabriel Harvey. Harvey refers twice to *Hamlet*, but uncertainty surrounds the dating of each reference. Virginia Stern, in *Gabriel Harvey: His Life, Marginalia and Library*, records both.[32] The first reference is in Harvey's copy of Guicciardini's *Detti, et Fatti*, printed in Venice 1571, and acquired by Harvey in 1580. Marginalia were added then, in 1590, and later, according to Stern. The critical passage runs thus: "Greene's quip for an upstart Courtier; & his art of connie catching: Diets drie dinner: a fresh supplie of Mensa philosophica; the Tragedie of Hamlet: Richard 3."[33] This passage is noted, little discussed, and is again problematic. Greene's *Quip for an vpstart Courtier* was published in 1592. He wrote several coney-catching pamphlets, for example *The Second Part of Conycatching* (1591), and *A Disputation between a Hee Conny-catcher and a Shee Conny-catcher* (1592). *Mensa Philosophica* (a tract including sententiae) was written by Michael Scot, whose dates are c. 1175–c. 1234. He was a mathematician, physician and scholar, and *Mensa Philosophica* was published in Frankfurt in 1602. *The Tragedie of Hamlet* is the beginning of Q1 and Q2's titles, and published in 1603, 1604 and 1605, and (Shakespeare's) *Richard III* was first published in 1597. Regrettably, this mixture of publication dates doesn't help with the dating of *Hamlet*.

The second reference is the more familiar one, found in the margins of Harvey's copy of Thomas Speght's *Works of Chaucer*, published in 1598. The significant part of the passage runs:

> The Earle of Essex much commends Albions England: ... The Lord Mountjoy makes the like account of Daniels peece of the Chronicle, touching the Vsurpation of Henrie of Bullingbrooke. Which in deede is a fine, sententious, & politique peece of Poetrie: as profitable, as pleasurable. The younger sort takes much delight in Shakespeares Venus, & Adonis: but his Lucrece, & his tragedie of Hamlet, prince of Denmarke, have it in them to please the wiser sort.... His [Sir Edward Dyer's] Amaryllis, & Sir Walter Raleighs Cynthia, how fine and sweet inuentions? Excellent matter of emulation for Spencer, Constable, France, Watson, Daniel, Warner, Chapman, Siluester, Shakespeare, & the rest of owr flourishing metricians ... & I haue a phansie to Owens new Epigrams....[34]

Discussion usually relates to the date at which Harvey added this manuscript note. A second issue for discussion might be why *Lucrece* and *Hamlet* are thus juxtaposed, when the qualities of the two are, at least today, assessed markedly differently, and when *Lucrece* is a narrative poem which, it is assumed here, Harvey read, while *Hamlet* is a drama which he could either have seen or read.

The Earl of Essex appears to be alive in the quotation ("commends" is present tense), so it is assumed Harvey inscribed the entry before Essex's execution on 25th February 1601, earlier than any known printed text of *Hamlet*. A present historic tense is possible, though perhaps unlikely. (The third earl was only born in 11.1.1591 and is therefore unlikely to be recommending such a text.) However, Harvey refers to Thomas Watson, as among "owr florishing metricians," although Watson died in 1592. It is a little difficult to comprehend "flourishing" when the poet is dead. Harvey has "a phansie to Owens new Epigrams...," but these are not published until 1607, although there is one, addressed to Burghley and dated 1596. Perhaps Harvey forgot Watson's demise, and had seen Owen's epigrams in manuscript, which is what Moore Smith suggests.[35] Stern gives it as her opinion that the marginalia above were probably written after 1st June 1599. *Hamlet* editors differ in their opinions, with Jenkins suggesting Harvey "even without a reading text" commended *Hamlet* before February 1601,[36] while Thompson and Taylor, recognizing the contradictions in Harvey's note, agree with Edwards that Harvey is "of little use in trying to date *Hamlet*."[37]

What is arguably more significant is the juxtaposition of *Lucrece* and *Hamlet*. Their written texts share one very distinctive feature, namely the presence of "pointing" or commonplace markings, the use of quotation marks at the beginning of a line to draw attention to it. Indeed, ninety-one quotations of a line or two were extracted from *Lucrece* by Anthony Munday and John Bodenham for their 1600 commonplace collection, *Bel-vedére*. Q1 *Hamlet* also has pointing, for some of Corambis' speeches (sig. C2r.23–32, 35, and sig. C2v.26–7 and 30). The quotation from Harvey, above, has been carefully presented to include what he celebrates in "Daniels peece of the Chronicle," namely that it is "a fine, sententious, & politique peece of Poetrie: as profittable, as pleasurable." Harvey admires Daniel's piece because it is "sententious," and *Lucrece* and Q1 *Hamlet* are marked to show their "sententiae." This may suggest why Harvey regards those written texts as pleasing the "wiser sort." This is entirely in keeping with Harvey's known character (master of rhetoric, yet also a "Pedantius"[38]), and it may indicate that Harvey saw *Hamlet* in its *written* form. That could have been Q1 or Q2 *Hamlet*, both of which have commonplace markings, though these are different. Could the marginalia's significance only be that they indicate Harvey saw a written text of *Hamlet*? If that written text was also a published text, it presumably postdates the publication of Q1 in 1603 or Q2 in 1604–5. Harvey's marginalia seem potentially valuable, but really contribute little to dating Shakespeare's *Hamlet*. The marginalia in Speght's Chaucer do firmly link Shakespeare and *Hamlet*—that is all. And it appears, though this is not certain, that Harvey is linking the two after the date, *c.* 1600, by which time most scholars propose Shakespeare has written his (Q2) *Hamlet*.

1601: Thomas Dekker's Satiromastix

Since Shakespeare is supposed to have written *Hamlet* by *c.* 1600, this may be why few do much more than mention briefly Thomas Dekker's play, *Satiromastix*, registered for publication in November 1601. In it one character called Tucca replies to another, Asinius:

> *Tucca.* No, Fye'st; my name's Hamlet reuenge: thou hast been at Parris garden, hast not? [TLN 1511-4].[39]

There is little discussion of this. While the date is just after many think Shakespeare has written his Q2 *Hamlet*, yet Dekker/Tucca could be referring to the continuing acting of the *Hamlet* of 1589, 1594, and 1596, since Dekker will obviously have completed his play at some point before its 1601 publication. Curiously, Tucca has the same "soundbite" of "Hamlet reuenge" that Lodge used. It appears that while Lodge's soundbite of 1596 is *not* taken by many as alluding to a Shakespearean *Hamlet*, Dekker's soundbite of at the latest 1601 *could* be doing so. If so, there would be an inconsistency in how "Hamlet, revenge" and "Hamlet reuenge" are interpreted. Logically, the interpretation should be the same for Lodge's soundbite in 1596 and Dekker's Tucca in 1601.

We may also note that while Dekker/Tucca does emphasize the popularity of *Hamlet*, once again there is no hint of an author.

1602 Stationers' Register

The Stationers' Register entry for 26th July 1602 names only the play, "A booke called the Revenge of Hamlett Prince of Denmarke." This title links with Lodge's reference to the ghost crying "Hamlet, revenge," and with Dekker's line, "my name's Hamlet reuenge," and with the protagonist and the main theme. The entry does not name the author. It is entered for James Roberts, who prints Q2 in 1604. It would be consistent to accept Lodge, Dekker and this entry as referring to the same *Hamlet*.

1603: Q1 Hamlet

Q1's title is "The Tragicall Historie of Hamlet Prince of Denmarke," apparently echoing the source's title, *Les Histoires Tragiques*. It appears that this printing is of the play entered in 1602. While Q1 is printed by Valentine Simmes for Nicholas Ling and John Trundell, Q2 is printed by James Roberts for Nicholas Ling. It means that we have six texts with two types of reference to a Hamlet story, three references focusing on *revenge*, and three on the *tragic history* of the Prince. All three can be found in Shakespeare's adulthood. The S. R. entry (*revenge*) and Q1 and Q2 (*tragic history*) are handled by people who overlap, James Roberts being associated with the S.R. entry and Q2, and Nicholas Ling with Q1 and Q2. Table 15 shows these overlaps and links juxtaposed. We do have to ask ourselves whether it is credible to claim Lodge's allusion "Hamlet, revenge" is to a non–Shakespearean text, but perhaps Dekker's "Hamlet reuenge" is to a Shakespearean one. We should then wonder what to make of "the Revenge of Hamlett," which seems to refer to Shakespeare's *Hamlet*. Table 15 brings these linked phrases together as a summary.

Table 15. Linking the *Hamlet*s

Date	Text	Title	Allusion	Entered by	Printed by	Printed for
1576 onwards	Source	*Les Histoires Tragiques*				
1596	*Wits miserie*		"Hamlet, revenge"			
1601	*Satiro-mastix*		"Hamlet reuenge"			
1602	S. R. entry	*Revenge of Hamlett*		James Robertes		
1603	Q1	*Tragicall Historie of Hamlet*			Valentine Simmes	N[icholas] L[ing], John Trundell
1604	Q2	*Tragicall Historie of Hamlet*			I[ames] R[oberts]	N[icholas] L[ing]

Q1 states on its title page that the play is by Shakespeare. Since he is by now a successful playwright, it would not be surprising if his name appeared on the title page whether it were his, or an abridgement of his, or even if it were a not entirely legitimate version (like a memorial reconstruction), because Shakespeare's name would have been associated with the play, and might "sell" the quarto.

The title page also claims that the play was "diuerse times acted by his Highnesse seruants in the Cittie of London: as also in the two Vniversities of Cambridge and Oxford, and else-where." It would be rewarding to find a *Hamlet* play recorded at one of these locations. Boas did make a proposal: "The Lord Chamberlain's Men are mentioned in the Cambridge accounts in 1594–5, and it may have been then, and not as generally thought, in 1601–2, that *Hamlet* (as is stated on the title page of the quarto of 1603) was acted at Cambridge."[40] Alan Nelson, editing the *Records of Early English Drama*, notes the university records relate to payments made for plays and for players to go away. Payments for plays were made in 1586–7, and 1587–8. Players were paid to leave Cambridge University in 1579–80, 1583–4, 1590–1, and 1591–2. Nelson writes that "the connection of *Hamlet* to a performance in 1594–5 (Boas' view) must remain doubtful."[41] Certainly where titles are not given a performance of *Hamlet* cannot be corroborated, but where titles are not given the possibility of one can also not be excluded.

Despite Boas' suggestion that *Hamlet* was performed in the city of Oxford in 1593, and in Cambridge in 1594–5, locations mentioned on Q1's title page, there is no known, dated reference to a performance of *Hamlet* in Oxford, or Cambridge. Burkhart, however, is one who accepts that Q1's "title-page, then, explicitly tells us that Q1 was used in provincial performances."[42] Paul Menzer considers that "Q1's title page may again be stretching back in time to include performances at Cambridge and Oxford" in the 1590s.[43]

There are further gaps and hints in the records. We know that the common players visited Oxford in the 1580s, since Robert Leicester, Chancellor of Oxford, is the signatory to a text dating to 1583–4 noting that:

> this vniuersitye of late hath often times bin greuoslye visited by reson of the extraordenary concurse of people at vnsesonable times of the yeare to see stage playse and games ... no common stage players be permitted ... with in the precinct of the vniversitye ... and if it happen by extraordinary means yat stage players shall get or obtane leaue ... yet it shall not be lawfull for anye master bachiler or scoller aboue the age of eighteen to repaire or go to see anye such thinge vnder paine of imprisonment ... and if any vnder the age of eighteen shall so presume ... the party so offending shall suffer open punishment....

It seems a real effort was to be made to ban enjoyment of such plays. The note continues: "...the prohibicion of common stage players very requisite so wolde I not haue it meant theare bye theat the tragedies commodies & other shewes of exercises of learning ... should be forbidden...."[44] There is also a Privy Council letter relating to performances at Cambridge, including the comment: "the common Plaiers do ordinarily resorte to the Vniversytie of Cambridge there to recite Interludes and Plaies ... besides the gathering together of multitudes of People...."[45] The numbers—"multitudes"—might contribute to how Nashe or Lodge can allude to a *Hamlet* with the apparent expectation it will be known to their readers. Such "common stage players" and "Plaies" may accommodate the possibility of a *Hamlet* performance at one or other university. We might suspect that some of these banned players and their plays did perform at Cambridge despite the "prohibicion," since the Cambridge *Parnassus* plays show the students' familiarity with the actors Richard Burbage and William Kempe, and with "sweet Mr Shakspeare" and Ben Jonson. So while the university records do not confirm any performance of *Hamlet*, their incompleteness and some supplementary evidence do not rule out such a performance.

In 1604 Q2 is published, and debate about whether subsequent *Hamlet*s are Shakespeare's ceases. In the same year Anthony Scoloker's *Diaphantus or the Passions of Love* is published, in which he writes that a book should "please all, like Prince Hamlet."[46] It is a play which has delighted theatre-goers and readers for over four hundred years, even if its origins remain unclear.

One of the many mysteries associated with Shakespeare is that we do not know when he began to write. A cursory glance at some of Shakespeare's contemporaries shows they were writing and published or their plays were performed, when they were in their twenties. John Lyly, born in 1554, had his first romance *Euphues* published in 1579, age twenty-five, and his first comedy, *The Woman in the Moon*, produced by 1583. Christopher Marlowe, born the same year as Shakespeare, had plays performed in the 1580s. *Dido, Queen of Carthage* seems to have been his first, and was acted between 1587 and 1590, and *Tamberlaine the Great* was on stage in 1587 when Marlowe was twenty-three. Thomas Nashe, born three years after Shakespeare, had his *Epistle* published when he was twenty-two. Ben Jonson's *Every Man in His Humour* was performed in 1598 when he was twenty-six. If Shakespeare wrote in his twenties, it would not be surprising if he were writing in the 1580s. Ben Jonson dates *Titus Andronicus* to 1584–9, in his *Induction to Bartholomew Fair*,[47] and Shakespeare is also linked to at least two history plays by 1592.[48] *Venus and Adonis* is published in 1593, when Shakespeare was twenty-nine. If Nashe's reference is to an early Shakespearean *Hamlet* play, of 1588–9, Shakespeare would be writing in his early to mid-twenties and would be just as precocious as his contemporaries, even if some of his greatest writing would come later.

The key question in Part Three is whether any of the pre-publication references to *Hamlet* are to someone else's play, or to Q1, or Q2, or even to F1. There is nothing in the writings of Nashe, Henslowe, Lodge, Harvey or Dekker to indicate whether it is Shakespeare's play to which they refer, or to which version of *Hamlet* they allude. There *is* a general consensus among scholars that Q2 is greater in literary and philosophical content (and maturity), and it might be supposed that if Nashe's *Hamlet* allusion was to a Shakespearean *Hamlet*, it is more likely to be to Q1, as Knight, Dyce, Staunton and others thought. This supposition is based on scholars' assessments of Q1 and Q2, and on an absence of evidence to the contrary.

This leads to the most critical question: do any of the references to a *Hamlet* pre–1603 unambiguously point towards, or away from, Shakespeare as its author? Nashe's *Epistle* does include "*Hamlets*" and "Kid" within seven lines of each other. Nothing stylistically, grammatically, or semantically, links them. "Kid" can be explained wholly in reference to Spenser's *May Eclogue*. It is entirely possible (and very likely) that "Kid" is simply a fortuitous homophone of "Kyd." While Thomas Kyd may be included in the criticisms of the "sort of shifting companions" (as perhaps Shakespeare is too), Nashe does not explicitly link Kyd and "*Hamlets*." Nashe's *Epistle* does not point to any author of a *Hamlet*. Malone's reasoning regarding the entry in Henslowe's *Diary* is clearly erroneous in four respects. Malone is a respected and significant authority, which may be why it is that his views on this minor matter do not appear to be questioned. Henslowe's *Diary* entry for "hamlet" gives no indication of author, but it is close to other entries of plays which have titles similar to some now associated with Shakespeare. Consequently the Henslowe entry cannot exclude, and may even support, Shakespeare as the author of that *Hamlet*.

Lodge gives no indication of the authorship of the *Hamlet* tragedy. However, the analogies of "chast Matilda," "great *Gaueston*" and "the downfal[s] of valiant *Robert of Normandy*" show that it is reasonable to identify "Hamlet, revenge" as just an Elizabethan soundbite, enough for Lodge to reference the play and amuse the reader. That we cannot find the exact phrase in any *Hamlet* does not mean Lodge cannot be alluding to Shakespeare's *Hamlet*—that is faulty and possibly anachronistic reasoning. Meres, as several Shakespearean scholars recognize, offers no proof of whether or not *Hamlet*, or other unnamed plays, had been written by 1598. An absence of citation proves nothing. Harvey's marginalia in Guicciardini's *Detti, et Fatti* probably refer to a written text, not a performance; his marginalia in Speght's *Chaucer* probably refer to a written *Hamlet*, since he pairs it with *Lucrece*. Harvey praises "sententious" writing in the same note, and claims the two texts would appeal to the "wiser sort"; both include commonplace markings for the written texts' *sententiae*. However, Harvey offers us nothing useful or certain regarding the date of Shakespeare's *Hamlet*. The *Satiromastix* reference to *Hamlet* in 1601 comes close upon the heels of Shakespeare's alleged composition of Q2. If its "Hamlet reuenge" refers to a Shakespearean *Hamlet*, we ought to reconsider how to interpret Lodge's "Hamlet, revenge."

Part Three's question about whether there was an *Ur-Hamlet* can only have a qualified answer. We cannot escape from the fact that Shakespeare is not unambiguously associated with *Hamlet* before the title page of Q1. However, no other author is connected with a play of that name prior to 1600, and Shakespeare's name *is* associated with it from 1603. The evidence for Shakespeare having an "early" or "late" start as a writer is very limited; the evidence for which version of *Hamlet* is referred to *c.* 1589 is non-existent. We can hardly see Nashe, Henslowe, Meres, Harvey, Dekker and the S. R. entry for "the Revenge of Hamlett" as providing evidence for the concept of an *Ur-*

Hamlet. The contemporary evidence does not indicate that anyone other than Shakespeare was associated with a *Hamlet* play; it does not indicate that there was an *Ur-Hamlet* by Thomas Kyd or anyone else. In fact the contemporary evidence leaves wide open the possibility that Nashe et al. were referring to a version of *Hamlet* by Shakespeare.

Conclusion: Closing with the Consequences

Greg's Foreword to Duthie's *"Bad" Quarto of Hamlet* included this comment:

> It is not to be supposed that Dr Duthie's monograph will be accepted as offering a final solution of the problem. It is hardly to be desired that it should. But I do think that it will prove an important step towards such a solution, and hope that it may, even in these days, arouse further interest in the subject.[1]

Many scholars accept Duthie's argument for a pre–Shakespearean *Hamlet* and for memorial reconstruction. As we noted in the Introduction, his book on the alleged MR of Q1 is by far the most detailed exploration of any of the principal theories of how the *Hamlet*s are related. Some add to his proposals, but others demur, disagree, or refer to them guardedly.[2] He has certainly aroused "further interest" in the relationship of the quartos.

This book includes a review of many of Duthie's points and offers fresh evidence, but it is not to be supposed that this monograph will be the last solution offered for the *Hamlet* quartos either. One reason might be that *The First Two Quartos of Hamlet*'s review of mainstream views on the *Hamlet*s questions several aspects of scholarly work on a much loved play, whichever *Hamlet* we most value. However, those scholars' ideas have been vital stepping stones for the investigations behind this study. It is their discussions which have led to the three crucial questions at the heart of the book: which quarto came first, how secure the hypothesis of MR is, and whether an *Ur-Hamlet* existed. By no means has every line of the *Hamlet*s been scrutinized and there is more to consider, but the book seeks to answer the basic question of the quartos' chronology first. As Wells and Taylor write, aspects of the dating of *Hamlet* do "depend on the validity of the hypothesis of memorial reconstruction."[3]

The First Two Quartos of Hamlet underlines the different views of scholars, and distinguishes between what is opinion or hypothesis, and what is supported by evidence. The book recognizes that some believe that Q1 comes first, while others believe that Q2 does; some believe in a first sketch and revision, others in MR, some in abridgement and some in a combination of those. These beliefs are incompatible. And it shows that while some give credit to the hypothesis of an *Ur-Hamlet*, others don't. Yet if we are to study the *Hamlet*s and make progress in our understanding of Shakespeare and the canon, these differences and the reasoning behind them need to be examined.

The methodology behind this book avoids speculation as far as possible. "Reasoned speculation," said one conference delegate at the Shakespeare Institute in 2013, is a legitimate part of the Humanities approach to subjects.[4] While this is true, when hypotheses and speculations are put forward we ought to try to establish their validity. It is the norm to propose and test hypotheses and, if a weakness or weaknesses are found, or if new evidence comes to light, to review the hypotheses. *The First Two Quartos of Hamlet* seeks to be objective and precise in its reassessment of the quartos and the beliefs surrounding them. It employs literary, linguistic and measurable techniques, and it attempts to minimize speculation. It tries to avoid biased terminology like "addition," "omission," "cut," "elimination" and so forth, which is often used in a context which connotes the unproven priority of Q2. It deliberately uses "hedges."[5] Although hedges may clutter the text, adverbs like "possibly," "perhaps," "probably," and modal verbs like "could," "may," "might" and so on, do signal where speculation is taking over from fact. The aim here is to discover what is certain and what else can be ascertained through reproducible evidence.

Let us return to the carefully phrased summary of the dominant narrative about *Hamlet*.

> In 1603 appeared an inferior text apparently assembled from actors' memories.... It is our belief that Shakespeare wrote *Hamlet* about 1600, and revised it later; that the 1604 edition was printed from his original papers; that the Folio represents the revised version; and that the 1603 edition represents a very imperfect report of an abridged version of the revision.[6]

Even though the summary is some twenty-five years old these are still basically the views expressed in recent *Hamlet* editions. For example, Bate and Rasmussen in their RSC edition of *Hamlet* (2008), write: "Scholars ... suppose that Shakespeare's play was written about 1600, but that it was a reworking of an older, now lost play.... The old *Hamlet* is sometimes speculatively attributed to Thomas Kyd.... A few scholars suppose that Shakespeare himself wrote the early version.... Though there is no firm evidence as to authorship or content, we may safely assume that the old *Hamlet* play (sometimes known as the *Ur-Hamlet*)...."[7]

We have noted already that the phrasing in the summary is careful ("belief") and cautious ("apparently"), and avoids presenting the account as fact. The phrasing may mean that if other or further evidence emerges the authors might be persuaded to adjust their beliefs. The description of the 1603 text as "inferior" shows that Q1 is not their preferred *Hamlet*, but it is not as damning as "corrupt" and "garbled." The authors are literary academics and prefer perhaps Q2, or F1, or a conflation. We have seen, however, that theatre practitioners can find Q1 effective in performance. The evaluative "inferior" reasonably assumes a certain kind of reader or audience.

"[A]ssembled from actors' memories" is qualified by "apparently"; the writers do not wholly commit themselves to this account of Q1's composition. Part Two shows us that there are serious reasons to doubt both that assemblage and the hypothesis of MR. Doubt begins with what seems to have been the legitimate printing of Q1, and the continuing association of those involved in that publication with the publishing of other Shakespeare plays. The lack of contemporary evidence for MR is another reason. The quantitative analysis of the key analogy, Bernard's reconstruction of Sheridan's *School for Scandal* in 1779, undermines that analogy substantially. The "forgetfulness" of "Marcellus" as an actor/reporter in not recalling all his lines nor being totally accurate, and of "Voltemand" not recalling his name, add to the reasons. Duthie ingeniously proposes that the parallel phrases between other Shakespearean plays and Q1 are actor/reporter'(s) "borrowings" from a wide range of different acting roles in different plays. He appears to overlook alternative suggestions and evidence, such as Shakespeare himself using such vocabulary and phrasing more than once. We need to be cautious about accepting some of Duthie's inventive descriptions of the operation of the memorial reconstructor(s): "the reporter remembered, though not very distinctly"; the reporter "misplaced" the phrase[8]; he "confuses"[9]; he "had a hazy memory of...,"[10] and his "memory temporarily broke down."[11] The list of near synonyms is extensive, and really each has an implied modal verb, such as the reporter *might have* "misplaced" the phrase, or he *may have* "had a hazy memory of...," or an adverb connoting possibility (not certainty), such as *perhaps* his "memory temporarily broke down." In other words, Duthie's narrative is speculative. The parallel phrases between Q1 and *The Spanish Tragedy*—selectively edited by Duthie, and dismissed by Maguire—also have more than one explanation. Additionally they depend on *The Spanish Tragedy* being the earlier text, when we do not know the date of either text. Neither set of verbal echoes, from other Shakespearean texts and from *The Spanish Tragedy*, provide proof of MR. Duthie's "objectionable" pronouns of scene 14 are, upon simple analysis, consistent and skilful ways of conveying asides. They reflect how a character's thoughts are conventionally conveyed on stage, and natural usage in speech. They show some subtle stage craft, and appear in the one scene which is quite different in the two quartos, the one scene we would have to argue is solely the creation of a "reporter" if we accept the MR hypothesis. The three way comparison between the source and the quartos provides major, further challenges to the hypothesis of MR.

Together these analyses "test" the "reasoned speculation" that has given us the hypothesis of MR. Together they reduce the credibility of MR; in reality, they show that the hypothesis is untenable for *Hamlet*, just as it is for the first quarto of *King Lear*, rather as Laurie Maguire shows that nearly thirty claims for the memorial reconstruction of other Elizabethan or Jacobean plays are unsustainable. As a little Danish boy in a Hans Christian Andersen story once said of his emperor, "han har jo ikke noget på."[12]

The first "belief" given in the summary is that "Shakespeare wrote *Hamlet* about 1600," a date widely given for Q2. That depends upon another hypothesis, that of the putative *Ur-Hamlet*, and upon the earlier mentions of a *Hamlet* not being to a Shakespearean *Hamlet*. Part Three reviews the undoubted evidence for a *Hamlet* played and known by or in at least 1589, 1594, and 1596, in other words before this "*Hamlet* about 1600." We have seen that the hypothesis linking Nashe's "*Hamlets*" and "the Kid in *Æsop*" to a Kyddian *Ur-Hamlet* is weakened by several factors. These include the lack of grammatical or semantic link between the two quotations, the fact that the list of criticisms in the extract in Chapter 11 do not apply consistently or exclusively to Kyd, Nashe's undoubted use here of Spenser's fable in *The May Eclogue*, the contemporary gloss to *The May Eclogue* which clearly identifies Nashe's second "*Æsop*" as the "diuine Master *Spencer*," and the stylistic quirk Nashe uses there and later in the *Epistle*. McKerrow did try to stem the speculations in his notes in 1910 with his aside that no one had associated Nashe's earlier Æsop anecdote with a Mr Glowworm.[13] Chapter 12 shows that Malone's conjecture and conclusions about the "hamlet" performed at Newington Butts are erroneous on *four* separate counts. We can say that Henslowe confirms the existence of a *Hamlet* play, but his entry tells us nothing about the author, the value of the play, or the frequency with which it was played. Lodge's "Hamlet, revenge" is paralleled by Meres' "soundbites," like "chast Matilda," so that Lodge also confirms the existence of a *Hamlet*, though not its author.

Yet someone has to have written that early *Hamlet*. There is nothing at present to prove it wasn't Shakespeare's. We also know that not all Elizabethan plays are attributed to their authors when the titles first appear. An obvious example of that, and an ironic one, is *The Spanish Tragedy*. It was performed on 23rd February 1592, and therefore written before that date, but its earliest recorded link to Kyd is in Thomas Heywood's *Apology for Actors* in 1612.[14] That's a gap of at least twenty years. It is a maximum of fourteen years between the first mention of a *Hamlet* (by Nashe) and the link between a *Hamlet* and "William Shake-speare" (Q1's title page). The gap we find today for linking *The Spanish Tragedy* to Kyd could be used as an analogy for linking the early mentions of a *Hamlet* to Shakespeare. And if Shakespeare were considered an "upstart" in 1592,[15] it would not be surprising that he is not named three years earlier as the author of the early *Hamlet*.

We might note in passing that the second belief is that Shakespeare "revised it later." This means that it is acceptable to see Shakespeare revising *King Lear*, and Q2 *Hamlet* into F1 (presumably), but not to see him revising Q1 into Q2 (presumably). Perhaps "revising" connotes a limited amount of change. The difference between Q1 and Q2 may better be described as redrafting, connoting substantial revision.

The last "belief" presented in the summary and examined in *The First Two Quartos of Hamlet* is that "the 1603 edition represents a very imperfect report of an abridged version of the revision." This belief places Q1 as the posterior text, certainly later than Q2 (and perhaps F1). The literature on the subject of the priority of the quartos tends to be summative rather than exploratory, perhaps because within twenty years of Q1 becoming known to scholars there was criticism of it and doubts about it being Shakespeare's. (Q1 was rediscovered in 1823, reprinted in 1825, and Collier is expressing doubts by 1842.) However, Part One has shown us that there are several significant problems associated with claiming the priority of Q2. One measurable, external reference point is given by the evolution of the English language. Albert Baugh describes Modern English (*c.* 1500 to today) as "the period of lost inflections," because in comparison with Old English we have very few inflections.[16] Chapter 1's analysis shows that Q1 has proportionally more dated third person singular present tense inflections than Q2. If we insist Q2 comes first, that finding needs a supplementary explanation or another hypothesis. A second reference point is the trend scholars themselves have identified, of Shakespeare's progression from fewer colloquialisms to more, as sampled in Q1's scene 16 and in Q2's corresponding scene, in V.i. The overview of such features in Q1 and Q2, in Chapter 1 and Appendix A, confirms the trend. Those findings also need a supplementary explanation if the trend is right and if we insist Q2 comes first.

Some may be happy to attribute those differences to actors, reporters, and/or compositors. Certainly it would be wrong to assume that Shakespeare's plays were not touched up and/or altered in the process of transcribing them for actors' parts, for a prompt copy, adapting them for the stage, and/or for the printing press. But on the evidence of the surviving texts there is a further indication of Q1's priority. Chapters two to five give us reproducible evidence which shows that Q1 is subtly closer than Q2 to *Les Histoires Tragiques*, the text which all scholars agree is the underlying source of the *Hamlet*s. This evidence lies in the parallels in phrasing and plot, with Q1's echoes of the source being almost double the density of those in Q2. More evidence lies, for example, in the order of specific ideas: both the source and Q1 have the "test" using "quelque belle femme" or Ofelia almost immediately after the proposal for the "test," while Q2 delays it for nearly 600 lines. The source and Q1 label the King a murderer quite explicitly; in Q2 the accusation is oblique. The phrasing of the Prince's request for secrecy and the Queens' responses are close in the source and Q1; Q2's are both different, in content and in style. Placing Q1 first gives us an explanation for scene 14 where the Queen learns of Hamlet's return, because it leans upon the Prince in *Les Histoires Tragiques* telling his mother he will return. In Q2 a Messenger delivers letters to the King for both him and the Queen. She is not present, and there is nothing in Q2 to confirm that she receives the letter, or to tell us what her reaction to his return is. The chapters show this and more; they underline Q1's closeness to the source, and Q2's slightly more distant relationship with it.

Neither the MR nor the abridgement hypotheses can account for those parallels and differences. To try to do so requires us to create yet more hypotheses, as well as to suggest a putative *Ur-Hamlet*. It might require the speculation, for instance, that the hypothetical *Ur-Hamlet* was closer to the French source, *and* that it was available to the actor/reporter(s) *and* that he/they used it. Nor would this resolve all the problems associated with MR. Duthie admits to a dilemma over Hamlet's age in Q2—thirty—but it is much less of a dilemma if Q1 has priority. *Les Histoires Tragiques* gives us a story about an uncle who kills a King to gain a kingdom and a Queen. It gives us a Prince who is on the verge of adulthood, and feels acutely his lack of "advancement"/ "preferment" (*Les Histoires Tragiques* and Q1). The Prince feels so vulnerable he deliberately adopts an appearance of madness and an equivocating manner in speech, as defense mechanisms. This is the young man we see in *Les Histoires Tragiques* and in Q1. Why Hamlet is thirty in Q2 can puzzle ordinary readers of the play, and we can only speculate about it. Shakespeare might have read Nashe's rant about the Danes, their aversion to learning and bearded boys learning their ABC at thirty,[17] though this is *not* put forward as a serious suggestion. Or perhaps Shakespeare "aged" his Prince for Burbage to play him (Burbage was thirty-seven in 1604), or decided that the philosophical aspects of his Q2 protagonist were more appropriate to a thirty year old Hamlet. Whatever his reasons, Shakespeare set up the Q2 (and F1) Hamlet to be thirty. Most actors of Hamlet are at least that age today. David Tennant was thirty-seven in 2008, Rory Kinnear was thirty-two in 2010, and Jonathan Slinger forty-one in 2013. A young Hamlet would carry additional vulnerability.[18] His lack of "preferment" (Q1) would be that of a Prince perhaps not quite old enough to be King. The Prince's pain in seeing his mother's switch of affections would be the greater, particularly when Ofelia obeys her father in the "nunnery" scene, and for the reader/audience the loss of a young Prince might well be more poignant, more tragic.

But these last comments about the vulnerability of a young Hamlet are subjective. The similarity in the Prince's age in the source and in Q1 does not logically fit a source (young Prince) > (*Ur-Hamlet*? >) Q2 (older) > (F1 [older]>) Q1 (younger) > later editions (older) model.[19] What renders that possible sequence even less believable are the subtleties in characters and their relationships which chapters four and five begin to develop. Most significant is the Queen's role. Her prominence and the intimacy of her relationship with Hamlet is slightly reduced across several scenes from (*Les Histoires Tragiques* to) Q1 to Q2. A sequence from source to Q1 to Q2 offers an uncomplicated, consistent and logical evolution in the handling of Queen and Prince. To reject that is to argue that an actor/reporter, suspected of having a "defective memory,"[20] was nevertheless sophisticated enough to handle the development of several characters—King, Queen, Prince—across a series of scenes, coincidentally returning some aspects of these characters to their former selves in *Les Histoires Tragiques*.

The analyses and new evidence in Parts One, Two and Three provide a basis for a re-evaluation of the dominant narrative about Q1 and Q2 *Hamlet*. They also open up further areas for research. For instance, this book is concerned with the first two quartos, and largely neglects F1, though Appendix C does show that F1, like Q2, is further from the French source than Q1. The subtleties of character development and changes between the quartos—or rather, from Q1 to Q2—are still only touched upon. There is potential for elaboration, and the chance to increase our knowledge of how Shakespeare worked on this play. Since *King Lear* (1608) is seen as a first draft, and there is now firm evidence to show Q1 *Hamlet*'s priority, there may be implications for the whole hypothesis of MR in Elizabethan and Jacobean times.

If we remove the complex web of hypotheses and assumptions of an *Ur-Hamlet* and of MR and of Q2's priority, what might replace it? It is difficult to create a comprehensive new narrative when there are still so many unknowns: for example, exactly what Shakespeare learnt in school, exactly which sources he used, how he accessed them, when he learnt French, when he began to write, whether there were juvenilia, if so what they were like, and how far he collaborated with other playwrights. However, the findings in this book are just enough to begin to construct a brief, coherent, referenced and evidenced narrative about the *Hamlet* quarto. It is a narrative which needs no major hypotheses, one where there are a small number of possibilities, clearly signaled, each of which can be accepted or rejected without affecting the basic account. It is one which suggests a precocious young playwright who wrote an early *Hamlet*, and returned to it a decade or so later, and "[n]ewly ... enlarged [it] to almost as much againe as it was."[21] The narrative draws upon the findings of the previous chapters, presenting them this time not as counter-arguments to some scholars' claims but instead as evidence contributing to an account about the *Hamlet* quartos.

Q1 and Q2: An Alternative Narrative

A tentative, alternative narrative still begins with Saxo Grammaticus and his *Historiae Danicae*, prose tales written in Latin by a Dane somewhere towards the end of the twelfth century. The tale of Amlethus is still translated by François de Belleforest into a French story about Amleth, by 1570. Volume V of Belleforest's *Histoires Tragiques*, including the tale of Amleth, is published in 1576, 1582 and 1583. One of these, perhaps the 1576 version (suggested by A. Stabler[22]) is the version a young Shakespeare, probably in his early twenties, seizes upon to rewrite as an English drama. The title *Les Histoires Tragiques* is echoed in Q1's title, *The Tragicall Historie of Hamlet Prince of Denmarke*.

We cannot be certain exactly what appealed in *Les Histoires Tragiques*, but we can see in simple terms which parts of the tale Shakespeare kept or cut, and what he added for Q1 *Hamlet*. (In this narrative Q1 is identified with the early *Hamlet*. Harold Bloom writes that in his view "Peter Alexander was correct in his surmise that Shakespeare himself wrote the "*Ur-Hamlet*," no later than 1589,"[23] which may indicate that Bloom is one who believes there was a Shakespearean pre–Q1 *Hamlet*. In the absence of such a text, this narrative takes a simple approach.) Shakespeare kept the story of the warrior King who was murdered by his brother who then took the widowed Queen to wife. Shakespeare kept the Prince, who is both nephew and stepson to the new King; Shakespeare kept the Prince's assumed "antic disposition," his equivocation, his rejection of the new King, and the affection he inspires in a particular young woman. Shakespeare re-used specific plot elements: the test with the young woman to check the Prince's real state of mind, the eavesdropper in the Queen's room and the eavesdropper's death, the Prince's awareness of how he lacked advancement, and his intention to avenge his father's death. The King's servants remain, and act as the Prince's escorts to England where their instructions say he should be killed. The Prince still returns and exacts revenge with a swapped sword, having confided in his mother.

In this narrative it is Shakespeare who cuts out significant parts of the Amleth story. Amleth is a brutal, proactive avenger and a bigamist. He seduces the (willing) young woman in the first test, finds and dismembers the eavesdropper's body, and feeds it to swine. Before he is sent to England he has already decided when he will return, and informs his mother accordingly. In England he proves himself to the English King, and wins a wife, before returning to Denmark to kill his father's murderer and take his throne; later he takes a second wife. Shakespeare omits all this.

As a consequence Shakespeare gives himself two major challenges. The first is how to present his protagonist, because the playwright has rejected the bloodthirsty, proactive, avenging aspects of Amleth. Instead Q1's Hamlet is Amleth with his hands tied. Hamlet doesn't have two friends warning him, separately, that the visit of the young woman is a trap or "test" (as Amleth does). He doesn't seduce Ofelia in the "nunnery" scene (as Amleth does), and he doesn't kill the eavesdropping counselor before he has spoken to his mother (as Amleth does). Hamlet doesn't calculatedly plan the day he will take revenge (as Amleth does), he doesn't receive assistance from his mother (as Amleth does), and he doesn't engineer the success of his act of revenge by totally disabling the court with alcohol (as Amleth does). Secondly, in turning his protagonist into an honorable, reflective and tragic figure, Shakespeare cannot just cut out the year-long escape to England which takes up a sizeable part of Amleth's story. Shakespeare cannot have his Prince move straight from becoming aware of his father's murder into becoming a murderer himself, albeit an avenger. Briefly, Shakespeare seems to fill the time or gap not so much with what is sometimes described as a delay as with showing his hero's hesitancy in accepting the word of a spirit from another world, with intensifying the tragedy of losing his father by creating a nearly parallel subplot, with the murder of his father reflected in the play within a play, and with the creation of the indefinable, philosophizing enigma that is Hamlet.

Inspiration for the Ghost may come from at least two sources. In this narrative Shakespeare is writing shortly after Thomas Newton's 1581 collection of translations of Senecan tragedies is published, with its revenge themes, ghosts, and "Tragicall speeches." Perhaps Seneca does influence Shakespeare at some level. It may be that Shakespeare notes the classical "ombre(s)" in *Les Histoires Tragiques*. He then turns the "ombre(s)" into a Ghost who appears earlier in the story, to inform his son of the murderous uncle/King's actions (as noted in Chapter 2, as well as by Stabler and Jenkins[24]). It might therefore be that Belleforest inspires the concept of a Ghost who comes to tell us what has happened, not just because of the "ombre(s)" but also because the French writer tells us Amleth was taught the art in which evil spirits can tell men of past events.[25] The mention of the "ombres" in the "chambre" scene is then transformed into Hamlet's father's Ghost. Just as it is only Amleth who speaks about the "ombres" in the "chambre" scene, so it is only Hamlet who sees the Ghost in the Queen's closet. Another addition, Hamlet's more philosophical thoughts, may be influenced by Montaigne's *Essais*, published in 1581.[26] And somehow Shakespeare seems to have heard or read about the case of *Hales v. Pettit*.[27] Belleforest, Montaigne, and the legal case were all available in French.

This early *Hamlet* is written and performed in the second half of the 1580s. One speech is exclusive to Q1, about adlibbing, extemporizing actors. It could be that Shakespeare is alluding to Richard Tarleton who was notorious for his extemporizing wit—Meres tells us so, for example.[28] A couple of Tarleton's jokes appear to be echoed in Q1, but are not in the later Q2 or F1. Tarleton's death in September 1588 may mean that by the time Shakespeare is revising, or redrafting, *Hamlet*, this reference is passé, no longer the "brief abstract or chronicles of the times." Or, as Wilson puts it, "Tarleton died in September 1588, after which a sneer at him would be, to say the least of it, old-fashioned."[29]

Shakespeare is an unknown in the 1580s, and for the audiences "the play's the thing." Consequently he is not initially named as its author, just as Thomas Kyd isn't initially named as the author of *The Spanish Tragedy*. But the early *Hamlet* is performed. Perhaps the play is one of the untitled "interludes or Plaies" at Cambridge University mentioned in the Privy Council letter in 1593.[30] Perhaps a performance of *Hamlet* is covered in the "tragedies commodies & other shewes of exercises of learning" which were not to be forbidden at Oxford.[31] Duncan-Jones sees Shakespeare as a "cult" writer at the two universities, *c.* 1600.[32] At any rate, at some point between its composition and its printing *Hamlet* is performed "in the two Vniuersities of Cambridge and Oxford" and in London and elsewhere, as Q1's title claims. Those performances may be earlier rather than later, for in 1589 Nashe, himself a young Cambridge graduate and about twenty-two years old, has his first opportunity to be published. He writes an *Epistle*, a preface to Robert Greene's *Menaphon*, addressing it "To the Gentlemen Stvdents of both Vniuersities." It is assumed that Nashe believes his readership will understand what he is writing about. Wittily, he tosses in a reference to Senecan elements in contemporary plays, like "whole Hamlets, I should say handfuls of Tragicall speeches." His wordplay here shows a stylistic quirk which he likes sufficiently well to repeat later in the *Epistle*, when railing against Richard Stanihurst, "whose heroicall poetry, infired, I should say inspired, with a hexameter furie." Nashe's quirky phrasing occurs as an aside in a list of criticisms of "shifting companions," who try different professions, perhaps like a "Johannes fac totum," as actor/playwright Shakespeare would be called in 1592.[33]

Whether Nashe knew the name of the author of the "*Hamlets*" is unknown. Shakespeare was not a "university wit," and in the 1580s would still be close to the beginning of his playwriting career. Nashe's priority is clearly in trying to ingratiate himself with the established writers of the day, like his "friend" Robert Greene, and the "diuine Master *Spencer*," the Elizabethan Æsop. But Nashe is referencing *Hamlet* in a way which permits us to infer he expected his audience to understand the allusion. Four years later Shakespeare's name appears on *Venus and Adonis* (1593) and then in 1594 on *The Rape of Lucrece*; in other words, he is published and named as a poet. That's the year Philip Henslowe records nine performances at Newington Butts by the Lord Admiral's or Chamberlain's men or both. Henslowe writes down 9th June and "hamlet" and eight shillings, but doesn't mention the author of "hamlet." He doesn't mention any authors of any of the plays in his play lists. The performances at Newington Butts don't bring in much money—an average of nine shillings and four pence—unlike those at the Rose. It may be the particularly unseasonable weather in June 1594, or the long trek from the south bank of the Thames, or the undrained marshy lands, but Newington Butts doesn't pull the crowds in.

In 1596 Thomas Lodge, another university wit, gets his *Wits Miserie* into print and shows how up to date he is with mention of three key features of a popular play: the pale visage of the Ghost, and the protagonist and the theme: "Hamlet, revenge." We may infer that Lodge too expects his audience to understand the reference, so the play is still being performed. Lodge, an Oxford man, may have seen it at university.

A number of Shakespeare's plays are known to have been written by now, like *Titus Andronicus*, which Ben Jonson tells us was known in 1584–9,[34] which may be the "andronicous" Henslowe also mentions at Newington Butts, and there is *1 Henry VI*, with "braue *Talbot* (the terror of the French)" whom Nashe mentions in *Pierce Penniless* (1592).[35] In 1598 the first of Shakespeare's plays to bear his name are published (for instance, *Richard III* and *Love's Labours Lost*). The same year Francis Meres' derivative *Palladis Tamia* comes out. In one chapter he lists comparisons between classical and English authors, for he is in part celebrating contemporary English writers. Meres is not wholly interested in the poetic arts, for he also mentions how Marlowe was "stabd to death by a bawdy Seruingman, a riuall of his in his lewde loue."[36] Meres doesn't mention Marlowe's plays, but does name him as a poet who has written on the love of Hero and Leander.[37] When Meres reaches Plautus and Seneca he lists twelve plays by the now established and quite prolific playwright, Shakespeare, and because Meres is a stylistic fetishist he opposes six comedies with six tragedies by Shakespeare. As Morris notes, Meres is not seeking to give a comprehensive list of Shakespeare's plays.[38] Meres' categorization is a bit shaky; he mixes histories and tragedies, and then he races on. *Palladis Tamia* is a physically small book—a copy is in the British Library—and the pages are very thin and crammed with print. In addition to maintaining his appositive style, and raiding Textor's *Officina* and Puttenham's *Arte of English Poetry* among others[39] for authors' names, genres and titles, Meres has many other chapters on other topics to write. He would not know "how important his list would be for future scholars" as Thompson and Taylor write.[40]

By 1598 Shakespeare has written nearly half of his plays, plus at least two narrative poems, and many sonnets. He is known to have written some dozen or so plays. He is "sweet Mr Shakspeare" in the Cambridge *Parnassus* plays (1598–1601).[41] "Will Shakespeare" is at the head of the cast list in front of Jonson's *Every Man in His Humour* (1598), and in the cast list for *Sejanus* (1603) as "Will. Shake-spear."[42] It is also in 1598 that Polish courtier Goslicki's *De Optimo Senatore* is translated into English, as *The Counsellor*. "Polonia" is a name used by Elizabethans for Poland, by for example John Gerard, author of *The Great Herball*.[43] It is possible that "Poloni-" plus the Latin masculine suffix, <us>, gave Shakespeare the idea for renaming Corambis in Q1. Polonius *is* a counselor; it is a fitting name. Shakespeare may be attending performances of his own plays. There is an anecdote which claims Shakespeare played "the Ghost in his own *Hamlet*," though this is reported by Rowe in 1709, nearly a century after Shakespeare's death.[44] At some point, perhaps in the late 1590s or early 1600s, the idea of revising, or improving, or redrafting *Hamlet* occurs to Shakespeare, for it was written in his early days as a playwright. Perhaps he did play the Ghost and noticed what worked well on stage; now he can see how to heighten the tragedy of his protagonist. The play's popularity may be reflected in a play written *c*. 1599 by John Marston, *Antonio's Revenge*, which has similarities with some of *Hamlet*'s plot.

Shakespeare has already created a major shift in character from Amleth in *Les Histoires Tragiques* to Hamlet in Q1. In Q2 it is not so much that Hamlet's hands are tied even more tightly as that the vulnerability that results is heightened. Some of that heightening is suggested by the comparison of colloquialisms in the quartos with its surprisingly high number of verbs beginning with the prefix "o'er" (over a dozen: see Appendix A). And because—as chapters two to five show—Q2 is further away from *Les Histoires Tragiques* and therefore logically later than Q1, and because we might assume that Shakespeare knew what he was doing as a playwright, it is a reasonable assumption that Shakespeare is seeking quite deliberately in Q2 to increase that vulnerability, Hamlet's status as a tragic hero, and the cathartic effect the play has upon us. We can see, for example, through his opening speech that Claudius is more kingly, more in control and more manipulative than Q1's King. Shakespeare also rewrites the four soliloquies, each time adding to Hamlet's sense of betrayal and despair. In Q2 there is an additional soliloquy, in IV.iv. There Hamlet marvels at the effort the army passing by will put into defending a "little patch of land" (IV.iv.17). If this is a contemporary reference—Hamlet sees plays as the "abstract and brief chronicles of the times"—it may be alluding to the English defense of the sand-dunes of Ostend from the Spaniards between July 1601 and the spring of 1602 (as Wilson once thought[45]). The defense of Ostend continued until 20th September 1604. G. A. Henty wrote about this siege: "On the 5th July 1601, the Archduke Albert began the siege of Ostend with 20,000 men.... The garrison at first consisted of but 2000 men...."[46] It is a little disconcerting to find those figures matched in Q2 IV.iv. Hamlet listens to the Captain telling him about how he and his men "goe to gain a little patch of land" (sig. K3r.21), and then comments on how "Two thousands soules..." (sig. K3r.28) go to fight for so little. Hamlet feels shame at the thought of "The iminent death of twenty thousand men" (sig. K3v.28). If *Hamlet* really is referring to the siege of Ostend, this would push Q2 *Hamlet*'s date forward to "the late summer or early autumn of 1601," in Wilson's opinion.[47] It might then place Shakespeare's redrafting of Q1 as after the news of the English defense reaches England—from approximately mid–July 1601 to mid-year 1602.

It is therefore perhaps at some time after 1598, and obviously before 1604, that Shakespeare begins his revision of *Hamlet*. Shakespeare is at least ten years older than when he drafted the early *Hamlet*, at least thirty-four (in 1598). We might reasonably expect that his own language has changed a little; it is reasonable to think he may be shifting slightly towards more modern <(e)s> inflections on third person singular present tense verbs. He is also even more flexible in his spelling to convey the natural elisions and contractions and relaxed pronunciations of speech. His spelling, provided that is reflected in the plays as printed, shows a considerable awareness of how words are actually pronounced. He seems to have noticed how "he" is often unstressed, and reduced in speech to not much more than a schwa, /ə/, which from time to time he renders as "a" in Q2. He also knows what's worked on stage with *Hamlet*. Q1 Corambis' role is enlarged for Polonius' role in Q2 by just over 70 percent.[48] Paul Menzer notes that there is an unusually high correspondence between the cues for Corambis and Polonius[49] and that "Some plausible mechanism is needed ... to account for the cue fidelity of Corambis/Polonius across the three texts of *Hamlet*."[50] Menzer also comments that "The longer Q2 version expands the counselor's volubility and, in the first ten lines, his sycophancy."[51] If Shakespeare wrote Q1, saw it performed and discovered the popularity of the toadying old man, it would not be surprising if he "expanded" (connoting Q1 as the prior text) that role to build on what the audience is enjoying. The cues and other parallels between Q1 and Q2 suggest Shakespeare had a Q1 copy to hand when he revised.

Shakespeare's refinements in Q2 include the further diminution of the Queen's role, the rewriting of scene 14 to give us IV.vi, and the lessening of the intimacy between the Prince and his mother. Each of these shows Shakespeare drawing further away from *Les Histoires Tragiques*, in a simple source > Q1 > Q2 sequence. The sequence and the evidence that the three texts provide suggest that Shakespeare had access to the French source and Q1 when he redrafted. There are a small number of verbal echoes of *Les Histoires Tragiques* that survive in Q2 but not in Q1,[52] like the use of "advancement"/ "advancement" while Q1 has "preferment," which is why we might speculate that Shakespeare re-read the source. The earlier parts of Q1 have more lines reproduced in Q2 than the later parts with minor roles like Marcellus, and Voltemar barely changed. This suggests that those roles satisfied the revising playwright. But the very beginning of Q2 (which Chapter 10 shows is not obviously "cut" to Q1's opening lines) does enhance the sense of apprehension among the night watch, for now both the guard on duty and the relief guard want to know "who's there." The increase in build up to the arrival of the Ghost may be because Shakespeare is working to increase the "willing suspension of disbelief" in his readership/audience. Later in the play Shakespeare seeks to enhance the climax, so the news of Rosencrans and Guyldensterne's death is delayed until the final scene too.

In the process of redrafting Shakespeare irons out a small number of "disparity gaps" or minor inconsistencies in Q1. It is true he does not resolve how or when Hamlet realizes there are eavesdroppers present in the "nunnery" scene. Perhaps Shakespeare has already seen that resolved in performance. At any rate, there is no longstanding male friend or the young woman herself to warn Hamlet. When we know *Les Histoires Tragiques*, Hamlet appears noticeably more isolated in Q2, and this is one example of that isolation. Shakespeare does remove the half line from Q1's scene 11, so there is no hint of any suspicion on Hamlet's part, no desire to "make all safe"; Hamlet is not proactive. Shakespeare does revise the Queen's promise. She cannot now "consent" to and "conceal" Hamlet's plans for revenge, because he does not confide in her. We might even wonder whether the change comes about because Shakespeare wishes to distance himself from the "conceal" and "consent" that Kyd echoed and repeated in *The Spanish Tragedy*.

Three possible contemporary allusions—Tarleton, *The Counsellor*, the defense of Ostend—fit an early Q1 and later Q2 sequence here. In this suggested narrative all three are cautiously interwoven. The "adlibbing" speech in Q1 would allude to Tarleton and would be dropped in Q2 because Tarleton died in September 1588; it need not be an interpolation by an actor or another. *The Counsellor* would give us Polonius from 1598, and the "How all occasions" soliloquy and scene would allude to the sand-dunes of Ostend, an event later than Q1. Perhaps that allusion too would be out of date when Shakespeare finishes F1 and is therefore excised.

Meanwhile, *Hamlet* is still "pleasing," according to Gabriel Harvey, reader in rhetoric at Cambridge. Harvey likes annotating books. His marginalia contain authors and titles and events and tenses which are not logically compatible. Once he mentions *Richard III* and *Hamlet*,[53] brief versions of the titles of two Shakespearean plays, but mentions no author, and the date of the annotation is unknown. Elsewhere he mentions the Earl of Essex in the present tense (he was executed in 1601), and the "flourishing" poet Watson (who died in 1592) and *Hamlet*. But Harvey does seem to value *Lucrece* and *Hamlet*, perhaps because their "sententiae" please the "wiser sort," such as himself. If that is the case, then it would suggest Harvey had *read* not just *Lucrece* (first published in 1594) but also *Hamlet*. Others are now confirming *Hamlet*'s[54] success: Dekker's *Satiromastix* refers to "Hamlet reuenge," being played at "Parris garden," suggesting another place where *Hamlet* has been performed, and there is Anthony Scoloker who writes that a book should "please all, like Prince Hamlet."[55] Edward Pudsey writes scraps of (misquoted) *Hamlet* in his commonplace book, Cyril Tourneur (or Thomas Middleton) pays tribute by writing *The Revenger's Tragedy* (performed in 1606) with all its parodying of *Hamlet*, and in 1607 and 1608 there are performances of *Hamlet* aboard ship.[56]

Despite the "chare" of rewriting (*pace* Hart) it looks as if Shakespeare did so. It looks as if he had an overall plan which changed some roles and relationships and sequences of events. The text looks as if he reread a scene or two, and transferred to his new script, Q2, what he wished to keep. Some lines are kept intact, some have the same words but not in quite the same order, some have only one or two words the same, and other lines are completely new. This is essentially what Irace notes in *Reforming the "Bad" Quartos*, though her interpretation of that pattern is not first draft and revision. Many who have redrafted poems, or essays or articles will recognize that pattern of copying across the lines or parts to be kept.

The above narrative embeds and contextualizes contemporary references to *Hamlet* and a number of the key differences between (*Les Histoires Tragiques* and) Q1 and Q2. It also begins to suggest possible dates for the composition of Q1 and the proposed revision of Q2. One of the unspoken results of positing Q2's priority is the tightness of the timeframe. If Q2 is Shakespeare's first *Hamlet*, written *c.* 1600, revised as F1, adapted for the stage, possibly abridged at some point, performed, memorially reconstructed, and taken on tour in the provinces, this is quite a tight schedule to meet its printing as Q1 in 1603. It is even tighter if it is Q1 which is entered on the Stationers' Register on 26th July 1602, as seems to be accepted. It is also difficult to understand why those putative actors/reporters didn't take the easy route and use the alleged earlier *Ur-Hamlet* script, since that was supposedly well-known enough to be alluded to by Nashe, put on by Henslowe, alluded to by Lodge, and was popular for at least seven years from 1589–96.

A *Les Histoires Tragiques* > Q1 > Q2 sequence is noticeably more leisurely. If Q1's adlibbing speech does target Tarleton, and Nashe does reference Q1, Q1 needs to have been written by, say, 1588. If modern courtesies are not anachronistic, it may be that Shakespeare wrote the Q1 "adlibbing" speech beginning "Let not your clown speak more than is set down" (9.17) before Tarleton's death in September 1588. That gives an opportunity for *Hamlet* to be performed a fair number of times, and for Nashe to feel confident his readership would understand the allusion by August 1589.

The considerable differences in Q1 and Q2 are then accommodated by the time span and the revision process. Q2 is revised after 1598 (*The Counsellor*) and perhaps after the start of the defense of Ostend (July 1601). Q2 keeps some 450 lines of Q1, but this Shakespeare is a reviser, obsessively reworking his ideas and changing many lines. Q1—perhaps Shakespeare's original draft, perhaps a prompt copy—might then be printed in 1603; it may be at the behest of the theatre company, to gain profits from it as a printed text as well as for performances.[57] Q1 might even have been published because it was known that Shakespeare was revising *Hamlet*, and it was suspected that a "new" *Hamlet* would or might displace the theatre company's profits from Q1. It might be that Q2 represents a literary text for readers (Erne's argument[58]), or that Shakespeare was one of those who made a "double sale of their labours, first to the Stage, and after to the press"[59] as Thomas Heywood says some playwrights did. It may also be that we are wrong to assume that Q2 was too long for performance then.

This account marries the familiar contemporary references to a *Hamlet* and the evidence of Part One. It doesn't contradict any documentary evidence, but does include a small number of speculative links, clearly marked as such. It does not require actor/reporters, abridgers, interpolations by others, hypotheses like that of an *Ur-Hamlet* or MR, or compositors' alterations. It also simplifies the writing of the *Hamlet*s by attributing them to Shakespeare, rather than to unknown others and their half recollected memories of performing in minor roles in *Hamlet* and nearly a dozen roles in other Shakespeare plays and *The Spanish Tragedy*. Menzer rejects a simple approach—"we need to shelve Occam's razor"[60]—without saying why, but this alternative narrative too has its complications and gaps. A first sketch and a revised Q2 narrative is not new in outline, for it is essentially what Elze, Knight, Caldecott, Furnival, and Sams *inter alia* have suggested, even without the supporting evidence offered here. *The First Two Quartos of Hamlet* begins to flesh out the narrative, just as Duthie fleshed out the memorial reconstruction hypothesis. It incorporates the linguistic evidence, the French source whose importance is considerable, and the age of our protagonist, none of which should be disregarded. It offers an unbiased examination of parts of Q1, a *Hamlet* that theatre practitioners have found dynamic and full of energy in performance. It recognizes what Hibbard notes in considering F1 in relation to Q2, that there is an "informed understanding of the matter," a "critical sense" that distinguishes what might be "indispensable"[61] and where best to develop the first quarto. It suggests we might gain from a full review of the relationship of the *Hamlet*s, leaning more carefully upon facts and less upon hypotheses, and admitting where our knowledge falls short. And if all three *Hamlet*s can be seen as his, we might recognize Shakespeare as not only a "supremely inventive poet"[62] but also a grafter.

Appendix A: Colloquialisms—Q1 and Q2

Feature	Q1 occurrence(s)	Q1 first occurrence Sig.	Q2 occurrence(s)	Q2 first occurrence Sig.
Personal pronoun + verb elision				
Ile, I'le	34	B2v	48	C1v
I'de	1	F2r		
th'owt			1	M4v
thou'lt			1	N1r
th'art			1	O1r
hee's, he's	4	D1r	10	D4r
hee'le, heele	3	F1v	1	H1v
shee's	2	D4r	1	M3r
shee'le			2	H1v
s'hath			1	G4v
tis, it's	40	B1r	60	B1v
is't, ist, i'st	17	B2r	14	B2r
t'will	3	B1v	3	B1v
wil't			1	K3r
t'was	1	E3r	4	F2v
twere, t'were			12	B3v
t'would			1	L4r
weele	7	D3v	13	C1v
lets	5	C3v	9	B3v
y'are, ya're	5	E2r		
you'l	5	C2v	2	C4v
you'ld	1	I4r		
tha'r			1	L3r
thei'le, they'le	1	F3r	1	H1v
Pronoun/existential particle/adverb + verb elision				
that's	7	B1v	15	E1v
ther's, there's, theres	12	D1r	16	D4r
heere's, heer's	4	F3r	7	E1v
what's, whats	4	B3r	11	B4r
wher's, where's	3	E1v	1	G3r
all's *for* all is	1	10	1	N3v

Feature	Q1 occurrence(s)	Q1 first occurrence Sig.	Q2 occurrence(s)	Q2 first occurrence Sig.
(Pronoun/existential particle/adverb + verb elision, continued)				
who's	1	H1v		
whol'd *for* who'd	1	D4v		
who'le	1	G2v		
howe's	1	I2v		
more's	1	H4r		
Noun + verb elision				
wit's	1	D2v		
end's	1	F3v		
mother's	1	G3r	1	O1r
brother's	1	G4v		
funerall's	1	I1v		
world's (has)			1	F1v
play's			1	G1r
thing's			1	K3v
honour's			1	K3v
nothing's			1	L2r
sisters			1	M1r
kings			1	O1r
Past tense <ed> marked as <'d>, <d> (/d/)				
appear'd	2	B1r	1	B2r
appeard			2	B1v
Past tense <ed> marked as <t> (/t/)				
sharkt	1	B2v	1	B2v
prickt	1	B2r	1	B2r
Verb + pronoun elision				
doo't	2	B3r	8	B3v
belieu't	1	C2r		
saw't			1	C2v
bear't			1	C4r
know't			1	D2v
sworn't			1	D3v
swear't			1	D4r
ento't			1	F3r
call't			1	L2v
see't			1	M2v
gau't			1	N1v
pardon't			1	N3v
think't			1	N4v
Contraction of infinitive marker to *+ verb*				
t'illume			1	B1v
t'have			1	G3r
t'expell			1	M4r
to'retop			1	M4v

Colloquialisms

Feature	Q1 occurrence(s)	Q1 first occurrence Sig.	Q2 occurrence(s)	Q2 first occurrence Sig.
*Preposition + **it** contraction*				
in't	2	B2v	12	B2v
for't	1	E3r	1	F2r
too't, to't	4	E3v	8	D1r
on't, ont	1	F1v	7	B2r
*Preposition + **faith** contraction*				
ifaith, yfaith	5	D2r	1	H1r
Preposition + possessive determiner/demonstrative pronoun/pronoun contraction				
with's	1	H4v		
in's			2	E1v
within's			1	H1r
neer's			1	H3v
for's			1	N3r
Pronoun + possessive determiner				
all's			1	N2v
*Conjunction + **it***				
y'ft			3	E1r
an't			2	I4v
*Enclitic **the***				
it'h, i'th			20	D4v
to'th			1	F2r
by'th			1	H3r
a'th			1	N4r
*Proclitic **the***				
e.g., arganian	1	E4r		
e.g., th'extravagant			1	B3r
(further e.g.s)			39	
Reduction by one syllable round <v> (/v/)				
ore, o're *for* over	5	C3v	11	B3v
or'emaister	2	D1v		
ore-grow'th			1	D1r
ore-leavens			1	D1r
orehanging			1	F2r
oer-cised			1	F3r
ore-raught			1	G1v
orethrowne			1	G3r
ore-dooing			1	G4r
ore-steppe			1	G4r
ore-doone,			1	G4r
ore-weigh			1	G4r
ore-heare			1	I1r

Feature	Q1 occurrence(s)	Q1 first occurrence Sig.	Q2 occurrence(s)	Q2 first occurrence Sig.
(Reduction by one syllable round <v> (/v/), continued)				
ore-beares			1	L1r
ore-rule			1	L3v
ore-reaches			1	M2v
ore-swayes			1	M4r
ore-crowes			1	O1r
ne're	5	D2v		
heau'n, heau'ns	5	D3r		
e're	2	F2v		
soe're	1	G3v		
giu'n	1	H1v		
eene, een			7	G4r
ha *for* have	2	D2v	2	M2r
Reduction of one syllable round <k> (/k/)				
tane			1	C4v
Dropping of syllable				
gin's *for* begins	1	C4v		
twixt *for* betwixt	1	H3v		
s'bloud *for* God's blood			1	F2v
s'wounds *for* God's wounds			2	F4v
"a"—not indefinite article				
a *for* have	5	C1v	1	G1r
a *for* of	4	E3r	1	F4v
a *for* on	2	E3r		
a *for* he			25	C2r

Appendix B:
Table of Comparisons from *Les Histoires Tragiques*, Q1 and Q2

The lines are presented to show parallels, and follow the order in *Les Histoires Tragiques*.

Texts Used

Sir Israel Gollancz, ed., *The Sources of Hamlet* (London: Humphrey Milford, Oxford University Press, 1926).
Kathleen O. Irace, ed., *The First Quarto of Hamlet* (Cambridge: Cambridge University Press, 1998).
Ann Thompson and Neil Taylor, eds., *Hamlet* (Q2). The Arden Shakespeare (London: Thomson Learning, 2006).

Notes

Page (*Les Histoires Tragiques*), scene and line (Sc.l) (Q1), and act, scene and line (A.sc.l) (Q2) give references for quotations.

APPENDIX B

Les Histoires Tragiques	Page	Q1 Hamlet	Sc.l	Q2 Hamlet	A.sc.l
[treason of brother against brother] *la trahison de frere conte frere*	170	*by a brother's hand*	5.58	*by a brother's hand*	I.v.74
Chrestiens	178	*Saviour*	1.116	*Saviour's birth*	I.i.158
de la divinité	184	*Oh God* (etc)	2.65	[Claudius] *incorrect to heaven... a fault to heaven*	I.ii.95, 101
du Chrestien	196	[Corambis] *to my God*	7.23	[Ghost] *doomed for a certain term... purged away*	I.v.10–13
les Dieux [Belleforest has already explained the events took place in a pre-Christian era]	208	[Ofelia] *Good God* (etc)	7.170,177, 178,184	[Ghost] *Unhouseled... on my head*	I.v.77–9
Priant les Dieux	222	[King] *trespass... sins... contrition... prayer*	10.3, 7, 9, 12,	[Ophelia] *Heavenly powers*	III.i.140
les Dieux	250	[Hamlet] *sins... purging of his soul... salvation... heaven*	17, 20, 26, 27	[Claudius] *prayer... repentance*	III.iii.51, 65
si Dieu	260	*Christian burial* (etc)	16.1, 10, 109	[Hamlet] *A took my father grossly full of bread... purging of his soul*	III.iii.80
		Heaven receive my soul	17.104	[Hamlet to Queen] *Confess yourself to heaven* (etc)	III.iv.147
		Thanks be to heaven	14.31	[King] *bring the body to the chapel* [Laertes] *To cut his throat i'th' church* [Priest in gravedigger's scene] *Christian burial* (etc)	IV.i.37 IV.vii.124 V.i.1, 5, 25
[the king of Norway] *deffié au combat, corps a corps*	178	[the king of Norway] *Dared to the combat*	1.73	[the king of Norway] *Dared to the combat*	I.i.83
l'art d'escumuer et pirate sur mer [Horvvendille was a pirate]	180			*A pirate of very warlike appointment* [a pirate took the ship Hamlet travelled on to England]	IV.vi.15–6
[the loser would forfeit...] *Celuy qui seroit vaincu perdroit toutes les richesses qui seroit en leurs vaisseaux*	182	*Did forfeit... all those lands/Which he stood seized of by the conqueror*	1.77–8	*Did forfeit... all those lands/Which he stood seized of to the conqueror*	I.i.87–8
[of Horvvendille] *vaillante*	182	[of Old Hamlet] *valiant*	1.73	[of Old Hamlet] *valiant*	I.i.83

Les Histoires Tragiques	Page	Q1 Hamlet	Sc.l	Q2 Hamlet	A.sc.l
il avoit incestueusement souillé la couche fraternelle	186	[Ghost] *incestuous wretch*	5.37	[Ghost] *Let not the royal bed of Denmark be/A couch for luxury and damnèd incest*	I.v.82–3
[Fengon] *osa enor s'accoupler par marriage... d'adultere incestueux*	188	[married old Hamlet's queen— incest]	2	[married old Hamlet's queen— incest]	I.ii.
[Geruthe] *s'estre incestueusement accouplee avec le tyran meurtrier de son espoux*	208	[Ghost] *incestuous wretch* e.g., *incestuous sheets*	5.37 2.70	[Claudius] *our sometime sister, now our Queen* [Hamlet] *married with.../My father's brother... incestuous sheets* [Ghost] *that incestuous, that adulterate beast* [Ghost] *damnèd incest*	I.ii.8 I.ii.152 I.ii.157 I.v.42 I.v.83
s'il venoit à perfection d'age [i.e., Amleth not yet "adult," or has not reached the then equivalent of his majority]	192	[Horatio] *young Hamlet* [Ofelia] *young Prince Hamlet* [Corambis] *the young Prince Hamlet* [Corambis] *young Hamlet*	1.127 6.40 7.58 11.1	[Horatio] *young Hamlet* [young Fortinbras] [Polonius] *that be is young*	I.i.170 [I.i.94, I.ii.28] I.iii.123
un jeune Prince	194			[Grave-maker] *young Hamlet*	V.i.140
le jeune seigneur	202	*a skull—Yorick's—that has rotted for] this dozen year... young Hamlet's father*	16.67–9	[Yorick's skull] *hath lien you i'th' earth three and twenty years*	V.i.163–4
[Amleth to mother] *de sauver vostre enfant ou en Suece en cest enfant*	214 218			4	
[Geruthe embracing Amleth] *avec la mesme amitié qu'une mere vertuese peut baiser, et caresser sa portee*	220				
L'Adolescent	254				
du jeune Prince	282				
[Amleth feigns losing his senses] *faignit d'avoir tout perdu le sens faire le sot, et contrefaire le fol il faut dissimuler* [dissemble] *Amleth donc se façonnant à*	192 196	[the Ghost might] *drive* [Hamlet] *into madness* [Ofelia] *his wit's bereft him* [Corambis] *Mad for thy love!... that hath made him mad*	4.43 6.43 6.57, 60	[Hamlet] *I know not "seems"* [the Ghost might] *draw* [Hamlet] *into madness* [Hamlet] *put an antic disposition on* [Polonius] *that hath made him mad*	I.ii.76 I.iv.74 I.v.170 II.i.107

Les Histoires Tragiques	Page	Q1 Hamlet	Sc.l	Q2 Hamlet	A.sc.l
l'exercice d'une grande folie sous ceste folie	198	[King, of Hamlet] *lost the very heart of his sense*	7.2	[Polonius] *mad... mad madness*	II.ii.92, 94, 147
il estoit insensé	202	[Corambis] *Hamlet's lunacy*	7.28	[Claudius] *dangerous lunacy*	III.i.4
et subtilitez de ce fol dissimulé	204	[Corambis] *mad.../Mad*	7.59, 60	[King] *his madness*	III.iii.2
faisoit le fol dissimulations				[Hamlet] *It is not madness*	III.iv.139
en ses ruses		[Corambis] *madness*	7.91	[Queen] *Mad as the sea*	IV.i.7
ce fol sage		[King] *Hamlet's lunacy*	8.2	[Queen] *his very madness*	IV.i.25
pour guerir le Prince de sa folie continuant en ses façons de faire, folles et naiases	206	[Hamlet] *It is not madness* [King] *his madness* *Mad... mad... losing his wits* (etc)	11.88 11.112 16.69–79	[King] *Hamlet in madness* [Gravedigger] *a was mad... the men are as mad as he... losing his wits*	V.i.34 V.i.142–150
[Amleth] *je sois constrainct de faire le fol... d'un insensé*	214	[Queen] *Mad as the sea his madness* [Hamlet] *in his madness ... madness ... madness*	16.134 16.140 16.46, 47, 49	[Claudius] *he is mad* [Queen] *mere madness* [Hamlet] *His madness* (etc)	V.i.261 V.i.273 V.ii.215
chacun me tienne pour privéde sens et cognoissance					
[Amleth] *il vaut mieux faindre l'un Le visage de un insensé*	216				
les ruses, dissimulations, et secretes menees					
pour surprendre Amleth en sa sagesse dissimulee	228				
sa fainte folie					
dissimulant accortement un grand desvoyement de sens	258				
faignant l'insensé	276				
j'ay fainte ceste sottise	278				
souz la fard d'une grande folie					
Prince Romain, qui pour se faindre fol, fut nommé Brutus	192	*Brutus killed me*	9.58–9	*Brutus killed me*	III.ii.100
à son avancement	194	[Hamlet] *I want preferment*	7.231	[Hamlet] *For what advancement* [Hamlet] *I lack advancement*	III.ii.52 III.ii.331
[e.g.] *s'en venger*	194	[e.g., Ghost] *Revenge*	5.20	[e.g.] *revenge*	I.v.7

Les Histoires Tragiques	Page	Q1 Hamlet	Sc.1	Q2 Hamlet	A.sc.l
venger, vengeance	196	[Hamlet] my revenge	5.26	revenge	I.v.25
venger la mort de mon pere	198	and so I am revenged	10.15	revenged	III.iii.75
les desirs de le venger	216	in revenge	11.93	and so am I revenged … revenge … revenged my dull revenge	III.iii.75, 79, 84 IV.iv.32
[Amleth ambiguous] parlant ainsi ambiguement [in answers e.g., re] les deux bastons [also in England; [242, he equivocates, riddles] 252]	198	[Hamlet equivocates e.g., to Corambis]	7.201	[Hamlet equivocates e.g., to Rosencrantz and Guildenstern, Polonius]	II.ii.316 II.ii III.ii
les hommes … donnerent conseil au Roy de tenter… decouvert … de la tromperie de l'adolescent [the king is given advice about how to discover the deceitfulness of the young man]	198	[Corambis hopes he has] found/The very depth and cause of Hamlet's lunacy	7.17–8	[Polonius] I have found/The very cause of Hamlet's lunacy	II.ii.48–9
[to discover the truth of Amleth's inclinations] l'atraper … quelque belle femme	198	to entrap the beart [Corambis claims Hamlet seeks to do this to Ofelia]	3.68		
un Gentil-homme, qui… esté nourry avec [Amleth]	200	fellow student	2.91	fellow student	I.i.176
[Amleth is warned twice of the entrapment by the young woman and by a childhood friend] elle asseuré encore de la trahison avec certain signes	200–1	[It is common for Hamlet to be enabled to deduce that Ofelia and he are being overheard; Ofelia's formal 2nd person plural may help to point to this]	7	[It is common for Hamlet to be enabled to deduce that Ophelia and he are being overheard; Ophelia's formal 2nd person plural may help to point to this]	III.i
[Amleth is stirred by the young woman's beauty] esmeu de la beauté de la fille	200–1	Ofelia./Thine ever… Hamlet I loved Ofelia	7.75–6 16.125	I did love you once I loved Ophelia	III.i.114 V.i.258
[she has loved him since childhood] elle l'aymoit des son enfance	202	[Ofelia's affection implicit in her receipt and belief of Hamlet's]	3	[Ophelia's affection implicit in her receipt and belief of Hamlet's]	
[Amleth] trompe le courtisans, et la fille	202	[Ofelia] The courtier, soldier, scholar, all in him/All dashed	1.185–6	[Ophelia] O what noble mind's here o'erthrown!	III.i.149

Appendix B

Les Histoires Tragiques	Page	Q1 Hamlet	Sc.l	Q2 Hamlet	A.sc.l
		and splintered	7.188	[King] Love! His affections do not that way tend	III.i.161
Qu'il ne s'estoit avancé en sorte à la violer, quoy qu'il dict du contraire	202	[King] Love? No, no, that's not the cause	13.94–5	[Ambiguity about Hamlet/Ophelia's relationship: Ophelia's song] Let in the maid, that out a maid/Never departed more	IV.v.54–5
		[Ambiguity about Hamlet/Ofelia's relationship: Ofelia's song] Let in the maid, that out a maid/Never departed more	9.179–80	[Equivocation/ambiguity in Hamlet's speech e.g.] A little more than kin and less than kind	I.ii.65
		[Indirectness/ambiguity in Hamlet's speech e.g.] Besides, to be demanded by a sponge			
[trap] *filet*	204	[Corambis] *Springes to catch woodcocks!*	3.61	[Polonius] *Springes* to catch woodcocks	I.iii.114
		[Corambis] *snares to entrap the heart*	3.68	[Laertes] As a woodcock to my own springe	V.ii.291
[to enclose Amleth in the same room as his mother, with someone hiding under the quilt] *on enferme Amleth seul avec sa mere dans une chambre, dans laquelle soit caché se cachant souz quelque loudier*	204	[Corambis] *Madam, send you in haste to speak with him,/And I myself will stand behind the arras*	9.32–3	[Polonius] *Let his Queen-mother all alone entreat him*	III.i.181
[the same man offers to hide] *s'offrist pour estre l'espion*	206	[Corambis] *Myself will be that happy messenger*	9.39	[Polonius] *And I'll be placed ... in the ear/of all their conference*	III.i.183–4
le conseil entra secrettement en la chamber de Royne	206	[Corambis] *And I myself will stand behind the arras*	9.33	[Polonius] *Behind the arras I'll convey myself/To hear the process*	III.iii.28–9
[Amleth as soon as he is in the queen's chamber] *sauta sur ce lourdier* [because he expects treason] *trahison*	206	[Hamlet at the beginning of the scene] *but first we'll make all safe*	11.6		
donner dedans à tout son glaive ... l'acheva d'occir [kills with his sword]	206	[Queen] *whips out his rapier...And in his rage the good old man kills*	11.109, 111	[Gertrude] *whips out his rapier... The unseen good old man*	IV.i.8, 12
[Geruthe regrets the failure of those	208	[Hamlet] *What devil thus hath*	11.38	[Hamlet] *What devil was't/That thus*	III.iv.74–

Les Histoires Tragiques	Page	Q1 Hamlet	Sc.l	Q2 Hamlet	A.sc.l
who following their desire for a moment's pleasure, cover their eyes [*bandé les yeux*] [and reject the fidelity required of those of her status]		*cozened you at bob-man blind?*		*hath cozened you at hoodman-blind?* (Jenkins, p. 94)	5
Harangue d'Amleth à la Royne sa mere [Includes comparison between Horvendille and Fengon]	210	[Includes comparison between Old Hamlet and new king]	11	[Includes comparison between Old Hamlet and Claudius]	III.iv
[Hamlet the "image" of his father] *voyant la vive image de sa* [Horvendille's] *vertu et sagesse en cest enfant*	218	[Hamlet to Queen] *behold this picture*	11.23	*Look here upon this picture*	III.iv.51
le meurtrier de mon pere [my father's murderer]	210	*him/That slew my father*	11.39–40	[Hamlet] *a murderer and a villain* [Hamlet does not declare Claudius has murdered Old Hamlet]	III.iv.94
de suivre des apetits des bestes	210	*A beast of reason/Would not have made such speed...Why she would hang on him as if increase/ Of appetite had growne...*	2.65–6 2.68	*appetite* *a beast that wants discourse of reason*	I.ii.144 I.ii.150
[Geruthe went running to Fengon with her arms outstretched] *allez courant les bras tendus... caresses incestuesement*	210	[Hamlet] *To make such/Dexterity the incestuous pleasure*	2.69–70 11.41	[Hamlet] *O most wicked speed! To post/With such dexterity to incestuous sheets* (Jenkins, p. 94) *th' incestuous pleasure*	I.ii.155–6 III.iv.90
vilain	210	[Hamlet] *A damned pernicious villain ... damned villain ... and be a villain* [Hamlet] *Having my father murdered by a villain ... damned villain ... murderous villain*	5.79, 80, 82 7.367, 374, 375	[Hamlet] *O villain, villain, smiling damned villain...* *a villain kills my father* [Hamlet to Queen] *A murderer and a villain*	I.v.106–8 III.iii.76 III.iv.94
lascive	210	[Ghost] *leudness... lust*	5.41–2 11.53	[Ghost] *Leudness... lust*	I.v.54, 55
[Amleth rejects Fengon as parent or	210–	*Farewell mother*	11.148–151	*Farewell dear mother*	IV.iii.48–

Les Histoires Tragiques	Page	Q1 Hamlet	Sc.l	Q2 Hamlet	A.sc.l
as uncle] *Je ne veux l'estimer mon parent et ne puis le regarder comme oncle....*	212	[King] *Your loving father, Hamlet.* [Hamlet] *My mother I say: you married my mother/My mother is your wife, man and wife is one flesh./And so (my mother) farewell*	11.149–150	[King] *Thy loving Father, Hamlet.* [Hamlet] *My mother. Father and mother is man and wife./Man and wife is one flesh. So—my mother.*	IV.iii.48–50
[source of concept of Ghost? Amleth accuses the Queen of embracing Fengon] *sans respecter les ombres* ["shades"] *de Horvvendille*	212	[Ghost in bedchamber]	11	[Ghost in bedchamber]	III.iv
[Later Amleth asks Fengon to report that vengeance has been exacted] *son ombre s'appaise parmy les esprits bien-heureux*	256	[Ghost requests revenge in earlier scene]	5	[Ghost requests revenge in earlier scene]	I.v
[Amleth] *Ne vous offencez... si je vous parle rigoureusement* [sword mentions, e.g.s] *en lieu de m'adextrer aux armes ayant les armes au poing luy voyant le glaive nud en main a main à l'espee clouée*	214 214 226 256	[Hamlet] *I will speak daggers* [Hamlet asks watchmen to swear] *upon my sword* (etc) [Gertred] *but whips out his rapier Among the foils six French rapiers*	10.203 5.125, 134 11.109 15.21 17.14	[Hamlet] *I will speak daggers to her* (also noted by Jenkins, ed., p. 94) [Hamlet asks the watchmen to swear] *Upon my sword ... sword* [Gertrude] *whips out his rapier* [King] *After the Danish sword Rapier... escrimeurs* [= fencers, swordsmen] *a sword unbated* [Osric] *for his weapon rapier and dagger*	III.ii.86 I.v.146, 148,154 IV.i.8 IV.iii.59 IV.vii.96, 98 IV.vii.136 V.iii.127 V.ii.129
[Amleth speaks of the shame which has soiled his mother's family's name] *pour celle infamie qui a souillee celle ancienne renomme infamie*	216 278	*And in his death your infamy shall die*	11.94	*That not your trespass but my madness speaks Confess Repent*	III.iv.144 III.iv.147 III.iv.148
Toutesfois faut il attendre le temps,	216	[Hamlet] *Yet I.../Stand still and let it*	7.366–8	[Hamlet to Ghost] *your tardy son to*	III.iv.104

Les Histoires Tragiques	Page	Q1 Hamlet	Sc.1	Q2 Hamlet	A.sc.l
et les moyens et occasions [Amleth is awaiting the time, the means and the occasion]		pass [Hamlet] your tardy son	11.59	chide [Hamlet—whole speech] How all occasions...	IV.iv.31 ff
[Geruthe] n'y t'avancer plus que raison à l'effect de ton dessein	222	[Ghost] Do not neglect nor long time put it off	11.67		
le Roy ny autre ne soit en rien informé de cecy [do not tell the king of this]	218				
duquel je feindray ne sçavoir rien je tiendray secrette, et ta sagesse, et ta gaillarde enterprinse [I will pretend to know nothing of your plans for revenge, and will keep secret both your wisdom and your bold enterprise/plan]	222	[Gertred] I will conceal, consent, and do my best,/What stratagem soe'er thou shalt devise	11.97–8	[Queen]... if words be made of breath/ And breath of life, I have no life to breathe/ What thou hast said to me	III.iv.195–7
[Queen] mon filz, et doux amy [Queen—essentially be careful] conduire sagement tes affaires, n'estre haste, ny trop boüillant en tes entreprises	220 222	Sweet Hamlet [Queen to Horatio regarding Hamlet] Bid him a while be wary of his presence	11.45 14.19	sweet Hamlet	III.iv.94
[Amleth faces two choices, to fight or to be dishonoured] il faut ou qu'une fin glorieuse mette fin à mes jours, ou qu'ayant les armes au poing, chargé de triomphe et victoire... ou la honte, et l'infamie, sont les bourreaux [executioners, hangmen, tortures] qui tormentent nostre conscience, et la poltronnerie est celle qui retarde le cœur des gaillardes entreprises	226	The scorns and flattery of the world... this conscience makes cowards of us all	7.113–35	To take arms against a sea of troubles... Th' oppressor's wrong, the proud man's contumely... Thus conscience does make cowards— ... and enterprises of great pitch and moment...	III.i.55–87
[Amleth, whom Geruthe loves]	230	[King, of Hamlet] Being the joy and	2.30	[Queen's affection implicit in	III.iv.118

APPENDIX B

Les Histoires Tragiques	Page	Q1 Hamlet	Sc.l	Q2 Hamlet	A.sc.l
qu'elle aymoit		half heart of your mother		phrasing e.g.] O gentle son [Claudius] He's loved of the distracted multitude	IV.iii.4
				[Claudius] The Queen his mother /Lives almost by his looks	IV.viii.12–3
[Fengon] feit le Roy des Anglois le ministre du massacre	230	the king of England…that Hamlet lose his head	11.154, 157	[Claudius] The present death of Hamlet. Do it, England!	IV.iii.63
[NB Amleth cuts off Fengon's head]	[256]	[King] That Hamlet lose his head	11.157	[Hamlet] my head should be struck off	V.ii.25
et le prier par lettre d'en despecher le monde	230	[Hamlet] found the packet sent to the king of England,/Wherein he saw himself betrayed to death	13.6–7	[Hamlet] fingered their packet	V.ii.15
Amleth entendant qu'on l'envioit en la grande Bretaigne vers l'Anglois, se douta tout aussi tost de l'occasion de ce voyage, pour ce ayant parlé à la Royne… [Amleth, hearing/ understanding he will be sent to Britain…]	230			[Hamlet, to Queen] There's letters sealed and my two schoolfellows—/Whom I trust as adders fanged	III.iv.200–1
				[King] So is it if thou knewest our purposes	IV.iii.46
				[Hamlet] I see a cherub sees them	IV.iii.47
[Amleth asks his mother that she celebrast ses obsequies et funerailles	230–2	funeral baked meats	2.94	funeral baked meats	I.ii.179
banquet funebre	252				
[the queen is told to prepare for Amleth's return] le verroit de retour	232	[Horatio] Madam, your son is safe arrived in Denmark	14.1		
[two of Fengon's faithful ministers] deux des fideles ministres de Fengon, portans des lettres, gravees du bois	232	[King addresses Rossencraft and Gilderstone] Right noble friends by Rossencraft and Gilderstone/ Our letters to our dear brother of England	7.1 11.127–8	[Claudius] dear Guildenstern and Rosencrantz	II.ii.1
		[Hamlet] a sponge that soaks up the	9.182	[Hamlet] a sponge… that soaks up the king's countenance	IV.ii.13–14

Les Histoires Tragiques	Page	Q1 Hamlet	Sc.l	Q2 Hamlet	A.sc.l
[Amleth erases the instruction for his death and in its place carves an order to the English to hang and throttle his companions] *rasa les lettres mentionans sa mort, et au lieu y grava et cisa un commandement à l'Anglois de faire pendre et estrangler ses compaignons*	232	king's countenance [Horatio] *in that packet there writ down that doom/To be perform'd on them pointed for him*	14.27–8	[Hamlet of instructions: the king of England] *should those bearers put to sudden death a royal knavery* [Hamlet] *devised a new commission*	V.ii.46 V.ii.19 V.ii.32
[Amleth is perhaps subject to malign influences] *avoit esté endoctriné en celle science, avec laquelle le malin esprit abuse les hommes … ce Prince, pour la vehemence de la melancholie… ainsi que les Philosophes*	236	[Hamlet] *The spirit I have seen may be the devil,/And out of my weakness and my melancholy,/As he is very potent with such men…* [Hamlet] *There are more things in heaven and earth, Horatio,/Than are dreamt of in your philosophy*	7.382–4 5.142–3	[Hamlet] *… the de'il hath power/T'assume a pleasing shape. Yea, and perhaps/Out of my weakness and my melancholy,/As he is very potent with such spirits,/Abuses me to damn him!* [Hamlet] *There are more things in heaven and earth, Horatio, Than are dreamt of in your philosophy*	II.ii.534–8 I.v.165–6
[the king of England] *feit prendre les deux serviteurs du Roy Fengon*	248	[Horatio] *in that packet there writ down that doom/To be perform'd on them "pointed for him*	14.27–8	[Ambassador] *Rosencrantz and Guildenstern are dead*	V.ii.355
[Amleth's return astonishes everyone] *ne fut sans donner un grand estonnement à chacun*	250	[Horatio] *Observe the king and you shall quickly find,/Hamlet being here, things fell not to his mind* [King] *Hamlet from England! Is it possible?*	14.24–5 15.1	[Claudius, of letters] *From Hamlet!* *If he be now returned*	IV.vii.38 IV.vii.59
[drain the goblet…] *baucer le gobelet … ne laissant jamais les hanaps vides … tous estans chargez de vin*	252	drink deep dreams his draughts of Rhenish down taking his carouse,/Drinking drunk	2.85 4.7 10.22–3	to drink a custom/More honoured in the breach than the observance drains his draughts of Rhenish	I.ii.174 I.iv.15–16 I.iv.10

Les Histoires Tragiques	Page	Q1 Hamlet	Sc.l	Q2 Hamlet	A.sc.l
de force de trop boire, vice assez familier ces corps assoupis de vin les autres vomissans le trop de vin le trop de ligueur	254	stoup of drink, stoup of beer a whole flagon of Rhenish the king doth drink	16.14, 23 16.82 16.65	down drunkards drink... chalice stoup of liquor a flagon of Rhenish stoups of wine (etc) [Queen] the drink, the drink	I.iv.19 IV.viii.157–8 V.i.56, 170 V.ii.244 V.ii.294
[Amleth seizes his father's murderer's sword] saisit l'espee du meurtrier de son pere... y laissa la sienne au lieu	256	[Hamlet and Leartes] They catch one another's rapiers	17.77	[Hamlet and Laertes] In scuffling they change rapiers	V.i.285
[Amleth asks Fengon to give an account of Amleth's revenge to the "ombre" of Horwvendille] mes angoisses ... quelle misere	256	[Hamlet to Horatio] What tongue should tell the story of our deaths,/If not from thee? [king, of Hamlet] sad and melancholy moods [Hamlet] suits of woe	17.100–1 2.27 2.39	[Hamlet to Horatio] report me and my cause aright/To the unsatisfied [Claudius] How is it that the clouds still hang on you? [Hamlet] shapes of grief... suits of woe	V.ii.323–4 I.ii.66 I.ii.82, 86
tout confit en larmes	274	[Hamlet] the tears that still stand in my eyes	2.34	[Hamlet] nor the fruitful river in the eye	I.ii.80
[Amleth presents himself as] le ministre et executeur	278			[Hamlet] I must be their scourge and minister (Jenkins, p. 95.)	III.iv.173
[Amleth to Danes] j'ay lavé les tasches, qui denigroient la reputation de la Royne	280	[Hamlet to Queen] I'll make your eyes look down into your heart/And see how horrid there and black it shows	11.20–1	[Queen to Hamlet] Thou turn'st my very eyes into my soul /And there I see such black and grieved spots	III.iv.87–8
la femme est facile à promettre, aussi est elle pesante et paresseuse à tenir (etc)	306	[Hamlet] Frailty, thy name is woman	2.66	[Hamlet] Frailty, thy name is woman	I.ii.146

Appendix C: A Summative, Four Way Comparison Between *Les Histoires Tragiques*, Q1, Q2 and F *Hamlet*

The lines are presented to show parallels, and follow the order in *Les Histoires Tragiques*.

Texts Used

Sir Israel Gollancz, ed., *The Sources of Hamlet* (London: Humphrey Milford, Oxford University Press, 1926).

Kathleen O. Irace, ed., *The First Quarto of Hamlet* (Cambridge: Cambridge University Press, 1998).

Ann Thompson and Neil Taylor, eds., *Hamlet* (Q2). The Arden Shakespeare (London: Thomson Learning, 2006).

Nick de Somogyi, ed., *Hamlet: The Tragedie of Hamlet, Prince of Denmark*. The Shakespeare Folios (London: Nick Hern Books, 2001).

Notes

"Y" represents "yes," this character / feature / event is present.

Appendix C

Feature	Les Histoires Tragiques	Q1	Q2	F1
Characters				
Previous king	Horvvendille	Old Hamlet	Old Hamlet	Old Hamlet
Opponent	Collere, Roy de Norvege	Fortenbrasse of Norway	Old Fortinbras of Norway	Old Fortinbras of Norway
Wife	Geruthe	Gertred	Gertrad	Gertrude
Murdering brother	Fengon	King	Claudius	Claudius
Prince/son	Amleth	Hamlet	Hamlet	Hamlet
Counsellor	Counsellor	Corambis	Polonius	Polonius
Woman to test prince	Belle femme	Ofelia	Ophelia	Ophelia
Friend of prince	un Gentil-homme, qui... esté nourry avec [Amleth]	Horatio	Horatio	Horatio
"shade"/ghost	Ombre(s)	Ghost	Ghost	Ghost
Pair of escorts	Deux serviteurs de roi	Rossencraft & Gilderstone	Rosencrans & Guyldensterne	Rosincrance & Guildenstern
King of England	Le Roy des Anglois	King of England	King of England	King of England
Scenes/plot elements				
Losses in battle	All the riches in his ships/vessels	*All his lands*	*All his lands*	*All his lands*
Murder of brother/king	Y	Y	Y	Y
Marriage to widow/queen	Y	Y	Y	Y
New king supported by court	Y	Y	Y	Y
Youth of prince	Hasn't yet reached *à perfection d'aage* i.e., not yet adult	About 19; 12 years + around 7	30 years old	30 years old
Prince + madness	deliberate simulation of madness	Antic disposition a possibility	Antic disposition a possibility	Antic disposition a possibility
Counsellor suggests testing madness with woman	Y	Y	Y	Y
Woman known to prince	Y	Y	Y	Y
Woman is fond of the prince	Y	Y	Y	Y
Prince is fond of the woman	Y	Y	Y	Y
Relationship between them is ambiguous	Y	Y	Y	Y
Counsellor suggests eavesdropping on conversation between prince and mother	Y	Y	Y	Y
Counsellor hides in bedchamber	*sous lourdier* (under a quilt)	Behind arras	Behind arras	Behind arras
Prince is armed	Y	Y	Y	Y

A Summative, Four Way Comparison

Feature	Les Histoires Tragiques	Q1	Q2	F1
(Scenes/plot elements, continued)				
Counsellor killed by prince	Y	Y	Y	Y
Prince reproaches mother for incestuous marriage to lesser man	Y	Y	Y	Y
Queen loves son	[Amleth] qu'elle [Geruthe] aymoit	Being the joy and half heart of your mother	The Queen his mother / Lives almost by his looks	The Queen his mother / Lives almost by his looks
King decides to send prince to England for English king to kill...	Y	Y	Y	Y
...with two escorts...	Y	Y	Y	Y
...bearing instructions to that effect	Y	Y	Y	Y
Prince intercepts instructions...	Y	Y	Y	Y
...changes them so escorts are to be killed	Y	Y	Y	Y
Escorts are killed	Y	Y	Y	Y
Queen expects Prince's return	elle verroit le retour [he says he will return a year hence]	? Madam your son is safe arrived		
Queen asks Prince to be careful	Y	[Queen asks Horatio] Bid him a while be wary of his presence		
Prince returns; it is a surprise	donner un grand estonnement à chacun [it astonishes everyone]	[King] Hamlet from England! Is it possible?	[King] Hamlet from England! Is it possible?	[King] From Hamlet?
Prince kills usurping king	Y	Y	Y	Y
Prince equivocates	Y	Y	Y	Y
Verbal echoes				
Old king is valiant	vaillante	valiant	valiant	valiant
Old king challenged opponent	deffié au combat	Dared to the combat	Dared to the combat	Dared to the combat
Old king is betrayed by his brother	la trahison de frere conte frere	by a brother's hand	by a brother's hand	by a brother's hand
Marriage is incestuous	incestueuse	incestuous	incestuous	incestuous
King is adulterer...	d'adultere		adulterate	adulterate
... the old king's	couche		couch	couch

Feature	Les Histoires Tragiques	Q1	Q2	F1
(Verbal echoes, continued)				
couche/bed had been defiled				
Prince desires *avancement*/advancement	*avancement*	*preferment*	*advancement*	*advancement*
Verb used in context of using woman to test Hamlet	*atraper*	*entrap*		
Image of blindness applied to Queen	[Geruthe regrets the failure of those who following desire for a moment's pleasure] *bandé les yeux* [and reject the fidelity required of those of her status]	*What devil thus hath cozened you at hob-man blind?*	*What devil was't /That thus hath cozened you at hoodman-blind?*	*What devil was't /That thus hath cozened you at hoodman-blind?*
Prince's rejection of new "father"	*Je ne veux l'estimer mon parent et ne puis le regarder comme oncle*	*My mother, I say*	*My mother. Father and mother is man and wife*	*My mother. Father and mother is man and wife*
Prince comments on Queen	*infamie*	*infamy*	*trespass*	*trespass*
Prince [in]explicit about murder of father	*le meurtrier de mon pere*	*him/That slew my father*	[*Almost as bad ...as kill a king and marry with his brother*]	[*Almost as bad ... as kill a king and marry with his brother*]
Prince's view of mother's sexual appetites	*de suivre des apetits des bestes*	*A beast of reason /Would not have made such speed appetite*	*appetite a beast that wants discourse of reason*	*appetite a beast that wants discourse of reason*
Upon rapidity of re-marriage	[Geruthe] *allez courant les bras tendus ... caresses incestuesement*	*To make such/ Dexterity*	*O most wicked speed! To post/ With such dexterity to incestuous sheets*	*O most wicked speed! To post/ With such dexterity to incestuous sheets*
New king a villain	*vilain*	*villain*	*villain*	*villain*
Prince conscious of how he will speak to mother	*Ne vous offencez ... si je vous parle rigoureusement*	*I will speak daggers*	*I will speak daggers*	*I will speak daggers*
Prince requires the opportunity	*Toutesfois faut il attendre le temps, et les moyens et occasions*		*How all occasions...*	
Queen's promise to son	*je tiendray secrette, et ta sagesse,*	*I will conceal, consent, and do*	*if words be made of breath/ and*	*if words be made of breath/ and*

A Summative, Four Way Comparison

Feature	Les Histoires Tragiques	Q1	Q2	F1
(**Verbal echoes**, continued)				
	ta gaillarde enterprinse	*my best,/What stratagem soe'er thou shalt devise*	*breath of life, I have no life to breathe/ What thou hast said to me*	*breath of life, I have no life to breathe/ What thou hast said to me*
Queen's affection for son	*Doux amy*	*Sweet Hamlet*	*Sweet Hamlet*	*Sweet Hamlet*
Two choices	[Amleth faces two choices]	Y	Y	Y
Second choice	*et l'infamie, sont les bourreaux* [executioners, hangmen, tortures] *qui tormentent nostre conscience, et la poltronnerie est celle qui retarde le cœur des gaillardes entreprises*	*this conscience makes cowards of us all*	*Thus conscience does make cowards—... and enterprises of great pitch and moment...*	*Thus conscience does make cowards—... and enterprises of great pitch and moment...*
Influences upon prince...	[Amleth is perhaps subject to malign influences] *avoit esté endoctriné en celle science, avec laquelle le malin esprit abuse les hommes ... ce Prince, pour la vehemence de la melancholie...*	*The spirit I have seen may be the devil,/And out of my weakness and my melancholy,/As he is very potent with such men...*	*the de'il hath power/T'assume a pleasing shape. Yea, and perhaps/ Out of my weakness and my melancholy,/As he is very potent with such spirits,/ Abuses me to damn him!*	*the de'il hath power/T'assume a pleasing shape. Yea, and perhaps/ Out of my weakness and my melancholy,/As he is very potent with such spirits,/ Abuses me to damn him!*
...in context of philosophy	*ainsi que les Philosophes*	*There are more things in heaven and earth, Horatio, /Than are dreamt of in your philosophy*	*There are more things in heaven and earth, Horatio, /Than are dreamt of in your philosophy*	*There are more things in heaven and earth, Horatio, /Than are dreamt of in our philosophy*
Prince speaks of his distress (at his father's death)... death)...	*mes angoisses ... quelle misere*	*suits of woe*	*shapes of grief... suits of woe*	*Shewes of grief... suites of woe*
...and his tears	*tout confit en larmes*	*the tears that still stand in my eyes*	*nor the fruitful river in the eye*	*nor the fruitful river in the eye*
...and the stain upon his mother's honour [Queen speaks]	*les tasches, qui denigroient la reputation de la Royne*	*how horrid there and black it shows*	[*And there I see such black and grieved spots*]	[*And there I see such black and grained spots*]

Appendix C

Feature	Les Histoires Tragiques	Q1	Q2	F1
(Verbal echoes, continued)				
Prince's view of his role as avenger	[Amleth presents himself as] *le ministre et executeur*		*I must be their scourge and minister*	*I must be their Scourge and Minister*
A view of women	*la femme est facile à promettre, aussi est elle pesante et parasseuse à tenir* etc	*Frailty, thy name is woman*	*Frailty, thy name is woman*	*Frailty, thy name is woman*
Themes/motifs/"color"				
Madness, real/illusionary	Y	Y	Y	Y
Revenge	Y	Y	Y	Y
Incest and the repulsion it evokes	Y	Y	Y	Y
"filet"/springs for woodcocks; entrapment	Y	Y	Y	Y
Excessive drinking	At banquet for Amleth's funeral	Earlier, in opening scenes	Earlier, in opening scenes	Earlier, in opening scenes
Transpositions				
"nunnery" scene; proposal to test prince followed immediately by that test	Y	Y	Moved <u>later</u>	Moved <u>later</u>
Decapitation of character	Amleth decapitates uncle [<u>later</u>]	King asks for Hamlet to be decapitated by king of England [<u>earlier</u>]	King asks for Hamlet to be decapitated by king of England [<u>earlier</u>]	King asks for Hamlet to be decapitated by king of England [<u>earlier</u>]
Sword swap	Prince swaps with uncle	Hamlet swaps with Leartes	Hamlet swaps with Laertes	Hamlet swaps with Laertes
Prince's expression of grief	After revenge is exacted	From beginning ie <u>earlier</u>	From beginning ie <u>earlier</u>	From beginning ie <u>earlier</u>
Ombre/Ghost	In bedchamber scene and <u>later</u> when king is killed	In bedchamber scene and <u>earlier</u> in opening scenes of play	In bedchamber scene and <u>earlier</u> in opening scenes of play	In bedchamber scene and <u>earlier</u> in opening scenes of play
Concern for the peace of mind of the ombre/Ghost	When King is killed	*Rest, rest perturbed spirit* is <u>earlier</u>	*Rest, rest perturbed spirit* is <u>earlier</u>	*Rest, rest perturbed spirit* is <u>earlier</u>
Pirates	Horvvendille was a pirate, *escumeur*		Pirates board Hamlet's ship	Pirates board Hamlet's ship
Mention of Brutus	[<u>earlier</u>]	[<u>later</u>]	[<u>later</u>]	[<u>later</u>]

A Summative, Four Way Comparison

Feature	Les Histoires Tragiques	Q1	Q2	F1
(*Transpositions*, continued)				
King (usurper)	*un fin et rusé* [shrewd and cunning]		The cunning and cleverness of Claudius in 1.2 and in playing Laertes	The cunning and cleverness of Claudius in I.ii and in playing Laertes
"Disparity gaps"				
Young woman "test"	Prince warned twice	No warning; Hamlet must deduce there are eavesdroppers	No warning; Hamlet must deduce there are eavesdroppers	No warning; Hamlet must deduce there are eavesdroppers
Mother in chamber "test"	Prince enters with suspicion	No reason for *But first we'll make all safe*		
Request for promise	Promise requested and given	Promise given	[different request and promise given]	[As Q2: different request and promise given]
Prince's return	Queen expects son's return	?Queen expects son's return		
Evolution of plot/character				
Prince confides in mother	Prince confides most in mother, about revenge and return	Prince confides greatly still in mother about revenge	Less confiding, no comment on revenge	As Q2, less confiding, no comment on revenge
Role of Queen	Greatest	Great	Less	As Q2, less
Wash away black spots of infamy	Prince tells Danes he has washed away blackening of queen's reputation	Prince tells Queen about blackness in her heart	Queen tells Prince about *black and grieved spots* in her soul	Queen tells Prince about *black and grained spots* in her soul
Development of King's character	King is shrewd and cunning	King flatters, Leartes and instructs him in three ways to kill Hamlet	King flatters Laertes more, and manipulates him into suggesting one way to kill Hamlet	King flatters Laertes more, and manipulates him into suggesting one way to kill Hamlet
Two "friends" of Hamlet	Servants of the King [*fideles ministres, deux serviteurs du Roy Fengon*]	*Right noble friends* of King, the King's *liegemen*	Less marked allegiance to King: *dear*, and *friends*, though their own lines reveal their obeisance to King	As Q2: less marked allegiance to King: *dear*, and *friends*, though their own lines reveal their obeisance to King

Chapter Notes

Introduction

1. From *Pierce Penniless*, in *Thomas Nashe. The Unfortunate Traveller & Other Works*, ed. by J. B. Steane (Middlesex: Penguin Books, 1972), pp. 49–145 (p. 74). Words set in bold by author for emphasis.

2. Ann Thompson and Neil Taylor, eds, *Hamlet*. The Arden Shakespeare (London: Thomson Learning, 2006). All Q2 quotations come from this text unless otherwise noted.

3. Kathleen O. Irace, ed., *The First Quarto of Hamlet* (Cambridge: Cambridge University Press, 1998). All Q1 quotations come from this edition unless otherwise noted.

4. Horace Howard Furness, ed., *A New Variorum Edition of Shakespeare. Hamlet*, 2 vols. (Philadelphia: J. B. Lippincott, 1905), II, p. 13.

5. G. R. Hibbard, ed., *Hamlet* (Oxford: Oxford University Press, 1987), p. 74.

6. Kathleen Irace's figures. The same figures are used in all relevant calculations in this book, for consistency (Irace, ed., *The First Quarto*, p. 2).

7. Thomas Caldecott, quoted by Furness, ed., *Variorum Hamlet*, II, p. 14.

8. John Payne Collier, quoted by Furness, ed., *Variorum Hamlet*, II, p. 14.

9. George Ian Duthie, *Elizabethan Shorthand & the First Quarto of "King Lear"* (Oxford: Basil Blackwell, 1949).

10. From W.W. Lloyd, "Critical Essay on *Hamlet*," quoted by Furness, ed., *Variorum Hamlet*, II, p. 24.

11. Ibid., p. 14.

12. Grant White, quoted by Furness, ed., *Variorum Hamlet*, II, p. 27.

13. Alfred W. Pollard, *Shakespeare's Fight with the Pirates and the Problems of the Transmission of His Text* (Cambridge: Cambridge University Press, 1967), p. 99.

14. Sidney Thomas, "*Hamlet* Q1: First Version or Bad Quarto?," in *The Hamlet First Published: Origins, Form, Intertextualities*, ed. by Thomas Clayton (Newark: University of Delaware Press, 1992), pp. 249–256 (pp. 251–2).

15. From Tycho Mommsen, *Athenæum*, quoted by Furness, ed., *Variorum Hamlet*, II, pp. 25–6.

16. William Henry Widgery, *The First Quarto of Hamlet. 1603*. Harness Prize essay, 1880 (London: Smith, Elder, 1880. British Library reference 11766.bbb.), pp. 87–204 (p. 18).

17. F. G. Hubbard, "The 'Marcellus' Theory of the First Quarto of *Hamlet*," *Modern Language Notes*, vol. 33, no. 2 (1918), pp. 73–80 (p. 74).

18. George Ian Duthie, *The "Bad" Quarto of Hamlet. A Critical Study* (Cambridge: Cambridge University Press, 1941).

19. Eric Sams, "Assays of Bias," *Notes and Queries*, CCXXXVI (March 1991), pp. 60–3.

20. John J. Burke Jr., Review of Eric Sams' *The Real Shakespeare. Retrieving the Early Years, 1564–1594*, *South Atlantic Review*, vol. 62, no. 4 (South Atlantic Modern Languages Association, Autumn 1995), pp. 81–4 (p.82).

21. Harold Jenkins, ed., *Hamlet*. The Arden Shakespeare, 2nd ed. (London: Methuen, 1982), p. 19.

22. Stanley Wells and Gary Taylor, general editors, *William Shakespeare. The Complete Works*. Compact edition (Oxford: Clarendon Press, 1988), p. 653. It is necessary to stress that the "Compact" edition from which this quotation is taken gives a "compact" summary of a complex situation concerning the *Hamlet*s, and that elsewhere the authors acknowledge both that complexity and how dating Q2 *Hamlet* 1600–1 does "depend upon the validity of the hypothesis of memorial reconstruction" ("Works Included in this Edition," in *William Shakespeare: A Textual Commentary*, ed. by Stanley Wells and Gary Taylor [London: W.W. Norton, 1997], p. 122).

23. Charles Harold Herford, ed., *The Works of Shakespeare*, 8 vols. (London: Macmillan, 1926), VIII, pp. 121, 123.
24. E. K. Chambers, ed., *Hamlet*. Arden edition (Boston: D.C. Heath, 1904), p. 11.
25. Philip Edwards, ed., *Hamlet Prince of Denmark*. The New Cambridge Shakespeare (Cambridge: Cambridge University Press, 2000), p. 3.
26. G. Blakemore Evans, ed., *The Riverside Shakespeare* (Boston: Houghton Mifflin, 1974), p. 1137.
27. Geoffrey Bullough, *Narrative and Dramatic Sources of Shakespeare*, 8 vols. (London: Routledge and Kegan Paul, 1973), VII, p. 49.
28. F. J. Furnival, *Forewords* [sic] to William Griggs, ed., *Shakspere's Hamlet: The Second Quarto, 1604* (London: W. Griggs, n. d.), p. viii.
29. In Weiner's Introduction, pp. 1–60. Albert B. Weiner, ed., *William Shakespeare: Hamlet: The First Quarto; 1603* (New York: Barron's Educational Series, 1962).
30. Karl Elze suggests the earlier date in his Einleitung to his *Hamlet* (Hrsg.von Karl Elze, ed., *Shakespeare's Hamlet* [Leipzig: G. Mayer, 1857], p. xvi). Dr. Richard Farmer implies the latter, since the English translation is dated 1608, in "An Essay on the Learning of Shakespeare" (British Library, 641.e.27, 1767).
31. Steven Urkowitz, "Back to Basics: Thinking about the *Hamlet* First Quarto," in *The Hamlet First Published: Origins, Form, Intertextualities*, ed. by Thomas Clayton (Newark: University of Delaware Press, 1992), pp. 257–291 (p. 257).
32. Alan Nelson, "Calling All (Shakespeare) Biographers! Or a Plea for Documentary Discipline," ed. by Takashi Kozuka and J. R. Mulryne, *Shakespeare, Marlowe, Jonson. New Directions in Biography* (Aldershot, Hampshire: Ashgate, 2006), pp. 45–67 (p. 56).

Chapter 1

1. John Dover Wilson and George Ian Duthie, eds., *King Lear* (Cambridge: Cambridge University Press, 1960), pp. 131, 132.
2. Steven Urkowitz, *Shakespeare's Revision of "King Lear"* (Princeton Essays in Literature) (Princeton, NJ: Princeton University Press, 1980).
3. Gary Taylor and Michael Warren, eds., *The Division of the Kingdoms* (Oxford: Clarendon Press, 1983).
4. Wells and Taylor, eds., *William Shakespeare*. Compact Edition.

5. Alfred Hart, *Stolne and Surreptitious Copies. A Comparative Study of Shakespeare's Bad Quartos* (Melbourne and London: Melbourne University Press in Association with Oxford University Press, 1942), p. 159.
6. Jenkins, ed., pp. 19, 5.
7. Terms like "first draft," and "first version" are used to denote the earliest surviving version by Shakespeare. This note acknowledges that we simply do not know what early drafts or "foul" papers existed. We can only talk about what survives.
8. Eric Sams, *The Real Shakespeare. Retrieving the Early Years, 1564–1594* (New Haven and London: Yale University Press, 1995), pp. 121–2.
9. E. K. Chambers, *William Shakespeare. A Study of Facts and Problems*, 2 vols. (Oxford: Clarendon Press, 1951), I, p. 425.
10. John Dover Wilson, ed., *Hamlet* (Cambridge: The University Press, 1934), p. 230.
11. Geoffrey Bullough, *Narrative and Dramatic Sources of Shakespeare*, 8 vols. (London: Routledge and Kegan Paul, 1973), VII, pp. 31–3.
12. Ibid., VII, opposite p. 31.
13. Ibid., VII, p. 30.
14. Ibid., VII, p. 18.
15. T. S. Dorsch, ed., *Julius Caesar*. The Arden Shakespeare (London: Methuen, 1975), p. vii.
16. Ibid., p. vii.
17. Peter Alexander, ed., *William Shakespeare. The Complete Works* (London and Glasgow: Collins, 1951).
18. The "error" with which Shakespeare kills off Caesar in the Capitol may have been something he read in Chaucer's *Monk's Tale* (Thompson and Taylor, eds., *Hamlet* [Q2], p. 50). In Plutarch Caesar is killed in the Senate House.
19. E. K. Chambers, *The Elizabethan Stage*, 4 vols. (Oxford: Clarendon Press, 1923), III, p. 309.
20. Bullough, V, p. 33.
21. Thompson and Taylor, eds., *Hamlet* (Q2), p. 50.
22. Andrew Cairncross, ed., *King Henry VI Part 1*. The Arden Shakespeare (London, Methuen, 1992).
23. "These wilde Pines do growe vpon the colde mountains of Liuonia, Polonia..." John Gerard's *Great Herball, or Generall Historie of Plantes* (British Library reference MIC.c.7401, 1597), p. 1177.
24. John Dover Wilson, "The "Hamlet" Transcript," *The Library*, 3rd series, 9 (1918), pp. 217–47 (p. 241).
25. Wilson, ed., *Hamlet* (1934), p. 197.
26. John Dover Wilson, ed., *Hamlet* (Cambridge: The University Press, 1936), p. 302.

27. John Dover Wilson, *The Manuscript of Shakespeare's Hamlet and the Problems of its Transmission*, 2 vols. (Cambridge: Cambridge University Press, 1963), I, p. xxii.
28. Wilson, ed., *Hamlet* (1934), p. 221.
29. George Rylands, ed., *Hamlet* (Oxford: Clarendon Press, 1969), p. 218.
30. Jenkins, ed., p. 527.
31. George Alfred Henty offers an account of the siege of Ostend which curiously mentions both the numbers of men that Shakespeare gives: "On the 5th July 1601 the Archduke Albert began the siege of Ostend with 20,000 men..." and "The garrison at first consisted of but 2000 men..." (G. A Henty, *By England's Aid or the Freeing of the Netherlands*, 1585–1604. Chapter XXIII, The Siege of Ostend (1890) http://www.online-literature.com/ga-henty/by-englands-aid-or-the-freeing/24/ [accessed 23rd September 2013].
32. James Shapiro, *1599. A Year in the Life of William Shakespeare* (London: Faber and Faber, 2005), p. 347.
33. Wilson, ed., *Hamlet* (1934), p. viii.
34. Found for example in the 1561 *Gorboduc*, and in Thomas Hughes' slightly later *Misfortunes of Arthur* (1588).
35. His elaborate language includes "Three of the carriages, in faith, are very dear to fancy, very responsive to the hilts, most delicate carriages and of very liberal conceit" (V.ii.133–5). John Lyly's *Euphues*, which set the trend for the style, was published in 1579.
36. For example, *Thyestes*, where Tantalus and Fury rise from hell to call for revenge. *Thyestes* was first translated by Jasper Heywood in 1560, but a collection of "Englished" Senecan plays, put together by Thomas Newton, was published in 1581. There are other elements which suggest a Senecan influence, such as the long speeches, and the technique of stichomythia, which proves a welcome contrast with the set speeches.
37. The essence of the courtier, a certain recklessness and nonchalance, was perhaps drawn from *Il Cortegiano* by Baldassarre Castiglione, translated into English by Sir Thomas Hoby in 1561 (reprinted 1577, 1588, 1603) and into Latin by Bartholomew Clerke in 1577. Book 1 of 4 outlines the perfect qualities of the courtier, qualities such as knowledge, great courage, skills in weaponry, a grace in all circumstances, magnanimity, and to be learned in humanity, classical languages and poetry. Ofelia/Ophelia's description no doubt recalled the concept of the perfect courtier to those of the audience familiar with *The Courtier*.
38. These may have contributed to *Hamlet*. Stuart Gillespie is one of several commentators who notes how Shakespeare and Montaigne share some interests, but "their expressing the same sentiments is not evidence of a direct relationship" (Stuart Gillespie, *Shakespeare's Books. A Dictionary of Shakespeare Sources* (London and New Brunswick, NJ: The Athlone Press, 2001), p. 344).
39. Robert Norman, *The Newe Attractive*, published in 1581, with later editions in 1585 and 1596. It was one of the first books on magnetism to be published in England.
40. Sidney uses the single compounded phrase "tragi-comical" in *The Defense of Poetry* (Arnold Whitridge and John Wendell Dodds, *An Oxford Anthology of English Prose* [New York: Oxford University Press, 1937], pp. 31–45 [p. 36]).
41. Jenkins, ed., p. 303n.
42. J. R. Mulryne, ed., *The Spanish Tragedy*. The New Mermaids, 2nd ed. (London: A. & C. Black, 1991), p. xiv.
43. Ibid., p. xv.
44. Edwards, ed., p. 3.
45. Thompson and Taylor, eds., *Hamlet* (Q2), pp. 60–1.
46. Thomas, p. 252.
47. Urkowitz, "Back to Basics: Thinking About the *Hamlet* First Quarto," pp. 264–5.
48. Steven Urkowitz, "'Well-sayd olde Mole': Burying Three *Hamlets* in Modern Editions," in *Shakespeare Study Today*, ed. by Georgianna Ziegler (New York: AMS Press, 1986), pp. 37–70 (p. 56).
49. The grammar of the first example is subject ("my hart"), verb ("is"), adverbial ("on the sodaine"), complement ("very sore"), adverbial ("all here about"). This is a common enough word order. The grammar of the second is less common: complement ("ill"), subject ("all"), verb ("'s"), adverb ("here"), and adverbial ("about my hart"). E. A. Abbott, *A Shakespearean Grammar* (London: Macmillan, 1901) has been consulted for aspects of Elizabethan grammar here and elsewhere.
50. Alexander, ed., *William Shakespeare*.
51. Richard Hodges, *A Special Help to Orthographie* (London, 1643), p. 26, quoted by Albert C. Baugh, *A History of the English Language* (London: Routledge & Kegan Paul, 1968), p. 298.
52. MacDonald P. Jackson, "Hand D of *Sir Thomas More*," reported by Sir Brian Vickers, *Shakespeare, Co-Author* (Oxford: Oxford University Press, 2004), pp. 89–90.
53. A. C. Partridge, "Orthography in Shakespeare and Elizabethan Drama: A Study of Colloquial Contractions, Elision, Prosody and Punctuation," reported by Vickers, p. 87.

54. The exercise was carried out by downloading originals of Q1 and Q2, and carrying out a "global" search on the respective endings. Each computer find was checked, to avoid mismatches.
55. F. O. Waller, "The Use of Linguistic Criteria in Determining the copy and Dates for Shakespeare's Plays," reported by Vickers, p. 88.
56. Wells and Taylor, *Textual Commentary*, pp. 102–5.
57. Duthie, *The "Bad" Quarto*, pp. 230–1.

Chapter 2

1. Bullough comments: "an undistinguished author." Bullough, VII, p. 10.
2. Sir Israel Gollancz, ed., *The Sources of Hamlet* (London: Humphrey Milford, Oxford University Press, 1926), p. 318.
3. From now on, *Les Histoires Tragiques* signifies not the collection of such stories but the volume giving the specific source of *Hamlet*.
4. Bullough, VII, p. 11n.
5. Jenkins, ed., p. 96.
6. All translations from the French are by the author.
7. Quotations from the French text are from Gollancz, ed., *The Sources of Hamlet*, for which page numbers are given in the text. Quotations from Q1 are from Irace, ed., *The First Quarto*, for which scene and line numbers are given, and for Q2, quotations are from Thompson and Taylor, eds., *Hamlet* (Q2), for which act, scene and line numbers are given. This order is adhered to in each example.
8. Jenkins, ed., p. 93.
9. Ibid., p. 94.
10. Evans, ed., p. 1137.
11. Vocabulary has been verified in *La Dictionnaire de la Langue Francais du seizième siècle*, 9 vols. ed. by Edmond Huguet (Paris: Libraire Ancienne Honoré Champion, 1932). The corrected version of this noun is found in vol. II.
12. Faire + infinitive is used to indicate causative action.
13. Kenneth Muir, *The Sources of Shakespeare's Plays* (London: Methuen, 1977), p. 4.
14. J. W. MacKail, ed., *The Aeneid* (Oxford: Clarendon Press, 1930), p. 228.
15. Jenkins, ed., p. 95.
16. Arthur P. Stabler, "King Hamlet's Ghost in Belleforest?" in *The Publication of Modern Languages Association*, vol. 77, No 1 (March 1962), pp. 18–20 (p. 19). Jenkins, ed., p. 93.
17. Tycho Mommsen, quoted in Furness, ed., *Variorum Hamlet*, II, p. 25.
18. Jenkins, ed., p. 95. Jenkins has obviously looked very closely at the French source, though he is not seeking to distinguish between the echoes of the French source in Q1 and Q2.
19. Thompson and Taylor, eds., *Hamlet* (Q2), p. 141.
20. Duthie, *The "Bad" Quarto*, pp. 230–1.
21. Thompson and Taylor, eds., *Hamlet* (Q2), p. 453n.

Chapter 3

1. Lene Petersen, *Shakespeare's Errant Texts. Textual Form and Linguistic Style in Shakespearean "Bad" Quartos and Co-Authored Plays* (Cambridge: Cambridge University Press, 2010), p. 70.
2. Lukas Erne, *Shakespeare as Literary Dramatist* (Cambridge: Cambridge University Press, 2003), pp. 220–244.
3. Duthie, *The "Bad" Quarto*, p. 183. Further discussion of *The Spanish Tragedy* and these promises follows in chapter eight.
4. Mulryne, ed., *The Spanish Tragedy*, p. xiv.
5. Wells and Taylor, *Textual Companion*, p. 398.
6. Wells and Taylor do not specify which "narrative accounts," but Saxo's and Belleforest's are the only extant earlier narrative accounts (ibid., p. 398).

Chapter 4

1. Irace, ed., *The First Quarto*, p. 111.
2. Naseeb Shaheen, *Biblical References in Shakespeare's Plays*, (London: Associated University Press, 1999), p. 535. Specific parallels are given by A. Davenant in "Shakespeare and Nashe's 'Pierce Penilesse,'" *Notes and Queries* (September 1953), pp. 371–374 (pp. 371–3), and by J. J. M. Tobin in the 1980s (Thompson and Taylor, eds., *Hamlet* [Q2], p. 72).
3. Steane, ed., p. 77. All page numbers from *Pierce Penniless* in the chapter and the table come from Steane's edition.
4. John Dover Wilson explores the need for Hamlet to realise there are eavesdroppers in *What Happens in Hamlet*, 3rd edition (Cambridge: Cambridge University Press, 1964).
5. Brian Morris, ed., *The Taming of the Shrew*. The Arden Shakespeare (London: Methuen, 1988), pp. 18–19.
6. Peter Quennell, *Shakespeare* (London: Readers Union, Weidenfeld & Nicholson, 1964), p. 21.

7. Park Honan, *Shakespeare: A Life* (Oxford: Oxford University Press, 1998), p. 45.
8. Muir, pp. 4, 6.
9. Katherine Duncan-Jones, *Ungentle Shakespeare: Scenes from His Life* (London: Thomson Learning, 2001), p. 5.
10. The information comes from the Belott-Mountjoy case. Details in e.g. Samuel Schoenbaum, *William Shakespeare. A Documentary Life* (Oxford: Clarendon Press, 1975), pp. 210–13.
11. O. Hood Phillips, *Shakespeare & the Lawyers* (London: Methuen, 1972), p. 78.
12. Jenkins, ed., p. 547.
13. The basis of the three way analysis between the source and the two quartos was first published in *Parergon*, in 2012 (Margrethe Jolly, "*Hamlet* and the French Connection: The Relationship of Q1 and Q2 *Hamlet* and the Evidence of Belleforest's *Histoires Tragiques*," in *Parergon*, Vol. 29, No. 1 [2012], pp. 83–105).

Chapter 5

1. Martin Rosenberg, reporting on how Q1 was received in 1881, in "The First Modern English Staging," in *The Hamlet First Published*, ed. by Thomas Clayton, pp. 241–8 (p. 247).
2. Bryan Loughrey reporting an interview with Peter Guinness, in "Q1 in Recent Performance," in *The Hamlet First Published*, ed. by Thomas Clayton, pp. 123–136 (p. 128).
3. Bryan Loughrey reporting an interview with Sam Walters, who in turn was quoting B. A. Young in the *Financial Times*. Ibid., p. 133.
4. Graham Holderness and Bryan Loughrey, eds., *The Tragicall Historie of Hamlet Prince of Denmark* (Maryland: Barnes and Noble Books, 1992), p. 13.
5. Alexander, ed., p. xxix.
6. Samuel Schoenbaum, *William Shakespeare: A Compact Documentary Life* (Oxford: Oxford University Press, 1987), p. 358.
7. Schoenbaum, quoting from Ben Jonson: *Timber, or Discoveries; Made Upon Men and Matter* (1641), from Ben Jonson, *Workes*, pp. 97–8 (ibid., p. 259).
8. Shapiro, p. 342.
9. Vickers, p. 39.
10. Q2's order *might* be preferable because "hallowed" ends with a long, unstressed syllable (diphthong plus consonant), while "gratious" ends with a shorter syllable (monophthong plus consonant) and because the vowel sound is a schwa, /ə/. The shorter syllable is perhaps a more decisive conclusion to the line.
11. Alfred Hart, *Shakespeare and the Homilies; And Other Pieces of Research into the Elizabethan Drama* (New York: AMS Press, 1971), p. 128.
12. Ibid., p. 142. Rather a sweeping comment; for example Philip Sidney's *Arcadia* was revised at an earlier date than this.
13. Heywood wrote: "It neuer was any great ambition in me to bee in this kind Voluminously read" (ibid., p. 143).
14. Ibid., p. 136.
15. Erne, p. 104 and elsewhere.
16. Heywood, quoted by Paul Werstine, in "Narratives about Printed Shakespeare Texts: 'Foul Papers' and 'Bad' Quartos Author(s)," in *Shakespeare Quarterly*, Vol. 41, No. 1 (Spring, 1990), pp. 65–86 (p. 84).
17. Grace Ioppolo, *Revising Shakespeare* (Cambridge, MA: Harvard University Press, 1991), p. 134.
18. G. Wilson Knight, *The Wheel of Fire* (Oxford: Oxford University Press, 1993), p. 33.
19. The small number of borrowings from the French source which are exclusive to Q2 legitimize the speculation that the playwright may have extended his borrowings slightly on a (later) reading.
20. Bullough's section on possible historical allusions records extracts from the C.S.P. Foreign Elizabeth 1588, July–December, and intermittently thereafter, commenting on the pirates, in the North Sea, and in the Great Belt, the seaway offering access to the Baltic (Bullough, VII, p. 184).
21. Hart, *Stolne and Surreptitious Copies*, p. 164.

Chapter 6

1. Wells and Taylor, *A Textual Companion*, pp. 102–5. Ants Oras, *Pause Patterns in Elizabethan and Jacobean Drama: An Experiment in Prosody*. University of Florida Monographs, Humanities No 3 (Florida: University of Florida Press, [Gainsville], Winter 1960).
2. Caldecott (1832), paraphrased by Furness, ed., *Variorum Hamlet*, II, p. 14.
3. Thomas, p. 251.
4. Mommsen, quoted by Furness, ed., *Variorum Hamlet*, II, pp. 25–6.
5. Mommsen, quoted by Furness, ibid., p. 25.
6. Widgery, p. 18.
7. Hubbard, pp. 73–77. Hubbard juxtaposes Widgery's and Gray's theories in the article in 1918, principally to rescue Widgery from oblivion, though Hubbard also makes a contribution to the debate.

8. Kathleen O. Irace, *Reforming the "Bad" Quartos. Performance and Provenance of Six Shakespearean First Editions* (Newark: University of Delaware Press. London and Toronto: Associated University Presses, 1994), p. 119.
9. John Dover Wilson, *The Copy for Hamlet, 1603 and the Hamlet Transcript, 1593* (London: Alexander Moring, The De La More Press, 1918. British Library reference: 011765.k.31), p. 22.
10. Chambers, *Facts and Problems*, I, p. 438.
11. Ibid., pp. 401–2.
12. Ibid., p. 331.
13. Ibid., p. 312.
14. All details from Chambers, *Facts and Problem*, I, pp. 408–9.
15. Ibid., p. 368.
16. Ibid., pp. 348, 294.
17. Ibid., p. 376.
18. Ibid., pp. 332, 408–9.
19. Walter W. Greg, "The Laws of Elizabethan Copyright: The Stationers' View," in *The Library*, XV, no. 1, 5th series (1960), pp. 8–20.
20. Robert Burkhart, *Shakespeare's Bad Quartos: Deliberate Abridgements Designed for Performance by a Reduced Cast* (The Hague: Mouton, 1979), p. 22.
21. Chambers, *Facts and Problems*, I, pp. 294–5.
22. Gollancz, ed., p. 319.
23. W. Tydeman, ed., *Two Tudor Tragedies* (London: Penguin Books, 1992), p. 50.
24. Paul Werstine discusses the significance of this in "Narratives about Printed Shakespeare Texts: 'Foul papers' and 'Bad' Quartos," *Shakespeare Quarterly*, 41:1 (1990) pp. 65–86.
25. Laurie E. Maguire, *Shakespeare's suspect texts: The "bad" quartos and their contexts* (Cambridge: Cambridge University Press, 1996), p. 103.
26. Duthie, *Elizabethan Shorthand & the First Quarto of "King Lear."*
27. William Bracy, *The Merry Wives of Windsor. The History and Transmission of Shakespeare's Text*. University of Missouri Studies, vol. XXV (Columbia: The Curators of the University of Missouri, 1952), p. 26.
28. G. N. Giordano-Orsini, "The Copy of *If You Know Not Me, You Know Nobodie*" Part I, in *The Times Literary Supplement* (4th December 1930), p. 1037, quoted by Maguire, p. 103.
29. L. S. Marcus, J. Mueller, and M. B. Rose, eds., *Elizabeth I: Collected Works* (Chicago and London: University of Chicago Press, 2000), p. 59.
30. "Edward Pudsey's booke": British Library reference: 117.e.62.
31. Maguire, p. 101.
32. Ibid., p. 101.
33. Ibid., p. 102.
34. Wells and Taylor, *Textual Companion*, p. 27.
35. Ibid., pp. 23–5.
36. Alexander, ed., p. xxvii.
37. Werstine, "Narratives About Printed Shakespeare Texts," p. 85.
38. Wells and Taylor, *Textual Companion*, p. 23.
39. Fred M. Clark, *Objective Methods for Testing Authenticity and the Study of Ten Doubtful Comedias Attributed to Lope de Vega* (Chapel Hill: University of North Carolina Press, 1971).
40. Clark, pp. 13–14.
41. Duthie, *The "Bad" Quarto*, p. 10.
42. Hugo Albert Rennert, *The Life of Lope de Vega* (Glasgow: Gowans & Gray, 1904).
43. Ibid., p. 287. One inference must be that Lope de Vega did not own or possess all his plays, suggesting Spanish playwrights handed over the play and copyright to the theatre company. The fact that he wrote at least 1500 plays makes it even less surprising that de Vega did not have control of all of them.
44. Ibid., p. 291.
45. Ibid., p. 294.
46. This information is attributed to Hartzenbusch: *Comedias Escogidas de Lope de Vega*, (Bib. de Autores Esp.) vol. IV: xxiiin (ibid., p. 292n).
47. Ibid., p. 294.
48. Wells and Taylor, *Textual Companion*, p. 23, and Maguire, p. 105.
49. Rennert, p. 176.
50. The quotation given in *A Textual Commentary* omits the last four clauses, although they directly follow the quotation offered (Wells and Taylor, *Textual Companion*, p. 23).
51. Rennert, p. 272.
52. Maguire, p. 106.

Chapter 7

1. Wells and Taylor, *Textual Companion*, pp. 23–5.
2. Duthie, *The "Bad" Quarto*, p. 37.
3. Ibid., p. 35.
4. Bracy reports Crompton Rhodes' opinion that Tate Wilkinson's "excellent opera" was "an inferior, almost illiterate, paraphrase from first to last, the songs alone being the genuine text of Sheridan" (R. Crompton Rhodes, "The Early Editions of Shakespeare: *The Duenna*," in *The Times Literary Supplement* (17th September 1925), p. 599 (Bracy, p. 49).

5. The text used is in Ernest Rhys' edition of Sheridan's *Poetry and Drama* (London: J. M. Dent, 1909); the line count is the author's.
6. Bracy, p. 51.
7. Alfred Pollard, quoted in Erne, *Shakespeare as Literary Dramatist*, p. 198.
8. R. Crompton Rhodes, quoted in Duthie, *The "Bad" Quarto*, p. 34.
9. Ibid., p. 10.
10. Wells and Taylor, *Textual Companion*, p. 27.
11. Hibbard, referring to the work by T. J. King (unreferenced) (Hibbard, ed., *Hamlet*, p. 77).
12. Ibid., p. 76.
13. Maguire, p. 104.
14. Jenkins, ed., p. 20.
15. Peter Blaney, "The Publication of Playbooks," ed. by John D. Cox and David Scott Kastan, *A New History of Early English Drama* (New York: Columbia Press, 1997), pp. 383–422 (p. 385).
16. Irace, *Reforming the "Bad" Quartos*, p. 151.
17. Irace, *Reforming the "Bad" Quartos*, p. 152.
18. Widgery, p. 138.
19. Ibid., pp. 139–40.
20. Ibid., p. 175.
21. Henry David Gray, "The First Quarto of 'Hamlet,'" *Modern Languages Review*, 10 (1915), pp. 171–80.
22. John Dover Wilson, *The Tragedie of Hamlet Prince of Denmark* (Weimar: Cranach Press, 1930. British Library reference C.100.1.16), p. 174.
23. Wilson, *The Copy for Hamlet*, p. 22. Wilson did not seem to support such a "chase after the Hamlet pirate of 1603" by 1934 (Wilson, *The Manuscript of Shakespeare's Hamlet*, I, p. xvi).
24. Irace, *Reforming the "Bad" Quartos*, p. 119.
25. Hibbard, ed., *Hamlet*, p. 76.
26. The number of lines for each character is taken from Irace's edition of Q1 *Hamlet* (Irace, ed., *Hamlet*, 2). Those concerned with 100 percent accuracy may argue that to mix scholars' line counts is not sufficiently precise, but the results will vary minimally and are unlikely to vary as much as 1 percent, and even a 5 percent variation does not affect the conclusions.
27. Wells and Taylor, *Textual Companion*, p. 27.
28. Or one in ten or 10 percent if all possible "actors" were included.
29. Duthie, *The "Bad" Quarto*, p. 134.
30. Irace, *Reforming the "Bad" Quartos*, p. 117.
31. Duthie, *The "Bad" Quarto*, p. 273.
32. Wilson and Duthie, ed., *King Lear*, pp. 131–2.
33. Maguire, pp. 324–5.
34. Steven Urkowitz, "Texts with Two Faces: Noticing Theatrical Revisions in *Henry VI*, Parts 2 and 3," in *Henry VI: Critical Essays*, ed. by Thomas A. Pendleton, (New York: Routledge, 2001), pp. 27–37 (p. 27).
35. Irace, *Reforming the "Bad" Quartos*, p. 137.
36. Sams, *The Real Shakespeare*, p. 130.
37. Holderness and Loughrey, ed., *Hamlet*, p. 8.

Chapter 8

1. Frederick Samuel Boas, ed., *The Works of Thomas Kyd* (Oxford: Clarendon Press, 1901), p. xlix.
2. Wilson, *The Copy for Hamlet*, 1603, p. 15.
3. Edward Dowden, ed., *Hamlet*. The Arden Shakespeare (London: Methuen, 1933), p. xix.
4. Duthie, *The "Bad" Quarto*, p. 91.
5. Ibid., pp. 52, 53.
6. Ibid., p. 91.
7. Ibid., pp. 128, 129.
8. Ibid., p. 128.
9. Ibid., p. 112.
10. Ibid., p. 93.
11. Mulryne, ed., *The Spanish Tragedy*, p. xiv.
12. Bullough, VII, p. 17.
13. Jenkins, ed., *Hamlet*, p. 97.
14. Duthie, *The "Bad" Quarto*, p. 185.
15. Ibid, pp. 184–185.
16. Ibid, pp. 182–4.
17. Ibid., p. 183.
18. Alexander, ed., *William Shakespeare*.
19. Maguire, pp. 165–6.
20. Duthie, *The "Bad" Quarto*, p. 196.
21. Ibid., p. 197.
22. Ibid., p. 196.
23. Ibid., p. 200.
24. Ibid., p. 203.
25. Ibid., p. 204.
26. Ibid., p. 163.
27. Ibid., p. ix.
28. Hibbard, ed., *Hamlet*, p. 96.
29. Thomas, p. 255.

Chapter 9

1. Jenkins, ed., pp. 19–20.
2. Loughrey, "Q1 in Recent Performance," p. 125.

3. Maguire, pp. 216–7.
4. Ibid., p. 219.
5. Ibid., p. 181.
6. Ibid., p. 185. (F1 is actually prose at this point.)
7. Ibid., p. 198.
8. Thompson and Taylor, eds., *Hamlet* (Q2), p. 417n, attributing the idea to J. D. Wilson.
9. Leah S. Marcus, *Unediting the Renaissance* (London: Routledge, 1996), p. 133.
10. Loughrey, "Q1 in Recent Performance," p. 125.
11. Thomas, p. 251.
12. Andrew S. Cairncross, *The Problem of Hamlet: A Solution* (London: Macmillan, 1936).
13. J. H. P. Pafford, ed., *The Winter's Tale*. The Arden Shakespeare (London: Methuen, 1963), pp. 165–6.
14. Maguire, p. 255.
15. Irace, *Reforming the "Bad" Quartos*, pp. 118–119. The role of "Prologue" as a possible memorial reconstructor is omitted later in her introduction to her Q1 *Hamlet* edition in 1998. This might be due to the absence of an "exit" for the Prologue before the appearance of Lucianus, in Q1.
16. Ibid., pp. 180–5.
17. Ibid., p. 114.
18. Wilson, *The Copy for Hamlet*, p. 22.
19. The additional problem of speculation upon either an abridged or adapted intermediate script between Q2 and Q1, or of the actor/reporter(s) adapting during reconstruction is acknowledged by, for example, Duthie (*The "Bad" Quarto*, p. 53); Irace speculates upon "inattention" and/or "deliberate abridgement" (Irace, *Reforming the "Bad" Quartos*, p. 119), and Maguire upon "two hands" (Maguire, p. 255).
20. Irace, *Reforming the "Bad" Quartos*, p. 122.
21. Writers, for example students, who need to edit to a specific length close to the current word count may excise a few words by deleting adverbs, or changing passives to actives, or substituting phrasal verbs with more formal equivalents; any who are required to expunge larger amounts of text will consider cutting out an idea, an aspect, a point that may be interesting but not in the foreground of the argument. It is difficult to scale down text proportionally, even if the overall word count is reduced by, say, two in five words, which is approximately what is needed to reduce Q2 to Q1 length.
22. A literature class, invited to produce a shortened version of a (conflated) *Hamlet*, cut out the subplot and magnified the role of the Ghost. Judicious and dramatically effective, yes.

Proportional, no. Similarly, the Reduced Shakespeare Company's rendering of *Hamlet* is hardly proportional.

Chapter 10

1. C. H. Herford & Percy Simpson, eds., *Ben Jonson*, 11 vols. (Oxford: Clarendon Press, 1927), III, 419.
2. William Hazlitt, ed., *The Dramatic Works of John Webster*, 4 vols. (London: John Russell Smith, Soho Square, 1857), II, 145.
3. The Rev. Alexander Dyce, ed., *The Works of Beaumont and Fletcher*, 11 vols. (London: Edward Moxon, Dover Street, 1843), I, pp. vii–viii.
4. It has been suggested that memorial reconstruction might lead to a simpler text.
5. M. L. Wine, ed., *John Marston: The Malcontent* (London: Edward Arnold, 1965), p. 11.
6. Herford and Simpson, VI, p. 15.
7. Hart, *Shakespeare and the Homilies*, p. 136.
8. Cook, quoted by Urkowitz, "Back to Basics: Thinking About the *Hamlet* First Quarto," pp. 268–9.
9. Hart, *Shakespeare and the Homilies*, p. 106n1.
10. Ibid., p. 96.
11. Ibid., p. 121.
12. Chambers, *Facts and Problems*, I, p. 420.
13. Hart, *Stolne and Surreptitious Copies*, pp. 447–8.
14. Hart, *Shakespeare and the Homilies*, p. 135.
15. Kathleen O. Irace, "Origins and Agents of Q1 *Hamlet*," in *The Hamlet first Published (Q1, 1603): Origins, Form, Intertextualities*, ed. by Thomas Clayton (Newark: University of Delaware Press, 1986), pp. 90–122 (p. 100).
16. Shapiro, p. 341.
17. Those arguing for abridgement as the primary explanation for the differences between a "bad" quarto and another version of a play are in a minority. These three seem to offer the most detail.
18. Bracy, p. 54.
19. Marvin Rosenberg, quoting from a sympathetic reviewer, in "The First Modern English Staging of *Hamlet* Q1," in *The Hamlet first Published*, ed. by Thomas Clayton, pp. 241–248 (p. 242).
20. Weiner, ed., p. iii.
21. Loughrey, "Q1 in Recent Performance: An Interview," pp. 124–5.
22. Burkhart, p. 115.
23. Ibid., p. 114.

24. Ibid., p. 97.
25. Bracy, p. 77.
26. Weiner, ed., pp. 35-7.
27. Ibid., p. 43.
28. Ibid., p. 52.
29. Ibid., p. 51.
30. Ibid., p. 51.
31. Ibid., p. 57.
32. Ibid., p. 44.
33. Bracy, p. 94.
34. The line count of matching lines is the author's, and the total number of lines is again taken from Irace.
35. Hart, *Shakespeare and the Homilies*, p. 121.
36. Ibid., p. 121.

Chapter 11

1. Robert Miola, *Shakespeare's Reading* (Oxford: Oxford University Press, 2000), p. 169. Readers are reminded that "*Ur-Hamlet*" is a label used to denote an early *Hamlet* whose existence is hypothetical, no more.
2. Frederick Gard Fleay, *A Biographical Chronicle of the English Drama 1559-1642*, 2 vols. (London: Reeves and Turner, 1891), II, p. 33.
3. Edmond Malone, "An Attempt to Ascertain the Order of Shakespeare's Plays" (British Library reference: 642.f.1, 1778), pp. 269-346.
4. Ibid., p. 292.
5. Chambers, *Facts and Problems*, I, p. 411.
6. Malone, "An Attempt to Ascertain," p. 292.
7. Ronald B. McKerrow, ed., *The Works of Thomas Nashe: Edited from the Original Texts*, 5 vols. (London: Sedgwick & Jackson, 1910), III, pp. 311-325. Subsequent page numbers in this chapter between 311 and 325 are to McKerrow's edition.
8. William Oldys, 1696-1761, English antiquarian and bibliographer.
9. Malone, "An Attempt to Ascertain," pp. 294-5n.
10. Ibid., p. 295.
11. Edmond Malone and James Boswell, eds., *The Plays and Poems of William Shakespeare*, 21 vols. (London: printed for F.C. and J. Rivington et al, 1821), II, p. 370.
12. Malone, quoted by Furness, ed., *Variorum Hamlet*, II, p. 5.
13. Richard Farmer, D.D. *An Essay on the Learning of Shakespeare*. The *Hystorie of Hamlet*'s deviation from the French source is mentioned in chapter twelve, towards the end of the section discussing "hamlet" and Newington Butts.
14. Malone and Boswell, *The Plays*, vol. II, pp. 371-2.
15. Sir Sidney Lee, *A Life of William Shakespeare*, 4th edition (London: John Murray, 1925), p. 1357.
16. Dowden, ed., pp. xiii, xiv.
17. John W. Cunliffe, "Nash and the Earlier Hamlet," *The Publication of the Modern Languages Association*, vol. 21 (1906), pp. 193-199 (p. 193).
18. Boas, ed., *The Works of Thomas Kyd*, p. xlix.
19. Chambers, *Facts and Problems*, I, p. 424.
20. Duthie, *The "Bad" Quarto*, p. 75.
21. Peter B. Murray, ed., *Thomas Kyd*. Twayne's English Authors Series (New York: Twayne, 1969), 88, pp. 5, 9. Murray's discussion includes the speculative attributions to Kyd (only *The Spanish Tragedy* being unquestionable) including the pre-Shakespearean *King Leir*, *Troublesome Reign* and *Titus Andronicus*: "most of them are so bad that one hopes Kyd did not write them" (ibid., p. 5).
22. J. Schick, ed., *The Spanish Tragedy* (London: J.M. Dent, 1898), p. xvi.
23. Ashley H. Thorndike, "Hamlet and Contemporary Revenge Plays" (*The Publication of the Modern Languages Association*, 1902), pp. 125-220 (pp. 126, 169).
24. Hibbard, ed., *Hamlet*, p. 13.
25. A. E. Jack, "Thomas Kyd and the Ur-Hamlet," *Modern Languages Association*, vol. 20 (4) (1905), pp. 729-748.
26. Chambers, ed., *Hamlet*, pp. 7, 11.
27. Chambers, *Facts and Problems*, I, p. 412.
28. Thompson and Taylor, eds., *Hamlet* (Q2), p. 46.
29. Sams, *The Real Shakespeare*, p. 21.
30. McKerrow comments upon printing from the 1610 edition (McKerrow, III, p. 309).
31. A. E. Jack, p. 748.
32. McKerrow, III, p. 315n.
33. McKerrow, IV, p. 449.
34. McKerrow, I, p. 20.
35. G. R. Hibbard, *Thomas Nashe: A Critical Introduction* (London: Routledge and Kegan Paul, 1962), p. 31.
36. Duthie, *The "Bad" Quarto*, p. 71.
37. The Glosse to the Eclogue by "E. K." gives: "The gate) the Gote: Northernely spoken to turne O into A" (J. C. Smith, and E. De Selincourt, eds., *Spenser, Poetical Works* [London: Oxford University Press, 1966], p. 440).
38. Ibid., p. 438, lines 227, 225-6, 236, 276, 299.
39. Duthie, *The "Bad" Quarto*, p. 74.

40. Smith and Selincourt, eds., p. xiv.
41. Ibid., p. 440.
42. McKerrow, ed., IV, p. 449.
43. Smith and Selincourt, eds., p. 440, under note beginning "Such ende."
44. McKerrow, ed., III, p. 312.
45. Boas, ed., *The Works of Thomas Kyd*, p. xx.
46. M. Truman, "The View from Here." *Compass*, Wessex (Ashford, Kent, UK: Headley Bros, 2010), pp. 73–4 (p. 74).
47. Mulryne, ed., *The Spanish Tragedy*, 1991, p. xi.
48. Boas, ed., *The Works of Thomas Kyd*, pp. xviii, xx.
49. It might be noted, however, that the translator of *Padre di Famiglia* is referred to only by the initials "T. K." "T. K." is assumed to be Thomas Kyd (McKerrow, ed., III, p. 450).
50. As Arber's transcription of The Stationers' Register shows.
51. Andrew Gurr, in his Introduction to Mulryne's 2009 edition of *The Spanish Tragedy* (J. R. Mulryne, ed., *Thomas Kyd: The Spanish Tragedy* [London: Methuen Drama, A. & C. Black, 2009], p. 20).
52. Mulryne, ed., *The Spanish Tragedy*.
53. G. Sarrazin, quoted in Duthie, *The "Bad" Quarto*, p. 70.
54. For example, IV.i.89–91, 100–1, 103–5 (*Titus Andronicus*, in Alexander, ed., *William Shakespeare*).
55. Duncan-Jones, p. 50.
56. Duthie, *The "Bad" Quarto*, p. 75.

Chapter 12

1. Chambers, *Facts and Problems*, I, p. 411.
2. R. A. Foakes and R. T. Rickert, eds., *Henslowe's Diary* (Cambridge: Cambridge University Press, 2002), p. 21.
3. Furness, ed., *Variorum Hamlet*, II, p. 9.
4. Ibid., p. 9.
5. Amanda Mabillard, *Newington Butts*. http://www.Shakespeare-online.com/theatre/nbutts.html [accessed 12th November 2010].
6. William Ingram, *The Business of Playing: The Beginnings of the Adult Professional Theatre in Elizabethan London* (New York: Cornell University Press, 1992), p. 159.
7. Foakes and Rickert, eds., pp. 21–2.
8. The examples given are no more than samples, but anyone examining the accounts will find that Newington Butts receipts are noticeably lower than the average of those at the Rose.
9. Howard Horace Furness, ed., *A New Variorum Edition of Shakespeare. A Midsummer Night's Dream* (Philadelphia: J.B. Lippincott, 1895, reprint 1923), p. 252.
10. Furness, ed., *Variorum Hamlet*, II, p. 10.
11. Walter W. Greg, ed., *Henslowe's Diary*, Part I, Text (London: A. H. Bullen, 1904), p. 13 F7r., and p. 17 F9r.
12. Malone and Boswell, *The Plays*, II, p. 293.
13. The French reads: [Amleth] "sauta sur ce lourdier, ou sentant qu'il y avoit dessous quelque cas cache, ne failait aussi tost d'y donner dedans a tout son glaive, puis tyrant le gallant demi mort, l'acheva d'occir..." (206).
14. Arthur Freeman, ed., *Francis Meres. Palladis Tamia; wits treasury* (London: Garland, 1973), p. 281r. All quotations are from this reprint of the original edition published by P. Short for Cuthbert Burbie. Page numbers are right hand side only, so r(ecto) and v(erso) are given, and paragraphs are numbered for clarity.
15. Ibid., p. 281r.
16. Walter W. Greg, ed., *Henslowe's Papers* (London: A.H. Bullen, 1907), p. 115.
17. Ibid., p. 121.
18. Ibid., p. 52.
19. Foakes and Rickert, eds., *Henslowe's Diary*, p. 217.
20. Freeman, ed., p. 279r.
21. Ibid., p. 282r.
22. Morris, ed., p. 63.
23. Agnes Latham, ed., *As You Like It*. The Arden Shakespeare (London: Methuen, 1975), p. xxvi.
24. A. R. Humphreys, ed., *Much Ado About Nothing*. The Arden Shakespeare (London: Methuen, 1981), p. 3.
25. F. H. Mares, ed., *Much Ado About Nothing* (Cambridge: Cambridge University Press, 2003), p. 8.
26. Jenkins, ed., p. 1. This is not a criticism; scholarly work on Shakespeare is so extensive it is impossible to read it all *and* make a contribution.
27. Don Cameron Allen, *Francis Meres's Treatise, "Poetrie." A Critical Edition. University of Illinois Studies in Language and Literature*, vol. XVI (Urbana: University of Illinois, 1933).
28. Ibid., p. 60.
29. Freeman, ed., p. 286v, paragraph 56.
30. Ibid., p. 282r, paragraph 26.
31. Ibid., pp. 281r–281v, paragraph 20.
32. Virginia Stern, *Gabriel Harvey: His Life, Marginalia and Library* (Oxford: The Clarendon Press, 1979).
33. Ibid., p. 128.
34. G. C. Moore Smith, *Gabriel Harvey's Marginalia* (Stratford-upon-Avon: Shakespeare

Head Press, 1913), p. 232. The actual handwritten marginalia, at the bottom of the page, offers no extra clues (Thomas Speght, Chaucer's *Works*. British Library reference: 42518, f422b).
35. Ibid., p. x.
36. Jenkins, ed., p. 6.
37. Thompson and Taylor, eds., *Hamlet* (Q2), p. 48.
38. The title of the comic play which "unmistakeably parodied Harvey" (Stern, p. 69).
39. Hans Scherer, ed., *Satiro-Mastix or The Vntrussing of the Humorous Poet. By Thomas Dekker* (Louvain: A. Uystpruyst, 1907), p. 46.
40. Frederick Samuel Boas, *University Drama in the Tudor Age* (Oxford: Oxford University Press, 1914), p. 344.
41. Alan Nelson, ed., *Records of Early English Drama*: "Cambridge. The Records," 2 vols. (Toronto: University of Toronto Press, 1989) I, pp. 984–985.
42. Burkhart, p. 111.
43. Paul Menzer, *The Hamlets: Cues, Qs and Remembered Texts* (Newark: University of Delaware Press, 2008), p. 165.
44. J. R. Elliot, Jr., ed., *Records of Early English Drama*. "Oxford: The Records," 2 vols. (Toronto: University of Toronto Press, 2004), I, p. 195. Folio reference: f242v. Date: 1583–4.
45. Nelson, *REED*. "Cambridge: The Records," I, p. 348. The letter from the Privy Council to the University is PRO: PC2/20, pp. 516–7, and dated 19th July 1593.
46. Thompson and Taylor, eds., *Hamlet* (Q2), p. 49. Although *Diaphantus* was published in 1604, there is some suggestion that it was written earlier, as Thompson and Taylor comment.
47. Jonson: "Hee that will sweare, *Ieronimo*, or *Andronicus* are the best playes, yet, shall passe vnexcepted at, here, as a man whose Iudgement shews it is constant, and hath stood still, these fiue and twentie, or thirtie yeeres" (J. R. Maxwell, ed., *Titus Andronicus*. The Arden Shakespeare [London: Routledge, 1993], p. xxii).
48. Chambers, *Facts and Problems*, I, p. 287.

Conclusion

1. Greg's conclusions to his Foreword, prefacing Duthie's book, *The "Bad" Quarto*, p. xi.
2. Examples already mentioned include: Burkhart, Bracy, Weiner, Sams and Urkowitz. Holderness and Loughrey include the comment: "even if the theory of memorial reconstruction is correct (and it is considerably more controversial than is generally recognised)" in the introduction to their *Hamlet* (Holderness and Loughrey, eds., p. 8).

3. Wells and Taylor, *Textual Commentary*, p. 122.
4. The Shakespeare postgraduate conference in June 2013, in the Shakespeare Institute, Stratford-upon-Avon, England.
5. Shapiro writes: "Rather than awkwardly littering the pages that follow with one hedge after another—"perhaps," "maybe," "it's most likely," "probably," or the most desperate of them all, "surely"—I'd like to offer one global qualification here: this is necessarily my reconstruction of what happened to Shakespeare in the course of this year and when I do qualify a claim it signals that the evidence is inconclusive or the argument highly speculative." Shapiro, p. xxiii.
6. Wells and Taylor, eds., *The Complete Works*. Compact Edition. p. 653.
7. Jonathan Bate and Eric Rasmussen, eds., *William Shakespeare. Hamlet*. The Royal Shakespeare Company Shakespeare (Basingstoke, Hampshire: Macmillan, 2008), p. 5.
8. Duthie, *The "Bad" Quarto*, p. 96.
9. Ibid., p. 97.
10. Ibid., p. 105.
11. Ibid., p. 109.
12. "Yet he does not wear anything," from *Kejserens nye klæder, The Emperor's New Clothes*.
13. This is Æsop's fable of the ape and the glowworm, mentioned earlier in the *Epistle*. McKerrow, ed., IV, p. 449.
14. J. R. Mulryne, ed., *The Spanish Tragedy*, p. xiii.
15. Robert Greene, *A Groats-worth of Witte*, quoted by S. Schoenbaum, *A Documentary Life*, p. 115.
16. Baugh, p. 59.
17. See the quotation opening the Introduction.
18. Perhaps like Ben Whishaw, who was twenty-four when he played the role at Old Vic in 2004.
19. It is acknowledged that the relationship of the source, hypothetical text and three surviving *Hamlet*s need not be linear; this is a simplified model. On the evidence, however, it could be right.
20. Duthie, *The "Bad" Quarto*, p. 53.
21. From the title page of Q2 *Hamlet*. Griggs, p. 2.
22. Bullough, VII, p. 11n.
23. Harold Bloom, *Shakespeare. The Invention of the Human* (London: Fourth Estate, 1998), p. 383.
24. Stabler, p. 19. Jenkins, ed., p. 93.
25. Gollancz, ed., p. 236. See also appendix B.
26. Gillespie, pp. 342–9. The lack of certainty about whether Shakespeare drew upon

Montaigne in *Hamlet* is also discussed by Jenkins, ed., pp. 108–110.

27. Jenkins, ed., p. 547.

28. Meres' chapter includes: "As *Antipater Sidonius* was famous for extemporall verse in Greeke, and *Ouid* for his *Quicquid conabar dicere versus erat*: so was our *Tarleton*, of whome Doctour *Case* that learned physitian thus speaketh in the seventh Booke, & seventeenth chapter of his Politikes; *Aristoteles suum Theodoretum Laudauit quendam peritum Tragœdiarum actorem; Cicero suum Roscium: nos Angli Tarletonum, in cuius voce & vultu omnes iocoli affectus, in cuius cerebroso capite lepidæ facetiæ habitant.* And so now is our wittie *Wilson*..." Freeman, ed., p. 285v–286r paragraph 52.

29. Wilson, "The 'Hamlet' Transcript," p. 241.

30. Nelson, *REED*. "Cambridge: The Records," I, p. 348.

31. Elliot, Jr., *REED*. "Oxford: The Records," I, p. 195.

32. Duncan-Jones, p. 136.

33. Robert Greene, *A Groats-worth of Witte*. Quoted in Diana Price, *Shakespeare's Unorthodox Biography* (Westport, CT: Greenwood Press, 2001), p. 48.

34. Maxwell, p. xxii.

35. Chambers, *Facts and Problems*, I, p. 292, in his discussion of *Henry VI*.

36. Freeman, ed., p. 287r paragraph 59.

37. Ibid., p. 282r paragraph 26.

38. Morris, ed., p. 63.

39. See chapter twelve under the section headed "1598: Francis Meres' *Palladis Tamia: Wits treasury*," and chapter twelve, note 27.

40. Thompson and Taylor, eds., *Hamlet* (Q2), p. 47.

41. *The First Part of the Returne from Parnassus*, lines 1001 and 1201. J. B. Leishman, ed., *The Three Parnassus Plays 1598–1601* (London: Ivor Nicholson & Watson, 1949).

42. S. Schoenbaum, *A Documentary Life*, p. 150.

43. Gerard, p. 1177. An alternative view is proposed by Abraham Samuel Shiff, in his essay, "The Forgotten Pun on a Diplomatic Scandal in a *Hamlet* Q2 Stage Direction," which recalls an incident in 1597. Queen Elizabeth was addressed by a Polish ambassador, whom she expected to be a legate but who came as a herald. She responded angrily to his hostile address, with *legatum expectavi, heraldum inveni*. Shiff's point is that "Polonius' puns upon the nationality of the Pole sparking off this incident. Shiff also sees "Corambis" as the earlier name, and "Polonius" as the revised name in the "Q2 revision." Abraham Samuel Shiff, "The Forgotten Pun on a Diplomatic Scandal in a *Hamlet* Q2 Stage Direction," http://trigs.djvu.org/global-language.../CorambisPoloniusDraft09.pdf [accessed 2nd October 2013] p. 15. Chambers hints at this incident (Chambers, *Facts and Problems*, I, p. 418), as does Bullough (Bullough, VII, pp. 185–7).

44. E. K. Chambers, *Sources for a Biography of Shakespeare* (Oxford: Oxford University Press, 1970), p. 60.

45. Wilson, ed., *Hamlet* (1934), p. 221.

46. G. A. Henty, *By England's Aid or the Freeing of the Netherlands* (1585–1604). Chapter XXIII, The Siege of Ostend. http://www.online-literature.com/ga-henty/by-englands-aid-or-the-freeing/24/ [accessed 23rd September 2013].

47. In 1604 the Spanish finally achieved victory (Wilson, ed., *Hamlet*: [1936], p. 221, and quoted by Rylands, ed., p. 218).

48. Q1's Corambis has 197 lines, Q2's Polonius has 339. Author's count.

49. Menzer, p. 59.

50. Ibid., p. 128.

51. Ibid., p. 121.

52. See chapter two.

53. Stern, p. 128.

54. It is not possible to ascertain which *Hamlet* this was, whether it was Q1 or Q2 or a stage version of either. It may be that when Burbage began to play the role its success increased.

55. Chambers, *Facts and Problems*, II, pp. 214–5.

56. Roland Mushat Frye, *Shakespeare's Life and Times* (London: Faber and Faber, 1967), section 66. The ship was called the *Dragon*, and Captain William Keeling had the crew perform *Hamlet* on 5th September 1607 and 31st March 1608.

57. Peter Blayney's article, "The Publication of Playbooks," investigates the profits from plays generally, doubting their profitability. It is tempting to wonder whether *Hamlet* might be an exception, since the text of the second quarto is reprinted in 1611. Blayney, pp. 383–422.

58. Erne, e.g. p. 104.

59. Werstine, "Narratives About Printed Shakespeare Texts," p. 84. Werstine is quoting from Heywood's address to his "Reader" in the 1608 edition of his *Rape of Lucrece*.

60. Menzer, p. 17.

61. Hibbard, ed., p.107.

62. Jenkins, ed., p. 5.

Bibliography

Abbott, E.A. *A Shakespearean Grammar*. London: Macmillan, 1901.

Alexander, Peter, ed. *William Shakespeare. The Complete Works*. London and Glasgow: Collins, 1951.

Allen, Don Cameron. "Francis Meres's Treatise, 'Poetrie.' A Critical Edition," *Studies in Language and Literature*, vol. XVI. Urbana: University of Illinois, 1933.

Arber, Edward, ed. *A Transcript of the Registers of the Company of Stationers of London 1554–1640 A.D.*, Vols. 1 & II. London: privately printed, 1875.

Bate, Jonathan, and Eric Rasmussen, eds. *William Shakespeare. Hamlet*, The Royal Shakespeare Company Shakespeare. Basingstoke, England: Macmillan, 2008.

Baugh, Albert C. *A History of the English Language*. London: Routledge & Kegan Paul, 1968.

Blaney, Peter. "The Publication of Playbooks," in *A New History of Early Modern English Drama*, ed. by John D. Cox and David Scott Kastan. New York: Columbia Press, 1997, pp. 383–422.

Bloom, Harold. *Shakespeare, The Invention of the Human*. London: Fourth Estate, 1998.

Boas, Frederick S. "*Hamlet* at Oxford: New Facts and Suggestions," *The Fortnightly Review*, 1913, pp. 245–253.

_____. *University Drama in the Tudor Age*. Oxford: Oxford University Press, 1914.

_____, ed. *The Works of Thomas Kyd*. Oxford: Clarendon Press, 1901.

Bodenham, Iohn. *Bel-vedére or the Garden of the Muses*. British Library reference: c.40.b.34, 1600.

Bracy, William. *The Merry Wives of Windsor. The History and Transmission of Shakespeare's Text*, University of Missouri Studies, vol. XXV. Columbia: The Curators of the University of Missouri, 1952.

Bristol, Michael D. Review of Eric Sams' *The Real Shakespeare*, *Renaissance Quarterly*, vol. 50, no. 2. University of Chicago Press, Summer 1997, pp. 607–9.

Bullough, Geoffrey. *Narrative and Dramatic Sources of Shakespeare*, 8 vols. London: Routledge and Kegan Paul, 1973.

Burke, John J., Jr. Review of Eric Sams' *The Real Shakespeare*, *South Atlantic Review*, vol. 62, no. 4, South Atlantic Modern Languages Association. Autumn 1995, pp. 81–4.

Burkhart, Robert E. *Shakespeare's Bad Quartos: Deliberate Abridgements Designed for Performance by a Reduced Cast*. The Hague: Mouton, 1979.

Cairncross, Andrew S. *The Problem of Hamlet: A Solution*. London: Macmillan, 1936.

_____, ed. *King Henry VI Part 1*. The Arden Shakespeare. London, Methuen, 1992.

Chambers, E.K. *The Elizabethan Stage*, 4 vols. Oxford: Clarendon Press, 1923.

_____. *Sources for a Biography of Shakespeare*. Oxford: Oxford University Press, 1970.

_____. *William Shakespeare. A Study of Facts and Problems*, 2 vols. Oxford: Clarendon Press, 1951.

_____, ed. *Hamlet*. Arden edition. Boston: D.C. Heath, 1904.

Clark, Fred M. *Objective Methods for Testing Authenticity and the Study of Ten Doubtful Comedias Attributed to Lope de Vega*. Chapel Hill: University of North Carolina Press, 1971.

Clayton, Thomas, ed. *The Hamlet First Published (Q1, 1603): Origins, Form, Intertextualities*. Newark: University of Delaware Press, 1986.

Cox, John D., and David Scott Kastan, eds. *A New History of Early Modern English Drama*. New York: Columbia Press, 1997.

Crystal, David, and Ben Crystal, eds. *Shake-*

speare's Words. A Glossary & Language Companion. London: Penguin, 2002.
Cunliffe, John W. "Nash and the Earlier *Hamlet*," *The Publication of the Modern Languages Association*. Baltimore, 1906, pp. 193–199.
Davenant, A. "Shakespeare and Nashe's 'Pierce Penilesse,'" *Notes and Queries*. September 1953, pp. 371–374.
Delius, William, ed. *The Leopold Shakspere: The Poet's Works in Chronological Order*. London, Paris & Melbourne: Cassell, 1881.
Diderot et D'Alembert, eds. *Encyclopédie*, 9 Tomes. JU-MAM, Geneve: chez Cramer L'Ainé & Compagnie, 1772.
Dorsch, T. S., ed. *Julius Caesar*. The Arden Shakespeare. London: Methuen, 1975.
Dowden, Edward, ed. *Hamlet*. The Arden Shakespeare. London: Methuen, 1933.
Duncan-Jones, Katherine. *Ungentle Shakespeare: Scenes from His Life*. London: Thomson Learning, 2001.
Duthie, George Ian. *The "Bad" Quarto of Hamlet. A Critical Study*. Cambridge: Cambridge University Press, 1941.
_____. *Elizabethan Shorthand & the First Quarto of "King Lear."* Oxford: Basil Blackwell, 1949.
Dyce, The Rev. Alexander, ed. *The Works of Beaumont and Fletcher*, 11 vols. London: Edward Moxon, Dover Street, 1843.
Edwards, Philip, ed. *Hamlet Prince of Denmark*. The New Cambridge Shakespeare. Cambridge: Cambridge University Press, 1985.
Elliot, J. R., Jr., ed. *Records of Early English Drama*. "Oxford: The Records," 2 vols. Toronto: University of Toronto Press, 2004.
Elze, Hrsg.von Karl. *Shakespeare's Hamlet*. Leipzig: G. Mayer, 1857.
Erne, Lukas. *Shakespeare as Literary Dramatist*. Cambridge: Cambridge University Press, 2003.
Evans, G. Blakemore, ed. *The Riverside Shakespeare*. Boston: Houghton Mifflin, 1974.
Farmer, Richard. "An Essay on the Learning of Shakespeare." British Library reference: 641.e.27, 1767.
Fleay, Frederick Gard. *A Biographical Chronicle of the English Drama 1559–1642*, 2 vols. London: Reeves and Turner, 1891.
Foakes, R. A., and R. T. Rickert, eds. *Henslowe's Diary*. Cambridge: Cambridge University Press, 2002.
Freeman, Arthur, ed. *Meres: Palladis Tamia; Wits Treasury*, Reprint of the 1598 edition published by P. Short for Cuthbert Burbie in London. London: Garland, 1973.

Frye, Roland Mushat. *Shakespeare's Life and Times*. London: Faber and Faber, 1967.
Furness, Horace Howard, ed. *A New Variorum Edition of Shakespeare. Hamlet*, 2 vols. Philadelphia: J. B. Lippincott, 1905.
_____. *A New Variorum Edition of Shakespeare. A Midsummer Night's Dream*. Philadelphia: J. B. Lippincott, 1923.
Furnivall, F. J. (Introduction) in *The Leopold Shakspere: The Poet's Works in Chronological Order*, ed. by Professor William Delius. London, Paris & Melbourne: Cassell, 1881.
Gerard, John. *The Great Herball, or Generall Historie of Plantes*. British Library reference MIC.c.7401, 1597.
Gillespie, Stuart. *Shakespeare's Books. A Dictionary of Shakespeare Sources*. London and New Brunswick, NJ: The Athlone Press, 2001.
Gollancz, Sir Israel, ed. *The Sources of Hamlet*. London: Humphrey Milford, Oxford University Press, 1926.
Gray, Henry David. "The First Quarto of 'Hamlet,'" *Modern Languages Review*, 10, 1915, pp. 171–80.
Greg, Walter W. "The Laws of Elizabethan Copyright: The Stationers' View," *The Library*, XV, no. 1, 5th series, 1960, pp. 8–20.
_____, ed. *Hamlet. First Quarto, 1603*. London: The Shakespeare Association & Sidgwick and Jackson, 1951.
_____, ed. *Henslowe's Diary*, Part I, Text. London: A.H. Bullen, 1904.
_____, ed. *Henslowe's Diary*, Part II, Commentary. London: A.H. Bullen, 1904.
_____, ed. *Henslowe's Papers*. London: A.H. Bullen, 1907.
Griggs, William. *Shakspere's Hamlet: The Second Quarto, 1604*. London: W. Griggs, n.d. [but dedicated to W.E. Gladstone: d. 1898].
Gurr, Andrew. Introduction in *Thomas Kyd: The Spanish Tragedy*, ed. by J. R. Mulryne. London: Methuen Drama, A. & C. Black, 2009.
Hart, Alfred. *Shakespeare and the Homilies; And Other Pieces of Research into the Elizabethan Drama*, reprint from 1934. New York: AMS Press, 1971.
_____. *Stolne and Surreptitious Copies. A Comparative Study of Shakespeare's Bad Quartos*. Melbourne and London: Melbourne University Press in Association with Oxford University Press, 1942.
Hazlitt, William, ed. *The Dramatic Works of John Webster*, 4 vols. London: John Russell Smith, Soho Square, 1857.
Henley, W.E. ed. *Hoby's Courtier*. London: David Nutt, 1900.

Henty, G. A. *By England's Aid or the Freeing of the Netherlands*, 1585–1604, Chapter XXIII, The Siege of Ostend (1890). http://www.online-literature.com/ga-henty/by-englands-aid-or-the-freeing/24/ [accessed 23rd September 2013].

Herford, Charles Harold. *The First Quarto of Hamlet*. 1603, Harness Prize essay, 1880. London: Smith, Elder, 1880. British Library reference 11766.bbb.18.

———. *A Sketch of Recent Shakespearean Investigation, 1893–1923*. London: Blackie & Son, 1923.

———, ed. *The Works of Shakespeare*, 8 vols. London: Macmillan, 1926.

———, and Percy Simpson, eds. *Ben Jonson*, 11 vols. Oxford: Clarendon Press, 1927.

———, and William Henry Widgery. *The First Quarto of Hamlet*. London: Smith, Elder, 1880.

Hibbard, G. R. "The Chronology of the Three Substantive Texts of Shakespeare's *Hamlet*," ed. by Thomas Clayton, *The Hamlet first Published (Q1, 1603): Origins, Form, Intertextualities*. Newark: University of Delaware Press, 1986, pp. 79–89.

———. *Thomas Nashe: A Critical Introduction*. London: Routledge and Kegan Paul, 1962.

———, ed. *Hamlet*. The Oxford Shakespeare. Oxford: Oxford University Press, 1987.

Holderness, Graham, and Brian Loughrey, eds. *The Tragicall Historie of Hamlet Prince of Denmark*. Maryland: Barnes and Noble Books, 1992.

Honan, Park. *Shakespeare: A Life*. Oxford: Oxford University Press, 1998.

Honigmann, E. A. J. *Shakespeare: The "Lost Years."* Manchester: Manchester University Press, 1985.

———. *The Stability of Shakespeare's Text*. London: Edward Arnold, 1965.

Hubbard, F. G. "The "Marcellus" Theory of the First Quarto of Hamlet," *Modern Language Notes*, vol. 33, no. 2, February 1918, pp. 73–79.

Hubler, Edward, ed. *Hamlet*. Signet Classics. London: The New American Library, 1963.

Hughes, Thomas and Others. *The Misfortunes of Arthur*. n.d. Students' facsimile edition. Sheffield University reference: B822.308, 1911.

Huguet, Edmond, ed. *Dictionnaire de la Langue Francais du seizième siècle*, 9 Tomes. Paris: Libraire Ancienne Honoré Champion, 1932.

Humphreys, A. R., ed. *Much Ado About Nothing*. The Arden Shakespeare. London: Methuen, 1981.

Hunter, G. K. *John Lyly. The Humanist as Courtier*. London: Routledge & Kegan Paul, 1962.

———, ed. *Marston: Antonio's Revenge*. London: Edward Arnold, 1966.

Ingram, William. *The Business of Playing: The Beginnings of the Adult Professional Theatre in Elizabethan London*. New York: Cornel University Press, 1992.

Ioppolo, Grace. *Revising Shakespeare*. Cambridge, MA: Harvard University Press, 1991.

Irace, Kathleen O. "Origins and Agents of Q1 Hamlet," in *The Hamlet First Published (Q1, 1603): Origins, Form, Intertextualities*, ed. by Thomas Clayton. Newark: University of Delaware Press, 1986, pp. 90–122.

———. *Reforming the "Bad" Quartos. Performance and Provenance of Six Shakespearean First Editions*. Newark: University of Delaware Press; London and Toronto: Associated University Presses, 1994.

———, ed. *The First Quarto of Hamlet*. Cambridge: Cambridge University Press, 1998.

Jack, A.E. "Thomas Kyd and the Ur-Hamlet," *The Publication of the Modern Languages Association*, Baltimore, 1905, pp. 729–748.

Jenkins, Harold, ed. *Hamlet*. The Arden Shakespeare, 2nd ed. London: Methuen, 1982.

Jolly, Margrethe. "*Hamlet* and the French Connection: The Relationship of Q1 and Q2 Hamlet and the Evidence of Belleforest's *Histoires Tragiques*," *Parergon*, vol. 29, no. 1, 2012, pp. 83–105.

Knight, G. Wilson. *The Wheel of Fire*. Oxford: Oxford University Press, 1993.

Latham, Agnes, ed. *As You Like It*. The Arden Shakespeare. London: Methuen, 1975.

Lee, Sir Sidney. *A Life of William Shakespeare*. London: John Murray, 1925.

Leishman, J. B., ed. *The Three Parnassus Plays 1598–1601*. London: Ivor Nicholson & Watson, 1949.

Loughrey, Bryan. "Q1 in Recent Performance: An Interview," in *The Hamlet First Published (Q1, 1603): Origins, Form, Intertextualities*, ed. by Thomas Clayton. Newark: University of Delaware Press, 1986, pp. 123–134.

Mabillard, Amanda. *Newington Butts*. Shakespeare Online. http://www.shakespeare-online.com/theatre/nbutts.html [accessed 12th November 2010].

MacKail, J.W., ed. *The Aeneid*. Oxford: Clarendon Press, 1930.

Maguire, Laurie E. *Shakespeare's Suspect Texts: The "bad" Quartos and Their Contexts*.

Cambridge: Cambridge University Press, 1996.
Malone, Edmond. "An Attempt to Ascertain the Order of Shakespeare's Plays." British Library reference: 642.f.1., 1778.
———, ed. *The Plays and Poems of William Shakspeare*. London: H. Baldwin, 1790.
———, and James Boswell, eds. *The Plays and Poems of William Shakespeare*, 21 vols. London: printed for F. C. and J. Rivington et al., 1821.
Marcus, L. S., J. Mueller, and M. B. Rose, eds. *Elizabeth I: Collected Works*. Chicago and London: University of Chicago Press, 2000.
Marcus, Leah. *Unediting the Renaissance*. London: Routledge, 1996.
Mares, F. H., ed. *Much Ado About Nothing*. Cambridge: Cambridge University Press, 2003.
Maxwell, J.C., ed. *Titus Andronicus*. The Arden Shakespeare. London: Routledge, 1993.
McKerrow, Ronald B., ed. *The Works of Thomas Nashe: Edited from the Original Texts*, 5 vols. London: Sedgwick & Jackson, 1910.
McMillin, Scott. "Casting the Hamlet Quartos: The Limit of Eleven," in *The Hamlet First Published (Q1, 1603): Origins, Form, Intertextualities*, ed. by Thomas Clayton. Newark: University of Delaware Press, 1986, pp. 179–194.
Menzer, Paul. *The Hamlets: Cues, Qs and Remembered Texts*. Newark: University of Delaware Press, 2008.
Miola, Robert. *Shakespeare's Reading*. Oxford: Oxford University Press, 2000.
Moltke, Max, and Gericke Moltke, and Dr. Robert Weiland. *Shakespeare's Hamlet-Quellen*. Leipzig: Verlag Von Johann Ambrosius Barth, 1881.
Morris, Brian, ed. *The Taming of the Shrew*. The Arden Shakespeare. London: Methuen, 1981.
Muir, Kenneth. *The Sources of Shakespeare's Plays*. London: Methuen, 1977.
Mulryne, J. R., ed. *The Spanish Tragedy*, 2nd ed. London: A. & C. Black, 1991.
———, ed. *Thomas Kyd: The Spanish Tragedy*. London: Methuen Drama, A. & C. Black, 2009.
Murray, Peter B., ed. *Thomas Kyd*. New York: Twayne, 1969.
Nelson, Alan H. "Calling All (Shakespeare) Biographers! Or a Plea for Documentary Discipline," in *Shakespeare, Marlowe, Jonson: New Directions in Biography*, ed. by Takashi Kozuka and J. R. Mulryne. Aldershot, Hampshire: Ashgate, 2006, pp. 55–67.

———, ed. *Records of Early English Drama: "Cambridge: The Records,"* 2 vols. Toronto: University of Toronto Press, 1989.
Norton, Thomas, and Thomas Sackville, Earl of Dorset. *The Tragidie of Ferrex and Porrex*, STC (2nd ed.) 18685.
Oras, Ants. *Pause Patterns in Elizabethan and Jacobean Drama: An Experiment in Prosody*. University of Florida Monographs, Humanities, no. 3. Gainsville: University of Florida Press, Winter 1960.
Pafford, J. H. P., ed. *The Winter's Tale*. The Arden Shakespeare. London: Methuen, 1963.
Pendleton, T. A., ed. *Henry VI: Critical Essays*. New York: Routledge, 2001.
Petersen, Lene. *Shakespeare's Errant Texts. Textual Form and Linguistic Style in Shakespearean "Bad" Quartos and Co-Authored Plays*. Cambridge: Cambridge University Press, 2010.
Phillips, O. Hood. *Shakespeare & the Lawyers*. London: Methuen, 1972.
Plumptre, James. "Observations on Hamlet." British Library reference: T.3.6.3. (1,2.), 1796.
Pollard, Alfred W. *Shakespeare's Fight with the Pirates and the Problems of the Transmission of His Text*. Cambridge: Cambridge University Press, 1967.
———, and John Dover Wilson. *Shakespeare Problems. The Manuscript of Shakespeare's Hamlet and the Problems of Its Transmission*, 2 vols. Cambridge: Cambridge University Press, 1934.
Price, Diana. *Shakespeare's Unorthodox Biography*. Westport, CT: Greenwood Press, 2001.
Pudsey, Edward. "Edward Pudsey's booke." British Library reference: 117.e.62, n.d.
Quennell, Peter. *Shakespeare*. London: Readers Union, Weidenfeld & Nicholson, 1964.
Rees, J. "Shakespeare and 'Edward Pudsey's Booke,'" 1600, *Notes and Queries*. September 1992, pp. 330–31.
Rennert, Hugo Albert. *The Life of Lope de Vega*. Glasgow: Gowans & Gray, 1904.
Rhys, Ernest, ed. *Sheridan: Poetry and Drama*. London: J. M. Dent, 1909.
Richmond, Hugh M. Review of Eric Sams' *The Real Shakespeare*, *Albion, a Quarterly Journal Concerned with British Studies*, vol. 28, no. 1, Spring 1996, pp. 95–6.
Rosenberg, Marvin. "The First Modern English Staging of *Hamlet* Q1," in *The Hamlet First Published (Q1, 1603): Origins, Form, Intertextualities*, ed. by Thomas Clayton. Newark: University of Delaware Press, 1986, pp. 241–248.

Rowse, A. L. *Discovering Shakespeare*. London: Weidenfeld & Nicolson, 1989.
Rylands, George, ed. *Hamlet*. Oxford: Clarendon Press, 1969.
Sams, Eric. "Assays of Bias." *Notes and Queries*, CCXXXVI. March 1991, pp. 60–3.
———. *The Real Shakespeare. Retrieving the Early Years, 1564–1594*. New Haven and London: Yale University Press, 1995.
———. Shakespeare, or Bottom? *The Myth of "Memorial Reconstruction."* Encounter, January 1989. http://www.ericsams.org/sams_bottom.html [accessed 6th April 2012].
———. *Taboo or Not Taboo? The Text, Dating and Authorship of Hamlet*, 1589–1623. http://www.ericsams.org/sams_taboo.pdf [accessed 15th February 2012].
Scherer, Hans, ed. *Satiro-Mastix or The Vntrussing of the Humorous Poet. By Thomas Dekker*. Louvain: A. Uystpruyst, 1907.
Schick, J., ed. *The Spanish Tragedy*. London: J.M. Dent, 1898.
Schoenbaum, Samuel. *William Shakespeare: A Compact Documentary Life*. Oxford: Oxford University Press, 1987.
———. *William Shakespeare: A Documentary Life*. Oxford: Clarendon Press, 1975.
Shaheen, Naseeb. *Biblical References in Shakespeare's Plays*. London: Associated University Press, 1999.
Shapiro, James. *1599: A Year in the Life of William Shakespeare*. London: Faber and Faber, 2005.
Sidney, Sir Philip. "The Defense of Poetry," in *An Oxford Anthology of English Prose*, ed. by Arnold Whitridge and John Wendell Dodds. New York: Oxford University Press, 1937, pp. 31–45.
Smith, G. C. Moore. *Gabriel Harvey's Marginalia*. Stratford-upon-Avon: Shakespeare Head Press, 1913.
Smith, J. C., and E. De Selincourt, eds. *Spenser, Poetical Works*. London: Oxford University Press, 1966.
Somogyi, Nick de, ed. *Hamlet*. The Shakespeare Folios. London: Nick Hern Books, 2001.
Speght, Thomas. Chaucer's *Works*. Gabriel Harvey's annotated copy. British Library reference: L. 42518, f422b, 1598.
Stabler, Arthur P. "King Hamlet's Ghost in Belleforest?" *The Publication of the Modern Languages Association*, vol. 77, no. 1. March 1962, pp. 18–20.
———. "Melancholy, Ambition and Revenge in Belleforest's *Hamlet*," *The Publication of the Modern Languages Association*, vol. 81, no. 3. June 1966, pp. 207–13.
Steane, J. B., ed. *Thomas Nashe. The Unfortunate Traveller & Other Works*. Middlesex: Penguin Books, 1972.
Stephens, Sir Leslie, and Sir Sidney Lee, eds. *The Dictionary of National Biography*, 18 vols, reprint of 1963–4. Oxford: Oxford University Press, 1921–22.
Stern, Virginia. *Gabriel Harvey: His Life, Marginalia and Library*. Oxford: The Clarendon Press, 1979.
Stevenson, J., A. J. Crosby, A. J. Butler, S. C. Lomas, and R. B. Wernham, eds. *Calendar of State Papers, Foreign Series*, 1564–5, 23 vols. London: 1863–1950.
Taylor, Gary, and Michael Warren, eds. *The Division of the Kingdoms*. Oxford: Clarendon Press, 1983.
Thomas, Sidney. "*Hamlet* Q1: First Version or Bad Quarto?," in *The Hamlet First Published (Q1, 1603): Origins, Form, Intertextualities*, ed. by Thomas Clayton. Newark: University of Delaware Press, 1986, pp. 249–256.
Thompson, Ann, and Neil Taylor, eds. *Hamlet: The Texts of 1603 and 1623*. The Arden Shakespeare. London: Thomson Learning, 2007.
———, and ———, eds. *Hamlet* (Q2). The Arden Shakespeare. London: Thomson Learning, 2006.
Thorndike, Ashley H. "*Hamlet* and Contemporary Revenge Plays," *The Publication of the Modern Languages Association*. Baltimore, 1902, pp. 125–220.
Timmins, Samuel, ed. *Hamlet*. London: Sampson Low, Son, 1860.
Truman, M. "The View from Here," *Compass*, Wessex. Ashford, Kent, UK: Headley Bros, 2010, pp. 73–4.
Tydeman, William, ed. *Two Tudor Tragedies*. London: Penguin Books, 1992.
Urkowitz, Steven. "Back to Basics: Thinking About the Hamlet First Quarto," in *The Hamlet First Published (Q1, 1603): Origins, Form, Intertextualities*, ed. by Thomas Clayton. Newark: University of Delaware Press, 1986, pp. 257–291.
———. *Shakespeare's Revision of "King Lear"* (Princeton Essays in Literature). Princeton, NJ: Princeton University Press, 1980.
———. "Texts with Two Faces: Noticing Theatrical Revisions in Henry VI, Parts 2 and 3," in *Henry VI: Critical Essays*, ed. by T.A. Pendleton. New York: Routledge, 2001, pp. 27–37.
———. "'Well-sayd olde Mole': Burying Three Hamlets in Modern Editions," in *Shakespeare Study Today*, ed. by Georgianna

Ziegler. New York: AMS Press, 1986, pp. 37–70.

Vickers, Sir Brian. *Shakespeare, Co-Author*. Oxford: Oxford University Press, 2004.

Vocht, H. de, ed. *Jasper Heywood and His Translations of Seneca's Troas, Thyestes and Hercules Furens*. Louvain: A. Uystpruyst, 1913.

Walker, Ralph, ed. *Ben Jonson's Timber; or Discoveries*, reprint. Westport, CT: Greenwood Press, 1976.

Weiner, Albert B., ed. *William Shakespeare: Hamlet: The First Quarto; 1603*. New York: Barron's Educational Series, 1962.

Wells, Stanley, and Gary Taylor, eds. *William Shakespeare: A Textual Companion*. London: W.W. Norton, 1997.

_____, and _____, general eds. *William Shakespeare. The Complete Works*. Compact edition. Oxford: Clarendon Press, 1988.

Werstine, Paul. "A Century of 'Bad' Quartos," *Shakespeare Quarterly*, vol. 50, no. 3 (Autumn 1999) Washington: Folger Shakespeare Library in association with George Washington Press, 1988, pp. 310–33.

_____. "Narratives About Printed Shakespearean Texts: 'Foul Papers' and 'Bad' Quartos," *Shakespeare Quarterly*, 41:1, 1990, pp. 65–86.

_____. "The Textual Mystery of Hamlet" *Shakespeare Quarterly*, vol. 39, no. 1 (Spring 1988) (Washington, Folger Shakespeare Library in association with George Washington Press), 1988, pp. 1–26.

Whitridge, Arnold, and John Wendell Dodds, eds. *An Oxford Anthology of English Prose*. New York: Oxford University Press, 1937.

Widgery, William Henry. *The First Quarto of Hamlet*. 1603, Harness Prize essay, 1880. London, Smith, Elder, 1880. British Library reference: 11766.bbb.18.

Wilson, John Dover. *The Copy for Hamlet, 1603 and the Hamlet Transcript, 1593*. London: Alexander Moring, The De La More Press, 1918. British Library reference: 011765.k.31.

_____. "The 'Hamlet' Transcript," *The Library*, 3rd series 9, 1918, pp. 217–47.

_____. *What Happens in Hamlet*. Cambridge: Cambridge University Press, 1964.

_____, ed. *Hamlet*. Cambridge: The University Press, 1934.

_____, ed. *Hamlet*. Cambridge: The University Press, 1936.

_____, ed. *The Sonnets*. Cambridge: Cambridge University Press, 1976.

_____, ed. *The Tragedie of Hamlet Prince of Denmark*. Weimar: Cranach Press, 1930. British Library reference: C.100.1.16.

_____, and George Ian Duthie, eds. *King Lear*. Cambridge: Cambridge University Press, 1960.

Wine, M. L., ed. *John Marston: The Malcontent*. London: Edward Arnold, 1965.

Ziegler, Georgianna, ed. *Shakespeare Study Today*. New York: AMS Press, 1986.

Index

a for *he* 29 (table)
abridgement: contraindications 59, 126, 131, 134–41, 182; as intermediate stage 32–3, 126, 136, 147; plausibility 53, 60, 131, 133, 138; as primary explanation for Q1 12, 16, 32, 40, 43, 45, 53, 59–60, 65, 69, 78–9, 87, 93, 96, 100, 128, 129–141, 147, 172, 178, 182
acting version 12, 67, 132, 133, 136
actor/reporter(s) 25–6, 30, 33, 39, 65, 71–4, 78, 84, 95–8, 100–1, 115–7, 127, 186, 192; his/their absence 97–8, 101, 125; and *Les Histoires Tragiques* 45, 47–49, 69; possible skills of 23, 25, 39, 71, 72; possible weaknesses of 25, 41, 72, 103, 116, 138, 179, 183; and *The School for Scandal* 90–5; and other Shakespearean plays 78, 103–5; and *The Spanish Tragedy* 22, 59, 105–9
adaptation 19, 32, 33, 40, 59, 60, 85, 87, 89, 96, 100, 126, 132, 135
additions 19, 20, 38, 63, 65, 66, 72, 131, 178, 185
adlibbing 186, 190, 192
adverbs 178
The Aeneid 38, 154, 155
Æsop 105, 148–52, 156–159, 180, 187
Alexander, Peter 184
All Fools 83
Allen, Don Cameron 166
allusions 2, 16, 17, 30, 31, 35, 63, 133, 134, 146, 190; to *Hamlet* 143, 158, 160; historical 17–21, 61; literary 17, 21–2
Amleth 21, 32, 35–41, 43, 53, 55, 58, 73, 108, 163, 184, 188; age 31, 41, 42; and "belle femme" 34, 44, 58; madness 34, 35, 46; and mother 34, 35, 36, 37, 41, 45–6, 47, 48–49, 54, 68, 108, 139; return to Denmark 39, 54, 55, 182, 185
analogy 10, 66, 67, 85, 87, 110, 119, 151, 164, 175, 181; of *The School for Scandal* 2, 99, 101, 127, 141, 179
Anatomie of Absurdities 149–50, 151, 154

Anatomie of Abuses 149–50, 151, 154
Andersen, Hans Christian 180
"andronicous" *see Titus Andronicus*
"antic disposition" *see* madness
"anticipations" 134
Antonio's Revenge 188
antonym 133, 146
An Apology for Actors 180
appositive style 167, 187
"*Arcadian Menaphon*" 149, 157
Arden of Faversham 78
The Arte of English Poetry 166, 187
As You Like It 27, 80, 165
asides 23, 24, 69, 110–11, 157, 158, 179, 180, 186
Asinius 171
assumptions 8, 19, 32, 60, 89, 114, 116, 125, 179, 181, 186, 188, 192; Q1 is memorial reconstruction 16, 45, 47, 51, 183; Q1's priority 65–6; Q2's priority 64, 126, 133, 183; Shakespeare's familiarity with French 61; *The Spanish Tragedy*'s priority over Q1 105; of *Ur-Hamlet* 33, 37, 47, 51, 178, 183
Astrophel and Stella 167, 168 (table)
"An Attempt to Ascertain the Order of Shakespeare's Plays" 144–5, 160, 163
aural error 117, 127
Austen, Jane 119

backlists 167
"bad" as descriptor 16, 62, 65, 81, 101, 103, 124, 125, 132
The "Bad" Quarto of Hamlet 1, 10, 31, 113, 177
Balthasar 106
Barnardo 73, 136–7
Bartholomew Fair 130, 174
Bate, Jonathan 2, 178
Baugh, Albert 181
Beaumarchais, Pierre 83, 89
Beaumont, Francis 84, 129, 131

237

INDEX

"beautiful woman" *see* "belle femme"
the "bedchamber" scene 35, 37–8, 45–6, 49, 58, 68–9, 74, 104, 108, 139
belief 2, 10, 12, 20, 67, 75, 106, 109, 133, 134, 146, 178–81
"belle femme" 35–6, 42, 44–5, 182; *see also* young woman
Belleforest, François de 2, 32–5, 37–8, 40–2, 45, 47–9, 51, 55, 65, 68, 70–1, 108–9, 184–6
Bellimperia 106, 108–9
Bel-vedére 170
Ben Greet Company 133
Bernard, John 13, 89–92, 94, 96–9, 101, 102, 179
Der Bestrafte Brudermord 3
binge drinking *see* drinking
Blaney, Peter 93
The Blind Beggar of Alexandria 78
Bloom, Harold 184
"blunders" 10, 25, 78; Kyd's 155
Blunt, Sir Christopher 84
Boas, Frederick S. 103, 106, 146, 153, 155, 172, 173
Bodenham, John 170
Bonian, Richard 79
"bookseller's hack" 10, 78
borrowings *see* parallels
Bracy, William 82, 92, 132, 133
Bright, Timothy 21
British Members of Parliament 153
Brudermord see Der Bestrafte Brudermord
Brutus 18–9
Buchanan, George 168 (table)
Bullough, Geoffrey 17–8, 33, 106
Bunbury, Sir Henry 8
Burbage, Richard 42, 173, 182
Burghley, Lord William 170
Burkhart, Robert 81, 132, 133, 173

Caesar Interfectus 18
Cairncross, Andrew 119
Caldecott, Thomas 8, 192, 219n7
Cambridge: city 99, 173; university 7, 82, 93, 152, 172, 173, 186, 188, 191
Camden, William 83
Castile 106
Chambers, E.K. 11, 17, 18, 79–81, 146, 147, 166
the "chambre" scene 35, 36, 37–8, 45–6, 48, 185
Chapman, George 78, 83, 84, 93, 169
Charlemagne 131
Charles Surface 90, 91–2 (tables)
"chast *Matilda*" 164, 175, 180
chiasmus 25, 49
the "churlish" Priest 79, 94
Clark, Fred M. 85
Claudius 47, 49, 66, 78, 125, 126, 136, 182, 183; character 68, 70–1, 72, 73, 135, 188; and Hamlet 22–3, 34, 44, 49, 58, 72, 74–5; Hamlet's rejection of King as father 205–6; and Laertes 68, 69, 72, 73; shared aspects 23, 34, 35, 39, 44, 74, 75, 126, 184; *see also* King
Clayton, Thomas 2
cohesion 49, 58, 59
Colin Clout comes home 167, 168 (table)
Collier, John Payne 9, 181, 219n8
colloquialisms 28–30, 60, 75, 77, 181, 188
comedias 85–6
"A comparative discourse of our English poets, with the Greeke, Latine and Italian Poets" 165, 166, 168
Compass magazine 153
compositor(s) 30, 117, 121, 136, 181, 192
"conceal" (and "consent") 49, 50, 58, 68, 108, 109, 190
Condell, Henry 84, 87
conflation 53, 77, 179
conjecture 16, 146, 161, 163, 180
connotations 47
consistency 13, 15, 26, 41–2, 69, 73, 75, 110, 112, 133, 139, 149, 171, 179, 183; *see also* inconsistency
Contention 100, 124, 167
contractions 25, 29–30, 189
The Copy for Hamlet, 1603, and the Hamlet Transcript, 1593 79
Corambis 18, 21, 23, 34, 35, 41, 42, 44, 45, 65, 73, 74, 78, 135, 143, 188, 189, 230n43; "closeth" 28; "pointing" of speech 134, 170
Cornelia 70
correlation 94, 99, 100, 124–7
correspondence 125–7, 189
The Counsellor 19, 30, 188, 190, 192
counterarguments 99, 184
The Countess of Pembroke's Arcadia 167, 168 (table)
Cox, John D. 2
Craig, Hardin 133
Crinitus, Petrus 166
criticisms of Q1 *see* descriptors
Crystal, Ben 56, 107
Crystal, David 56, 107
cues 2, 90, 91, 95, 96, 189
Cunliffe, John 146, 149
cuts 12, 33, 71, 73, 126, 129, 131–6, 138–9, 141, 184, 185, 190

Day, John 81
De Optimo Senatore 19, 188
De Poetis Latinis 166
"Death be not proud" 122
The Defense of Poetrie 21
deixis 48, 111

Dekker, Thomas 14, 160, 171, 172, 174, 175, 191
deletions 63, 65
descriptors (Q1): "blunders" 10, 78; the "complete collapse of sense and syntax" 119, 121, 122, 127; "corrupt" 39, 65, 132, 133, 179; "dynamo" 114; "a farrago of nonsense" 78, 119, 141; "garbled" 9, 26, 33, 65, 71, 78, 123, 133, 179; "inconsistencies" 78, 134, 190; "inferior" 11, 78, 178, 179; "maimed" 9, 62, 78, 84; "mangled" 9, 62, 82; "marred" 9, 78; "mistakes" 118; "misunderstandings" 78; "mutilated" 65, 78; "mutilated corpse" 114, 141; "skeletal version" 114; "travestied" 103; "truncated" 103; "ungrammatical" 65; "wrong" 118; *see also* "bad"
descriptors (Q2): "authentic" 94, 103, 108; "good" 16, 103
determiner 29, 29 (table), 110, 120, 153
Detti, et Fatti 14, 169, 175
"deux des fideles ministres de Fengon" 68, 74–5
de Vega Carpio, Lope Felix 85–7
Diaphantus, or the Passions of Love 14, 174
Dido, Queen of Carthage 155, 174
differences 63, 101, 105, 135, 138, 168, 178, 182, in colloquialisms 28–30; between Q1 and Q2 22, 24, 26–31, 48, 64, 67–7, 75, 87, 115, 118, 125–6, 129, 132, 136, 141, 181, 192; in Hamlet's age 8, 31, 41; scene 16 and V.i 28, 139–40; in source and *Hamlet*s 34, 40–1, 48, 191
A Discourse of English Poetrie 166
Discoveries 16
"disparity gaps" 57–9, 75, 190
A Disputation between a Hee Conny-catcher and a Shee Conny-catcher 169
The Division of the Kingdoms 15
Doctor Faustus 78, 155
Donne, John 122, 151
Doran, Madeleine 133
Dorsch, T. S. 220*n*15
"doth" 27 (table)
Dowden, Edward 103, 146
Drayton, Michael 164, 168 (table), 168
drinking 35, 39, 53, 55–7
drowning 17, 61
The Duchess of Malfi 129
duck houses 153
The Duenna 89–90
The Duke of Milan 117
Duke of Urbino, Francesco Maria della Rovere 17
dumb show 11, 21, 37, 115, 126
Duncan-Jones, Katherine 61, 156, 186
Duthie, George Ian 1–3, 10, 15, 67, 82, 89, 93, 177, 192; on actor/reporter(s) 78, 97, 102–6, 112, 113, 179, 183; on Hamlet's age 31, 42, 182; on *King Lear* 15, 98; on Nashe 146, 149, 151; on "objectionable" pronouns 102, 109–12, 118, 127, 179; on shorthand 9, 82; on *The Spanish Tragedy* 1, 22, 50, 59, 105–9, 113, 127, 141, 179
Dyce, Rev. Alexander 174

Edes, Richard 18
Edmund Ironside 131
Edwards, Philip 2, 22, 170
E. K. *see* Edward Kirke
Eld, G. 79
"elimination" 135, 178
elisions *see* contractions
Elizabeth I 18, 71, 82, 83
The Elizabethan Æsop 143, 152, 187
Elizabethan Shorthand 82
Elze, Karl 192
Embassador *see* English Ambassador
enclitic 29, 29 (table), 30
English Ambassador 79, 94, 95–6 (tables), 98 (table)
"entrapment" *see* test
An Epistle (to the Gentlemen Students of Both Universities) 2, 3, 55, 143–58, 160, 174–5, 180, 186
equivocation 184, 203
Erasmus, Desiderius 166
Erne, Lukas 48, 67, 134, 192
Ervin, Senator Sam 83
escorts 35, 66, 74, 138, 184; *see also* Rosencrans and Guyldensterne; Rossencraft and Gilderstone
Essais 21, 186
"An Essay on the learning of Shakespeare" 144
Essex, Robert, Earl of 20, 84, 169, 191
Essex rebellion 20
<eth> 26–29, 60
Euphues 174
euphuistic 21, 148
Evans, G. Blakemore 37
Every Man in His Humour 66, 174, 188
Every Man Out of His Humour 19, 67, 129, 131
evidence 2, 3, 8, 9, 11, 13, 15–7, 22, 33, 43–5, 65, 79, 98–101, 114–5, 146, 175, 180, 190; of abridgement 129, 132, 133; colloquialisms 28–30, 60; linguistic 26–30, 60, 192; of Meres 166; of postulated memorial reconstruction 83, 127, 133, 179; priority of Q1 68, 75, 140, 181–3; proximity of French source to Q1 59–60, 181
evolution of ideas 43, 46–9, 52, 94, 183
expansion (of Q1) 127, 133, 135, 189; Jonson's habit of 67
extra-metrical connectives 115–6
extra-metrical pleonasm 116
extras 97, 125

240 INDEX

fables 150, 152, 158
The Faerie Queene 152, 167, 168 (table)
Farmer, Dr. Richard 144, 145
The Februarie Eclogue 152
Fengon 36, 37, 38, 39, 40, 44, 46, 58, 68, 71, 74; character 70, 183; shared aspects 34, 48, 69, 108, 182, 184, 185
Field, Richard 61
1599 2
First Clown 8, 41
first draft 9, 16, 43, 60, 65, 114, 119, 121, 125, 133, 137, 140, 183, 191
first sketch 12, 32, 52, 67, 73, 75, 140, 147, 178, 192
Fitzgerald, F. Scott 67
Fleay, Frederick Gard 143, 146
Fletcher, John 84, 129, 131
"fluctuating correlation" 94, 124–5, 127
Foakes, R.A. 165, 228*n*2
Forman, Dr. Simon 162
Fortinbras 36, 70
Fortinbrasse 64, 70, 134
foul papers 84, 134, 136, 220*n*7
Fowles, John 67
fox 150 (table), 151–2, 158
Francisco 73, 136–7
The French Lieutenant's Woman 67
French source 2, 31, 33–6, 40, 43, 44–6, 50–61, 68, 69, 74, 77, 81, 105, 106, 108, 127, 135, 140, 163, 182, 183, 190, 192; *see also Les Histoires Tragiques*
Furness, Horace Howard 219*n*4, 228*n*9
Furnival, F.J. 11, 192

Gabriel Harvey: His Life, Marginalia and Library 169
A Game of Chess 99
"garbled" *see* descriptors
Gentleman 91 (table), 138
Gerard, John 19, 188
Gertrard (Q2's Queen) 53, 137, 139, 182, 189; promise 47, 49, 58, 60, 190; reputation 47; shared aspects 34, 35, 36, 37, 46, 184, 185; and son 35, 42, 47, 54, 68–9, 73, 140, 183, 189
Gertred (Q1's Queen) 71, 72; promise 47, 49, 50, 51, 58, 60, 107, 113, 190; reputation 47, 51; scene 14 53, 109–112, 137–9, 140, 182; shared aspects 34, 35, 36, 37, 46, 51, 55, 59, 139, 182, 184, 185; and son 35, 46, 47, 53, 54, 60, 68–9, 71, 140, 183
Gertrude 51, 108
Geruthe (Queen in *Les Histoires Tragiques*) 70, 182; promise 47, 48, 49, 50, 51, 58, 60, 107–8; reputation 46–7, 51; shared aspects 34, 35, 36, 45, 46, 59, 139, 182, 184, 185; and son 35, 37, 41, 48, 54, 68–9, 140, 183
Ghost 33, 40, 42, 48, 69, 70, 73, 116, 117, 126, 158, 190; in armor 17; and "l'ombre(s)" 37, 39, 108, 185; and revenge 11, 14, 21, 37, 144, 160, 164, 171, 187; Shakespeare playing Ghost 188
Gilderstone *see* Rossencraft and Gilderstone
Giordano-Orsini, G. N. 82
glowworm 149–51, 180
Goethe, Johann Wolfgang von 10
Gollancz, Sir Israel 2, 33, 41
Gonzago 17
Goslicki, Wawrzyniec Grzymala 19, 30, 188
grafter 3, 193
grammatical points 24–5, 49, 64, 109–13, 119, 122–3, 127, 146, 221*n*49; in Harvey's marginalia 169–70; in Meres' *Palladis Tamia* 166; in Nashe's *Epistle* 153, 156, 157–8, 174, 180
Gran Memoria 86
Gravedigger 7, 8, 28, 42, 79, 94, 95–6 (tables), 117, 118
Gray, Henry D. 10, 79, 94
The Great Herball, or Generall Historie of Plantes 19, 188
Greene, Robert 37, 143, 145, 149, 152, 157, 169, 186, 187
Greg, Walter W. 1, 81, 85, 95, 112, 132, 136, 177
Griffith, William 81
Griggs, William 96*n*
Guicciardini, Lodovico 14, 169, 175
Guilpin, Everard 167, 168
Guinness, Peter 62, 114, 118, 133
Gurr, Andrew 2, 155
Guyldensterne *see* Rosencrans and Guyldensterne

"hack-poet" 103
Hales v. Pettit 61, 186
Hamlet (F1) 8, 15, 32, 33, 62, 77, 103, 105, 125, 126, 129, 131, 132, 136, 144, 145, 161, 164, 174, 179, 190, 193; closer to Q1 24–6, 116; closer to Q2 7, 19, 25, 30, 45, 51, 140, 147, 182, 183, 186; "cut" 134; as a revised play 12, 25, 67, 141, 181, 191
Hamlet and Ofelia/Ophelia *see* Ofelia; Ophelia
"*Hamlet* and the French Connection" vi, 223*n*13
Hamlet and the King *see* Claudius; King
Hamlet and the Queen *see* Gertrard; Gertred
The Hamlet first Published (Q1, 1603): Origins, Form, Intertextualities 2
"Hamlet reuenge" 14, 171–2, 175, 191
"Hamlet, revenge" 14, 37, 144, 160, 164, 171–2, 175, 180, 187
Hamlet's age 1, 7–8, 13, 31, 41–3, 57, 122, 140, 182, 183, 192
The Hamlets: Cues, Qs and Remembered Texts 2
"Hamlets, I should say handfuls" 13, 144, 156–8, 186

Index

Hamlet's return 2, 52, 53–4, 57, 59, 68–9, 71–3, 75, 102, 138, 139, 140, 182
Hamlett, Katherine 17
Hardy, Thomas 67
harey the vj 99, 163
Hart, Alfred 16, 65–7, 72, 115, 131–2, 136, 191
Harvey, Gabriel 14, 160, 169–70, 174, 175, 190–1
"hath" 27–8
Haza, José Ruano de la 87
"*Hecuba*" 25–6
hedges 178
Hekatompathia 21, 50
Heminge, John 84, 87
1 Henry IV 79–80
2 Henry IV 80, 124
Henry V 61, 80, 100, 104, 105, 124, 165
2 Henry VI 79, 167
3 Henry VI 104, 105, 167, 168 (table)
Henslowe, Philip 14, 144, 159, 164, 174, 180, 187, 191
Henslowe's *Diary* 37, 98–9, 143, 160–3, 175
Henty, G. A. 189
Herford, Charles 11
Hermione 119–20
Hero and Leander 167, 187
Heywood, Thomas 67, 82, 87, 88, 93, 167, 180, 192
Hibbard, G.R. 2, 93, 94, 112, 146, 193
Hieronimo 50, 106, 108–9, 155
his Highness' servants 82, 93, 172
Les Histoires Tragiques 2, 21, 22, 81, 113, 139, 140, 163, 171–2, 188, 190–2; comparison with *Pierce Penniless* 55–7; comparison with Q1 and Q2 31–43, 44, 46–8, 50–1, 53–61, 68–9, 71, 74, 181–5; comparison with *The Spanish Tragedy* 105, 107–8
Historiae Danicae 32, 184
Hodges, Richard 27
The Hog Hath Lost His Pearl 83
Hogg, Douglas 153
Holderness, Graham 62, 101
homophone 117, 149, 156, 158, 175
The Honest Man's Fortune 131, 136
Hoppe, Harry 114, 226*n*3
Horatio 7, 8, 24, 36, 41–2, 53–4, 63–4, 69, 71–2, 75, 109–11, 126, 138–9
Horvvendille (Amleth's father) 34, 35, 36, 38, 70; warrior King 184
Hubbard, Frank 183
Humphreys, A.R. 228*n*24
Hunsdon, Lord Henry 131
hypotheses *see* abridgement; first sketch; interpolation; memorial reconstruction; revision; *Ur-Hamlet*
The Hystorie of Hamblet 145, 163

If You Know Not Me 82
inconsistency 78, 115, 117, 134, 149, 165, 171, 180, 190
Induction to *Bartholomew Fair* 174
Induction to *The Malcontent* 130
"infamie," "infamy" 47, 48, 49, 51, 68, 105, 108
infinitive marker 29, 30
inflections 6, 26–30, 60, 140, 181, 189
informal features *see* colloquialisms
insertions 63, 116, 117, 127, 131
internal rhyme 64, 112
interpolation 20, 87, 112, 190, 192
Ioppolo, Grace 63, 65, 67, 84
Iovii, Paulus 17
Irace, Kathleen O. 1, 27 (table), 79, 94, 95–6 (tables), 97, 100, 112, 132, 191
Isabella 106

Jack, A. E. 146, 148
Jackson, MacDonald P. 27, 59
James I 18, 82
Jenkins, Harold 2, 16, 20, 33, 35, 36, 38, 41, 60, 61, 93, 106, 170, 185, 222*n*18
Jenkins, Thomas 60
The Jew of Malta 99, 162 (table)
Joan of Brainford 150
John a Kent and John a Cumber 131
Johnson, Gerard 93
Jonson, Ben 16, 19, 129, 130–1, 167, 173, 174, 187, 188; as reviser 65–7; suggesting Shakespeare revised 62
Joseph Surface 90, 91–92 (tables)
Julius Caesar 18, 19
Julius Caesar 18, 19

Kastan, David Scott 2
Kempe, William 19, 173
"Kid in *Æsop*" 105, 148–52, 156–8, 159, 180
the King (Q1) 54, 71, 73, 110–2, 183; character 40, 65, 68, 70, 72, 73, 182, 188; and Hamlet 22–4, 34, 44, 48, 54; Hamlet's rejection of King as father 205–6; and Leartes 68, 71; shared aspects 22, 23, 34, 35, 39, 44–5, 46, 48, 69, 74, 108, 126, 184; *see also* Claudius; Fengon
King John 103, 104
King John 103, 104, 105, 165
King Lear 15, 16, 26, 82, 98, 163, 180, 181, 183
the King of England 35, 39, 74, 185
the King of Norway 34, 35, 70, 125
Kinnear, Rory 182
Kirke, Edward 152
Knight, Charles 163, 174, 192
Knight, L.C. 70
Koeppel, Emil 151
Kyd, Thomas 1, 3, 22, 108, 149, 176, 181, 186;

as borrower? 50, 108, 190; date of *The Spanish Tragedy* 50, 113; homophone 158, 175; linked to "Kid in *Æsop* ?" 105, 148–9, 152, 154–6, 158; as possible author of early *Hamlet* 2, 50, 105, 109, 143, 145–7, 157, 158, 164, 176, 178, 180

Lady Teazle 90, 91–2 (tables)
Laertes 36, 68, 69, 72, 73
Latham, Agnes 228n23
Law, Jude 126
Leartes 36, 68, 71, 134
Lee, Sir Sidney 146
Leicester, Robert, Chancellor of Oxford 173
Leontes 119–22
The Life of Lope de Vega 85
Ling, Nicholas 80, 81, 94, 171, 172
Linley, Thomas (the elder and the younger) 89
Lodge, Thomas 14, 37, 99, 144, 147, 159, 164, 171, 173, 174, 175, 180, 187, 191
London 20, 61, 81, 82, 92, 93, 94, 99, 132, 161, 172, 186
Lorenzo 106, 155
Loue labours wonne 165
Loughrey, Bryan 62, 101
Love à-la-Mode 83, 89
Love's Labours Lost 80–1, 165, 187
Lucianus, "Lucianus" 13, 25, 33, 79, 94, 95, 96 (table), 97, 98 (table), 100, 115, 125, 127
Lyly, John 174

Macklin, Charles 83, 89
madness 34–6, 41, 42, 44, 104, 108, 182, 184; reporter's recall 103–4
Maguire, Laurie 1, 78, 82, 83, 86, 93, 99–100, 107, 115–7, 124, 179–80
The Malcontent 83, 130
Malone, Edmond 2, 105, 143–5, 158, 160–4, 175, 180
Mamillius 119–20
manipulation: by Amleth 55; by Claudius 65, 72–3, 188
The Manuscript of Shakespeare's Hamlet and the Problems of its Transmission 22, 79
Marcellus, "Marcellus" 10, 13, 25, 33, 51, 64, 73, 79, 94–8, 100, 125–7, 135, 179, 190
Marcus, Leah S. 226ch9n9
Mares, F.H. 228n25
marginalia 14, 169–70, 175, 191
Le Mariage de Figaro 83, 89
Marlowe, Christopher 7, 78, 155, 167, 174, 187
Marston, John 83, 130, 188
Mary Queen of Scots 18
Massinger, Philip 117
Matilda the faire and chaste Daughter of Lord Robert Fitzwater 164
The May Eclogue 151–2, 158, 175, 180

McKerrow, Ronald 148–9, 152, 180
McMillin, Scott 93
memorial reconstruction (by actors) 1, 39, 82–8, 147, 180, 193; *The Duenna* 89–90; *King Lear* 15, 98; Lope de Vega's plays 85–7; *Love à–la-mode* 83, 89; *Le Mariage de Figaro* 83, 89; Q1 *Hamlet* hypothesis 3, 10–3, 15–6, 19–20, 23, 26, 30, 32–3, 39–47, 51, 59–67, 69, 77–141, 172, 177–80, 182–3, 192; rejection of hypothesis 10, 101, 180; *The School for Scandal* 2, 13, 90–2, 98, 141, 127
Memorilla 86
memoriones 86–7, 101
Menaphon 143, 145, 148–9, 152, 157, 186
Mensa Philosophica 169
Menzer, Paul 2, 173, 189, 192
The Merchant of Venice 79, 80, 165
Meres, Francis 2, 14, 159–60, 164–8, 175, 180, 186, 187–8
The Merry Wives of Windsor 93, 100, 124, 132, 133
The Merry Wives of Windsor: the History and Transmission of Shakespeare's Text 132
Messenger 72–3, 135, 182
Middleton, Thomas 99, 191
Midsummers night dreame 165
Miola, Robert 143, 146
Mirabellius, Dominicus Nanus 166
The Mirror of Martyrs 18
Mr. Oldys 144
moat 153
modal verbs 1, 178
Mommsen, Tycho 9–10, 25, 77–8
Montaigne, Michel Eyquem de 21, 186
Montano 78, 134
"moral agenda" 124, 127
morphology *see* inflections
Morris, Brian 59, 187, 222n5
Moseley, Humphrey 84, 130
motive: Amleth's 47; Bernard's 90, 92, 99, 101; Hamlet's 47; for memorially reconstructing Q1 *Hamlet* 92–3, 99, 127
MR *see* memorial reconstruction
MRA *see* memorial reconstruction (by actors)
Mrs. Candour 90, 91–2 (tables)
Much Ado About Nothing 80, 165, 167
Los Muertos Vivos 86
Muir, Kenneth 37, 61
Mulryne, J. R. 21, 155
Munday, Anthony 167, 170
Murray, Peter B. 146

Nashe, Thomas 16; *Epistle* 2, 3, 13, 37, 50, 99, 105, 143–58, 160–1, 164, 173,–6, 180–1, 186, 187, 191–2; *Pierce Penniless* 7, 55–7, 167, 182

Nelson, Alan 13, 173
A New History of Early English Drama 2
Newington Butts 14, 143, 144, 160–3, 180, 187, 228*ch*12*n*8
Newton, Thomas 167, 185, 221*n*36
non sequitur 161
Norman, Robert 21, 221*n*39
Norwegian Captain 135
noverint 145, 148, 152, 155, 158
the "nunnery" scene 44–5, 51, 57, 59, 60, 65, 73, 78, 140, 183, 185, 190, 222*ch*4*n*4

"objectionable" pronouns 78, 102, 109–112, 118, 127, 179
Objective Methods for Testing Authenticity and the Study of Ten Doubtful Comedias Attributed to Lope de Vega 85
Ofelia 17, 21, 34, 35, 41, 42, 100, 115, 134, 193, 185; used to test Hamlet 44–5, 58, 65, 73, 135, 182
Officina 166, 187
Old Hamlet (Hamlet's father) 34, 36, 38, 41, 42, 47, 48, 54, 140, 185
Old Rowley 90, 91–2 (tables)
"ombre(s)" 37–9, 108, 185
omissions 10, 63, 78, 130, 178; by Meres 165, 168
Ophelia 34, 35, 61, 72, 100, 115; used to test Hamlet 36, 44, 45, 58
opinions 28, 92, 178; actor's 114, 133; scholars' 3, 9, 16, 92, 102–3, 106, 146, 161, 163, 170, 189
Oras, Ants 26
Øresund 139
Ostend, the siege of 20, 189, 190, 192
Østerberg, V. 42, 146, 151, 158
Owen's epigrams 170
Oxford: city 99, 173; university 7, 18, 19, 82, 93, 172, 186

Palladis Tamia: wits treasury 2, 160, 164–8, 187
parallels: drunkenness 54–6; with French source 33, 34, 44, 55–6, 59–61, 107, 140, 182; in the *Hamlet*s 17, 25, 28, 30; in Nashe's *Epistle* 150–1, 158; in other Shakespearean plays 104, 179; in *Palladis Tamia* 166; soundbites 180; with *The Spanish Tragedy* 50, 105–78, 127, 141, 179
Parergon vi
Pause Patterns in Elizabethan and Jacobean Drama: an Experiment in Prosody 26, 223*ch*6*n*1
"Pedantius" 170
Pericles 100
Petersen, Lene 222*ch*3*n*1
Philip Stubbes 149–50, 154, 158
Pierce Penniless 21, 42, 55–7, 167, 187

piracy 80–2, 84, 85, 88, 92
pirates 71, 72, 139; as note-takers 94, 101
pivot word 24
Platter, Thomas 18
Plautus, Titus Maccius 165, 167, 168 (table), 187
player king 10, 94
Players 21, 45, 73, 79, 94, 95–8 (tables), 131
players 79, 80 (table), 83, 92, 93, 94, 96, 132, 134, 173
plurals (Nashe) 152–4
Poel, William 62, 133
pointing 134, 170
Polixenes 119
Pollard, Alfred 79, 92
Polonia 19, 188
Polonius 21, 34, 35, 36, 42, 45, 48, 69, 74–5, 131, 134; "closeth"/"closes" 28; reason for name 19, 30, 78, 188, 190, 230*n*43
Polyanthea 166
Pope, Alexander 116
Porter, Henry 167
possessive determiners 29, 110, 120, 153
preface: Day's 81; Nashe's (*Epistle*) 37, 105, 186
The Prelude 67
prepositions 29, 30
Pride and Prejudice 119
printing 16, 79–82, 163, 171, 186, 191; Q1 *Hamlet* 79, 80 (table), 81, 87, 93, 99, 127, 141, 179, 181
Privy Council letter 173, 186
proclitic "the" 29–30
The Prologue 79, 94, 95–8 (tables), 125
prompt book/copy 15, 84, 93, 181, 192
pronouns: "faulty" 109, 110–3; "misuse" of 109; "objectionable" 78, 102, 109–12, 118, 127, 179
proportionality 126, 131, 226*ch*9*n*22
propositions 165
proximal adverbs 24
publication *see* printing
Pudsey, Edward 14, 83, 191
puns 18–9
Puttenham, George 166, 187
quantitative analysis 2, 141, 179

Queen Elizabeth I *see* Elizabeth
Queen Gertrard *see* Gertrard
Queen Gertred *see* Gertred
Queen Gertrude *see* Gertrude
Queen Geruthe *see* Geruthe
Queen Margaret 104
Queens' promises *see* individual Queens
A Quip for an vpstart Courtier 169

Ramello, Giovanni 109
The Rape of Lucrece 82, 168 (table), 169, 170, 175, 187, 191

Rasmussen, Eric 2, 178
reader, address to 82, 84, 86, 130
The Real Shakespeare. Retrieving the Early Years, 1564–1594 1
recollections: actor/reporter's 59, 78, 106, 107; Hamlet's 41
Records of Early English Drama 173
redrafting 121, 181, 186, 188, 189, 190
reduction: of aspect of Q2 126, 135; of verb inflections 26
Reforming the "Bad" Quartos. Performance and Provenance of Six Shakespearean First Editions 1, 79, 191
Rennert, Hugo Albert 85, 86
The Return of the Native 67
revenge 21, 35, 143, 149, 156, 158; Amleth's 38, 40, 41, 47–8, 54, 58, 60, 68, 108, 184, 185; Hamlet's 11, 41, 47–9, 51, 58, 60, 68–9, 71, 184, 185, 190; Laertes' 72; in *The Spanish Tragedy* 22, 102, 108–9; Stationers' Register entry 171–2, 175; *see also* "Hamlet reuenge"; "Hamlet, revenge"
The Revenger's Tragedy 191
Revising Shakespeare 63
revision 61, 63–65, 67–8, 84, 94, 126, 181; for F1 11–2, 26, 67, 181, 191; *Les Histoires Tragiques* 81; hypothesis regarding Q2 9, 12–3, 16, 28, 32, 42, 43, 46, 48, 52, 59–62, 63–5, 67, 68, 70–4, 75, 87, 100, 116, 124–5, 133–7, 140, 147, 178, 186, 189–90, 191, 192; Jonson's 65–7; *King Lear* 15–6, 181; Shakespeare as reviser 10, 16, 62, 63, 127–8, 141; of an *Ur-Hamlet* 132
rewriting 11, 16, 63, 136, 189, 191; Jonson's 66, 67
Reynaldo 78, 134
Rhodes, R. Crompton 92
Richard II 79, 80, 165
Richard III 79, 80, 81, 165, 169, 187, 191
Rickert, R. T. 165, 228
Robert of Normandy 164, 175
Robert(e)s, James 80, 81, 171–2
Robertson, John M. 106
Romeo and Juliet 8, 12, 78, 100, 124, 130, 165
Rose Theatre 161, 162 (table)
Rosencrans and Guyldensterne 45, 68, 72, 74, 75, 190; *see also* escorts
Rossencraft and Gilderstone 68, 71, 74, 111, 112, 140; *see also* escorts
Rowe, Nicholas 188
Rylands, George 20

Sailors 138
Sams, Eric 1, 16, 101, 147, 192
Sarrazin, Dr G. 146, 155
Satiromastix 14, 99, 171, 175, 191
Saxo Grammaticus 32, 184
Schick, J. 146

Schiller, Friedrich 10
Schoenbaum, Samuel 62
The School for Scandal 2, 13, 90–2, 94–99, 101, 127, 141, 179
Scoloker, Anthony 14, 160, 191
Scot, Michael 169
The Scourge of Villainy 83
Second Gravedigger 79, 94
The Second Part of Conycatching 169
Sejanus 188
Seneca, Lucius Annaeus 37, 145–6, 148–9, 151, 154–8, 165, 167, 185, 187
Shaheen, Naseeb 222*ch*4n2
Shakespeare, William: as actor 66, 188; as author of Q1 8, 9, 13, 14, 16, 52, 119, 145, 147, 172, 178; beginning to write 60–1, 174, 175, 183; his "creative prime" 119, 124; as "cult" writer 186; debt to Seneca 37, 145, 147, 156, 158; on duration of plays 12, 67, 130; first writing of *Hamlet* 11–3, 16, 60–1, 141, 178, 180; as genius 3, 77; as grafter 3, 193; knowledge of French 61; knowledge of law 61, 118, 186; knowledge of stagecraft 23–24; as playwright 3, 47, 54, 96, 120–1, 131, 167, 184–90; as reviser *see* revision; "supremely inventive poet" 16, 193; use of *Les Histoires Tragiques* 33, 38–40, 46, 52, 55–6, 60, 70–1, 184–5, 188, 190; use of *Pierce Penniless* 42, 55–6, 182
Shakespeare and the Homilies 131
Shakespeare, Co-Author 27
Shakespeare Institute, Stratford-upon-Avon 178
Shakespeare's Bad Quartos: Deliberate Abridgements Designed for Performance by a Reduced Cast 132
Shakespeare's Revision of "King Lear" 15
Shakespeare's suspect texts. the "bad" quartos and their contexts 1–2, 100 (table)
Shakspere's Hamlet: the Second Quarto, 1604 220n28
Shapiro, James 2, 20, 21, 63, 132
The Shepherd's Calendar 151, 152, 167, 168 (table)
Sheridan, Richard Brinsley 89, 101
shorthand 9, 82, 94
Sidney, Sir Philip 21, 167, 168 (table)
siege of Ostend 20, 189, 190, 192
Simmes or Sims, Valentine 80, 171, 172 (table)
Sir Benjamin 90, 91–2 (tables)
Sir Oliver 90, 91–2 (tables)
Sir Peter Teazle 90, 91–2 (tables)
Sir Thomas More 63, 131
Skialethia 167, 168
Slinger, Jonathan 182
Smethwick, John 80
Smith, G.C. Moore 170
Smythick, John *see* Smethwick

soliloquy 65, 66, 73, 78, 103, 104, 118–24, 134, 188, 190
Sonnet 94 124
Sonnet 135 112
soundbites 164, 171, 175, 180
The Sources of Hamlet 33
The Spanish Tragedy 1, 127, 146, 155, 179, 180–1, 186, 190, 192; anterior to Q1 *Hamlet*? 22, 105–6, 113; date 21, 50, 105; postulated use for memorial reconstruction of Q1 50, 59, 78, 102, 105–9, 113, 141
speculation 2, 8, 42, 51, 63, 75, 82, 98, 126, 144, 163, 179, 182, 192; abridgement 126; Kyd as author of early *Hamlet* 145, 158, 178, 180; motive for memorial reconstruction 93–4, 99, 101; priority of Q1 75; Shakespeare re-reading *Les Histoires Tragiques* 60, 190; *Ur-Hamlet* 11, 32, 69, 141
Speght, Thomas 14, 169, 170, 175
Spenser, Edmund 151–2, 156, 158, 167, 168 (table), 175, 180
Stabler, Arthur P. 33, 38, 60, 184, 185
stage directions 23, 53, 63, 113, 114–5, 127
Stanihurst, Richard 154, 158, 186
Stationers' Register (S.R.) 14, 21, 79–81, 87, 165, 167, 171, 172, 175, 191
Staunton, Howard 174
stenography *see* shorthand
Stern, Virginia 169–70
Stoll, E.E. 106
"stolne and surreptitious copies" 84, 87, 88
"streamlining of action" 135
Stubbes, Philip 149, 150, 154, 158
stylistic quirk 180, 186
stylometrics 26, 30
"substitutions" 63, 64
suffixes *see* inflections
supers *see* extras
supposition 165, 174
sword swap 36, 38, 184
syntax 50, 119–22, 124, 127, 166

Tamberlaine the Great 99, 174
The Taming of the Shrew 59, 79, 100, 165, 168 (table)
"the tamynge of a shrowe" 162 (table), 163
Tarleton, Richard 19, 20, 186, 190, 192
Tarleton's Jests 19, 20, 186
Taylor, Gary 2, 15, 26, 28, 83, 86, 89, 93, 95, 177
Taylor, Neil 2, 19, 20, 42, 147, 170, 188
Taylor, Robert 83
Tender Is the Night 67
Tennant, David 182
test 34–5, 42, 73, 182, 184, 185
Textor, J. Ravisius 166, 187
Texts with Two Faces: Noticing Theatrical Revisions in Henry VI, Parts 2 and 3 100

theory 9–12, 15, 40, 94, 97, 98, 100, 101, 112, 125, 147
Thomas, Sidney 219*n*14, 221*n*46, 226*ch*9*n*11
Thompson, Ann 2, 19, 20, 42, 147, 170, 188
Thorndike, Ashley H. 146
The Three Parnassus Plays 1598–1601 160, 173, 188
Titian 17
title pages 8, 80–2, 87, 93, 99, 129, 141, 158, 172, 173, 175, 181
Titus Andronicus 80, 98, 103, 104, 105, 156, 163, 165; date 174, 187
"To be or not to be" 41, 78, 116, 118–19, 121–4, 135
tongue twister 28
topicality 17, 18, 21, 63, 71, 73
Tourneur, Cyril 191
The Tragedie of Ferrex and Porrex 81
The Tragedie of Gorboduc 81, 88
The Tragedy of Caesar and Pompey, or Caesar's Revenge 18
The Tragicall Legend of Robert, Duke of Normandie 164
transpositions 10, 33, 43, 63, 64, 65, 78; decapitation 39; escorts' deaths 73; "nunnery" scene 45, 65, 75; "ombre"/Ghost 38–9
"trap" *see* test
The Treatise of Melancholie 21
Troilus and Cressida 79
The True Tragedy of Richard Duke of York 100, 124
The True Tragedy of Richard III 21
Trundell, John 80–1, 171, 172 (table)
Tucca 14, 171
Twelfth Night 27
The Two Gentlemen of Verona 165

"ungrammatical" 65
Ur-Hamlet 68, 106, 141, 159, 160, 175–6, 177, 183, 192; considered as source for Shakespeare 33, 103, 132; hypothesis rejected 10, 178; possible attribution to Kyd 3, 50, 109, 143, 146, 158, 176, 180; possible attribution to Shakespeare 178, 184; possible contents 11, 37; used by actor/reporter? 32, 47, 48, 51–2, 59, 69, 109, 140, 182, 191
Urbano, Duke of 17
Urkowitz, Steven 15, 23, 24, 100, 101, 131

"A Valediction: Forbidding Mourning" 151
van Doren, M. 119
variant 22, 26, 64, 35, 139
Vautrollier 61
Venus and Adonis 168 (table), 174, 187
verb suffixes *see* inflections
verbal echoes *see* parallels
Vere, Sir Francis 20

Vickers, Sir Brian 27, 63
Viggars, Peter 153
Virgil (Publius Vergilius Maro) 37
Voltemand, "Voltemand" 10, 13, 25, 33, 51, 70, 73, 79, 95, 96 (table), 97, 98 (table), 125, 179
Voltemar 10, 70, 94, 95 (table), 97 (table), 98, 100, 125, 127, 190

Waller, F.O. 28, 59
Walleys, Henry 79
Warner, William 168 (table), 169
Watson, Thomas 21, 50, 167, 169, 170, 191
Webbe, W. 166
Webster, John 129, 130
Weever, John 18
Weiner, Albert B. 11, 12, 100, 132, 133, 134, 136
Wells, Stanley 2, 15, 26, 28, 83, 86, 89, 93, 95, 177, 219n22
Werstine, Paul 84

Whishaw, Ben 229n18
Widgery, William Henry 10, 79, 94
Wilkinson, Tate 89, 90, 92, 101, 102
William Shakespeare. a Study of Facts and Problems 79
William Shakespeare. A Textual Companion 26
Wilson, John Dover 22, 103, 132, 186, 189; on allusions 17, 19, 20–1, 186, 189; possible actor/reporters 79, 94, 95n (table), 96n (table), 97
The Winter's Tale 119, 120
Wits Miserie and the Worlds Madnesse 37, 144, 160, 164, 172 (table), 187
The Woman in the Moon 174
Wordsworth, William 67
The Works of Chaucer 14, 169, 170, 175

Yorick 7, 8, 41, 42
young woman 34–5, 36, 58, 184, 185, 190; *see also* "belle femme"